Measuring the Restrictiveness of International Trade Policy

Measuring the Restrictiveness of International Trade Policy

James E. Anderson and J. Peter Neary

The MIT Press
Cambridge, Massachusetts
London, England

MIT Press books may be purchased at special quantity discounts for business or sales promotional use. For information, please email special_sales@mitpress.mit.edu or write to Special Sales Department, The MIT Press, 55 Hayward Street, Cambridge, MA 02142.

This book was set in Times New Roman on 3B2 by Asco Typesetters, Hong Kong and was printed and bound in the United States of America.

Library of Congress Cataloging-in-Publication Data

Anderson, James E.
Measuring the restrictiveness of international trade policy / James E. Anderson and J. Peter Neary.
    p. cm.
Includes bibliographical references and index.
ISBN 0-262-01220-0 (alk. paper)
1. Commercial policy. 2. Tariff. 3. Non-tariff trade barriers. 4. Foreign trade regulation. 5. International trade. I. Neary, J. Peter. II. Title.
HF1411.A475 2005   381.3—dc22   2005049130

10 9 8 7 6 5 4 3 2 1

to the memory of my mother and father
J.E.A.

to my mother and to the memory of my father
J.P.N.

Contents

List of Figures

List of Tables

Preface

Karl Marx said that man was born free but is everywhere in chains. International trade, by contrast, has never been unfettered and remains significantly restricted, globalization notwithstanding. For students of the subject, this poses problems of theory, policy, and measurement. Measurement is the Cinderella of this trio, because theorists have paid little attention to the measurement of trade restrictions, leaving practitioners to make do with ad hoc solutions.

In this book we present an approach to the problem of measuring trade restrictiveness that we have developed over the past fifteen years. Whereas the standard theory of index numbers applies to prices, output, or productivity, we develop new index numbers that apply directly to policy variables. Our theoretical work builds on the standard theory of policy reform in open economies and extends it in a number of directions. We also illustrate how our indexes can be applied, under a variety of simplifying assumptions, and show that they make a big difference to the assessment of trade restrictiveness. The book thus attempts to present our results in a way that will appeal to both of our potential audiences: to convince our theoretically minded colleagues that the problem is an important one and that our answer is the correct one, and to give practitioners an analytical base and some practical tools for applying our ideas.

Like all authors we hope that every reader will read the book carefully from beginning to end. However, recognizing that life is short and books are long, let us give some recommendations for more selective readings. Those who want a nontechnical introduction to the book should read chapters 1 and 2 and look at some of the empirical results in part III, especially chapter 15. Theorists and graduate students will want to concentrate on part II. Here chapters 4 and 5 are the analytic core of the book, presenting the two principal indexes we propose. They are sandwiched between chapters that deal with the theory of trade policy reform. Chapter 3 summarizes the standard results in the field, while chapter 6 extends it in new directions, showing how the effects of trade policy on welfare and market access can be expressed in terms of the mean and variance of the tariff distribution. Chapters 7 and 8 detail the additional complications that arise for theory and measurement when trade is restricted by quotas as well as tariffs. Chapter 9 extends our indexes to economic environments other than the competitive small open economy, while chapter 10 shows how they relate to other ways of aggregating trade restrictions.

Finally, those interested mainly in applications will want to skim part II for background and concentrate on the empirical work in part III. Following a short methodological introduction in chapter 11, chapters 12 through 15 apply our approach to a range of issues, including the trade restrictiveness of domestic distortions and the use of a computable general-equilibrium model to calculate the measures of trade restrictiveness we propose. While these applications show the potential of our indexes in applied work, the principal contribution of our approach is conceptual. To take an analogy from better-known index numbers, the Konüs true cost-of-living index has not supplanted fixed-weight consumer price indexes in practice. In the same way we do not expect that our approach will put an end to the calculation of trade-weighted indexes of average tariffs. However, we hope that readers of this book will come away with a clearer understanding of their deficiencies and of the circumstances where they can be expected to approximate the theoretically ideal indexes we present.

Many individuals have contributed in person to our thinking on these issues. In addition to those mentioned elsewhere, we would like to thank Patrick Honohan, Ian Jewitt, Ron Jones, and Kala Krishna for helpful comments; Geoff Bannister (who co-authored the paper on which section 12.3 is based), Can Erbil, Chris Holmes and Ulrich Reincke for able research assistance; and Carl Hamilton for assistance with the data for section 14.5.

Portions of this book have appeared in different forms in a number of journals, including *Econometrica*, the *International Economic Review*, the *Journal of International Economics*, the *Review of Economic Studies*, the *Review of International Economics*, and the *World Bank Economic Review*, as well as in collected works edited by Ron Jones and Anne Krueger (*The Political Economy of International Trade*, published by Basil Blackwell) and by Bob Baldwin (*Empirical Studies of Commercial Policy*, published by University of Chicago Press). We are grateful to the editors and referees of these books and journals for invaluable comments and also to the publishers for permission to reprint excerpts here.

In addition to our home universities, Boston College and University College Dublin, a number of institutions have provided stimulating research environments and substantive support during the writing of this book. Some of the chapters originated as components of a World Bank project. Refik Erzan and Will Martin at the World Bank, with the support of Ron Duncan and Ravi Kanbur, provided indispensable moral and material sustenance for our efforts. Jim Anderson wishes to thank the Institute for International Economic Studies at the University of Stockholm. Peter Neary's work was made possible by a Visiting Research Professorship at the University of Ulster at Jordanstown in Northern Ireland. His more recent work on the project forms part of the Globalisation Programme of the Centre for Economic Performance at the London School of Economics, funded by the UK Social Science Research Council, and of the International Trade and Investment Programme of the Geary Institute at University College Dublin. He also wishes to thank the Social Science Research Council of the Royal Irish Academy and the European Community's Human Potential Programme under contract HPRN-CT-2000-00069 [EGEMTPS]. Finally, the Centre for Economic Policy Research helped circulate early versions of all our papers and also financed many of the workshops at which a number were presented. The hospitality and support of all these bodies is gratefully acknowledged, but they should not be held responsible for any of the views expressed.

I THE PROBLEM

1 Introduction

The influence of a country's trade policy on its economic well-being is one of the most widely debated topics in economics. Yet the prior question of how the stance of trade policy should be measured has received very little attention in the past. In practice this is done typically using a variety of ad hoc measures such as the trade-weighted average tariff, the coefficient of variation of tariffs, or the non-tariff-barrier coverage ratio. But all these measures lack any theoretical foundation and are subject to theoretical and practical drawbacks. Some researchers, such as Papageorgiou et al. (1991), have constructed subjective measures of trade restrictiveness. These have the advantage of incorporating important local considerations, but they are inherently difficult to compare across different countries or time periods.

The problem of how the restrictiveness of trade policy should be measured is not so severe in the textbook world where there is only a single trade barrier that takes a well-defined form, such as a single tariff or a single quota. But in most real-world situations, especially in developing countries, actual systems of trade intervention are pervasive and highly complex. This poses a challenge for analysts and policy makers alike. In the face of a bewildering array of tariffs and quantitative restrictions, it is extremely difficult to assess the true orientation of a country's overall trade policy or to evaluate the thrust of a package of policy changes that encourage trade in some product lines but discourage it in others.

Traditional analysis provides little guidance on how to aggregate restrictions across different markets. This makes it difficult to evaluate proposals for trade liberalization that form part of a stabilization package or to assess the progress made in moving toward less restricted trade. A further reason for seeking a framework within which trade policies can be compared consistently is of analytical as well as practical importance. Since

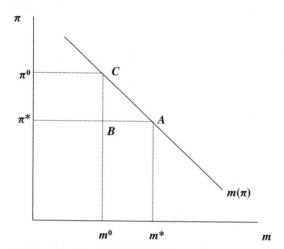

Figure 1.1
Trade policy restrictiveness and the cost of protection

ultimately the case for free trade is a scientific hypothesis, theoretically sound but potentially false, some measure of trade restrictiveness is necessary if satisfactory tests of the impact of trade on growth and economic performance are to be possible.[1]

This book describes an approach we have developed that provides theoretically satisfactory yet practically implementable procedures for measuring the restrictiveness of trade policy. Two relatively recent developments have made this approach possible. At a theoretical level, the normative theory of international trade has been formalized in a systematic way and extended to take account of varieties of trade policy other than tariffs.[2] And, at a practical level, the rapid increase in availability of cheap computing power has made possible the implementation of models with a disaggregated structure that comes closer than ever before to the complexity of real-world protective structures. Later in the book we describe how the approach we propose can be implemented on a personal computer. First, we examine the conceptual problem in more detail, show how different aspects of trade policy regimes can be incorporated

---

1. Leamer (1988b) and Edwards (1992) propose and implement tests along these lines, adopting the Heckscher-Ohlin explanation of trade patterns as a maintained hypothesis. Krishna (1991) and Pritchett (1996) review this and other approaches to measuring openness and trade restrictiveness.

2. Dixit (1986) and Anderson (1988, 1994) provide overviews of work in the field.

into a single measure, the Trade Restrictiveness Index, and review some of the theoretical extensions and applications of this Index.

The simplest context in which measuring trade restrictiveness arises is when tariffs are the only form of trade policy. Figure 1.1 illustrates the market for a single good whose world price (assumed given) is π^* and whose home import demand curve is $m(\pi)$. Domestic producers and consumers face a price that is raised by the tariff to π^0. By adopting a partial equilibrium perspective for the moment, we can measure the deadweight loss, or cost of protection, given by the Marshallian triangle ABC. As for the restrictiveness of trade policy, in this one-good context it can obviously and unambiguously be measured by the height of the tariff, the distance BC. However, once we move beyond the simple one-good case, it is not immediately clear what is meant by the restrictiveness of trade policy, far less how we might go about measuring it. Just as in figure 1.1, it is not the same as the welfare cost of protection, though we will see that one natural way to measure trade policy restrictiveness uses that welfare cost as a benchmark. The next chapter presents a mainly diagrammatic analysis of an extended two-good example that introduces these issues, and prepares the way for the general theoretical treatment in part II of the book.

2 Measuring Trade Policy Restrictiveness: A Nontechnical Introduction

What do we mean by a measure of "trade policy restrictiveness"? In principle, we mean some scalar index number that aggregates the trade restrictions that apply in a number of individual markets. Whether a particular index number formula is satisfactory depends on the uses to which the measure of restrictiveness is to be put. Some indexes are fully satisfactory for one purpose but quite misleading for another. Other indexes, lacking a clear theoretical foundation, are not satisfactory for any purpose. In this chapter we provide an intuitive introduction to the two main indexes introduced in this book, and discuss how other indexes used for the same purpose fall short.

The main focus of this book is on the Trade Restrictiveness Index, or TRI, an index that aggregates trade restrictions while holding constant the level of real income. This is the natural aggregate to use in studies that attempt to link growth in income to measures of a country's trade policy stance. It would not make sense to "explain" income growth in terms of a measure of trade policy that itself varies with income. The TRI is also the natural index to use in evaluating a country's progress toward trade liberalization, for example, in the context of the World Bank's Structural Adjustment Loans. Since loan conditionality is predicated on the assumption of a link between trade policy and income growth, it is desirable to measure the two concepts independently.

The book also discusses a different measure of trade restrictiveness that is appropriate for other purposes. In a trade negotiations context, where foreign exporters are concerned with domestic market access, it makes sense to aggregate trade restrictions in a way that holds constant the volume of imports rather than real income. An index of this type is discussed informally below and considered formally in chapter 5.

Before considering how an ideal measure of trade restrictiveness might be constructed, we review the measures that have been used in practice to aggregate across tariffs. (We postpone consideration of quotas until chapter 7.) These include different measures of average tariffs and alternative measures of tariff dispersion, such as the standard deviation and coefficient of variation of tariffs. We illustrate the properties of these measures and contrast them with those of our alternative welfare-based measure in a very simple context, a linear two-good partial-equilibrium model. In subsequent chapters we will see how our measure can be applied in much more general contexts.

2.1   The Trade-Weighted Average Tariff

Especially when data are particularly poor, it is not unknown for analysts to compute the simple (i.e., unweighted) average of tariff rates across different commodities. However, this measure has obvious disadvantages: it treats all commodities identically, and it is sensitive to changes in the classification of commodities in the tariff code. Clearly, tariffs should be weighted by their relative importance in some sense. The simplest and most commonly used method of doing so is to use actual trade volumes as weights. This leads to the *trade-weighted average tariff*, τ^a:

$$\tau^a \equiv \frac{\sum m_i t_i}{\sum m_i \pi_i^*},\tag{1}$$

where t_i is the specific tariff on good i, m_i is its import volume, and π_i^* its world price. This index is very easy to calculate: it equals total tariff revenue, $\sum m_i t_i$, divided by the value of imports at world prices, $\sum m_i \pi_i^*$. The average tariff can be rewritten as a weighted average of tariff rates:

$$\tau^a = \sum \omega_i^* \tau_i, \quad \omega_i^* \equiv \frac{m_i \pi_i^*}{\sum m_j \pi_j^*},\tag{2}$$

where τ_i (equal to t_i/π_i^*) is the ad valorem tariff rate on good i. Note that the weights ω_i^* are valued at world prices π_i^* rather than at domestic prices π_i.

Despite its convenience the trade-weighted average tariff runs into difficulties immediately. As the tariff on any good rises, its imports fall, so the now higher tariff gets a *lower* weight in the index. For high tariffs this fall in the weight may be so large that the index is *decreasing* in the tariff rate. (Recalling that the numerator of τ^a is tariff revenue, another way of putting this is that the tariff rate is on the wrong side of the Laffer curve.) More subtly, tariffs have greater effects on both welfare and trade volume

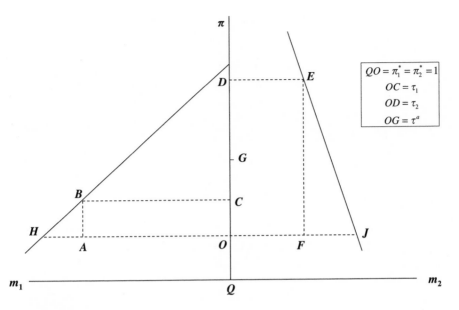

Figure 2.1
Trade-weighted average tariff: Tariff rates and import demand elasticities negatively correlated

when they apply to imports in relatively elastic demand, but it is precisely these goods whose weights fall fastest.

Figures 2.1 to 2.3 illustrate these considerations in a linear two-good example. Each panel of figure 2.1 depicts the domestic market for one of the goods, whose home import demand curve is $m_i(\pi_i)$, $i = 1, 2$. For ease of exposition the world prices of the two goods, π_1^* and π_2^*, are normalized at unity. Domestic producers and consumers face the tariff-inclusive prices π_i^0, represented by QC for good 1 and QD for good 2. As drawn, the import demand curve for good 1 is more elastic than that for good 2, whereas good 1 has a lower tariff than good 2. So in this example tariff rates and import demand elasticities are negatively correlated. The trade-weighted average tariff, obtained by weighting the two tariff rates by the imports (valued at world prices) of the two goods AO and OF, is indicated by τ^a. (We show in the appendix to this chapter how to locate the trade-weighted average tariff in the figure.)

Next consider a change in trade policy that leads to the situation illustrated in figure 2.2. The two import demand functions are the same, but the configuration of tariff levels is reversed: now the correlation between demand elasticities and tariff levels is positive rather than negative. In the

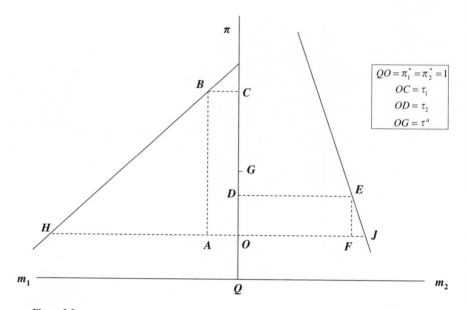

Figure 2.2
Trade-weighted average tariff: Tariff rates and import demand elasticities positively
correlated

left-hand panel, imports of the more elastic good 1 are almost eliminated,
so its high tariff receives a very low weight in the average tariff. In the
right-hand panel, the low tariff on the low-elasticity good 2 receives a
high weight. As a result the calculated average tariff (again denoted by
τ^a) is low, considerably lower than that in figure 2.1. Yet it seems intuitively obvious that trade is more restricted in figure 2.2 than in figure
2.1, since both welfare and the volume of trade have fallen. (Given the
partial equilibrium perspective of this chapter, the deadweight loss or
welfare cost of protection resulting from the two tariffs is measured by
the sum of the Marshallian triangles BAH and EFJ. The volume of
trade equals AF in both figures.) The index has thus moved in the wrong
direction, since its value has fallen even though trade is now more
restricted.

The comparison between figures 2.1 and 2.2 is extended and illustrated
from a different perspective in figure 2.3. For the same demand functions
as before, figure 2.3 plots the trade-weighted average tariff as a continuous function of the tariff rates on the two goods.[1] Clearly, for similar

---

1. The demand function slopes are 1.2 for good 1 and 0.3 for good 2. The tariff rates τ_1 and
τ_2 equal $\{1.5, 5.0\}$ and $\{3.0, 1.0\}$ in figures 2.1 and 2.2 respectively.

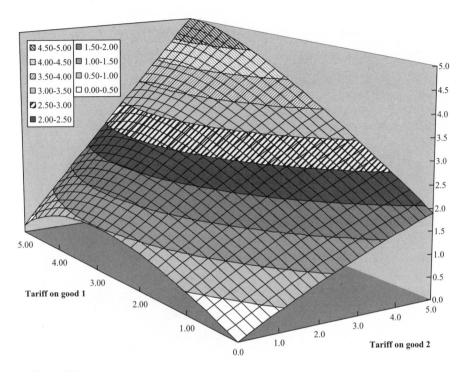

Figure 2.3
Trade-weighted average tariff

tariff rates the trade-weighted average tariff performs reasonably well. In the special case of identical tariff rates (along the diagonal of the three-dimensional surface), the index number problem disappears. However, for non-uniform tariffs, the trade-weighted average tariff gives a very misleading indication of the magnitude and even of the direction of change in trade policy. The most striking feature of figure 2.3 is that the trade-weighted average tariff actually *declines* in τ_1, the tariff rate on the higher elasticity good 1, when τ_1 is high and τ_2 is low.

2.2 Alternative Weights: Current or Free Trade? Imports or Production?

We have seen the difficulties caused by using current import volumes to construct trade-weighted average tariffs. In response, some authors have suggested using instead the import volumes that *would* prevail in free trade as weights. This view is well expressed by Loveday (1931), quoted with approval by Leamer (1974, p. 34): "The theoretically perfect weighting system would be the one under which each commodity were given a

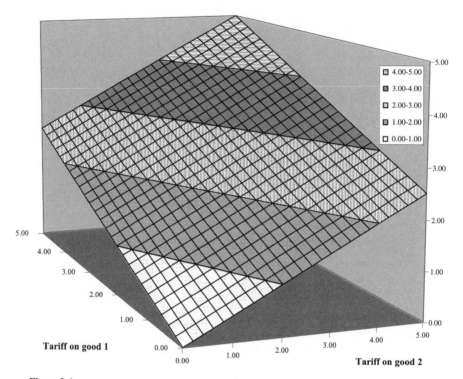

Figure 2.4
Average tariff weighted by free-trade imports

coefficient equivalent to the value which it would have in international trade of a free trade world."

But is this indeed the "theoretically perfect weighting system"? Figure 2.4 illustrates the behaviour of the trade-weighted average tariff in our example when free-trade import volumes are used as weights. Since free-trade import levels for the two goods have been (arbitrarily) set equal to each other, the behavior of the index is predictable: it increases linearly and symmetrically in the two tariff rates. But we have already seen that both import volumes and welfare fall faster as the tariff on the higher elasticity good 1 is increased. Using free-trade weights avoids the most obvious defect of using current trade weights in that the resulting index is always increasing in each individual tariff rate. But otherwise, it does not seem to measure trade restrictiveness very satisfactorily.

A further consideration is that the use of free-trade weights poses a major practical problem: the free-trade import volumes are not directly observable. In principle, they can be estimated (Leamer shows how this may be done), and even imperfect estimates would avoid the difficulty that weights based on actual import volumes are biased downward by tariffs. Nonetheless, the need to estimate the weights means that the informational requirements of this index are just as great as those of the "true" indexes that we discuss below: a complete model of import demand must be specified and estimated.

The choice between actual and free-trade import weights is identical, in principle, to that between Paasche (current-weighted) and Laspeyres (base-weighted) indexes in any other branch of economics. In practice, some plausible compromise between the two (e.g., their geometric mean, the Fisher Ideal index) is often used. However, a central theme of the economic approach to index numbers (e.g., see Pollak 1971 and Diewert 1981) is that the choice between alternative index-number formulas should primarily be based not on informal issues of plausibility but on the extent to which they approximate some "true" or benchmark index, which answers some well-defined economic question. We will return to this theme in section 2.4 below and address it more formally in chapter 4.

Many other weighting schemes have been proposed, but none has a superior theoretical foundation and all suffer from practical disadvantages. One possibility, discussed by Leamer (1974), is to use world exports. These have two advantages: like domestic imports, data on them are easily available, and unlike imports, they are much less likely to be influenced by domestic tariffs. However, this virtue reflects a basic problem with using any external variables as weights: they take no account of the special features of the country being studied.

Other possible sources of weights are domestic consumption or production levels. However, these also exhibit some odd features. Production shares give zero weight to tariffs on noncompeting imports, while consumption shares, like import shares, may be low for high tariffs precisely because they restrict trade so much. Finally, note that the implications of either consumption or production shares cannot be illustrated in figures 2.1 and 2.2, since these figures as drawn are consistent with an infinite range of consumption and production levels. Thus the high tariff on good 1 in figure 2.2 (which causes a large drop in imports and a considerable welfare cost) might get a low weight if sector 1 is less important than sector 2 in domestic consumption or production.

2.3 Measures of Tariff Dispersion

One implication of the previous two sections is that the problem of constructing a satisfactory aggregate tariff measure increases with the dispersion of tariff rates. This has led many practitioners to supplement weighted averages of tariff rates by measures of tariff dispersion to try and get a full picture of the restrictiveness of a tariff system.

Just as we discussed already in the context of average tariffs, a key issue in choosing between different measures of tariff dispersion is which weights, if any, should be used. In the absence of any theoretical basis for using measures of dispersion, the unweighted standard deviation or coefficient of variation of tariffs is often used. But this has little to recommend it. In our two-good example the unweighted standard deviation depends symmetrically on the two tariff rates, thus failing to give any indication that trade is more restricted by increases in the tariff on the high-elasticity good 1. The same is true if any fixed set of weights, such as the levels of free-trade imports, is used. This suggests that current import shares should be used as weights in calculating the standard deviation of tariffs.

However, using current imports as weights leads to additional problems, as figure 2.5 illustrates. When the low-elasticity good 2 has the

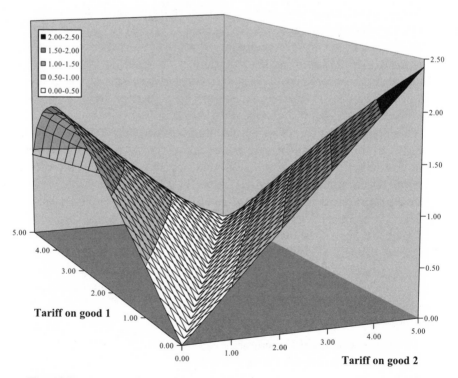

Figure 2.5
Trade-weighted standard deviation of tariffs

higher tariff, the import shares do not vary much, and so the trade-weighted standard deviation is approximately linear in the individual tariff rates. By contrast, when the high-elasticity good 1 has the higher tariff, its import share falls more rapidly and so the trade-weighted standard deviation rises at a decreasing rate in τ_1 and even declines for sufficiently high values of τ_1. This behavior gives exactly the wrong impression of the restrictiveness of the tariff structure, which is greatest when τ_1 is high. For example, the import-weighted standard deviation of tariffs is higher for the parameter values of figure 2.1 than for those of figure 2.2, suggesting once again that trade is more restricted in the former case whereas intuitively this is not so. These undesirable features are only partly avoided by using the coefficient of variation rather than the standard deviation of tariffs. The behavior of the coefficient of variation can be inferred from figures 2.3 and 2.5: it is very flat for all the parameter values shown, except for very high values of τ_1, when it increases rapidly, reflecting the fact that the average tariff is declining even more rapidly than the standard deviation. Once again, this behavior does not give a satisfactory depiction of the degree of trade restrictiveness.

Over and above the performance of the standard deviation of tariffs in this particular example, there are two general problems with using any measure of tariff dispersion as an indicator of trade restrictiveness. First, it implicitly assumes that a reduction in dispersion represents a reduction in trade restrictiveness. There are reasons, to be discussed in section 3.4 and chapter 6, why this may be true in some cases. However, as we will see, it is not a general presumption. Second, it is not clear how a measure of tariff dispersion can be combined with a measure of average tariffs. If both move in the same direction, there is a presumption that trade restrictiveness has unambiguously risen or fallen (although we have just noted the qualifications that must be made in interpreting changes in tariff dispersion). But this is no longer true if the two measures move in opposite directions. More generally, there is no satisfactory rule for combining the measures of average and dispersion to yield a scalar measure that might, even in principle, be comparable across countries or across time.

2.4   The Welfare-Equivalent Uniform Tariff

The discussion so far shows the problems with purely statistical measures such as the trade-weighted average tariff or the standard deviation of tariffs. All, in the memorable phrase of Afriat (1977), provide "answers without questions." Since they do not start from any explicit criterion of trade policy restrictiveness, their merits can be evaluated only on intuitive ad hoc grounds. And even on such grounds they do not correspond to measures of restrictiveness in any reasonable sense. A more formal approach, starting from an explicit concept of trade policy restrictiveness, is required.

The two central themes of this book are, first, that measures of trade policy restrictiveness should start from a formal criterion against which restrictiveness is measured and, second, that a natural criterion for an economist to adopt is the effect of the structure of trade policy on national welfare. As we will see in section 2.5 and in later chapters, our approach can easily be adapted to allow for other criteria. But the welfare-theoretic perspective is a natural starting point, and so it is the one with which we begin. It leads to an index number of tariffs that we call the "welfare-equivalent uniform tariff" or the "TRI uniform tariff," where TRI denotes the Trade Restrictiveness Index.

It is straightforward to see how this perspective leads to an alternative measure of trade policy restrictiveness in the example given earlier. Figures 2.6 and 2.7 repeat the tariff configurations of figures 2.1 and 2.2 respectively. Taking welfare as the standpoint, the appropriate way of

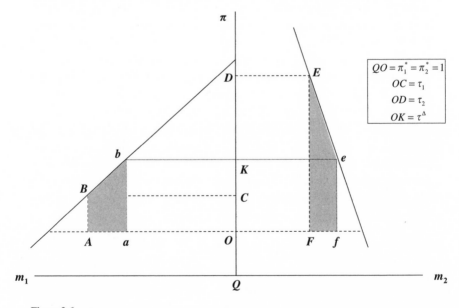

Figure 2.6
TRI or welfare-equivalent uniform tariff: Tariff rates and import demand elasticities negatively correlated

measuring trade restrictiveness is to ask: "What is the *uniform* tariff that, if applied to both goods, would be equivalent to the actual tariffs, in the sense of imposing the same welfare loss?" The answer to this question in figure 2.6 is a tariff equal to *OK*: the increase in the tariff on good 1 from *OC* to *OK* yields a welfare loss equal to the area *ABba*. By construction, *ABba* equals the welfare gain of *FEef* arising from the reduction in the tariff on good 2 from *OD* to *OK*. The same applies in figure 2.7 with appropriate modifications: the uniform tariff *OK* now implies a reduction in the tariff on good 1 and an increase in that on good 2. Evidently the welfare-equivalent uniform tariff is higher in figure 2.7 than in figure 2.6, in accordance with the intuitive presumption that trade is more restricted in figure 2.7. A corollary is that in both cases the welfare-equivalent uniform tariff is closer to the actual tariff on the high-elasticity good 1: this accords with the intuition that a high tariff on that good is more restrictive than a high tariff on good 2.

Figure 2.8 plots the welfare-equivalent uniform tariff as a function of the tariff rates on the two goods. Like the trade-weighted average tariff in figure 2.3, this index coincides with the actual tariff rates when they are equal to one another along the diagonal of the three-dimensional

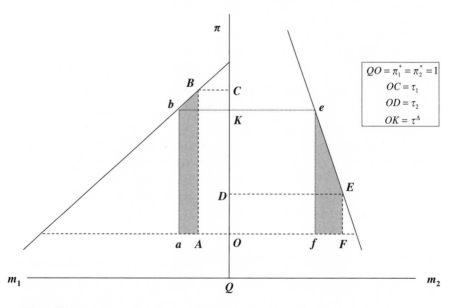

Figure 2.7
TRI or welfare-equivalent uniform tariff: Tariff rates and import demand elasticities positively correlated

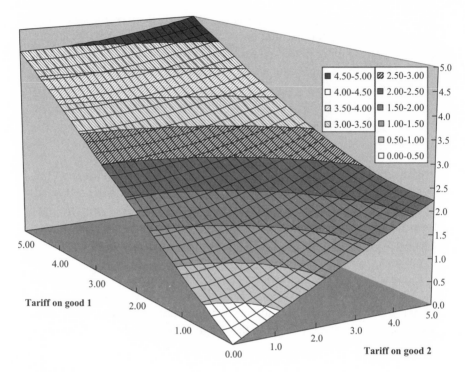

Figure 2.8
TRI or welfare-equivalent uniform tariff

surface. But, unlike the trade-weighted average tariff, it has satisfactory properties at other points too. It is always increasing in each individual tariff rate, and it responds more rapidly to increases in the tariff on the high-elasticity good 1.

These properties can be confirmed formally by deriving an explicit formula for the welfare-equivalent uniform tariff. Among the side-benefits of the resulting algebra, we can show that the approach extends to any number of goods. To solve for the welfare-equivalent uniform tariff, write the linear import demand function for good i as

$$m_i = \alpha_i - \beta_i \pi_i, \tag{3}$$

where β_i is the price-responsiveness of imports of good i (i.e., the slope of the import demand curve for good i relative to the *vertical* axes in figures 2.1 and 2.2). Now recall that with linear demands the welfare loss L_i from a tariff at rate τ_i on good i equals $(\tau_i \pi_i^*)^2 \beta_i / 2$. Hence the total welfare loss on all goods is $L = \sum L_i$, and so the welfare-equivalent uniform tariff τ^Δ is defined implicitly by the equation:

$$\sum \{\tau^\Delta \pi_i^*\}^2 \beta_i = \sum \{\tau_i \pi_i^*\}^2 \beta_i. \tag{4}$$

The right-hand side is the actual welfare loss from an arbitrary set of tariffs $\{\tau_i\}$, while the left-hand side is the hypothetical welfare loss from a uniform tariff rate τ^Δ. Equating the two and solving for τ^Δ gives the welfare-equivalent uniform tariff:[2]

$$\tau^\Delta = \left\{\sum \omega_i \tau_i^2\right\}^{1/2}, \quad \omega_i \equiv \frac{\{\pi_i^*\}^2 \beta_i}{\sum \{\pi_j^*\}^2 \beta_j}. \tag{5}$$

Note the differences from the formula for the trade-weighted average tariff τ^a in equation (1): τ^a is a weighted *arithmetic* mean of the tariff rates whereas τ^Δ is a weighted *quadratic* mean of the tariff rates, and, crucially, the weights used in constructing τ^a depend on the *levels* of imports, m_i, whereas those used in constructing τ^Δ depend on the *marginal import responses*, the β_i.

The weights in (5) can alternatively be written in terms of the elasticity of import demand for each good, evaluated at world prices, $\varepsilon_i \equiv \pi_i^* \beta_i / m_i$:

$$\omega_i = \varepsilon_i \omega_i^*, \tag{6}$$

where the ω_i^* weights are those used in (2) to construct the trade-weighted uniform tariff. Differentiating equations (5) and (6) shows that as required, the welfare-equivalent uniform tariff is increasing in each tariff rate, and by more so the greater the elasticity of import demand for the good in question.

The fact that the welfare-equivalent uniform tariff is related to the total welfare cost of the tariff structure gives it a firm theoretical basis. But does it mean that the welfare-equivalent uniform tariff is just another welfare index? It is true that the informational requirements of calculating the welfare-equivalent uniform tariff are similar to those of calculating the cost of protection. But the two measures are not the same, since they answer very different questions. The cost of protection answers the question "What is the welfare loss imposed by the tariff structure?" By contrast, we have already seen that the welfare-equivalent uniform tariff answers the very different question "What is the uniform tariff which

---

2. This expression for the TRI uniform tariff in the special case of independent linear demands is also derived by Feenstra (1995, p. 1562).

would be equivalent to the actual tariffs, in the sense of imposing the same welfare loss?"

An analogy with the theory of the true cost-of-living index (which we will pursue more formally in chapter 4) throws further light on this question. All economists agree that the fixed-weight consumer price index overestimates the true rate of inflation, which is more appropriately measured by a Konüs or true cost-of-living index. For example, the Boskin Commission Report estimated that substitution bias alone led to an overestimate of US inflation of about 0.3 percent per annum in the years prior to 1996, adding billions of dollars to the government deficit because of the index linking of taxes and benefits.[3] One response to this Report would be to assert that its estimates of true inflation are unnecessary, since it would be possible with the same underlying information to calculate the welfare cost of inflation over the period. But this ignores the usefulness and importance of being able to summarize in a single number the "true" rate of inflation. In the same way the welfare-equivalent uniform tariff summarizes in a single number the "true" height of tariffs.

To see the relationship between the welfare-equivalent uniform tariff and the cost of protection more formally, we rewrite the welfare cost equation (4) as follows:

$$L = \frac{(\tau^\Delta \pi^*)^2 \beta}{2} = \sum L_i, \tag{7}$$

where

$$L_i = \frac{(\tau_i \pi_i^*)^2 \beta_i}{2}.$$

Here π^*, defined as $[\sum \{\pi_i^*\}^2]^{1/2}$, is a quadratic mean of world prices, and β, defined as $\sum (\pi_i^*)^2 \beta_i / \sum (\pi_i^*)^2$, may be interpreted as the "aggregate price-responsiveness of imports." Inspection of this equation shows that the welfare-equivalent uniform tariff τ^Δ bears the same relationship to the aggregate welfare loss L as each individual tariff rate bears to the welfare loss in its own market. The two measures L and τ^Δ are closely linked, but they measure distinct concepts. Of course, the details of this derivation rely heavily on the linear partial-equilibrium specification of our example. However, we will see in chapter 4 that in general equilibrium our

---

3. See Labor Statistics Bureau (1996).

index of trade restrictiveness is also related in an appropriate manner to the true cost of protection.

2.5 The Import-Volume-Equivalent Uniform Tariff

In trying to measure the restrictiveness of a tariff system, it is natural for an economist to consider the equivalent uniform tariff that would yield the same level of welfare, and this is the benchmark on which we concentrate in this book. However, for some purposes and audiences, other benchmarks such as employment, output, or import volume may also be of interest. We will return to this topic in more detail in chapter 5. In the present example it is straightforward to illustrate the behavior of an index that equals the uniform tariff yielding a constant volume of imports (measured at world prices). Such an index was used by the Australian Vernon Committee (Commonwealth of Australia 1965) and its properties were investigated by Corden (1966). We may call it the "import-volume-equivalent uniform tariff" or the "Mercantilist TRI uniform tariff" ("MTRI" for short), since it recalls the concerns of Mercantilist writers with the balance of trade. Its behavior in the two-good example is illustrated in figure 2.9.

The key feature of figure 2.9 is that the MTRI uniform tariff is linear in both tariff rates but increases more rapidly in τ_1, the tariff on the more elastic good. Moreover the Mercantilist index behaves somewhat similarly to the welfare-equivalent uniform tariff (the surface in figure 2.9 never lies above that in figure 2.8) but very differently from the ad hoc indexes considered earlier in this chapter.

To derive an explicit expression for the import-volume-equivalent uniform tariff, note that it is defined implicitly by the equation

$$\sum \pi_i^*[\alpha_i - \beta_i(1 + \tau^\mu)\pi_i^*] = \sum \pi_i^*[\alpha_i - \beta_i(1 + \tau_i)\pi_i^*]. \tag{8}$$

The right-hand side is the total value of imports given an arbitrary set of tariffs $\{\tau_i\}$, while the left-hand side is the value of imports that would be generated by a uniform tariff rate τ^μ. Equating the two and solving for τ^μ gives the import-volume-equivalent uniform tariff:

$$\tau^\mu = \sum \omega_i \tau_i. \tag{9}$$

This has the same linear form as the trade-weighted average tariff τ^a but the same weights as the welfare-equivalent uniform tariff τ^Δ.[4]

---

4. It is also identical to equation (5) in Corden (1966), except that we ignore intermediate inputs, so Corden's v_i parameters (giving the share of value added in the domestic output of sector i) are set equal to one.

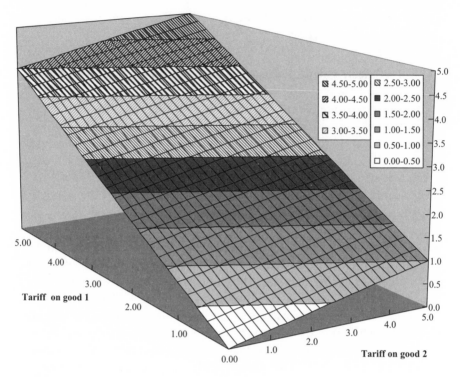

Figure 2.9
MTRI or import-volume-equivalent uniform tariff

2.6   Conclusion

In this chapter we have used a simple two-good linear example to introduce the issues that arise in measuring the restrictiveness of trade policy.
We have seen that the most commonly used measure, the trade-weighted
average tariff, has many undesirable features. Most strikingly, it is likely
to be decreasing in tariffs on highly elastic goods. This more obvious defect is overcome by using alternative weights, such as consumption, production, or the level of imports that would obtain in free trade. However,
indexes based on these weights have their own difficulties, and none of
them has any firm theoretical basis. Finally measures of dispersion such
as the standard deviation of tariffs have an intuitive appeal, since the
problems of average tariff measures are more acute the less uniform is
the tariff system. But such measures themselves have only a tenuous relationship to trade restrictiveness in our example. And even if this were not

so, there is no way of combining them with a measure of average tariffs to obtain an overall measure of trade policy restrictiveness.

All these problems with ad hoc or purely statistical measures of trade policy restrictiveness reflect a lack of clarity about what is being measured. The approach we propose in this book is to start with an explicit criterion against which trade policy restrictiveness is to be measured. Appropriate indexes can then be derived from these criteria, and we have illustrated in this chapter how this can be done in two cases. The most natural criterion from an economist's perspective is that of welfare. This leads to the welfare-equivalent uniform tariff, constructed to yield the same welfare loss as the actual (and typically nonuniform) tariff structure. An alternative criterion, with more appeal in a trade negotiations context, is the volume of imports. This leads to the import-volume-equivalent or Mercantilist uniform tariff, constructed to yield the same import volume (at world prices) as the actual tariff structure. We have seen that these measures have much more satisfactory properties and that, at least in our special example, they behave similarly to each other but very differently from the ad hoc indexes. In the remainder of the book we turn to show how these simple insights can be extended to more realistic contexts.

Appendix: The Geometry of the Trade-Weighted Average Tariff

In this appendix we show how the trade-weighted average tariff can be located in two-panel diagrams such as figures 2.1 and 2.2. Specializing equation (1) to the two-good case, the trade-weighted average tariff becomes

$$\tau^a \equiv \frac{t_1 m_1 + t_2 m_2}{\pi_1^* m_1 + \pi_2^* m_2}. \tag{10}$$

With world prices normalized to one, this can be rewritten in terms of tariff rates

$$\tau^a = \frac{\tau_1 m_1 + \tau_2 m_2}{m_1 + m_2}. \tag{11}$$

This in turn can be manipulated to equal

$$\tau^a = \tau_1 + \frac{(\tau_2 - \tau_1) m_2}{m_1 + m_2}. \tag{12}$$

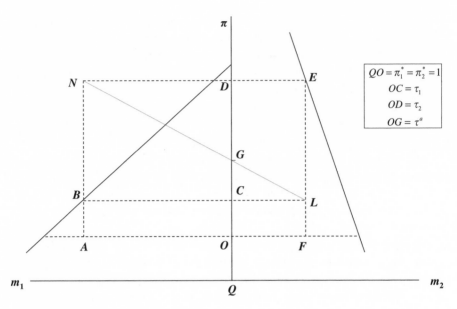

Figure 2.10
Locating the trade-weighted average tariff

Now repeat the same steps, expressed not in terms of symbols but of distances in figure 2.10, which repeats the essential features of figure 2.1:

$$\tau^a = \frac{OC \cdot AO + OD \cdot OF}{AF} = OC + \frac{CD \cdot OF}{AF}. \tag{13}$$

The final step is to locate the points N and L in figure 2.10. The coordinates of these points are the import volume of one good and the tariff rate of the *other* good. The straight line joining points N and L intersects the vertical axis at G. It is now easy to show that the distance OG denotes the trade-weighted average tariff. By similar triangles, $CL/BL = CG/BN$. This implies that $OF/AF = CG/CD$. Substituting into (13) gives

$$\tau^a = OC + CG = OG, \tag{14}$$

which proves the required result.

II TRADE POLICY REFORM AND THE TRI

3 Tariff Reform in General Equilibrium

We have seen in chapter 2 that most commonly used measures of trade policy restrictiveness are unsatisfactory on both theoretical and practical grounds. We have also seen that the *welfare-equivalent uniform tariff* provides, in principle, a much more satisfactory measure. However, the discussion so far has stayed in the realm of diagrammatic and partial equilibrium examples. In the remainder of this book we will show that the welfare-equivalent uniform tariff concept can be extended to and made operational in much more general contexts. The first steps we take are to allow for tariffs on many commodities and to model the general equilibrium interactions of firms and households in both goods and factor markets. To set the scene for this, the present chapter reviews the theory of tariff reform in competitive general equilibrium. Readers who are familiar with this topic may wish to skim this chapter to acquaint themselves with our notation and then proceed directly to chapter 4.[1]

3.1 Household and Firm Behavior

The setting we consider is that of a small open economy. This economy produces and consumes $n + 1$ commodities that are traded at exogenous prices with the rest of the world. Within this economy all agents face the same domestic prices, some or all of which differ from world prices because of trade policy. For convenience and with no loss of generality we assume that one of the commodities is an untaxed numéraire good and that all trade taxes are specific rather than ad valorem. This allows us to write the equilibrium price condition as

---

1. Textbook treatments of consumer and producer behavior using duality techniques may be found in Dixit and Norman (1980) and Woodland (1982). Our treatment of tariff reform draws on Anderson and Neary (1992) and Neary (1995).

$$\pi = \pi^* + t, \tag{1}$$

where π, π^*, and t are n-by-1 vectors of domestic prices, world prices and tariffs respectively. In general, the algebra is fully consistent with other types of trade taxes: import subsidies if commodity i is imported and t_i is negative, and export taxes or subsidies if commodity i is exported and t_i is either negative or positive, respectively. However, such policies raise issues of interpretation, which we postpone until chapter 12. As for quotas and other quantitative trade restrictions, they raise different issues which we will consider in chapter 7. For the present we therefore assume that tariffs are the only form of trade taxes, and subsume all export goods into the numéraire.

Two types of private-sector agents operate in the economy, households and firms. Households are assumed to be utility-maximizing price-takers who care only about their consumption of traded final goods. Thus a typical household maximizes its utility u, subject to its budget constraint $x_0 + \pi'x \leq I.$[2] Here x_0 and x denote consumption of the numéraire and nonnuméraire goods respectively, and I denotes household income. Utility is an increasing, quasi-concave function of the consumption vector $\{x_0, x\} : u = U(x_0, x)$.

It is more convenient to characterize the household's behavior in an alternative but fully equivalent way, as choosing its consumption vector to minimize the cost of attaining a given level of utility. This leads to the expenditure function

$$e(\pi, u) \equiv \min_{\{x_0, x\}} [x_0 + \pi'x : U(x_0, x) \geq u], \tag{2}$$

which equals the minimum cost of attaining u facing prices π. This function has some useful properties. It is increasing and concave in prices π; it is increasing in utility u, with e_u measuring the marginal cost of utility or the inverse of the marginal utility of income; and, by Shephard's lemma, its derivatives with respect to π equal the household's Hicksian or compensated demand functions for the nonnuméraire goods: $e_\pi(\pi, u) = x^c(\pi, u)$.[3] These coincide with the Marshallian demand func-

2. Throughout the book, all vectors are column vectors; a prime ($'$) denotes the transpose of a vector or matrix; and a dot ($\cdot$) denotes a vector inner product. Thus $\pi'x = \pi \cdot x = \sum_i \pi_i x_i$.

3. Subscripts generally denote matrices of partial derivatives, whose dimensions can be inferred from the context. So, for example, e_π is the partial derivative of the scalar e with respect to the n-by-1 vector π, and so is itself an n-by-1 vector; and $e_{\pi\pi}$ is the second partial derivative of the scalar e with respect to the n-by-1 vector π, and so is itself an n-by-n matrix. An exception to our subscript convention is x_0, which represents consumption of the numéraire.

tions $x(\pi, I)$ provided the levels of u and I are compatible, which gives the "Slutsky identity": $x^c(\pi, u) = x[\pi, e(\pi, u)]$. Differentiating this with respect to prices leads to the Slutsky equation, $x_\pi^c = x_\pi + x_I x'$, where x_π^c (which equals $e_{\pi\pi}$) is negative definite.[4] And differentiating it with respect to utility shows that the vector $e_{\pi u}$ is proportional to the vector of Marshallian income derivatives of demand x_I, where the factor of proportionality is the marginal cost of utility: $e_{\pi u} = x_I e_u$.

So far we have considered the behavior of a single utility-maximizing consumer. Obviously we wish to apply our results to the more realistic case of many heterogeneous households. One route to doing this would be to specify explicitly the distribution of tastes and endowments across households and the redistribution instruments available to the government. Instead, following much of the literature, we have chosen to ignore the aggregation problem altogether and to assume that the behavior of the aggregate household sector can be characterized in the same way as that of an individual household. This can be justified if the government continually implements a social welfare function using lump-sum taxes and transfers. However, a simpler justification is that we focus exclusively on efficiency and ignore issues of distribution. Whenever we state that the utility of the aggregate household rises, this should be interpreted as implying a potential Pareto improvement. Whether such a potential improvement is actually translated into an actual one for any or all households depends on the redistribution policies in force. Of course, this approach ignores a whole range of crucial issues concerned with distribution and inequality. However, we have nothing new to say on the subject here, so we set it aside to concentrate on the problem of devising policy rules that will increase efficiency.

Consider next the behavior of firms. Assuming that all goods and factor markets are competitive and all firms are price-takers, their aggregate behavior will maximize the value of GDP.[5] The resulting maximized value can be written as a function of exogenous variables:

$$g(\pi, v) \equiv \max_{\{y_0, y\}} [y_0 + \pi' y : F(y_0, y, v) \le 0]. \tag{3}$$

---

4. Concavity of the expenditure function in all prices implies that $e_{\pi\pi}$ is negative semidefinite. Provided we assume in addition that there is some substitutability in demand between the numéraire and nonnuméraire goods, this property is strengthened to negative definiteness, implying that all compensated demand functions are downward sloping.

5. GDP is used here to refer to the total value of goods and services produced in the economy, valued at domestic prices. It does not include tariff revenue which, as we will see in equation (7) below, is treated by convention as a separate source of income for the household sector.

Here y_0 and y are the net outputs of the numéraire and nonnuméraire goods respectively; v is a vector of exogenous factor endowments; and $F(y_0, y, v) \leq 0$ is the aggregate production constraint, summarizing in implicit form all the technological and institutional constraints on transforming primary factors into net outputs. For most of this book we hold factor endowments constant, so the v vector can be suppressed. As for the prices π, the GDP function is increasing and convex in them, and by Hotelling's lemma, its partial derivatives with respect to π equal the economy's net supply functions for nonnuméraire goods: $g_\pi(\pi, v) = y(\pi, v)$. The matrix $g_{\pi\pi}$ therefore equals y_π, the matrix of price-output responses, which from convexity can be assumed to be positive definite, implying that all general-equilibrium supply functions slope upward.[6]

3.2   The Trade Expenditure Function

Having considered the behavior of households and firms separately, we now wish to relate them. A convenient way of doing this is by introducing a new function, the *trade expenditure function*, which summarizes in a compact way the behavior of both sets of agents.[7] Its form reflects a number of assumptions about the economy. The first is that changes in tariffs affect both households and firms in the same way; for most of the book we will assume that they face the same prices. (This assumption is relaxed in chapter 12, where we consider domestic distortions.) The second assumption is the identity between GDP at domestic prices and factor income. We assume that the factors of production are fully owned by domestic households, so GDP and GNP are the same. (This assumption can easily be relaxed to allow for international factor mobility, using the approach of Neary 1985.) Hence the value of GDP is also the value of factor income that accrues to households.

With these assumptions the trade expenditure function is defined as the excess of household expenditure over GDP:

6. As in the case of demand, convexity itself implies that $g_{\pi\pi}$ is positive semidefinite and we must assume in addition that there is some substitutability between the numéraire and nonnuméraire goods in production to guarantee positive definiteness. A corollary is that there must be at least as many non-traded factors as there are traded goods, since otherwise the production possibilities schedule would have flat segments, and we would have to work with supply correspondences rather than functions.

7. Variants of this function have been used, under a variety of names, by different authors. Neary and Schweinberger (1986) coined the term "trade expenditure function" and presented the properties of the function in detail.

$$E(\pi, u) \equiv e(\pi, u) - g(\pi).$$ (4)

This function has very convenient properties. With respect to utility it behaves just like the standard expenditure function: $E_u = e_u$ is the marginal cost of utility and $E_{\pi u} = x_I e_u$ is proportional to the Marshallian income derivatives of demand. With respect to prices, Shephard's and Hotelling's lemmas together imply that its derivatives equal the difference between domestic demand and supply. Hence they give the compensated excess demand functions for the nonnuméraire goods:

$$E_\pi(\pi, u) = e_\pi(\pi, u) - g_\pi(\pi)$$

$$= x^c(\pi, u) - y(\pi).$$ (5)

These functions in turn are almost identical to compensated net import demand functions, except for one additional complication. It is convenient to assume that households have an additional source of income in the form of exogenous endowments of the nonnuméraire goods, $\bar{x}$. These can be thought of as representing foreign aid or other net transfers from abroad, in which case they represent an additional component of GNP not included in GDP. However, they are really introduced as a technical device to facilitate the derivation of shadow prices, which greatly help in interpreting the results. Since these exogenous endowments reduce domestic excess demand, they are subtracted from (5) to give the compensated net import demand functions for the nonnuméraire goods:

$$m^c(\pi, u, \bar{x}) = E_\pi(\pi, u) - \bar{x}.$$ (6)

We have assumed that e is concave in π and g is convex in π, so it follows that E is concave in π. Hence m_π^c, which equals $E_{\pi\pi}$, is negative definite: heuristically, the compensated net import demand functions $m^c(\pi, u)$ slope downward.[8] Note that the import demand functions are "net." If good i is exported, then m_i is negative, and negative definiteness implies that the (compensated) supply of good i is increasing in its price.

3.3 Shadow Prices and the Marginal Cost of Tariffs

We are now almost ready to examine the effects on welfare of endowment and tariff changes. The trade expenditure function E gives the excess of

---

8. As in the case of the individual $e(\pi, u)$ and $g(\pi)$ functions, $E_{\pi\pi}$ must be negative semi-definite and we assume sufficient substitutability that it is negative definite.

private-sector expenditure over GDP. This can be financed in only two ways. The first is from exogenous endowments. We have already discussed $\bar{x}$, the endowments of the nonnuméraire goods, which are valued at their domestic prices π. To them must be added any exogenous endowment of the numéraire good, which we denote b.[9] The second source of additional income is government activity, which in our model can take only one form, the redistribution of tariff revenue, $t'm$. It is convenient to assume that all of this is returned in a lump-sum fashion to the household sector. Given that we are ignoring distribution, this amounts to no more than the assumption that all the tariff revenue accrues to domestic residents in one way or another. In reality, of course, a government's use of tariff revenue may not accord with the marginal preferences of its citizens. However, this consideration raises issues that are not peculiar to tariff analysis and that are circumvented by our focus on efficiency.

The conditions for equilibrium in the economy can now be expressed in terms of a single equation:

$$E(\pi, u) = (b + \pi'\bar{x}) + t'm. \tag{7}$$

This equation is both the balance-of-payments equilibrium condition and the aggregate budget constraint. It states that any excess of domestic spending over income must be met either from exogenous endowments $b + \pi'\bar{x}$, or from redistributed tariff revenue. The import levels are determined in turn by equation (6). This is actually n individual equations, one for each nonnuméraire good. By Walras's law, they imply a corresponding equation for the numéraire good, when combined with the budget constraint (7).

To derive the welfare effects of endowment and tariff changes, it is helpful to begin by totally differentiating equation (7) without eliminating the change in imports. Since all tariff revenue is redistributed and since world prices are fixed (so that from equation 1, $d\pi = dt$), this simplifies to

$$e_u \, du = (db + \pi' \, d\bar{x}) + t' \, dm. \tag{8}$$

The left-hand side is the change in utility times the marginal cost of utility. This can be interpreted as the change in real income. As for the right-hand side, it says that real income is raised by any increase in endowments or by any expansion in tariff-constrained imports. Intuitively, tariffs induce import levels which are "too low," and any change

9. For consistency with our earlier notation, it might be more natural to write this as $\bar{x}_0$. However, later (when we suppress $\bar{x}$), it will prove convenient to interpret this as the exogenous balance-of-payments surplus, so writing it as b is appropriate.

that raises them above their distorted levels is welfare-enhancing, the more so the greater the distortion.

Equation (8) is very helpful in providing intuition for the effects of tariff changes. However, we cannot stop there since dm on the right-hand side is endogenous. To eliminate it, we must totally differentiate the import demand functions (6):

$$dm = -d\bar{x} + m_\pi^c \, d\pi + x_I e_u \, du. \tag{9}$$

Substituting for dm into (8), again using the fact that $d\pi = dt$ since world prices are exogenous, gives:

$$(1 - t'x_I)e_u \, du = (db + \pi^* \cdot d\bar{x}) + t'm_\pi^c \, dt. \tag{10}$$

This is the basic equation for the welfare effects of tariff changes in a small open economy, and in the remainder of this chapter we explore its implications.

Consider first the left-hand side of (10). It equals the change in real income, $e_u \, du$, multiplied by the term $1 - t'x_I$. Since the coefficient of db on the right-hand side is unity, the inverse of $1 - t'x_I$ can be interpreted as the shadow price of the numéraire, or, as it is more commonly known, the *shadow price of foreign exchange*. The inverse can also be interpreted, following Jones (1969), as the *tariff multiplier*. The "impact" effect of a unit increase in the endowment of the numéraire is to raise real income (measured in numéraire units) by one, which in turn raises demand for imports by x_I. From (8) this raises real income further, so causing a further increase in import demand, initiating a process which continues in a multiplier chain. Finally, a third way of looking at the inverse of $1 - t'x_I$ comes from rewriting it in an alternative way, using the fact that marginal propensities to consume sum to unity, $x_I^0 + \pi'x_I = 1$ (where x_I^0 denotes the income responsiveness of demand for the numéraire good). Substituting from this equation, we can rewrite the term $1 - t'x_I$ as the sum of income responses weighted by *world* prices, $x_I^0 + \pi^* \cdot x_I$, which, following Hatta (1977a), is often known as the *Hatta normality term*.

Each of the intuitive explanations just given for the term $1 - t'x_I$ suggests a route to establishing that it must be positive at all times, and not just in free trade (when it equals unity and so is trivially positive). First, writing it in the form suggested by Hatta shows that a sufficient condition for it to be positive is that all goods are normal; a negative value for the term is possible only if some goods are both inferior and subject to high tariffs. Second, the tariff multiplier interpretation suggests that if the term is not positive the multiplier process must be unstable. This is confirmed by Hatta (1977a), who shows that the term must be positive if the tariff-constrained equilibrium is stable under a tâtonnement-type adjustment mechanism. (See also Fukushima 1981.) Finally, interpreting the inverse of the term as the shadow price of foreign exchange suggests a direct argument why it must be positive, which is emphasized by Smith (1982, 1987): if it were not positive, the tariff reform problem would be trivial, since a welfare gain could be assured by throwing away some of the economy's endowment. On the basis of each of these three arguments, we will assume henceforward that the term is always positive.

Consider next the coefficient of $d\bar{x}$ in (10), which equals the vector of world prices. World prices are therefore the shadow prices appropriate for evaluating domestic activity in this tariff-distorted economy, and we may refer to the tariffs (the difference between domestic market and shadow prices) as the *shadow premia* of imports. This result, well known from Little and Mirrlees (1968), allows a useful interpretation of the coefficient of dm in (8): the welfare cost of a change in tariffs equals the sum of the compensated changes in distorted activities which it causes, valued by the shadow premia of those activities. This interpretation will continue to apply in many more complicated situations to be considered in later chapters.

Finally we come to our main focus of interest, the last term in (10). The coefficient of dt measures (minus) the *marginal cost of tariffs*. It shows that the welfare effects of tariff changes depend on the *compensated* changes in imports they induce, valued at the corresponding shadow premia. This result is the foundation of the two principal results in the theory of tariff reform, to which we turn next.

3.4 Welfare-Improving Tariff Changes: Radial Reductions and Concertina Reform

There is one simple case where the sign of the tariff reform term in (10) is unambiguous: when only a single good is subject to tariffs, m_π^c is a negative scalar (equal to the slope of the compensated import demand curve), and so a reduction in the sole tariff must raise welfare. The difficulty of the theory of tariff reform arises because this does not generalize to more than one tariff: even if all components of t are positive and all components of dt are negative, the fact that the matrix m_π^c is negative definite does not guarantee that the full expression $t'm_\pi^c dt$ is positive.

However, the spirit of the single-tariff case may be preserved if we assume that all tariff rates move together. In this *radial reduction* case the tariffed goods are aggregated into a sort of composite commodity, and the effect of reducing all tariffs by the same proportion is the same as that of reducing a single tariff when no other goods are subject to tariffs.[10] Formally, if each tariff is reduced by the same proportionate amount, we may write $dt_i/t_i = -d\alpha$, $d\alpha > 0$, for all i. In vector notation, this becomes $dt = -t\,d\alpha$, $d\alpha > 0$. Substituting into (10), we find that the change in welfare is proportional to $-t'm_\pi^c t$, which is minus a quadratic form in a negative definite matrix and so is necessarily positive. Thus, provided the shadow price of foreign exchange is positive, a radial reduction in tariffs always raises welfare. Summarizing,

Proposition 3.1 (Uniform Reduction Rule) Assume that the shadow price of foreign exchange is positive. Then a radial reduction in tariffs of the form $dt = -t\,d\alpha$ must raise welfare.

Of course, the requirement that all tariffs be reduced together and to the same extent is very demanding. An alternative approach to tariff reform is to reduce one tariff at a time. When this tariff is the highest, we have an example of what is called *concertina reform*. However, unlike the radial reduction rule, a concertina reform is not guaranteed to raise welfare without additional restrictions on the structure of the economy. Specifically, we need to assume that the good in question is a *net substitute* for all other goods:

Assumption (Net Substitutability) Good i is a net substitute for all other goods if the cross-effects in the compensated general equilibrium import demand functions are positive: $m_{ij}^c = m_{ji}^c > 0$ for $j = 0, 1, \ldots, n$, $i \neq j$.

With this assumption we can now derive the second main result in the theory of tariff reform. First, we disaggregate the tariff vector into t_1 (a scalar) and t_2, and assume that t_2 is fixed. The matrix m_π^c must then be partitioned conformably: for example, m_{12}^c is the matrix giving the effects on the compensated demand for imports of good 1 of changes in the prices of type-2 goods. Equation (10) with fixed endowments then gives the following:

$$(1 - t'x_I)e_u\,du = (t_1 m_{11}^c + t_2' m_{21}^c)\,dt_1. \tag{11}$$

---

10. Unless all initial tariff rates are equal, this does not yield a composite commodity in the usual Hicksian sense that all relative commodity prices are constant. Since $d\pi = dt = -t\,d\alpha$, we have $d\pi_i/\pi_i = -(t_i/\pi_i)\,d\alpha$ for all i. Hence prices fall fastest for goods with high initial tariff rates. We return to this issue in chapter 6.

This illustrates the basic problem of the second best. Lowering the tariff on good 1 has a direct effect, represented by $t_1 m_{11}^c$, which unambiguously raises welfare. However, it also has an indirect effect, represented by $t_2' m_{21}^c$, which is ambiguous in sign.

To derive the concertina rule from (11), it is convenient to switch to ad valorem tariffs, defined on the *domestic* price base. We write these as $T_i = t_i/\pi_i$, to be distinguished from the more familiar tariff rates defined on the world price base and already introduced in chapter 2, $\tau_i = t_i/\pi_i^*$. (Note that the change in base does not affect the ranking of tariffs: $T_1 > T_2 \Leftrightarrow \tau_1 > \tau_2$.) The key to the proof is the fact that E is linearly homogeneous in *all* prices (π_0, π), where π_0 denotes the price of the numéraire. This implies

$$\pi_1 m_{11}^c = -(\pi_0 m_{01}^c + \pi_2' m_{21}^c). \tag{12}$$

Making these substitutions, equation (11) can be rewritten as follows:

$$(1 - t'x_I)e_u \, du = \left(T_1 - \sum_{-1} \omega_{i1} T_i \right) \pi_1 m_{11}^c \, dt_1, \tag{13}$$

where $\sum_{-1}$ indicates that the summation is over *all* goods (including the numéraire) *except* good 1, and where the ω_{i1} coefficients, defined by $\omega_{i1} = \pi_i m_{i1}^c/(-\pi_1 m_{11}^c)$, sum to one: $\sum_{-1} \omega_{i1} = (\pi_0 m_{01}^c + \pi_2' m_{21}^c)/(-\pi_1 m_{11}^c) = 1$, from (12). The concertina rule now follows if we assume that good 1 has the highest tariff rate (so $T_1 > T_i$ for all $i \neq 0$ and $i \neq 1$) and is a general-equilibrium substitute for *all* other goods (so $m_{i1}^c > 0$ and hence $0 < \omega_{i1} < 1$ for all i). This implies that the term in brackets on the right-hand side of (13) must be positive, since it equals the difference between T_1 and a weighted average of all other tariff rates, $\sum_{-1} \omega_{i1} T_i$. Hence, recalling that m_{11}^c is negative, we have that a cut in t_1 must raise welfare. Summarizing,

Proposition 3.2 (Concertina Rule)   Assume that the shadow price of foreign exchange is positive, that good 1 has the highest tariff rate, and that good 1 is a general equilibrium substitute for all other goods (so $m_{j1}^c > 0$ for $j = 0, 2, \ldots, n$). Then a reduction in t_1 must raise welfare.

It is worth noting some common misunderstandings of the concertina rule. First, it does *not* require that all goods be substitutes, only that the good whose price is being lowered be a substitute for all others. Second, even this is an overly strong sufficient condition. In particular, the fact that good 1 is a complement for another good that is subject to a high tariff rate does not per se make a reduction in t_1 welfare-reducing. On the contrary, complementarities imply negative values of m_{i1}^c and ω_{i1}, which in themselves make it *more* not less likely that a cut in t_1 will raise welfare; see figure 3.3 below.[11] An exception to the concertina rule requires that good 1 be strongly *substitutable* with goods that are themselves subject to high tariffs, so much so that the bracketed term on the right-hand side of (13) becomes negative. As we will see in figure 3.4 below, this in turn requires that when there are two tariffed goods, good 1 and the numéraire good must be complements.

Finally, does the concertina rule justify a uniform tariff structure? We saw earlier that uniform reductions in all tariffs must raise welfare, and we have just shown that moving toward uniformity by progressively reducing the highest tariffs is likely to do so. However, this does not mean that uniformity itself is desirable. In particular, *raising* any tariff toward uniformity is unlikely to be desirable. This may be seen from (13), and by recalling that, by convention, the tax rate on the numéraire is zero, $T_0 = 0$. Because of this we cannot be sure that the term $T_1 - \sum_{-1} \omega_{i1} T_i$ is negative even if T_1 is less than all other tariff rates on nonnuméraire goods, which would be required for a rise in t_1 to raise welfare.[12]

3.5 Welfare and Tariffs: A Diagrammatic Illustration

When only two goods are subject to tariffs, the results of the last section can be conveniently illustrated, following Neary (1995), in a diagram drawn in the space of domestic goods prices. This diagram will also prove useful in the next chapter. Recall equation (11), which showed the welfare effects of changes in t_1 when t_2 is fixed. This can be reinterpreted as giving the condition for the optimal *second-best* choice of t_1. Setting du/dt_1 equal to zero implies

$$t_1^o = -t_2 m_{21}^c (m_{11}^c)^{-1}. \tag{14}$$

Since we have assumed that there is only one good in each of the sub-categories of imports, all the terms in (14) are scalars, and (since m_{11}^c is

---

11. This qualifies the criticisms of the concertina rule by Lopez and Panagariya (1992) who point out that complementarities are very likely in the presence of pure imported intermediate inputs.

12. It is true that raising tariffs towards uniformity must be welfare-improving if there is no numéraire good. However, in the absence of a numéraire, "uniform" tariffs are identical to free trade. See Neary (1998) for further details and see Fukushima and Hatta (1989) and Stern (1990) for contrasting views on the desirability of uniform taxation.

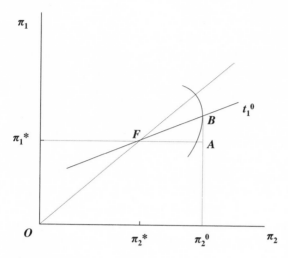

Figure 3.1
Optimal second-best tariff on good 1

negative) the sign of the relationship between t_1^o and t_2 hinges on the sign of the cross-price term m_{21}^c. Suppose, for concreteness, that the two goods are net substitutes at all times so that m_{21}^c is always positive. The relationship between t_1^o and t_2 is then as illustrated in figure 3.1 (since $t_i = \pi_i - \pi_i^*$). The t_1^o locus is upward-sloping and passes through the free-trade point (π_1^*, π_2^*).[13] For a given tariff on good 2, which implies a domestic price π_2^0, the second-best optimal value of t_1 is indicated by the point B. Since this point maximizes welfare subject to the constraint that we cannot move left of the vertical line through π_2^0, we can draw an iso-welfare contour which is vertical at point B, as shown.

Note a standard second-best implication: at point A imports of good 1 are unrestricted, yet welfare is increased if a tariff is imposed on this good. The intuition justifying this can be seen by recalling from (8) that the change in welfare is proportional to $t' \, dm$, which in our two-good case equals $t_1 \, dm_1 + t_2 \, dm_2$. At A, protection imposes a welfare cost because imports of good 2 are "too low" relative to the free-trade optimum. (Whether imports of good 1 are above or below their free-trade levels has

---

13. Equation (14) does not give a closed-form expression for t_1^o, and so the t_1^o locus is not a straight line, unless the trade expenditure function is quadratic in prices (so that Hicksian import demand functions are linear in prices and the m_{21}^c and m_{11}^c coefficients are constants). The qualitative properties of the diagram require only that m_{21}^c not change sign so that, in the relevant range of prices, goods 1 and 2 are either always substitutes or always complements.

no direct effect on welfare because t_1 is zero at A.) To raise welfare, it is therefore desirable to increase imports of good 2. The *direct* method of doing so would of course be to lower t_2, but this is precluded by assumption. There remains an *indirect* method: to raise the domestic price of its substitute, good 1, by imposing a tariff on it, so diverting demand from good 1 to good 2. Naturally this also serves to reduce imports of good 1 itself, but for a small tariff on good 1 the resulting welfare loss is small and so may be ignored: for a small movement from A toward B, $t' dm$ is approximately equal to $t_2 dm_2$. Only when point B is reached is the welfare gain from indirectly encouraging imports of good 2 exactly offset by the welfare loss from directly discouraging imports of good 1.

The relationship between t_1^o and t_2 is of interest both for itself and for the light it throws on the relationship between welfare and the values of *both* tariffs. Reversing the roles of the two tariffs, a series of steps identical to those that led to (14) gives the optimal second-best tariff on good 2, t_2^o, when the tariff on good 1 is fixed at an arbitrary level:

$$t_2^o = -t_1 m_{12}^c (m_{22}^c)^{-1}. \tag{15}$$

Bearing in mind that the direction of causation is now different, equation (15) can also be represented in price space. This locus too must be upward-sloping provided the two goods are always net substitutes; moreover it must be *more* steeply sloped than the t_1^o locus implied by (14).[14] We can go further if we assume that for each value of t_1 and t_2 there is a unique second-best optimal value of the other tariff. In that case there must be an iso-welfare contour tangential to the vertical line through B and another tangential to the horizontal line through C in figure 3.2. By appropriate choice of t_1 and t_2, these points can be linked to form a single iso-welfare contour that can also be extended into the other quadrants where either or both goods are subsidized. This gives the potato-shaped contour in figure 3.2:[15] the fact that it has an upward tilt follows from the assumption that the two goods are substitutes.

14. When the two goods are substitutes, the t_2^o locus is more steeply sloped than the t_1^o locus provided $m_{11}^c m_{22}^c - m_{12}^c m_{21}^c$ is strictly positive. This must hold since we have assumed that m_π^c is negative definite.

15. When the m_{ij}^c coefficients of the import demand equations are constant, each contour encloses a convex set. The proof is straightforward. Along such a contour: $d^2 t_1 / dt_2^2 = -AB/C$. Here A equals $m_{11}^c m_{22}^c - m_{12}^c m_{21}^c$, which is positive as already noted; B equals $t_1^2 m_{11}^c + 2t_1 t_2 m_{12}^c + t_2^2 m_{22}^c$ which is negative, being a quadratic form in the negative definite matrix m_π^c; and C is proportional to du/dt_1 and so is positive below the t_1^o locus. Hence along a given iso-welfare contour, dt_1/dt_2 is increasing in t_2 below the t_1^o locus and decreasing in t_2 above it. This proves that the contour is concave to the origin and so encloses a convex set.

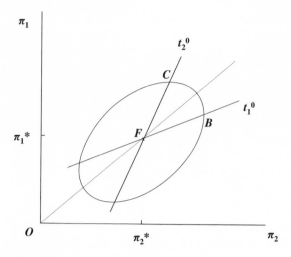

Figure 3.2
Iso-welfare contour when all goods are substitutes

The results of section 3.4 can now be illustrated in figure 3.2. The radial reduction rule implies that welfare rises as we move along any ray toward the free-trade point F. As for the concertina rule, it is convenient to normalize world prices to unity so that specific tariffs and ad valorem tariff rates are identical. With this normalization the uniform tariff rate locus OF is now the 45° line, and in the region northeast of F, a concertina reform implies a movement toward the 45° line, either vertically from above or horizontally from the right. To show that such a reform ensures a welfare increase, it is only necessary to show that the t_1^o and t_2^o loci lie on either side of the 45° line, provided all three goods are net substitutes. This follows because, from (13), the t_1^o locus can be written as $t_1^o = \omega_{21} t_2$ and with all goods substitutes ω_{21} is positive and less than one. Similarly the t_2^o locus can be written as $t_2^o = \omega_{12} t_1$, whose slope (in t_1, t_2 space) is positive and *greater* than one. Thus the two loci that determine the slope of the iso-welfare locus lie on either side of the 45° line, and a concertina reform must raise welfare.

Figure 3.3 shows that this result is strengthened rather than weakened when goods 1 and 2 are complements. Both the t_1^o and t_2^o loci are now downward-sloping, so a movement toward the 45° line from above or the right is unambiguously welfare-increasing. Indeed, any tariff cut now guarantees a welfare improvement, unlike in figure 3.2, where a highly nonproportional tariff cut (e.g., a reduction in t_1 with no change in t_2, starting from point B) could lower welfare.

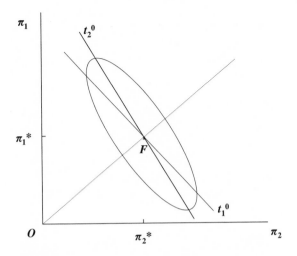

Figure 3.3
Iso-welfare contour when goods 1 and 2 are complements

Finally figure 3.4 shows how the concertina rule can fail because of complementarities. Good 1 is now a complement for the untaxed numéraire good 0. Hence ω_{01} is negative, and so ω_{21} is greater than one and the t_1^o locus is *more* steeply sloped than the 45° line. Cuts in t_1 in the cross-hatched region now lower welfare. Net imports of good 1 rise (which by itself is welfare-improving, as always), and so do net imports of its complement, good 0 (though since good 0 is not subject to tariffs, changes in its net imports have no welfare significance in themselves). However, good 2 is so strongly substitutable for good 1 that its imports fall sufficiently to reduce welfare overall. Note another implication: it is only in the shaded areas of figure 3.4 that an increase in the dispersion of tariffs raises welfare. We will return to the issue of tariff dispersion in chapter 6.

3.6   Conclusion

In this chapter we reviewed the theory of tariff reform in a competitive small open economy. Starting with consumer and producer behavior, we showed how a tariff-restricted equilibrium can be compactly specified in terms of the trade expenditure function. We then used this to derive the effects on welfare of arbitrary changes in tariffs, and to prove the two main results in the theory of tariff reform, the radial reduction and concertina reform rules. Armed with these technical tools and substantive

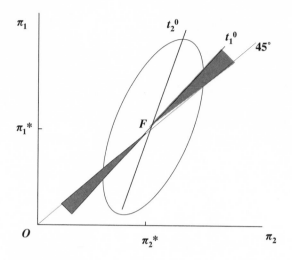

Figure 3.4
Iso-welfare contour when goods 0 and 1 are complements: The concertina rule fails in the shaded areas

results, we are now ready to proceed in the next chapter to see how a welfare-based measure of trade restrictiveness may be derived.

Appendix: Welfare-Improving Tariff Changes in a Large Open Economy

The discussion in the text of this chapter has concentrated on the case of a small open economy, facing parametric world prices. In this appendix we extend the analysis to economies that are large enough to influence world prices. The key results are, first, that the reference first-best point is no longer free trade but the optimal tariff point and, second, that welfare-improving tariff changes relative to that reference point can be characterized in the same way as in a small open economy.

To derive these results, we must repeat the derivations of section 3.3 allowing world prices to adjust endogenously. As before, we begin by differentiating the balance-of-payments equilibrium condition (7). Equation (8) is augmented by the change in the terms of trade, represented by the average of world price changes, weighted by net imports:

$$e_u \, du = (db + \pi' \, d\bar{x}) + t' \, dm - m' \, d\pi^*. \tag{16}$$

To eliminate the change in world prices, we need to make foreign behavior explicit. Rather than modeling the rest of the world in detail, we characterize it by its inverse net import demand functions, which give the prices offered by the rest of the world as a function of its net trades: $\pi^* = \pi^*(m^*)$. Since the rest of the world's net imports must match those of the home country $(m + m^* = 0)$, these demand curves can be written in differential form as

$$d\pi^* = \pi_m^* dm, \tag{17}$$

where π_m^* is the n-by-n matrix of the rest of the world's excess demand responses. Because of income effects in foreign demand this matrix cannot be signed in general. However, if substitution effects dominate abroad the matrix is positive definite.

Substituting from (17) into (16) yields

$$e_u du = (db + \pi' d\bar{x}) + \hat{t}' dm, \tag{18}$$

where

$$\hat{t}' \equiv t' - m' \pi_m^*. \tag{19}$$

This shows that changes in imports affect welfare to the extent that actual tariffs deviate from the optimal tariffs given by $m' \pi_m^*$. Equation (8) is the special case of (18) appropriate to a small open economy, where optimal tariffs are zero (since $\pi_m^* = 0$ and so $\hat{t} = t$). Computationally, the large open economy case is more complex, since the vector $m' \pi_m^*$ must be evaluated at the initial equilibrium not at the first-best optimum itself. Nevertheless, the underlying intuition is the same in both small and large open economies: an increase in imports raises welfare provided the tariffs on the goods in question are above their optimal levels.

In order to proceed, we need to eliminate the endogenous change in imports, just as in section 3.3. However, equation (9) cannot be used in its existing form, since the change in domestic prices $d\pi$ itself depends on import changes. To eliminate this, we differentiate (1) and substitute from (17):

$$d\pi = d\pi^* + dt = \pi_m^* dm + dt. \tag{20}$$

Substituting into (9) and collecting terms gives

$$dm = A[-d\bar{x} + m_\pi^c dt + x_I e_u du], \tag{21}$$

where

$$A \equiv (I - m_\pi^c \pi_m^*)^{-1}. \tag{22}$$

Equation (21) shows the effects on home net imports of changes in domestic variables (including utility), taking account of the induced changes in world prices. It is thus a type of general equilibrium import demand function (in differential form) and A may be interpreted as a matrix of *import demand multipliers* (where I is the n-by-n identity matrix). The A matrix shows how a unit increase in domestic demand for imports for whatever reason is dampened by the induced changes in the terms of trade. In the small open economy the matrix π_m^* is zero. Hence A reduces to the identity matrix, and equation (21) simplifies to (9).

To see the intuition for (21), consider the case of only one import good. Any positive shock to the right-hand side of the import demand equation (9) has an impact or first-round effect on domestic import demand. This raises the world price of imports (assuming that π_m^* is positive, so a rise in m raises π), which passes through to the domestic price, giving rise to a second-round *fall* in home import demand; this process continues as the multiplier chain works itself out. The final outcome is a value for A that is presumptively (though not necessarily) positive and less than one.

Returning to the general case, we arrive at the final step in evaluating the welfare effects of tariffs, which is to substitute from the change in imports from (21) into the welfare change expression (18). This leads to

$$(1 - T'x_I)e_u\, du = db + (\pi - T)'\, d\bar{x} + T'm_\pi^c\, dt, \tag{23}$$

where

$$T' \equiv \hat{t}'A. \tag{24}$$

Comparing this with the corresponding equation for the small open economy, (10), we see that it has exactly the same form, with the role of actual tariffs t in (10) taken by the shadow premia T in (23). These measure the difference between domestic prices and shadow prices for the tariff-constrained goods, and equal the import demand multiplier A premultiplied by the deviations of actual from optimal tariffs, $\hat{t}$. Clearly, the expressions for shadow premia are much more complex in the large open economy case. They are endogenous rather than exogenous, and they depend, in general, on all the variables characterizing the world equilibrium. Nonetheless, they permit an intuitive understanding of the principles of tariff reform along the same lines that apply in the small open economy. In particular, the uniform reduction and concertina reform results continue to apply with no additional qualifications, provided they are interpreted in terms of shadow premia rather than actual tariffs. (See Neary 1995 for details.) Hence, although the informational requirements of determining welfare-improving tariff changes are much greater when world prices are endogenous, the same basic principles apply.

4 The Trade Restrictiveness Index

In this chapter we formalize the intuitive arguments of chapter 2 using the general equilibrium tools developed in chapter 3. Our objective is a theoretically based index number that aggregates tariffs in an appropriate manner. To set the scene for this we begin in section 4.1 by reviewing the theory of the "true" or utility-based cost-of-living index, which is the appropriate aggregator for consumer prices. We then show in section 4.2 how the equilibrium of a competitive small open economy can be summarized in terms of a single function, the *balance-of-trade function*. These two steps pave the way for section 4.3, where we introduce the "true" or utility-based index of trade restrictiveness, which is the appropriate aggregator for tariffs. This index generalizes the welfare-equivalent uniform tariff introduced in chapter 2, and we call it the Trade Restrictiveness Index, or TRI. We explain the conceptual basis of this index, and in section 4.4 discuss its interpretation in both levels and rates-of-change form. Finally sections 4.5 and 4.6, which may be skipped without loss of continuity, show how the TRI relates to the trade-weighted average tariff and the cost of protection, respectively.

4.1 The True Cost-of-Living Index

In measuring changes in consumer prices, it is customary to compute some fixed-weight index number of current (period-1) relative to base (period-0) prices:

$$\Pi = \frac{\pi^1 \cdot x^r}{\pi^0 \cdot x^r}, \tag{1}$$

where x^r is a vector of reference quantities. A whole family of empirical index numbers can be defined depending on the choice of x^r. For example, setting x^r equal to base-period quantities x^0 gives the Laspeyres price index, while setting it equal to current quantities x^1 gives the Paasche price index. Alternatively, setting x^r equal to the arithmetic, geometric, or harmonic mean of current and base-period quantities yields the less well-known Edgeworth, Walsh, and Geary price indexes respectively.[1]

We already noted in chapter 2 the lack of conceptual foundations of fixed-weight indexes such as these. A different problem with them is that they make no allowance for changes in consumption patterns in response to price changes. Both these deficiencies are avoided by the "true" or Konüs cost-of-living index. The Konüs index is defined in terms of the household expenditure function, introduced in section 3.1. The index equals the expenditure needed to attain a reference utility level u^r at current prices, $e(\pi^1, u^r)$, scaled by the expenditure needed to attain the same utility level at base-period prices, $e(\pi^0, u^r)$:

$$\chi(\pi^1, \pi^0, u^r) = \frac{e(\pi^1, u^r)}{e(\pi^0, u^r)}. \tag{2}$$

The Konüs index answers the question "What is the cost of attaining the reference utility level u^r when prices equal π^1 relative to when prices equal π^0?"

If tastes are homothetic, the expenditure function can be written as $u\bar{e}(\pi)$, and the true cost-of-living index is independent of the reference utility level. But this is not true more generally, so there exists a whole family of true indexes, of which the two most widely used are the "Laspeyres-Konüs" index, which uses base-period utility $(u^r = u^0)$, and the "Paasche-Konüs" index, which uses current utility $(u^r = u^1)$. Notwithstanding this ambiguity, the Konüs index is preferable to any fixed-weight index because it allows for substitution away from commodities that have risen in price.

Since the expenditure function $e(\pi, u)$ is homogeneous of degree one in π, we can divide both sides of (2) by χ to rewrite it in a less familiar way:[2]

$$\chi(\pi^1, \pi^0, u^r) : e\left(\frac{\pi^1}{\chi}, u^r\right) = e(\pi^0, u^r). \tag{3}$$

1. See Diewert (1981) and Neary (1996) for discussion and further references.

2. This introduces a notational convention which we will use extensively in this book. The function preceding the colon is defined implicitly by the equation following it. This way of defining the true cost-of-living index was first introduced by Shephard (1953, 1970).

This defines χ in implicit form as the uniform scaling factor by which period-1 prices must be deflated to compensate the consumer for the change in prices from π^0 to π^1. The true cost-of-living index can therefore be interpreted as a utility-equivalent uniform price factor. It is this approach that extends to our true index of trade restrictiveness.

4.2   The Balance-of-Trade Function

In order to apply the same approach to measuring the restrictiveness of trade policy, we need to summarize the equilibrium of the economy in terms of a single function. We came close to this in chapter 3, where we saw that the trade expenditure function $E(\pi, u)$ permits a compact representation of the combined behavior of the household and producer sectors. However, this function does not take account of the effects of the government sector in redistributing tariff revenue to households. A function that remedies this deficiency and thus summarizes the whole economy as compactly as possible is the *balance-of-trade function*. In free trade it coincides with the trade expenditure function, but more generally the two functions have very different properties.

The balance-of-trade function is defined as the *deviation* from balance-of-payments equilibrium. For the small open tariff distorted economy of the last chapter, the function equals

$$B(\pi, u) \equiv E(\pi, u) - (\pi - \pi^*)' m^c(\pi, u). \tag{4}$$

The value of this function is the net transfer that is required to reach the level of aggregate national welfare u facing the vector of domestic prices π. Implicit in the function are all the variables that characterize the general equilibrium of the economy, including tastes, technology and factor endowments, world prices π^*, and the price of the numéraire good. In specific applications throughout the book we will make some of these arguments explicit.

The balance-of-trade function may also be written in an alternative way, using the fact that the trade expenditure function is homogeneous of degree one in domestic prices $\{1, \pi\}$, so $E(\pi, u) = E_0 + \pi' E_\pi$, where E_0 and E_π denote net imports of the numéraire and nonnuméraire goods, m_0 and m, respectively:

$$B(\pi, u) = m_0 + \pi^{*'} m. \tag{5}$$

Thus the balance-of-trade function equals the balance-of-payments deficit valued at world prices, or equivalently, it equals the amount of foreign exchange needed to sustain the utility level u when domestic prices equal π.

The values of π and u at which the balance-of-trade function is evaluated need not bear any relation to one another. In particular, they need not correspond to the same equilibrium. However, if they do, the function leads naturally to a compact way of expressing that the economy is in balance-of-payments equilibrium. All that is required is that the value of the function equal the exogenous balance-of-payments surplus b (which may be zero of course):

$$B(\pi, u) = b. \tag{6}$$

The results of chapter 3 may now be stated in an alternative way by differentiating (6):

$$B_u \, du = db - B'_\pi \, dt, \tag{7}$$

where, from (4), the derivatives of the balance-of-trade function are

$$B_u = (1 - t' x_I) e_u, \tag{8}$$

$$B'_\pi = -t' m^c_\pi. \tag{9}$$

This relates the change in real income (i.e., the change in utility times the marginal cost of utility e_u) to changes in the balance-of-payments surplus and the tariff vector. The term B_u equals e_u times the inverse of the shadow price of foreign exchange, discussed in chapter 3. As for the vector B'_π, it measures the *marginal cost of tariffs*: each element B_i equals $-\sum_j t_j \partial m^c_j / \partial \pi_i$, which gives the welfare cost of a unit increase in the tariff on good i. This is a weighted sum of induced changes in net imports, where the weights are the shadow premia (equal to the tariffs themselves). The whole expression $B'_\pi \, dt$ measures the foreign transfer that would be needed to restore the initial level of utility following a tariff increase.

4.3   The Trade Restrictiveness Index

We are now ready to generalize the welfare-equivalent uniform tariff that was developed heuristically in chapter 2. We wish to compare the degree to which trade is restricted by initial tariffs t^0 relative to a benchmark tariff vector t^1 (which may be zero if we are comparing with free trade). With given world prices, domestic prices are directly related to tariffs, so this is equivalent to comparing the restrictiveness of an initial price vector π^0 with a new one π^1. Using the balance-of-trade function, we can compactly write the assumption that equilibrium prevails under both the initial and the new trade policies as

$$B(\pi^1, u^1) = B(\pi^0, u^0) = b^0. \tag{10}$$

(For simplicity, we assume that the exogenous balance-of-payments surplus is the same in both periods, equal to b^0.) In some applications the new equilibrium may be identified with free trade so that $\pi^1 = \pi^*$, but the techniques also allow for more general comparisons between two distorted equilibria.

Now, by analogy with (3), define the TRI as the uniform scaling factor Δ by which period-1 prices must be deflated to compensate the aggregate consumer for the change in prices from π^0 to π^1:[3]

$$\Delta(\pi^0, \pi^1, u^r) : B\left(\frac{\pi^1}{\Delta}, u^r\right) = B(\pi^0, u^r). \tag{11}$$

This expresses the TRI as a function of an arbitrary reference utility level u^r. In practice, just as with the true cost-of-living index, it is very convenient to concentrate on the Laspeyres variant with $u^r = u^0$. Hence the TRI becomes

$$\Delta(\pi^0, \pi^1, u^0) : B\left(\frac{\pi^1}{\Delta}, u^0\right) = B(\pi^0, u^0). \tag{12}$$

This is the version of the TRI with which we will be concerned in the remainder of the book. Note that from (10), the right-hand side of the definition, $B(\pi^0, u^0)$, equals b^0. However, we do not make this substitution since (12) shows precisely what the TRI is: it equals a scalar index of the restrictiveness of the trade policy associated with domestic prices π^0, relative to that associated with domestic prices π^1, where restrictiveness is defined with respect to the initial utility level u^0.

Writing the TRI in the form given in (12) preserves the analogy with the true cost-of-living index from section 4.1. It is useful in applications where we want to measure the change in trade restrictiveness relative to an arbitrary initial equilibrium. In other applications it is more insightful to work instead with the inverse of Δ. This can be written as one plus a *uniform tariff surcharge* τ^Δ applied to the new prices π^1 (i.e., one plus the

---

3. Because of the presence of trade restrictions, the balance-of-trade function is not homogeneous of degree one in domestic prices $\{1, \pi\}$, and so the parallel between the TRI and the Konüs true cost-of-living index is not complete: there is no step which is analogous to equation (2) in the general-equilibrium derivation.

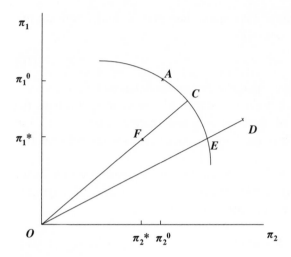

Figure 4.1
Trade restrictiveness index

uniform change in domestic prices, so $\tau^\Delta = (1 - \Delta)/\Delta$:

$$\tau^\Delta(\pi^0, \pi^1, u^0) : B[(1 + \tau^\Delta)\pi^1, u^0] = B(\pi^0, u^0). \tag{13}$$

This form is particularly useful when we wish to compare the initial tariff vector with free trade, so $\pi^1 = \pi^*$:

$$\tau^\Delta(\pi^0, u^0) : B[(1 + \tau^\Delta)\pi^*, u^0] = B(\pi^0, u^0). \tag{14}$$

τ^Δ is then the uniform tariff which just compensates for the abolition of period-0 tariffs. It is also a true index number, giving a scalar tariff rate that yields the same level of utility as the tariff vector π^0. We will refer to it as the "TRI uniform tariff."

Figure 4.1, drawn in price space for the case where only two goods are subject to tariffs, illustrates the interpretation of Δ and τ^Δ. Let point A, with coordinates (π_1^0, π_2^0), denote the initial protected equilibrium. Through this point is drawn an iso-welfare locus, representing those combinations of prices of the two goods that yield the same level of welfare as A and also preserve balance-of-payments equilibrium.[4]

4. The properties of this locus were considered in section 3.5. As shown there, the case illustrated in figure 4.1 is where all three goods (both the two goods whose prices are shown and the implicit numéraire good) are general-equilibrium net substitutes for each other. However, none of the conclusions drawn are affected by this.

Consider first the comparison with free trade, represented by point F (with coordinates (π_1^*, π_2^*)). The ray from the origin through F meets the iso-welfare locus through A at point C. Thus FC/OF measures τ^Δ, the uniform tariff rate that would compensate for the abolition of the initial tariffs (the move from A to F). Following our convention, the value of Δ is therefore the ratio of OF to OC. This is less than one, and so, relative to free trade, Δ is an *inverse* measure of trade restrictiveness.

Keeping A as the initial equilibrium, consider next the comparison with an arbitrary protected equilibrium represented by point D. To compensate for the policy change from A to D requires an equiproportionate reduction in domestic prices along the ray OD toward point E. Tariffs are not uniform along this ray (since it does not pass through the free-trade point F), so we describe this move as the imposition of a uniform tariff factor equal to minus the ratio of ED to OD. Our convention therefore implies that the value of Δ for this case is the ratio of OD to OE, which is clearly a welfare-consistent measure of the restrictiveness of trade policy at D relative to A. So, for a *given* initial equilibrium, Δ is an *increasing* measure of the trade restrictiveness of the new equilibrium.

4.4 The TRI and the Trade-Weighted Average Tariff I

What is the relationship between the TRI uniform tariff and the trade-weighted average tariff? In this section we show that both can be written as weighted averages of domestic prices, in either levels or rates-of-change form. In the next we provide sufficient conditions for the TRI uniform tariff to exceed the trade-weighted average tariff.

To write τ^Δ as a weighted average, we first apply the mean value theorem to the balance-of-trade function:[5]

$$B[(1 + \tau^\Delta)\pi^*, u^0] - B(\pi^0, u^0) = B_\pi(\tilde{\pi}, u^0) \cdot [(1 + \tau^\Delta)\pi^* - \pi^0] \tag{15}$$

where $\tilde{\pi}$ is some price vector intermediate between the uniform tariff and the initial equilibrium: $\tilde{\pi} = \alpha(1 + \tau^\Delta)\pi^* + (1 - \alpha)\pi^0$ for some α between zero and one. From the definition of τ^Δ in (14), the left-hand side of (15) is zero. Hence the right-hand side is also zero. By manipulating this, we

5. The mean value theorem states that, for any continuous differentiable vector-valued function $f(x)$, the increment in the function's value between any two points equals the difference between them, times the gradient of the function evaluated at *some* intermediate point: $f(x^1) - f(x^0) = f_x(\tilde{x}) \cdot (x^1 - x^0)$, where $\tilde{x} = \alpha x^1 + (1 - \alpha)x^0$, for some α such that $0 \le \alpha \le 1$.

can write the TRI uniform tariff as follows:[6]

$$\tau^{\Delta} = \frac{B_{\pi}(\tilde{\pi}, u^0) \cdot (\pi^0 - \pi^*)}{B_{\pi}(\tilde{\pi}, u^0) \cdot \pi^*}. \tag{16}$$

Recall from equation (9) that B_{π} can be interpreted as the vector of marginal costs of tariffs. Equation (16) then implies that the TRI uniform tariff equals the ratio of a weighted sum of tariffs to a weighted sum of free-trade prices, where the weights are the marginal costs of tariffs.

Equation (16) can be written in an alternative form, using τ_i to denote the tariff rate on good i, $(\pi_i^0 - \pi_i^*)/\pi_i^*$:

$$\tau^{\Delta} = \sum \omega_i^{\Delta} \tau_i, \tag{17}$$

where

$$\omega_i^{\Delta} \equiv \frac{B_i(\tilde{\pi}, u^0)\pi_i^*}{B_{\pi}(\tilde{\pi}, u^0) \cdot \pi^*}.$$

Thus τ^{Δ} is a weighted average of the tariff rates, where the weights depend on the marginal costs of tariffs B_i, evaluated at the intermediate price vector $\tilde{\pi}$. (Not all weights need be positive but they sum to unity.) Each weight equals the share of good i in the cost of a uniform increase in trade restrictiveness. Heuristically we can describe the weights as *marginal welfare weights*.

This may be compared with the conventional ad hoc measure of trade restrictiveness discussed in chapter 2, the trade-weighted average tariff τ^a. Like τ^{Δ} this is a weighted average of tariff rates, except that the weights are the actual trade shares:

$$\tau^a = \sum \omega_i^a \tau_i, \tag{18}$$

where

$$\omega_i^a \equiv \frac{E_i(\pi^0, u^0)\pi_i^*}{E_{\pi}(\pi^0, u^0) \cdot \pi^*}.$$

(This is equation 2 from chapter 2, with E_i replacing m_i.) Thus the weights in the TRI depend on the derivatives of the balance-of-trade function, while the weights in the trade-weighted average tariff depend on the deriv-

---

6. This is not well defined at free trade, since both numerator and denominator are zero there. (Recall from equation 8 that $B_{\pi}' = -(\pi^0 - \pi^*)m_{\pi}^c$.) However, since the numerator approaches zero faster than the denominator, there is a well-defined path along which the right-hand side of equation (16) converges to zero as π^0 approaches π^*.

atives of the trade expenditure function. Similar comparisons apply to the other ad hoc indexes discussed in chapter 2. For example, the weights in a tariff index based on consumption shares depend on the derivatives of the consumer expenditure function $(e_i \pi_i^* / e'_\pi \pi^*)$, and the weights in a tariff index based on production shares depend on the derivatives of the GDP function $(g_i \pi_i^* / g'_\pi \pi^*)$. This shows up the theoretical superiority of the TRI. Not only does it derive from an explicitly specified model of the economy and so have a firm basis in welfare economics, it also aggregates individual tariff rates using appropriate *marginal* welfare weights as opposed to aggregating by *average* shares in trade, consumption or GDP.

A different perspective on the comparison between the TRI uniform tariff and the trade-weighted average tariff comes from considering them in rate-of-change form. To see the effect on the TRI uniform tariff of a small change in the initial tariff vector π^0, totally differentiate equation (13). (We need to differentiate both sides of the equation: utility is fixed when we compare a *given* price vector π^0 with π^1, but utility changes when we change π^0.)

$$(B_\pi^\Delta \cdot \pi^1) \, d\tau^\Delta + B_u^\Delta \, du^0 = B_\pi \cdot d\pi^0 + B_u \, du^0 = 0 \tag{19}$$

In obvious notation, the derivatives of the balance-of-trade function are evaluated at two different points: B_π and B_u (without superscripts) are evaluated at the initial tariff-distorted price vector π^0, while B_π^Δ and B_u^Δ are evaluated at the uniform-tariff-surcharge price vector $\pi^\Delta \equiv (1 + \tau^\Delta)\pi^1$. From this we can derive the proportional change in the TRI uniform tariff:

$$\frac{d\tau^\Delta}{1 + \tau^\Delta} = \frac{B_u^\Delta}{B_u} \frac{B_\pi \cdot d\pi^0}{B_\pi^\Delta \cdot \pi^\Delta}. \tag{20}$$

This can be written more compactly as

$$\frac{d\tau^\Delta}{1 + \tau^\Delta} = \psi^\Delta \frac{B_\pi \cdot d\pi^0}{B_\pi \cdot \pi^0}, \tag{21}$$

where

$$\psi^\Delta \equiv \frac{B_u^\Delta}{B_u} \frac{B_\pi \cdot \pi^0}{B_\pi^\Delta \cdot \pi^\Delta}.$$

ψ^Δ is a correction factor needed because the balance-of-trade function is evaluated at two different points. It equals unity when the initial and reference price vectors are identical. In this convenient special case the change in τ^Δ takes the particularly simple form

$$\frac{d\tau^\Delta}{1+\tau^\Delta} = \frac{B_\pi \cdot d\pi}{B_\pi \cdot \pi}.$$ (22)

To interpret this, it is again helpful to draw the analogy with the true cost-of-living index χ, defined in (3). Define τ^χ as the uniform tariff surcharge corresponding to χ (i.e., $\tau^\chi = (1 - \chi)/\chi$). Using a similar chain of reasoning to that which led to (22), we can show that, as a result of an arbitrary price change $d\pi$, the proportional change in τ^χ equals $e'_\pi d\pi / e'_\pi \pi$. This gives the change in expenditure required to support the initial utility level following the actual price change $(e'_\pi d\pi)$, deflated by $e'_\pi \pi$, the additional expenditure needed to support the initial utility level following a uniform 1 percent rise in all prices. Similarly the numerator of the right-hand side of (22), $B'_\pi d\pi$, gives the change in foreign exchange required to support the initial utility level following a change in trade policy. This is deflated by $B'_\pi \pi$, the additional foreign exchange needed to support the initial utility level when all domestic prices of tariff-constrained goods rise by 1 percent. Thus, for small changes in tariffs, the change in the TRI uniform tariff equals the conventional measure of the cost of an *arbitrary* change in protection, normalized by the marginal cost of a *uniform* change in protection.

Finally, to compare the changes in τ^Δ and τ^a, equation (22) can be written in a different manner:

$$\frac{d\tau^\Delta}{1+\tau^\Delta} = \sum \omega_i \hat{\pi}_i,$$ (23)

where

$$\omega_i \equiv \frac{B_i \pi_i}{B'_\pi \pi}.$$

Just as we did with the level of the TRI uniform tariff in moving from (16) to (17), this equates the change in the TRI to a weighted average of the changes in domestic prices caused by the tariff changes, where the weights depend on the marginal costs of tariffs B_i. Compare this with the change in the trade-weighted average tariff. (To avoid discontinuities when all tariffs are zero, we consider the change in the trade-weighted average tariff *factor*, $1 + \tau^a$.[7])

---

7. The weights in (24) are valued at domestic prices, like the weights in the TRI. By contrast, as noted in section 2.1, the *level* of the trade-weighted average tariff is a weighted average of individual tariff rates where the weights are trade shares valued at *world* prices.

$$\frac{d\tau^a}{1 + \tau^a} = \sum \omega_i \hat{\pi}_i, \tag{24}$$

where

$$\omega_i \equiv \frac{E_i \pi_i}{E'_\pi \pi}.$$

Thus the weights in the TRI change depend on the derivatives of the balance-of-trade function, while the weights in the trade-weighted average tariff change depend on the derivatives of the trade expenditure function. Hence, both in levels and rates of change, the TRI uniform tariff aggregates individual tariffs or price changes using appropriate *marginal* welfare weights as opposed to the *average* import shares of the trade-weighted average tariff.

4.5   The TRI and the Trade-Weighted Average Tariff II

In the previous section, we showed that both the TRI uniform tariff and the trade-weighted average tariff can be written as weighted averages of individual tariff rates. Next we would like to be able to rank them. Unfortunately, we cannot do so directly. However, we can come close by introducing a new tariff index, which we call the *true average tariff*. In this section, we show how this new index is related to τ^Δ and τ^a.

The true average tariff is defined implicitly as

$$\tau^\delta : E[(1 + \tau^\delta)\pi^*, u^0] = E^0, \tag{25}$$

where E^0 is net expenditure in the tariff-distorted equilibrium: $E^0 = E(\pi^0, u^0)$. Equation (25) states that τ^δ is the uniform tariff that would induce the same level of net expenditure at the initial level of utility as the actual (and in general highly nonuniform) vector of initial tariffs. Like the trade-weighted average tariff, the true average tariff can be written as a weighted average of individual tariff rates, with the difference that the weights allow for substitution in import demand. To see this, we repeat the steps which we took with the TRI in the last section. Apply the mean value theorem to the trade expenditure function, and use equation (25), to write the true average tariff as follows:

$$\tau^\delta = \sum \tilde{\omega}_i \tau_i, \quad \tilde{\omega}_i \equiv \frac{\tilde{m}_i \pi_i^*}{\sum \tilde{m}_j \pi_j^*}, \quad \tilde{m}_i = E_i(\tilde{\pi}, u^0). \tag{26}$$

Thus τ^δ is a weighted average of the tariff rates, where the weights depend on import volumes evaluated at some price vector $\tilde{\pi}$ intermediate between the uniform tariff and the initial equilibria: $\tilde{\pi} = \alpha(1 + \tau^\Delta)\pi^* + (1 - \alpha)\pi^0$ for some α.

Next we can unambiguously rank τ^δ and the trade-weighted average tariff:

Proposition 4.1 The trade-weighted average tariff cannot exceed the true average tariff: $\tau^a \leq \tau^\delta$, with a strict inequality if there is any substitutability in import demand.

Proof The proof of proposition 4.1 is similar to standard bounds proofs in index number theory (see Pollak 1971) with the added complication that some goods are not subject to tariffs. Since the latter are subsumed into the numéraire, their domestic price and import volume equal one and m_0 respectively. Net expenditure by the private sector in the initial equilibrium is therefore

$$E^0 = E(\pi^0, u^0) = m_0^0 + \pi^0 \cdot m^0. \tag{27}$$

The trade expenditure function is a minimum-value function. (See Neary and Schweinberger (1986).) Hence net expenditure when the tariff-constrained goods are subject to a uniform tariff τ^δ satisfies the following:

$$E[(1 + \tau^\delta)\pi^*, u^0] \leq m_0^0 + (1 + \tau^\delta)\pi^* \cdot m^0, \tag{28}$$

with a strict inequality if there is any substitutability in import demand. From the definition of τ^δ, the left-hand sides of (27) and (28) are equal. Combining the right-hand sides, canceling m_0^0, and invoking the definition of τ^a from chapter 2, the result follows immediately. ∎

Equation (26) and proposition 4.1 show that the relationship between the trade-weighted average tariff and the true average tariff is identical to that between the Laspeyres price index and the Konüs true cost-of-living index in consumer theory: τ^a gives a fixed-weight approximation to τ^δ, and because it neglects substitution induced by tariff changes, it underestimates the true height of tariffs.

The preceding result might be interpreted to imply that the trade-weighted average tariff is "no worse" than the consumer price index, since both are fixed-weight approximations to theoretically based indexes. However, this is not the case because the true average tariff itself is of relatively limited interest. It has some potential uses, but they are all partial equilibrium in nature.[8] The true average tariff is not a valid general-equilibrium measure of average tariffs, since it does not equal the uniform tariff that would induce the same equilibrium as the initial tariff structure. Formally this is because it is defined in terms of the trade expenditure function rather than the balance-of-trade function. Thus it focuses on private-sector behavior only and ignores the government budget constraint. If a uniform tariff equal to τ^δ were imposed, with utility at u^0, private sector spending would equal the level it has in the initial equilibrium: $E[(1 + \tau^\delta)\pi^*, u^0] = E(\pi^0, u^0)$. However, the economy would not be in equilibrium, since the balance of trade would not equal its initial level b^0: $B[(1 + \tau^\delta)\pi^*, u^0] \neq b^0$. Hence τ^δ does not provide a valid benchmark for calculating a scalar equivalent to the initial tariff structure. By construction, only the TRI uniform tariff gives such a benchmark.

Can we relate the true average tariff and the TRI uniform tariff? The next proposition states the relationship between them but shows that it is indeterminate in sign:

Proposition 4.2 The true average tariff τ^δ exceeds the TRI uniform tariff τ^Δ if and only if replacing the initial tariff vector by the welfare-equivalent uniform tariff would lead to a fall in tariff revenue.

Proof The true average tariff is defined by (25), while the TRI uniform tariff is defined by (13). Writing the latter in full (using the definition of the balance-of-trade function) gives

$$E[(1 + \tau^\Delta)\pi^*, u^0] - \tau^\Delta \pi^* \cdot E_\pi[(1 + \tau^\Delta)\pi^*, u^0] = b^0. \tag{29}$$

Subtracting this from (25) gives

$$E[(1 + \tau^\delta)\pi^*, u^0] - E[(1 + \tau^\Delta)\pi^*, u^0]$$
$$= (\pi^0 - \pi^*) \cdot E_\pi(\pi^0, u^0) - \tau^\Delta \pi^* \cdot E_\pi[(1 + \tau^\Delta)\pi^*, u^0]$$
$$= R^0 - R^\Delta. \tag{30}$$

The trade expenditure function is increasing in prices, so the left-hand side is positive if and only if τ^δ exceeds τ^Δ. As for the right-hand side,

---

8. The true average tariff is the appropriate index to use to aggregate tariffs across subsectors in order to construct an index of the average level of tariffs facing consumers or producers. It has been used in this way (usually operationalized under Törnqvist or Cobb-Douglas assumptions) both in partial equilibrium studies (e.g., Aw and Roberts 1986) and in CGE models (e.g., Cox and Harris 1985). See chapter 10, section 10.2, for further discussion.

it equals the actual tariff revenue in the initial equilibrium (R^0) minus the revenue that would accrue if the tariff vector were replaced by the welfare-equivalent uniform tariff (R^Δ). This proves the proposition.   ∎

There is no way in general of determining whether moving from the initial tariffs to the welfare-equivalent uniform tariff would raise or lower tariff revenue. Hence we can conclude that the trade-weighted average tariff is a Laspeyres approximation to a "true" index, which is itself a flawed measure of trade restrictiveness and bears an indeterminate relationship to the correct measure. The trade-weighted average tariff does not allow for substitutability and is implicitly partial equilibrium; the true average tariff remedies the first deficiency, but only the TRI remedies both.

4.6   The TRI and the Cost of Protection

The fact that the TRI uses utility as benchmark suggests that it is related to the standard measure of the cost of protection. This turns out to be the case. However, it does *not* follow that the TRI is merely a rescaling of the cost of protection. On the contrary, the two indexes measure very different things and are related in exactly the same way as the height of a single tariff is related to the Harberger triangle measure of welfare cost. We have already demonstrated this in the linear example of chapter 2, where we noted that the two concepts have similar informational requirements but provide answers to very different questions. We now show that this continues to hold in the more general model of this chapter.

   Note first that the standard compensating variation measure of the cost of protection in this model is

$$L(\pi^0, u^0) = B(\pi^0, u^0) - B(\pi^*, u^0).\tag{31}$$

If only a single good is subject to a tariff, (31) may be written as an integral over the price derivative of the balance-of-trade function:

$$L(\pi^0, u^0) = \int_0^{\tau^0} B_\pi[(1 + \tau)\pi^*, u^0]\, d\tau.\tag{32}$$

Equation (32) does not extend to the general case of many tariffs. However, the general case may be reduced to a scalar representation by rewriting (31) using the definition of the TRI uniform tariff from (14):

$$L(\pi^0, u^0) = B[(1 + \tau^\Delta)\pi^*, u^0] - B(\pi^*, u^0).\tag{33}$$

Hence

$$L(\pi^0, u^0) = \int_0^{\tau^\Delta} B_\pi[(1 + \tau)\pi^*, u^0] \, d\tau. \tag{34}$$

Thus we have expressed the cost of protection with many tariffs as an integral over the scalar TRI uniform tariff in exactly the same way as the cost of protection with a single tariff equals an integral over the tariff. This confirms that the TRI is a correct measure of the average height of trade restrictions, and that it is conceptually distinct from the cost of protection itself. Indeed, the TRI bears the same relation to the welfare cost of protection as the true cost-of-living index bears to the true measure of welfare change in consumer theory.

4.7   Conclusion

This chapter has outlined one of the central contributions of the book, the Trade Restrictiveness Index. We explained how the TRI is derived, noted its resemblance to the true cost-of-living index in consumer theory, and outlined its properties and underlying intuition. An obvious next step is to proceed to empirical implementation, which involves specifying in more detail the model of the economy that has so far been subsumed inside the black box of the balance-of-trade function. However, before proceeding with this, some further conceptual matters must be addressed. First, the relationship between the TRI and the standard measures of tariff mean and dispersion merits further consideration. Second, the theory of the TRI must be extended to allow for quantitative trade restrictions as well as tariffs. Third, we need to compare the TRI with other indexes and to explore its robustness to relaxations of the assumptions made in this chapter. These themes are the focus of the remainder of part II.

5 The Mercantilist Trade Restrictiveness Index

In this chapter we turn to consider our second tariff index number, the Mercantilist TRI (MTRI). We call it "Mercantilist" because it takes as its starting point the Mercantilist preoccupation with the volume of trade. Modern avatars of Mercantilist thinking are everywhere, and their concern with trade volumes plays an important constraining role in policy formation. For one example, successive GATT rounds have interpreted reciprocity in tariff negotiations to mean equivalent import volume expansion. The WTO goes further, sanctioning retaliation by the offended party to displace a volume of trade equal to that displaced by the original offending protection. (See Bagwell and Staiger 1999 for a rationalization.) For another example, interest group pleading and even US government negotiators have focused in recent years on trade volumes in auto parts and in semiconductors, as well as on aggregate US–Japanese bilateral trade volumes. The ubiquity of such examples shows that there is a demand on the part of practical trade policy makers for measures of trade restrictiveness that take the volume of trade as reference. Such measures thus have a vital role to play both as an input to negotiations and as a performance measure of negotiations.

In the previous chapter we addressed the policy index number problem in a different context, that of the welfare effect of trade restrictions. We provided a rigorous theoretical foundation for the Trade Restrictiveness Index (TRI), which operationalizes the idea of finding a uniform tariff that yields the same *real income* as the initial differentiated tariff structure. We advocated its use in studies of openness and growth and in other applications where it is desirable to have a measure of the restrictiveness of trade policy that takes real income as its reference. In the trade negotiations context, however, comparing levels of protection with an index that holds constant the level of real income is less

appropriate.[1] Nations care about the effect of their partners' policies on
their own interests, not their partners' interests. This need is addressed
by the MTRI, which answers the question "What is the uniform tariff
rate that will yield the same *trade volume* as the current differentiated
tariff structure?"

Section 5.1 introduces the MTRI and sections 5.2 and 5.3 compare it
with the trade-weighted average tariff and the TRI, respectively.

5.1   The MTRI

Chapter 2 gave a diagrammatic derivation of the Mercantilist TRI in the
context of a simple two-good example. Here we wish to define it in the
much more general setting of chapters 3 and 4: a competitive small open
economy that imposes a vector of tariffs t on its imports m. We first show
how the total volume of imports can be expressed as a function of domestic prices and the trade balance, and we then use this function to define
the Mercantilist TRI.

We begin with the general-equilibrium import demand functions that
depend on domestic prices and the economy's exogenous income $b : m =
m(\pi, b)$. These have not been discussed before, but they are closely related
to the utility-compensated net import demand functions $m^c(\pi, u)$ that
were derived in chapter 3. The relationship between the two is set out
in full in the appendix to this chapter. Now we aggregate the vector of
net imports m using world prices to obtain the import volume function,
$M(\pi, b)$, which gives the volume of imports at world prices when domestic prices equal π and the trade balance equals b:

$$M(\pi, b) \equiv \pi^* \cdot m(\pi, b). \tag{1}$$

Then we can use this function to define the Mercantilist Trade Restrictiveness Index (MTRI) as the uniform tariff τ^μ that yields the same
volume (at world prices) of tariff-restricted imports as the initial tariffs,
$M(\pi^0, b^0)$:

---

1. An index of home country tariffs that holds constant the real income of the foreign country is appealing in a two-country world. In an n-country world (with $n > 2$), this loses its appeal because an index of one country's trade distortions can hold constant only one of its
trading partners' real incomes. Thus there would be $n - 1$ different indexes of each country's
trade policies, differing from each other in complex and unintuitive ways. A single constant-
volume index treats no one trading partner as special and is appealing as a summary of a
country's restrictiveness relative to the rest of the world.

$$\tau^{\mu}(\pi^0, b^0) : M[(1 + \tau^{\mu})\pi^*, b^0] = M(\pi^0, b^0).$$ (2)

Note that we get a different MTRI depending on which goods are included in the index. In international comparisons and multilateral negotiations it is natural to include all imports, regardless of trading partner and whether or not they are subject to tariffs. (This is the convention adopted in the applications of part III.) Alternatively, in bilateral negotiations it makes more sense to define the index as the uniform tariff that would yield the same volume of bilateral trade. For example, in US–Japan trade negotiations the MTRI for Japan might include all Japanese imports and exports to the United States, both distorted and undistorted. Separate indexes could also be calculated for particular product groups (e.g., reflecting concerns with bilateral trade in electronics or motor vehicles). The only group of goods for which the index cannot be defined is that of *all* traded goods, both exported and imported.[2]

In chapter 4 we used the intermediate value theorem to write the TRI as a weighted average of tariff rates. We can do the same for the MTRI by applying the theorem to the import volume function:

$$M[(1 + \tau^{\mu})\pi^*, b^0] - M(\pi^0, b^0) = M_{\pi}(\tilde{\pi}, b^0) \cdot [(1 + \tau^{\mu})\pi^* - \pi^0],$$ (3)

where $\tilde{\pi}$ is some price vector mean between the uniform tariff and the initial equilibrium: $\tilde{\pi} = \alpha(1 + \tau^{\mu})\pi^* + (1 - \alpha)\pi^0$ for some α such that $0 \leq \alpha \leq 1$. As before, we can set the left-hand side of (3) equal to zero from the definition of τ^{μ} to obtain

$$\tau^{\mu} = \frac{M_{\pi}(\tilde{\pi}, b^0) \cdot (\pi^0 - \pi^*)}{M_{\pi}(\tilde{\pi}, b^0) \cdot \pi^*} = \sum_{i} \omega_i^{\mu} \tau_i,$$ (4)

where

$$\omega_i^{\mu} \equiv \frac{M_i(\tilde{\pi}, b^0)}{M_{\pi}(\tilde{\pi}, b^0)}$$

Thus the MTRI is a weighted average of the tariff rates. The weights are marginal volume weights, as opposed to average volume weights in the

2. Heuristically it does not make sense to define trade restrictiveness without selecting an untaxed good or group of goods as reference. Technically the index is not defined over all goods, since (from the standard assumption of no money illusion) when b equals zero the import volume function is homogeneous of degree zero in the prices of *all* traded goods. Neary (1998) shows how the failure to select a reference untaxed good leads to misleading results in the theory of trade policy.

case of the trade-weighted average tariff and marginal welfare weights in the case of the TRI.

We can also derive the effects of small tariff changes, meaning changes in π^0, on the MTRI, just as we did for the TRI in chapter 4. Totally differentiate (2), using M^0 to denote $M(\pi^0, b^0)$, and holding π^* and b^0 fixed. This gives

$$\frac{d\tau^\mu}{1 + \tau^\mu} = \frac{M_\pi \cdot d\pi^0}{M_\pi^\mu \cdot \pi^\mu} = \psi^\mu \frac{M_\pi \cdot d\pi^0}{M_\pi \cdot \pi^0}. \tag{5}$$

As before, ψ^μ is a correction factor that is needed because the derivatives of the import volume function are evaluated at two different points:

$$\psi^\mu \equiv \frac{M_\pi \cdot \pi^0}{M_\pi^\mu \cdot \pi^\mu}. \tag{6}$$

M_π is evaluated at the initial tariff-distorted price vector π^0, and M_π^μ is evaluated at the uniform-tariff-equivalent price vector $\pi^\mu \equiv (1 + \tau^\mu)\pi^*$. The correction factor is likely to be close to unity, and can be ignored for small changes. The change in the MTRI can then be written as a weighted average of tariff changes:

$$\frac{d\tau^\mu}{1 + \tau^\mu} = \sum \omega_i \hat{\pi}_i, \tag{7}$$

where

$$\omega_i \equiv \frac{M_i \pi_i}{M_\pi' \pi}.$$

This should be compared with equations (23) and (24) in chapter 4, which give the corresponding changes in the TRI and the trade-weighted average tariff. The change in the MTRI weights changes in tariff rates on individual goods by their marginal contribution to import volume or marginal import share, whereas the change in the TRI weights changes in tariff rates on individual goods by their marginal contribution to welfare and the change in the trade-weighted average tariff weights changes in tariff rates on individual goods by their *average* import share.

5.2   The MTRI and the TRI

The first issue we address is the relationship between the MTRI and the TRI. We have already seen in chapter 2 that the MTRI is less than the

TRI in the two-good linear case. (Recall the discussion in section 2.5 and the comparison between figures 2.8 and 2.9.) Here we show that under very general conditions, the same unambiguous ranking continues to hold:

Proposition 5.1 The MTRI uniform tariff cannot exceed the TRI uniform tariff: $\tau^\mu \leq \tau^\Delta$.

This result can be explained intuitively as follows: Replacing an initial vector of nonuniform tariffs by the MTRI uniform tariff requires raising low tariffs and cutting high ones. Since the total volume of imports must remain fixed, the welfare cost of the tariff increases must be less (in absolute value) than the welfare gain from the tariff cuts. Hence, moving to the MTRI uniform tariff raises welfare. To restore welfare to its initial level would require a *higher* uniform tariff than the MTRI.

This result can be illustrated in figure 5.1, which repeats the initial position from figure 2.1 in chapter 2. With world prices of both goods QO normalized to equal one, the initial tariff OC on good 1 is much lower than that on good 2, OD. The initial level of imports measured at world prices equals AF. As in chapter 2, the MTRI uniform tariff can be con-

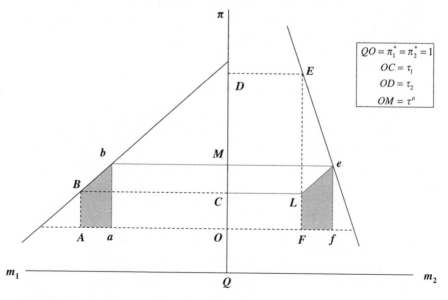

Figure 5.1
MTRI and TRI uniform tariffs compared

structed by first locating point L, which is horizontally aligned with the import point for good 1, B, and vertically aligned with that for good 2, E. Now draw through L the line Le parallel to the import demand curve for good 1, which meets the import demand curve for good 2 at point e. The uniform tariff OM therefore generates total imports of be, which, by construction, equal initial imports AF. What about welfare? Moving to the MTRI uniform tariff OM means that the welfare cost of raising the low tariff (AB) on good 1 is $ABba$, which by similar triangles equals $FLef$. This is clearly less than $FEef$, the welfare gain from cutting the high tariff on good 2 (FE). Hence a higher uniform tariff is needed if welfare is to remain unchanged, which implies that the TRI uniform tariff is greater than the MTRI uniform tariff.

Proposition 5.1 is an important result, since it means that the uniform tariff calculated according to the MTRI logic generally underestimates the uniform tariff appropriate when welfare is the standard of reference. In the remainder of this section we present a formal proof of the result, which readers less interested in technical details may skip without loss of continuity.

Proof of Proposition 5.1

Just as we defined the actual volume of trade function in (1), we can also define a utility compensated volume of trade function which uses world prices to aggregate the Hicksian import demand vector:

$$M^c(\pi, u) \equiv \pi^* \cdot m^c(\pi, u). \tag{8}$$

Since we are mostly concerned with uniform tariffs, it is convenient to define amended balance of trade and compensated volume of imports functions, both of which depend on the uniform tariff rate τ and the level of utility u (given world prices):

$$\bar{B}(\tau, u) \equiv B[(1+\tau)\pi^*, u], \quad \overline{M}^c(\tau, u) \equiv M^c[(1+\tau)\pi^*, u]. \tag{9}$$

(Note that τ is a scalar in this subsection.) The signs of the derivatives of these functions are given by the following lemma:

Lemma 5.1 (i) $\bar{B}_\tau > 0$; (ii) $\bar{B}_u > 0$; (iii) $\overline{M}^c_\tau < 0$; (iv) $\overline{M}^c_u > 0$.

The proof is immediate: $\bar{B}_\tau = B'_\pi \pi^* = -\tau \pi^{*\prime} E_{\pi\pi} \pi^*$ and $\overline{M}^c_\tau = M^{c\prime}_\pi \pi^* = \pi^{*\prime} E_{\pi\pi} \pi^*$, which are positive and negative respectively since $E_{\pi\pi}$ is negative definite from chapter 3; $\bar{B}_u > 0$ from equation (8) in chapter 4. Finally we show in the appendix that $\overline{M}^c_u$ has the same sign as M_b, the marginal propensity to import tariff-constrained goods, valued at world prices. We assume throughout that this is positive.

Now, to prove the proposition, start at the initial equilibrium with arbitrary tariffs so that domestic prices and utility equal π^0 and u^0 respectively. Consider the problem of finding the domestic price vector that minimizes the trade balance subject to maintaining the initial volume of imports at world prices, M^0, evaluated at the initial utility level:

$$\min_{\pi}\{B(\pi, u^0) : \pi^* \cdot E_\pi(\pi, u^0) \leq M^0\}. \tag{10}$$

The first-order condition (using the expression for B_π derived in chapter 4) gives

$$(t - \lambda\pi^*)'E_{\pi\pi} = 0, \tag{11}$$

so the solution (assuming $E_{\pi\pi}$ is of full rank) is a uniform tariff equal to the Lagrange multiplier λ. We can call this uniform tariff the *compensated* MTRI, since it is the uniform tariff that yields the same volume of trade as the initial tariff structure, subject to the constraint that utility is held constant.

Since trade is balanced in the initial equilibrium, meaning $B(\pi^0, u^0) = b^0$, and since B has been minimized, there must be a trade balance surplus at the new uniform tariff and the initial utility level: $\bar{B}(\lambda, u^0) < b^0$. From lemma 5.1 (ii), utility must rise to restore the initial trade balance $\bar{B}(\lambda, u) = b^0$, but from lemma 5.1 (iv) a rise in utility will raise $\overline{M}^c(\lambda, u)$. Restoring the $M^c = M^0$ constraint requires from lemma 5.1 (iii) an offsetting rise in the uniform tariff to the MTRI level, τ^μ. Finally, moving to the TRI uniform tariff τ^Δ requires from lemma 5.1 (i) a further rise in τ. This proves the proposition. ∎

All this can be conveniently illustrated in figure 5.2, drawn in the space of uniform tariffs τ and utility levels u. Point A, which corresponds to (λ, u^0), lies below the locus of points that give a trade balance equal to b^0. From lemma 5.1 (i) and (ii) this locus must be downward-sloping. To prove the proposition, we need to locate relative to A the points corresponding to the MTRI and the TRI. That corresponding to the MTRI must lie on the M^0 locus through A, which from lemma 5.1 (iii) and (iv) must be upward-sloping. That corresponding to the TRI must have the same utility level as λ but lie on the same b^0 locus as τ^μ. It follows immediately that the points must lie at F and C as shown, and so the TRI cannot be less than the MTRI.

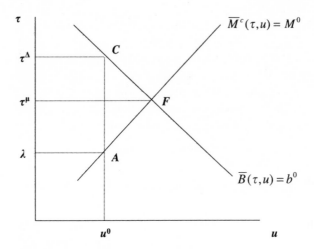

Figure 5.2
Proof of proposition 5.1

5.3   The MTRI and the Trade-Weighted Average Tariff

Next we want to rank the MTRI and the trade-weighted average tariff. We have just seen that the MTRI uniform tariff cannot exceed the TRI uniform tariff, and we saw in chapter 4 that the TRI uniform tariff and the trade-weighted average tariff cannot be ranked in general. Hence the same must be true of the MTRI uniform tariff and the trade-weighted average tariff. In partial equilibrium it is easy to show that their relative size depends on the composite elasticity of import demand: the MTRI uniform tariff exceeds the trade-weighted average tariff if this elasticity exceeds one. To see this, return to figure 5.1, and recall that the MTRI uniform tariff equals the line OM. This also equals the level of tariff revenue generated by the MTRI uniform tariff, $abef$, divided by the value of imports at world prices. Now recall from the discussion in section 2.1 that the trade-weighted average tariff equals the ratio of *actual* tariff revenue to the value of imports at world prices. In figure 5.1 the former equals $ABCO + ODEF$ to $JAFK$. Hence the MTRI uniform tariff exceeds the trade-weighted average tariff if and only if it leads to a higher level of tariff revenue. This is equivalent to requiring the composite elasticity of demand for imports to exceed one, which is what we wished to prove.

Of course, this argument is heuristic only, and needs to be extended to many goods and to general equilibrium. With many goods we need to be more careful in specifying the composite import demand elasticity; and in general equilibrium, the assumptions of no income effects and no cross-effects need to be relaxed. It turns out that the result continues to hold when the composite import demand elasticity is defined as the arc elasticity of demand for total imports with respect to the uniform tariff level, when perverse income effects are avoided by assuming that the composite import good is normal in demand, and (rather more restrictively) when the assumption of no cross-effects is weakened to the requirement that tariff-constrained goods are implicitly separable from other goods in the trade expenditure function. The full statement of the result is as follows:

Proposition 5.2 The MTRI uniform tariff τ^μ exceeds the trade-weighted average tariff τ^a if (i) the compensated arc elasticity of demand for the composite tariffed good exceeds one, (ii) the composite tariffed good is normal, and (iii) the trade expenditure function is implicitly separable in tariffed and other goods.

This proposition gives sufficient conditions only, and they are overly strong. The basic insight remains: the MTRI uniform tariff is more likely to be higher than the trade-weighted average tariff the more elastic is the demand for tariff-constrained imports. Once again, the proof in the remainder of this section can be skipped without loss of continuity.

Proof of Proposition 5.2

To compare the MTRI and the trade-weighted average tariff, we need to isolate the roles of substitution and income effects. Substitution effects are isolated by assuming that the tariff-constrained goods are *implicitly separable* from all other goods in the trade expenditure function. (In chapter 6 below we discuss the rationale and implications of this form of separability.) Income effects are isolated by using the *compensated* MTRI uniform tariff derived in (11). Recall that this is defined as the uniform tariff which maintains the initial volume of imports when utility is held constant:

$$\lambda : \overline{M}(\lambda, u^0) = \pi^* \cdot E_\pi(\pi^0, u^0). \tag{12}$$

Like the true average tariff τ^δ, introduced in section 4.5, this is a partial equilibrium concept and so of little interest in itself. (τ^δ is partial equilibrium because it ignores the government budget constraint; λ is partial equilibrium because it holds utility constant.) Nevertheless, a crucial intermediate step in the proof is that these two indexes can be unambiguously ranked under implicit separability. Formally,

Lemma 5.2   Under implicit separability, the true average tariff cannot be less than the compensated MTRI uniform tariff: $\tau^\delta \geq \lambda$.

Proof   First, recall the definition of τ^δ from equation (25) in chapter 4. We rewrite this using $E = \pi \cdot E_\pi + p \cdot E_p$, the decomposition of total net expenditure into net expenditure on tariff-constrained and other goods (using p to denote the price vector of the latter in this section only). Rearranging yields

$$\pi^0 \cdot E_\pi(\pi^0, u^0) - (1 + \tau^\delta)\overline{M}(\tau^\delta, u^0) = p^0 \cdot [E_p\{(1 + \tau^\delta)\pi^*, u^0\} - E_p(\pi^0, u^0)].$$
(13)

The right-hand side gives the change in net expenditure on unconstrained goods as a result of replacing the initial tariff vector by the uniform tariff τ^δ. This cross-price effect is of indeterminate sign in general. However, a sufficient condition for it to be zero is that the tariff-constrained goods are implicitly separable from other goods. We make this assumption in the remainder of this lemma. (See also chapter 7 below for further discussion.)

Now, with the right-hand side of (13) equal to zero, add (12) to it, and make use of the definition of the trade-weighted average tariff from chapter 2, written in matrix notation as $\tau^a \equiv (\pi^0 - \pi^*) \cdot E_\pi(\pi^0, u^0)/\pi^* \cdot E_\pi(\pi^0, u^0)$. Rearranging gives, under implicit separability,

$$(1 + \tau^a)\overline{M}(\lambda, u^0) = (1 + \tau^\delta)\overline{M}(\tau^\delta, u^0).$$
(14)

But τ^a cannot exceed τ^δ from proposition 4.1, and $\overline{M}$ is nonincreasing in τ as noted above. Hence it follows that λ cannot exceed τ^δ, with a strict inequality if there is any substitutability in import demand. This completes the proof of lemma 5.2.   ∎

The remainder of the proof is straightforward. First, add $\lambda\overline{M}(\lambda, u^0)$ to both sides of (14) and rewrite as follows:

$$(\lambda - \tau^a)\overline{M}(\lambda, u^0) = (1 + \lambda)\overline{M}(\lambda, u) - (1 + \tau^\delta)\overline{M}(\tau^\delta, u^0).$$
(15)

Since $\overline{M}$ is always positive by assumption, the left-hand side has the same sign as the difference between λ and τ^a. As for the right-hand side, it equals the change in total expenditure (at *domestic* prices) on imports when the uniform tariff changes from τ^δ to λ. But from lemma 5.2 we know that this implies a (non-strict) *reduction* in the uniform tariff. Hence the right-hand side is positive if and only if the arc elasticity of $\overline{M}$ between the two points is greater than one in absolute value.[3]

The final step in the proof is to show that τ^μ cannot be less than λ and is greater than it the more important are income effects. This follows immediately as a corollary of proposition 5.1 above: see, for example, figure 5.2. ∎

5.4 Conclusion

Most economists who work with index numbers are familiar with some of the problems they pose. However, it is not widely appreciated that these problems are even more acute in the context of international trade policy, and especially when import volume is the focus of concern. In particular, the deficiencies of the trade-weighted average tariff go far beyond those of standard fixed-weight indexes. First, the usual problem of substitution bias is accentuated: highly distorting tariffs get disproportionately low weights, and the index may be a *decreasing* function of tariff rates. Second, while it is true that the trade-weighted average tariff yields a Laspeyres-type approximation to a true tariff index, that index itself is inappropriate for evaluating tariff structures in general equilibrium. The problem is that it ignores the redistribution of tariff revenue, implicitly assuming that compensating transfers are made to offset the loss of tariff revenue. Remedying this deficiency leads to the Trade Restrictiveness Index (TRI), which we introduced in chapter 4. But this brings up the third difficulty: while the TRI is the appropriate index when the welfare effects of tariffs are considered, it is not at all relevant to the concerns of policy makers and trade negotiators with trade volume.

This chapter has introduced a new index number, the Mercantilist Trade Restrictiveness Index (MTRI), which deals satisfactorily with all these difficulties. It resembles the TRI in two respects: because it is based on optimizing behavior, it avoids substitution bias, and because it is a general-equilibrium index, it correctly accounts for tariff revenue. It differs from the TRI in taking trade volume rather than welfare as its reference. The MTRI is defined as the uniform tariff that yields the same

---

3. Define the arc elasticity of $\overline{M}$ as $-(1 + \tau)\Delta\overline{M}/\overline{M}\Delta\tau$, where $\Delta\overline{M} \equiv \overline{M}(\lambda, u^0) - \overline{M}(\tau^\delta, u^0)$, $\Delta\tau \equiv \lambda - \tau^\delta$, and where $\overline{M}$ and τ are evaluated at appropriate intermediate points: $\tau = \alpha\lambda + (1 - \alpha)\tau^\delta$ and $\overline{M} = \beta\overline{M}(\lambda, u^0) + (1 - \beta)\overline{M}(\tau^\delta, u^0)$. This arc elasticity is greater than one in absolute value if and only if the right-hand side of (15) is positive.

volume of imports as a given tariff structure.[4] Since the MTRI is a true
index number for tariffs, the performance of empirical measures should
be evaluated in terms of how closely they approximate it. In addition to
presenting and justifying the MTRI, we have been able to prove two
surprisingly strong results concerning its relationship with other indexes.
The MTRI uniform tariff can never exceed the TRI uniform tariff, and it
exceeds the trade-weighted average tariff if import demand is sufficiently
elastic.

Appendix: Properties of the Import Volume Functions

Since we are concerned with the volume of tariff-restricted trade (measured at world prices), it is convenient to express its equilibrium level
as a function of the variables characterizing the general equilibrium of
the economy. Consider first the import demand functions for individual
goods. Recall from chapter 3 that we can derive the vector of utility-
compensated net import demand functions $m^c(\pi, u)$ from the trade expenditure function.[5] As with an individual consumer, we can relate these
economywide Hicksian net import demand functions to their Marshallian
equivalents.[6] The latter depend on domestic prices and the economy's
exogenous income $b : m = m(\pi, b)$. In equilibrium, exogenous income
equals the balance of trade, which is related to domestic prices and utility
via the balance of trade function $B(\pi, u)$ introduced in chapter 4. Hence
we can write a "Slutsky identity" which, just as in the consumer case,
states that the Hicksian and Marshallian import demand functions coincide when the economy is in equilibrium:

$$m^c(\pi, u) = m[\pi, B(\pi, u)]. \tag{16}$$

Differentiating this with respect to u and recalling from chapter 3 that
$m_u^c = E_{\pi u} = x_I e_u$, and from chapter 4 that $B_u = (1 - t \cdot x_I)e_u$, yields

$$m_b = (1 - t \cdot x_I)^{-1} x_I. \tag{17}$$

4. This definition is appropriate for comparisons of an arbitrary tariff structure with free
trade. More generally, when two different tariff structures are compared, the MTRI is
defined as the uniform deflator that, applied to the new set of distorted prices, yields the
same trade volume as the initial tariffs. The cross-sectional and time-series applications in
part III illustrate these two alternative comparisons.

5. In chapter 3 we also included exogenous goods endowments as an additional argument of
m^c. They play no role in this chapter, so it is convenient to suppress them.

6. For a more formal derivation, see Neary and Schweinberger (1986).

Thus an increased transfer from abroad raises demand for imports to an extent determined by the marginal income responses x_I, grossed up by the shadow price of foreign exchange.

Aggregating the two vectors of import demand functions leads in turn to two scalar import volume functions, one compensated and the other uncompensated:

$$M^c(\pi, u) \equiv \pi^* \cdot m^c(\pi, u) \quad \text{and} \quad M(\pi, b) \equiv \pi^* \cdot m(\pi, b). \tag{18}$$

The derivatives of these functions are easily derived from the corresponding derivatives of the import demand functions. Here we note only that the derivative of the Marshallian import volume function with respect to exogenous income is

$$M_b = \pi^* \cdot m_b = (1 - t \cdot x_I)^{-1} \pi^* \cdot x_I, \qquad 0 < M_b < 1. \tag{19}$$

This is the marginal propensity to import tariff-constrained goods, valued at world prices, and we assume throughout that it lies between zero and one. The numerator, $\pi^* \cdot x_I$, is the marginal propensity to consume tariff-constrained goods at world prices. It also equals the inverse of the "Hatta normality term" for this subset of goods, which, as we noted in chapter 3, is customarily assumed to be positive.

Finally, by analogy with (16), we can relate the Hicksian and Marshallian import volume functions by a Slutsky identity:

$$M^c(\pi, u) = M[\pi, B(\pi, u)]. \tag{20}$$

Differentiating with respect to π gives a Slutsky decomposition of the price derivatives of the Marshallian import volume function:

$$M_\pi = M_\pi^c - M_b B_\pi. \tag{21}$$

Similarly, differentiating with respect to u relates the utility responsiveness of the Hicksian import volume function to the income responsiveness of the Marshallian import volume function:

$$M_u^c = M_b B_u = e_u \pi^* \cdot x_I \tag{22}$$

where the second equality makes use of the expression for M_b in (19).

6 Trade Reform, Trade Restrictiveness, and Tariff Structure

The issue of the structure of tariff rates has already come up at a number of points in this book. In chapter 2 we saw that the trade-weighted standard deviation of tariffs is a poor indicator of the restrictiveness of trade policy. And in chapter 3 we saw that a reduction in tariff dispersion may but need not increase welfare. Our discussion of the concertina rule derived plausible sufficient conditions on the pattern of substitutability between goods which ensured that lowering the highest tariff would raise welfare. However, figure 3.4 showed graphically how an increase in dispersion may raise welfare when these conditions fail. These results suggest that measures of tariff dispersion are not always helpful in assessing the implications of a given tariff structure.

Nonetheless, the widespread use of measures of tariff dispersion in practice may not be totally unjustified, despite its lack of a rigorous theoretical justification to date. It is intuitively plausible that both trade reform and trade restrictiveness should be in some way related to tariff dispersion. Consider first the trade reform context. The marginal welfare damage caused by a tariff is proportional to the height of the tariff, so large tariffs are more damaging than small ones, all else equal. Thus increases in dispersion that preserve the mean tariff in some appropriate sense should be welfare decreasing. To see this in the special case of no cross-effects and no income effects, consider figure 6.1. (This repeats the essential features of figure 5.1 in the previous chapter but reverses the chain of reasoning.) Start with a uniform tariff equal to OM (so $\tau_1 = \tau_2 = OM$). Next introduce dispersion in the tariff structure by lowering τ_1 to OC and raising τ_2 to OD. By construction, the volume of trade is unchanged: it equals af initially and AF after the change, and these volumes are equal since Le is drawn parallel to Bb. However, reversing the reasoning of section 5.2, we can see that welfare falls since the cut in τ_1 raises welfare by the smaller shaded area $ABba$, but the increase in

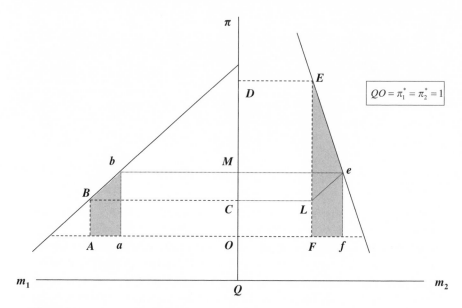

Figure 6.1
Effects of an increase in tariff dispersion on welfare for a given import volume

τ_2 lowers welfare by the larger shaded area *FEef*. Thus an increase in tariff dispersion that keeps trade volume constant lowers welfare in this example.

As for the problem of measuring trade restrictiveness, in the extreme case of no dispersion, where all tariff rates are equal, the index number problem disappears and all three indexes τ^a, τ^Δ, and τ^μ coincide. Figure 6.1 can also be used to show that increases in dispersion have different effects on the indexes. By construction, the move away from uniform tariffs in figure 6.1 leaves the volume of imports and hence the MTRI uniform tariff unchanged. But, since welfare falls, a higher uniform tariff would be required to generate the same level of welfare as the new dispersed tariff structure. Hence at least in this two-good example an increase in tariff dispersion raises the TRI by more than the MTRI.

In this chapter we explore how these partial-equilibrium insights can be formalized in general equilibrium, drawing on and extending the approach of Anderson (1995).[1] We first define two *generalized moments*

---

1. Anderson (1995) introduced generalized tariff moments (though defined in terms of world prices rather than, as here, in terms of domestic prices) and used them to elucidate the properties of the trade restrictiveness index of Anderson and Neary (1996). This chapter draws on Anderson and Neary (2004).

of the distribution of tariffs, the generalized mean and the generalized variance. We show how the standard results of trade reform, presented in chapter 3, can be expressed in terms of changes in these generalized moments. In addition we are able to extend these results significantly and to derive analogous results for the effects of tariff changes on trade volume. These results in turn lead us to explore how changes in the TRI and MTRI can be expressed in terms of changes in the generalized moments. Finally we show how the generalized moments can be related in some special cases to the observable moments of the tariff distribution, the trade-weighted average tariff and the standard deviation of tariffs, thus providing a partial rationale for the widespread use of these measures in applied work.

6.1 Generalized Tariff Moments

In order to characterize changes in the distribution of tariffs, we introduce *generalized* or *substitution-weighted* tariff moments. These are equal to weighted moments, where the weights are the elements of the substitution matrix $E_{\pi\pi}$ normalized by the domestic prices of nonnuméraire goods.[2]

The economic model in this chapter is identical to that in the previous three chapters, and we will continue to make extensive use of the trade expenditure function and related tools. In addition it is convenient to introduce some extra notation. It turns out to be easiest to work with both the level and the change in tariffs deflated by *domestic* prices. Hence, as in our discussion of the concertina rule in section 3.4, define the ad valorem tariff rate on good i relative to the domestic price base as $T_i \equiv t_i/\pi_i = (\pi_i - \pi_i^*)/\pi_i$. Note that tariff rates defined in this way must lie between zero and one: $0 \le T_i < 1$, which is why T_i is sometimes called the "power" of the tariff. They are related to tariff rates defined with respect to world prices by $T_i = \tau_i/(1 + \tau_i)$. Next, to express the vector of tariff rates in matrix notation, let $\underline{x}$ denote a diagonal matrix with the elements of the vector x on the principal diagonal. Then we can write the vector of tariff rates T as

$$T \equiv \underline{\pi}^{-1}t = \iota - \underline{\pi}^{-1}\pi^*, \tag{1}$$

---

2. This is more convenient than normalizing by world prices as in Anderson (1995), since it allows us to make use of the homogeneity restrictions on import demand.

where ι denotes an n-by-1 vector of ones. Furthermore the derivations are enormously simplified if we *define* the change in tariff rates as the changes in specific tariffs relative to domestic prices: $dT_i \equiv dt_i/\pi_i$, or in matrix notation

$$dT \equiv \underline{\pi}^{-1} dt. \tag{2}$$

Note that dt equals $d\pi$, since world prices are fixed. Hence the vector of changes in T, dT_i, equals the vector of tariff-induced proportional changes in domestic prices, $d\pi_i/\pi_i$.

Next define the matrix of substitution effects normalized by domestic prices as

$$S \equiv -\bar{s}^{-1}\underline{\pi}E_{\pi\pi}\underline{\pi}, \tag{3}$$

where

$$\bar{s} \equiv -\pi'E_{\pi\pi}\pi > 0.$$

By construction, S is a symmetric n-by-n positive definite matrix all of whose elements sum to one: $\iota'S\iota = 1$. We can use S_{ij} to denote both the individual elements of S and (when either i or j is zero) the corresponding cross-price effects with the numéraire good:

$$S_{ij} = -\bar{s}^{-1}\pi_i E_{ij}\pi_j, \qquad i,j = 0,1,\ldots,n. \tag{4}$$

Note the sign convention: the normalized own-price effects S_{ii} are positive for all i, while the normalized cross-price effects S_{ij} are negative if and only if goods i and j are general-equilibrium net substitutes. The standard homogeneity restrictions on the $E_{\pi\pi}$ matrix imply corresponding restrictions on the S matrix:

$$E_{0j} + \sum_{i=1}^{n} \pi_i E_{ij} = 0 \Leftrightarrow S_{0j} + \sum_{i=1}^{n} S_{ij} = 0 \qquad \forall j = 0,1,\ldots,n. \tag{5}$$

Thus the elements of column j of S sum to $-S_{0j}$, which is the normalized cross-price effect between the numéraire good and good j. (From symmetry the elements of row i of S sum to $-S_{i0}$.)

After these preliminaries we can define two generalized moments of the tariff structure. The first is the generalized average tariff:

$$\bar{T} \equiv \iota'ST. \tag{6}$$

This equals a weighted average of the individual tariff rates, where the weights are the row (or column) sums of S:

$$\bar{T} = \sum_{j=1}^{n} \omega_j T_j \tag{7}$$

where

$$\omega_j \equiv \sum_{i=1}^{n} S_{ij} = -S_{0j}$$

(The last equality follows from equation 5.) The weights must sum to one, since $\sum_j \omega_j = \sum_i \sum_j S_{ij} = \iota' S \iota = 1$. However, they need not lie in the $[0, 1]$ interval. It follows that $\bar{T}$ itself need not lie in the unit interval. Two conditions that are sufficient to ensure that it does are immediate. First, $\bar{T}$ must lie in the unit interval if tariffs are uniform. In that case $T = \iota\beta$ $(0 \leq \beta < 1)$, so $\bar{T} = \iota' S \iota \beta = \beta$. Second, because S is defined to be positive definite, the weight on a given tariff rate is more likely to be positive the higher the own-substitution effect for that good and the more it is a complement rather than a substitute for other tariff-constrained goods. Equation (7) implies a more succinct condition: the weight attached to the tariff rate on good j in the expression for $\bar{T}$ is positive if and only if that good is a substitute for the numéraire. Hence, if all goods are substitutes for the numéraire, $\bar{T}$ must be positive and less than one. For later reference we state these results formally:

Lemma 6.1 Sufficient conditions for the generalized average tariff to be positive and less than one are (i) that all tariff rates are the same, or (ii) that all goods subject to tariffs are general-equilibrium substitutes for the numéraire good.

Clearly, the conditions in lemma 6.1 are overly strong. $\bar{T}$ can only be negative if tariffs are disproportionately higher on goods that are relatively strong complements for the numéraire good, and it can only be greater than one if tariffs are disproportionately higher on goods that are relatively strong substitutes for the numéraire good.

The second generalized moment we introduce is the generalized variance of tariffs:

$$V \equiv (T - \iota\bar{T})' S(T - \iota\bar{T}) = T'ST - \bar{T}^2. \tag{8}$$

Unlike the generalized average tariff, V is unambiguously positive in sign, since it is a quadratic form in the positive definite matrix S. Finally we define the changes in the two generalized moments as follows:[3]

$$d\bar{T} \equiv \imath' S \, dT \quad \text{and} \quad dV \equiv 2(T' S \, dT - \bar{T} \, d\bar{T}). \qquad (9)$$

As we will see, these changes in generalized moments provide an invaluable intermediate step when we come to assess the effects of changes in actual tariffs on welfare and import volume.

6.2   Welfare and Trade Policy Reform

We begin with the effects of tariff changes on welfare. Recall the basic equation linking changes in welfare to changes in tariffs, equation (10) from chapter 3:

$$\mu^{-1} e_u \, du = t' E_{\pi\pi} \, dt. \qquad (10)$$

Here $\mu \equiv (1 - t' x_I)^{-1}$ is the scalar tariff multiplier, which for reasons discussed in chapter 3 we assume to be positive. We can rewrite (10) in terms of the normalized substitution matrix by using (1) and (2) to replace specific by ad valorem tariffs:

$$(\mu \bar{s})^{-1} e_u \, du = -T' S \, dT. \qquad (11)$$

Since both μ and $\bar{s}$ are positive, the sign of the change in welfare is given by the right-hand side of (11). Using (9), we can express this in terms of the changes in the generalized tariff moments:

$$(\mu \bar{s})^{-1} e_u \, du = -\bar{T} \, d\bar{T} - \tfrac{1}{2} dV. \qquad (12)$$

Hence we have shown that the change in welfare is related in a particularly simple way to the changes in the generalized moments of the tariff structure. We can summarize this result as follows:

Proposition 6.1   The effects on welfare of an arbitrary small change in tariffs are fully described by their effects on the generalized mean and variance of tariffs. An increase in the generalized mean lowers welfare if and only if its initial value is positive, while an increase in the generalized variance always reduces welfare.

---

3. These definitions are Laspeyres-type approximations which deliberately ignore tariff-induced changes in π and $E_{\pi\pi}$. The change in the variance of tariffs can be interpreted as twice the (generalized) covariance between initial tariff rates and their changes: $dV = 2(T - \imath\bar{T})' S(dT - \imath \, d\bar{T}) = 2 \operatorname{cov}(T, dT)$.

It is not too surprising that welfare is a decreasing function of the generalized mean tariff in a wide range of circumstances. (Recall lemma 6.1 and the associated discussion.) More important is the result that it is always decreasing in the generalized variance. This provides a rationalization for the common practice of viewing increases in the variance of tariffs as harmful. A corollary of proposition 6.1 is that a generalized mean-preserving spread, in the sense of an increase in V with no change in $\bar{T}$, must lower welfare. We will return to this theme in section 6.3 below.

Next we want to see how the standard results on trade policy reform that we presented in chapter 3 can be expressed in terms of the generalized tariff moments. We consider the radial tariff reduction result in this section and the concertina reform result in the next. If all specific tariffs are reduced by a given proportion, $dt_i = -t_i \, d\alpha \; (d\alpha > 0)$, then all ad valorem tariffs fall by the same proportion: $dT_i = -T_i \, d\alpha$, or in vector form $dT = -T \, d\alpha$. Substituting from this, we can write the expressions for the changes in generalized moments in (9) as

$$d\bar{T} = -\imath' ST \, d\alpha = -\bar{T} \, d\alpha \quad \text{and} \quad dV = -2(T'ST - \bar{T}^2) \, d\alpha = -2V \, d\alpha.$$

(13)

Summarizing,

Proposition 6.2 An equiproportionate reduction in all tariffs reduces the absolute value of the generalized average tariff by the same proportion, and lowers the generalized tariff variance by twice as much.

Note that if $\bar{T}$ is negative, then a uniform reduction in all tariffs paradoxically *raises* the generalized average tariff, moving it closer to zero. Notwithstanding this, the generalized variance falls sufficiently to ensure that welfare rises. From (11) the change in welfare is proportional to $T'ST \, d\alpha$, which is always positive. This is, of course, just the standard radial reduction result.

We can also derive a new result for the case of a uniform *absolute* reduction in the tariff rates T. In this case dT_i is the same for all goods, so $dT_i = -d\alpha$, or $dT = -\imath \, d\alpha$. The contrast between uniform proportionate and uniform absolute changes is illustrated in the first two rows of table 6.1. The former changes all tariffs in the same proportion however they are measured (whether in nominal units, or relative to either home or world prices). By contrast, a uniform absolute reduction in the tariff rates T leads to a fall in specific tariffs t in proportion to domestic prices: $dT = -\imath \, d\alpha$ implies that $d\pi = dt = -\pi \, d\alpha$, so domestic relative prices are unchanged. Table 6.1 also shows that this change has very simple effects

Table 6.1
Alternative tariff reduction formulas

	Effect on					
	$dt\ (=d\pi)$	$dT\ (\equiv \underline{\pi}^{-1}\,dt)$	$d\tau\ (\equiv (\underline{\pi}^{*})^{-1}\,dt)$	$d\bar{T}$	dV	$(\mu\bar{s})^{-1}e_u\,du$
Uniform proportionate reduction	$-t\,d\alpha$	$-T\,d\alpha$	$-\tau\,d\alpha$	$-\bar{T}\,d\alpha$	$-2V\,d\alpha$	$(\bar{T}^2 + V)\,d\alpha$
Uniform absolute reduction in T	$-\pi\,d\alpha$	$-\iota\,d\alpha$	$-(\iota+\tau)\,d\alpha$	$-d\alpha$	0	$\bar{T}\,d\alpha$
Uniform absolute reduction in τ	$-\pi^{*}\,d\alpha$	$-(\iota - T)\,d\alpha$	$-\iota\,d\alpha$	$-(1 - \bar{T})\,d\alpha$	$2V\,d\alpha$	$[\bar{T}(1 - \bar{T}) - V]\,d\alpha$
Uniform contraction in T	$-(\iota - \pi\beta)\,d\alpha$	$-(T - \iota\beta)\,d\alpha$	$-[\tau - (\iota + \tau)\beta]\,d\alpha$	$-(\bar{T} - \beta)\,d\alpha$	$-2V\,d\alpha$	$[\bar{T}(\bar{T} - \beta) + V]\,d\alpha$

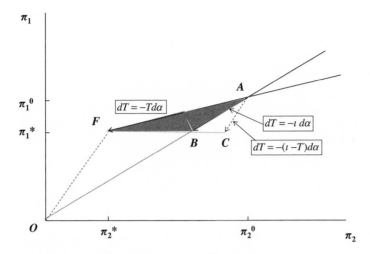

Figure 6.2
Uniform proportionate and uniform absolute changes in tariffs

on the generalized moments: the generalized mean definitely falls while the variance does not change. Hence welfare rises if and only if the generalized mean tariff is positive.

Figure 6.2 compares the effects on domestic prices of a uniform proportionate and a uniform absolute reduction in tariffs in the two-good case. Starting at point A, a uniform proportionate reduction in tariffs moves the equilibrium along a ray toward the free-trade point F. By contrast, a uniform absolute reduction in tariffs moves the equilibrium along a ray toward the origin O, as indicated by the vector AB. We know from the standard result in chapter 3 that a move toward F always raises welfare, and we have just seen that a move toward O raises welfare provided $\overline{T}$ is positive. Hence the shaded area between the two rays is a "cone of liberalization": a movement from A toward any point in this region must raise welfare if $\overline{T}$ is positive. (Similarly all points in the unshaded area above A and between the two rays have lower welfare than A if $\overline{T}$ is positive.) Such movements can be characterized by a convex combination of uniform proportionate and uniform absolute tariff reductions:

$$dT = -[\gamma T + (1 - \gamma)\iota]\, d\alpha, \qquad 0 \le \gamma \le 1. \tag{14}$$

The effects of such a change on the generalized moments are given by

$$d\overline{T} = -(\gamma \overline{T} + 1 - \gamma)\, d\alpha \quad \text{and} \quad dV = -2\gamma V\, d\alpha, \tag{15}$$

while its effect on welfare equals

$$(\mu \bar{s})^{-1} e_u \, du = [\gamma T' ST + (1 - \gamma)\bar{T}] \, d\alpha. \tag{16}$$

The implications of these results can be summarized as follows:

Proposition 6.3 Any convex combination of a uniform proportionate and a uniform absolute reduction in tariff rates as given by (14) (i) lowers the generalized average tariff if and only if $\bar{T} > -(1 - \gamma)/\gamma$, (ii) always lowers the generalized variance of tariffs, strictly so for $\gamma > 0$, and (iii) raises welfare if and only if $\bar{T} > -\gamma T' ST/(1 - \gamma)$.

This result substantially increases the scope of what is known about the welfare effects of across-the-board cuts in tariffs. It is particularly important because successive trade rounds under the GATT and the WTO have considered many different types of tariff-cutting formula. (Francois and Martin 2003 review the different approaches under consideration in the current round.) Most of these formulas can be closely approximated by (14), and so proposition 6.3 suggests that they increase welfare given reasonable restrictions on the degree of complementarity between the tariff-constrained goods and the numéraire.

Before leaving this topic, it is important to recall that the new results presented here refer to a uniform absolute reduction in T, the tariff rates measured with respect to *domestic* prices. This is not the same as a uniform absolute reduction in τ, the tariff rates measured with respect to *world* prices. Moreover the latter change is not guaranteed to raise welfare under reasonable conditions. The effects of this change are shown in the third row of table 6.1. It reduces domestic prices in proportion to *world* prices $(d\pi = -\pi^* \, d\alpha)$, and so corresponds to a movement away from A in figure 6.2 along the dotted line AC that is parallel to OF. This lowers the generalized mean tariff provided $\bar{T}$ is less than one (which from proposition 6.1 is ensured if all tariff-constrained goods are substitutes for the numéraire). However, it *raises* the generalized variance. The net effect on welfare is proportional to $\bar{T} - T' ST$, or $(\iota - T)' ST$, which cannot be unambiguously signed even when all goods are substitutes. Hence this type of tariff reform is not helpful from a welfare perspective, though we will see in section 6.4 that it is very important from the perspective of import volume.

6.3 Welfare Effects of Tariff Reforms That Reduce Dispersion

Consider next the concertina reform result. As in chapter 3, suppose without loss of generality that the highest tariff rate is on good 1. This implies an identical ranking whether tariff rates are defined relative to world prices, $\tau_1 > \tau_i$, $\forall i \neq 1$, or relative to domestic prices, $T_1 > T_i$, $\forall i \neq 1$. The fact that only the tariff on good 1 is changed can be expressed by setting $dT_1 = -d\alpha$, and by writing the vector of tariff changes as follows:

$$dT = \begin{bmatrix} dT_1 \\ 0 \\ \vdots \\ 0 \end{bmatrix} = -\varepsilon_1 \, d\alpha \qquad (17)$$

where

$$\varepsilon_1 \equiv \begin{bmatrix} 1 \\ 0 \\ \vdots \\ 0 \end{bmatrix}.$$

We use ε_i to denote an n-by-1 vector with one in the ith entry and zeros elsewhere. With a concertina-type reform specified in this way, the change in the generalized average tariff can be expressed as follows:

$$d\bar{T} = -\iota'S\varepsilon_1 \, d\alpha = -\omega_1 \, d\alpha = S_{01} \, d\alpha \qquad (18)$$

(where the final step uses equation (5)). Thus a reduction in the tariff on good 1 lowers the generalized average tariff if and only if that good is a substitute for the numéraire good: $S_{01} < 0$. As for the change in the generalized variance of tariffs, substituting from (17) into (9) gives

$$dV = -2(T'S\varepsilon_1 - \bar{T}\iota'S\varepsilon_1) \, d\alpha. \qquad (19)$$

To show that this is negative with substitutability, expand the expression in parentheses as follows:

$$T'S\varepsilon_1 - \bar{T}\iota'S\varepsilon_1 = \sum_1 T_i S_{i1} - \bar{T}\omega_1$$

$$= T_1 S_{11} + \sum_2 T_i S_{i1} + \bar{T} S_{01}$$

$$= S_{11}\left(T_1 - \sum_2 T_i \omega_{i1} - \bar{T}\omega_{01} \right). \qquad (20)$$

The expression in parentheses in the last row of (20) equals the tariff rate on good 1 less a weighted average of n other tariff rates, where from (5) the weights sum to one:

$$\omega_{i1} \equiv -\frac{S_{i1}}{S_{11}}, \qquad i = 0, 2, 3, \ldots, n,$$

$$\omega_{01} + \sum_2 \omega_{i1} = 1. \tag{21}$$

By assumption, all the other $n - 1$ individual tariff rates are less than T_1. If all goods are substitutes for good 1, then, from (7), $\bar{T}$ itself is less than T_i, and if all goods are substitutes for good 1, then, from (21), all the weights are positive. Hence substitutability is sufficient to ensure that the generalized variance is reduced by a concertina reform. Combining (18) and (19), we get the effect on welfare:

$$(\mu\bar{s})^{-1} e_u \, du = T' S \varepsilon_1 \, d\alpha = S_{11} \left(T_1 - \sum_2 T_i \omega_{i1} \right) d\alpha, \tag{22}$$

which, as we saw in chapter 3, must be positive if all tariff-constrained goods are substitutes for good 1. Using generalized moments thus throws a new perspective on why a concertina reform raises welfare. In addition the results found here for its effects on the generalized moments will prove useful when we consider the effects of tariffs on market access in section 6.5.

We can get a new result by considering a tariff reform that affects the dispersion of tariffs in a different way. Consider an equiproportionate reduction in the gap between all tariff rates and an arbitrary uniform tariff rate, denoted by β:[4]

$$dT = -(T - \iota\beta) \, d\alpha. \tag{23}$$

---

4. Equation (14) is a special case of this, with β less than one and $\gamma = 1/(1 - \beta)$. The tariff reform rule in (23) bears a superficial resemblance to a result of Fukushima (1979). However, the results are different. Fukushima shows that a welfare change of the form $d\tau = -(\tau - \iota\gamma) \, d\alpha$ raises welfare for *all* values of γ. However, a key difference is that Fukushima includes in the vector τ the distortions on *all* traded goods; that is, unlike our model, his does not allow for a numéraire traded good that is not subject to tariffs. As a result the level of welfare is the same in his model for all levels of γ, since a uniform distortion affecting all traded goods (both exports and imports) does not distort relative prices from their free-trade values, so it yields no revenue and imposes no welfare cost. Fukushima's result is thus a restatement of the uniform proportional reduction result. See Neary (1998) for further discussion.

This is a generalization of the uniform radial reduction rule, for which β is zero. Substituting from (23) into (9), the changes in the generalized moments become

$$d\bar{T} = -(\bar{T} - \beta)\,d\alpha \quad \text{and} \quad dV = -2V\,d\alpha. \tag{24}$$

(These and other effects of equation 23 are given in full in the last row of table 6.1.) Thus a tariff reform as in (23) reduces the generalized mean if and only if β is less than $\bar{T}$ and unambiguously reduces the generalized variance. The implications for welfare can be found by substituting into (12),

$$(\mu\bar{s})^{-1}e_u\,du = [\bar{T}(\bar{T} - \beta) + V]\,d\alpha. \tag{25}$$

Hence we have a new result for trade policy reform:

Proposition 6.4 A sufficient condition for welfare to rise following an equiproportionate reduction in the gap between all tariff rates and an arbitrary uniform rate β, as in (23), is that β is no farther from zero than the generalized mean tariff $\bar{T}$.

Note that this result holds whether $\bar{T}$ is positive or negative. A corollary is that, if β equals the generalized average tariff $\bar{T}$, then a rise in welfare is guaranteed. This makes intuitive sense, since in this case the reform is a generalized mean-preserving contraction of the tariff distribution: $d\bar{T} = 0$ and $dV = -2V\,d\alpha$.

This type of tariff reform can be illustrated in figure 6.3, which repeats the essential features of figure 6.2. Any reform of the type given in (23) can be represented by a movement along a line from the initial point A toward a point on the ray from the origin through F. The location of the point depends on β. For example, if β is zero, the point coincides with F; if β equals T_1, the point is given by D, which is horizontally aligned with A—the case of a "superconcertina" reform, where *all* tariffs are reduced equiproportionally toward the lowest tariff rate; while if β exceeds T_1, the point lies above D. A corollary of proposition 6.4 is that, provided $\bar{T}$ is positive, the tariff reform rule (23) is welfare-improving for all β such that $0 \le \beta \le \bar{T}$. Let E denote the point at which β equals $\bar{T}$. (In the two-good case, $\bar{T}$ exceeds T_1, and so E lies above D, provided good 2 is a substitute for the numéraire, since $\bar{T} - T_1 = \omega_2(T_2 - T_1)$. Note that the path from A to E is not a straight line, since unlike β the value of $\bar{T}$ changes as we move away from A.) Hence the region EAF can be added to the region FAB already derived in the last section to give an expanded cone of welfare-increasing liberalization, indicated by the full shaded area.

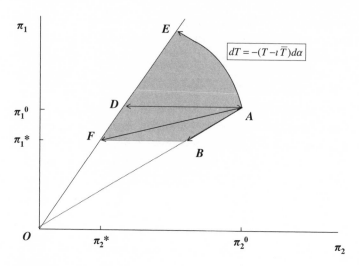

Figure 6.3
Cone of welfare-improving liberalization

6.4   Market Access and Changes in Tariff Moments

We turn next to see how changes in tariff moments can be used to summarize the effects of tariff changes on the volume of imports. As in chapter 5 we measure this at world prices: $M \equiv \pi^* \cdot m$. We will see later that this seemingly innocuous convention has important implications. The change in import demand can be expressed in terms of income and substitution effects as follows:

$$dM = \pi^* \cdot dm = \pi^* \cdot (E_{\pi\pi}\, d\pi + x_I e_u\, du). \tag{26}$$

However, we know from (10) that in general equilibrium the income effect is itself related to tariff changes via the substitution matrix $E_{\pi\pi}$. Substituting into (26), we can write the full effect of changes in tariffs on import volume as follows:[5]

$$dM = (\pi^* + M_b t)' E_{\pi\pi}\, dt. \tag{27}$$

As in chapter 5, M_b is the marginal propensity to import tariff-constrained goods, defined as follows:

$$M_b \equiv \mu \pi^* \cdot x_I = \frac{\pi^* \cdot x_I}{\pi^* \cdot x_I + x_{0I}}, \tag{28}$$

5. This is equation (15) in Ju and Krishna (2000).

where x_{0I} is the income derivative of demand for the numéraire good. Hence M_b must lie between zero and one provided only that both the tariff-constrained goods as a whole and the unconstrained good (i.e., the numéraire) are normal in demand, a very mild restriction.

The next step is to express equation (27) in terms of the generalized moments. Note first that the coefficient in parentheses can be written as follows:

$$\pi^* + M_b t = \pi - (1 - M_b)t = \underline{\pi}[\iota - (1 - M_b)T]. \tag{29}$$

A similar series of derivations to those in section 6.2 allows us to write the change in import volume as follows:

$$\bar{s}^{-1} dM = -[\iota - (1 - M_b)T]' S \, dT. \tag{30}$$

This can be expressed in terms of changes in the generalized moments:

$$\bar{s}^{-1} dM = -[1 - (1 - M_b)\bar{T}] \, d\bar{T} + \tfrac{1}{2}(1 - M_b) \, dV. \tag{31}$$

Equation (31) shows that as with the change in welfare in equation (12), the change in import volume is fully determined by the changes in the two generalized moments. However, a key difference is that the volume of imports is *increasing* in the generalized variance, for a given level of the generalized mean. Hence we can state a result that parallels proposition 6.1:

Proposition 6.5   The effects on import volume of an arbitrary small change in tariffs are fully described by their effects on the generalized mean and variance of tariffs. A sufficient condition for an increase in $\bar{T}$ to lower import volume is that $(1 - M_b)\bar{T}$ is less than one. A sufficient condition for an increase in V to *raise* import volume is that M_b is less than one.

The fact that import volume is increasing in the generalized variance of tariffs is an important and surprising finding that has a major influence on the results to be presented below. Some intuition for the positive relationship between V and M can be given using the linear two-good example of chapter 2. Imports of each good m_i equal $\alpha_i - \beta_i \pi_i$, $i = 1, 2$. Hence an iso-import-volume locus in price space must be downward sloping with constant slope:

$$\left. \frac{d\pi_1}{d\pi_2} \right|_{dM=0} = -\frac{\beta_2 \pi_2^*}{\beta_1 \pi_1^*}. \tag{32}$$

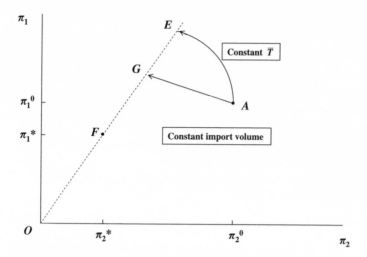

Figure 6.4
A variance-reducing tariff change that keeps $\bar{T}$ constant must lower M, since $\bar{T}$ is valued at domestic prices and M at world prices

Figure 6.4 illustrates. Starting from an initial point A, the iso-import-volume locus is downward-sloping as represented by the straight line AG. The locus AE along which $d\bar{T}$ is zero is also downward-sloping and has a slope equal to

$$\frac{d\pi_1}{d\pi_2}\bigg|_{d\bar{T}=0} = -\frac{\beta_2 \pi_2}{\beta_1 \pi_1} = -\frac{T_2}{T_1}\frac{\beta_2 \pi_2^*}{\beta_1 \pi_1^*}. \tag{33}$$

This slope is greater (in absolute value) than the slope of the iso-import-volume locus (32) at any point where T_2/T_1 exceeds one, meaning any point such as A to the right of the ray OF. Hence a movement toward OF along the $d\bar{T} = 0$ locus AE must lower the volume of imports. But it is evident that moving toward the free-trade relative price ratio OF must lower the variance of tariffs. Hence it follows that M is positively related to V. A variance-reducing tariff change that keeps $\bar{T}$ constant must lower the volume of imports, since $\bar{T}$ is valued at domestic prices and M at world prices.

With income and cross-substitution effects in general equilibrium, this intuition must be qualified, but the same general point applies. From (10), the change in welfare following any change in tariffs is proportional to $(\pi - \pi^*)' E_{\pi\pi} dt$. However, from the definitions of S and $d\bar{T}$ in (3) and (9), $\pi' E_{\pi\pi} dt$ is zero whenever $d\bar{T}$ is zero. Combining these expressions shows that the change in welfare is proportional to $-\pi^{*\prime} E_{\pi\pi}\,dt$. The latter can be written as $-dM^c$, meaning minus the compensated change in import volume. Thus welfare and import volume move in opposite directions when $d\bar{T}$ is zero, namely for any mean-preserving change in the variance of tariffs. Income effects complicate this argument but do not reverse it provided M_b is less than one. To see this, recall from (11) that $-T'S\,dT$ is proportional to the change in utility, so we can rewrite equation (30) to obtain the full expression linking changes in welfare and import volume:

$$dM + (1 - M_b)\mu^{-1} e_u\,du = -\bar{s}\,d\bar{T} \qquad (34)$$

Hence, if $d\bar{T}$ is zero, welfare and import volume must move in opposite directions, provided M_b is less than one.

Equation (34) also yields a generalization of proposition 4 in Ju and Krishna (2000):

Proposition 6.6 Both welfare and the value of imports cannot fall following a reduction in tariffs, defined as a fall in $\bar{T}$.

When combined with the result in (18) that a reduction in an arbitrary tariff lowers $\bar{T}$ if and only if the good in question is a substitute for the numéraire good, we have a corollary of proposition 6.6: if all goods are net substitutes for the numéraire, then *any* reduction in tariffs must lower $\bar{T}$, as a result of which either M or u or both must rise.

Before leaving the positive relation between import volume and tariff variance, it is worth noting that it does *not* hold if import volume is measured in domestic prices, which we denote by $\tilde{M} \equiv \pi'm$. A series of derivations similar to those that led to (31) above now yields

$$
\begin{aligned}
d\tilde{M} &= m'\,d\pi + \pi'\,dm \\
&= m'\,dt + (\pi + \tilde{M}_b t)'E_{\pi\pi}\,dt \\
&= (m'\pi^*)\,d\tau^a - \bar{s}(\iota + \tilde{M}_b T)'S\,dT \\
&= (m'\pi^*)\,d\tau^a - \bar{s}(1 + \tilde{M}_b \bar{T})\,d\bar{T} - \tfrac{1}{2}\bar{s}\tilde{M}_b\,dV. \qquad (35)
\end{aligned}
$$

This shows that the change in $\tilde{M}$ consists of two components. The first, $m'\,d\pi$, is a valuation effect that is proportional to the change in the trade-weighted average tariff τ^a. The second, $\pi'\,dm$, is the change in import volume at constant domestic prices. The latter in turn is *negatively* related to both $\bar{T}$ and V. Indeed, it is affected by changes in $\bar{T}$ and V in a very similar manner to the level of welfare, as a comparison between (12) and (35) makes clear.[6] In particular, radial reduction and variance reduction rules for tariff reform (including the concertina rule) can be shown to increase $\tilde{M}$ in a manner similar to those derived for welfare in sections 6.2 and 6.3. Unfortunately, however, these results are not of great interest. As far as trade negotiations are concerned, market access matters primarily from the perspective of *exporters* to the economy under consideration. Hence it is import volume at world rather than at domestic prices that is the main focus of interest, and we concentrate on it from now on.[7]

6.5   Tariff Changes and Market Access

We are now ready to consider the effects of various types of tariff reform on the volume of imports as measured by M. We begin with a uniform radial reduction in tariffs. It is clear from (27) that if only one good is subject to tariffs, then import volume rises monotonically as the tariff is reduced toward zero. However, it does not follow that import volume must rise following a uniform radial reduction when many goods are subject to tariffs. The reason is that, as we have seen in (13), both $\bar{T}$ and V fall in this case. Since, from (31), falls in $\bar{T}$ and V have opposite effects on import volume, we can therefore expect the overall effect to be ambiguous. To see this explicitly, substitute from (13) into (31) so that the change in import volume becomes

$$\bar{s}^{-1} \, dM = [\bar{T} - (1 - M_b) T' ST] \, d\alpha. \tag{36}$$

Rewriting this in terms of the generalized moments yields

$$\bar{s}^{-1} \, dM = [\{1 - (1 - M_b)\bar{T}\}\bar{T} - (1 - M_b)V] \, d\alpha. \tag{37}$$

---

6. A minor difference from the earlier case is that the marginal propensity to spend on importables in (35), $\tilde{M}_b \equiv \mu\pi' x_I$, is measured at domestic rather than world prices. Unlike M_b, this could be greater than one if tariffs are sufficiently high, even if all goods are normal in demand. The difference between the two marginal propensities depends directly on the size of the tariff multiplier: $\tilde{M}_b - M_b = \mu - 1$.

7. A different reason for being interested in import volume at domestic prices is that the difference between it and import volume at world prices equals tariff revenue: $R = t'm = \tilde{M} - M$. Hence the change in tariff revenue is $dR = d\tilde{M} - dM$. Substituting from (27) and (35) yields a particularly simple expression $dR = m' \, dt + e_u \, du$. This is important in discussions of trade policy reform subject to a tariff revenue constraint, where it leads to a version of the Ramsey rule for tariff rates, an application we do not pursue further here. See, for example, Anderson (1999) and Falvey (1994).

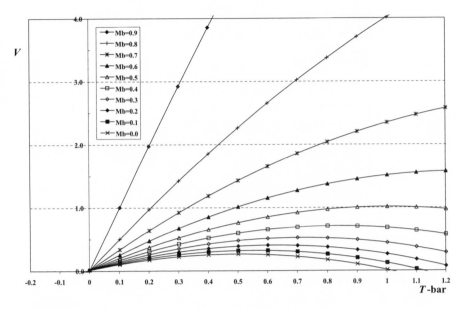

Figure 6.5
Threshold values of V above which a uniform radial reduction in tariffs lowers import volume

Even when $\bar{T}$ lies between zero and one, the expression on the right-hand side can be either positive or negative, as figure 6.5, drawn in $\{V, \bar{T}\}$ space, illustrates. Higher curves in the figure correspond to higher values of M_b, each curve showing the threshold value of V as a function of $\bar{T}$, above which a uniform radial reduction in tariffs lowers import volume. The implications of the figure can be summarized as follows:

Proposition 6.7 A uniform radial reduction in tariffs is more likely to raise import volume, the lower the generalized variance of tariffs, V, and the higher the marginal propensity to spend on importables, M_b.

Ju and Krishna (2000) consider the special case where all tariff rates are the same. This implies that V is zero, and so corresponds to the horizontal axis (when $\bar{T}$ lies in the unit interval) in figure 6.5. Proposition 6.7 shows that their result can be considerably relaxed, especially for high values of M_b.

While the effects on import volume of a uniform radial reduction are ambiguous, we can get much sharper results for other kinds of uniform tariff reductions. First, by inspecting (30), it is clear that import volume must rise (without any restrictions on substitutability or on the value of $\bar{T}$) if tariff rates are changed according to the following rule:

$$dT = -[\imath - (1 - M_b)T]\,d\alpha. \tag{38}$$

Substituting this into (30) yields a quadratic form in S, which must be positive. The rule for reducing tariff rates given by (38) implies, from (2), reducing domestic prices in proportion to a weighted average of domestic and world prices, where M_b is the weight attached to domestic prices:

$$d\pi = dt = \pi\,dT = -[\pi^* + M_b t]\,d\alpha$$

$$\qquad = -[M_b\pi + (1 - M_b)\pi^*]\,d\alpha. \tag{39}$$

We can state this formally as follows:[8]

Proposition 6.8   Import volume must rise if tariffs are reduced in a manner that reduces domestic prices in proportion to a weighted average of domestic and world prices, where M_b is the weight attached to domestic prices.

We saw in sections 6.2 and 6.3 that a radial reduction in tariffs is in the interior of a cone of welfare-increasing tariff reforms, and has the special feature that it ensures a welfare gain irrespective of the pattern of substitutability between goods. A similar set of results hold for import volume. The tariff change in proposition 6.8 does not require substitutability, and lies in the interior of a cone of import-volume-increasing tariff changes. To determine the extent of this cone, we turn next to the effects on import volume of uniform absolute reductions in tariff rates. Consider first a uniform absolute reduction in tariff rates measured with respect to domestic prices, T. From table 6.1 we know that this leaves the generalized variance unchanged and lowers the generalized mean, and so it raises import volume provided the coefficient of $d\bar{T}$ in (31) is positive:

$$\bar{s}^{-1}\,dM = [1 - (1 - M_b)\bar{T}]\,d\alpha. \tag{40}$$

As for a uniform absolute reduction in tariff rates measured with respect to *world* prices, τ, this must also raise import volume under similar conditions, since we know from table 6.1 that it lowers the generalized mean and increases the generalized variance. The full expression is

---

8. Ju and Krishna present this result in a rather different form without the weighted average interpretation: see the first part of their proposition 1.

$$\bar{s}^{-1} dM = [\{1 - (1 - M_b)\bar{T}\}(1 - \bar{T}) + (1 - M_b)V] d\alpha. \tag{41}$$

Finally consider a convex combination of these two types of uniform absolute reduction (where δ is the weight attached to the uniform absolute reduction in T):[9]

$$dT = -[\delta\iota + (1 - \delta)(\iota - T)] d\alpha = -[\iota - (1 - \delta)T] d\alpha. \tag{42}$$

The effect of this change on import volume is given by

$$\bar{s}^{-1} dM = [\{1 - (1 - \delta)\bar{T}\}\{1 - (1 - M_b)\bar{T}\} + (1 - \delta)(1 - M_b)V] d\alpha. \tag{43}$$

This is clearly positive for a wide range of parameters. Of course, when δ equals M_b, it is definitely positive and reduces to the case given in proposition 6.8. For other values of δ we can summarize these results as follows:

Proposition 6.9   Sufficient conditions for any convex combination of uniform absolute reductions in T and τ to raise import volume are that both M_b and $\bar{T}$ are less than one.

The resulting cone of import-volume-increasing tariff changes is represented in figure 6.6 by the shaded area between the rays AB and AC (which are repeated from figure 6.2).

   Consider next the changes in tariffs that explicitly reduce variance. In section 6.3 we were able to show that these often raise welfare. However, in the present context such changes are likely to *reduce* import volume, since it is positively related to the generalized variance. Consider first a concertina reform, or, more generally, a reduction in the tariff on good 1 only. The changes in generalized moments in this case are given by equations (18) and (19). Substituting from these into the expression for changes in import volume in (31), we have, after a series of derivations similar to those preceding to (20),

$$\bar{s}^{-1} dM = -[(1 - M_b)T'S\varepsilon_1 - \bar{T}\iota'S\varepsilon_1] d\alpha$$

$$= -(1 - M_b)S_{11}\left(T_1 - \sum_2 T_i\omega_{i1} - \frac{\omega_{01}}{1 - M_b}\right) d\alpha. \tag{44}$$

The expression in parentheses can be unambiguously signed in some special cases. In many such cases it is positive, implying that a *rise* in T_1 (i.e.,

---

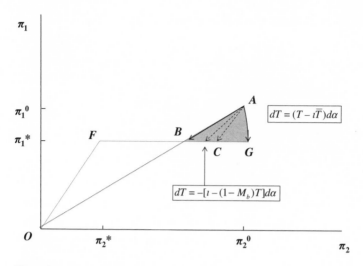

Figure 6.6
Cone of import-volume-increasing liberalization

a negative value for $d\alpha$) raises import volume. For completeness we state these conditions formally:[10]

Proposition 6.10 Assume that M_b is positive and less than one. Then a reduction in the highest tariff will raise import volume if that good is a substitute for all other tariff-constrained goods and unrelated to or a complement for the numéraire good ($\omega_{01} \leq 0$). A reduction in the *lowest* tariff will *lower* import volume if that good is a substitute for all other goods, including the numéraire.

Finally consider the effects on import volume of a variance-reducing tariff reform as in (23):

$$\bar{s}^{-1}\, dM = [(\bar{T} - \beta)\{1 - (1 - M_b)\bar{T}\} - (1 - M_b)V]\, d\alpha. \qquad (45)$$

Not surprisingly, this kind of reform may lower import volume. It must do so if β is greater than the generalized mean, assuming that M_b is less than one and $\bar{T}$ lies between zero and one. In particular, if β equals $\bar{T}$, the case of a generalized mean-preserving contraction of the tariff distribution, then import volume definitely falls. Turning this result around, we can state sufficient conditions for a variance-*increasing* tariff reform to raise import volume:

---

10. This extends propositions 2 and 3 of Ju and Krishna.

Proposition 6.11 Sufficient conditions for a variance-increasing tariff reform (i.e., $dT = (T - \imath\beta)\,d\alpha$) to raise import volume are that M_b is less than one, $\bar{T}$ lies between zero and one, and β is greater than or equal to $\bar{T}$.

This result allows us to expand further the cone of import-volume-increasing tariff changes in figure 6.6. When β equals $\bar{T}$, the tariff change is represented by the curve AG (opposite in direction to AE in figure 6.3 and, like it, drawn under the assumption that $\bar{T}$ is positive). When β equals one, the tariff change becomes $dT = -(\imath - T)\,d\alpha$, which is equivalent to a uniform absolute reduction in τ. (Recall the third line in table 6.1.) It is therefore represented by the line AC as in figure 6.2. From proposition 6.11, all movements from A between these two extremes (i.e., all tariff changes in the cone CAG) raise import volume provided that $\bar{T}$ lies between zero and one. But we have already seen in proposition 6.9 that all changes in the cone BAC also raise import volume. Hence, combining the two results, we denote the full cone of import-volume-increasing tariff changes by the shaded area BAG.

Comparing figures 6.3 and 6.6, we see that the cones of liberalization that raise welfare and import volume are nonintersecting. It should be emphasized that each cone shows only those regions in which an unambiguous increase in the target of interest is guaranteed, given the mild assumptions that $\bar{T}$ and (in the case of import volume) M_b are between zero and one. They therefore show tariff reforms that can be recommended to attain either target subject to minimal informational requirements. If additional information is available, then it may be possible to identify further tariff changes that can attain the desired goal. For example, proposition 6.7 gives additional assumptions that ensure that import volume rises following a uniform radial reduction in tariffs, which we know will always raise welfare. Nevertheless, the conclusion is inescapable that there is likely to be a conflict between the objectives of raising welfare and increasing market access. The only tariff change that is guaranteed to achieve both goals, with no assumptions other than that $\bar{T}$ and M_b lie between zero and one, is a uniform absolute reduction in T, which reduces domestic prices proportionally.

6.6 Changes in the TRI and MTRI and Measures of Tariff Dispersion

Next we want to relate changes in the TRI and the MTRI to changes in the distribution of tariffs, as summarized by changes in the generalized tariff moments. Fortunately, most of the hard work has already been done. Explicit expressions for changes in the TRI and the MTRI as functions of arbitrary tariff changes were derived in chapters 4 and 5. It remains to re-express these in terms of changes in the generalized tariff moments using the results from earlier sections.

Begin with the TRI. From equation (21) in chapter 4 the proportional change in the TRI uniform tariff can be written as follows:

$$\frac{d\tau^\Delta}{1+\tau^\Delta} = \psi^\Delta \frac{B_\pi \cdot d\pi}{B_\pi \cdot \pi}. \tag{46}$$

Here ψ^Δ is a correction factor, which is needed because the derivatives of the balance-of-trade function B are evaluated at two different points:

$$\psi^\Delta \equiv \frac{B_u^\Delta}{B_u} \frac{B_\pi \cdot \pi}{B_\pi^\Delta \cdot \pi^\Delta}. \tag{47}$$

The derivatives B_π and B_u are evaluated at the initial tariff-distorted price vector π, while the derivatives B_π^Δ and B_u^Δ are evaluated at the uniform-tariff-equivalent price vector $\pi^\Delta \equiv (1+\tau^\Delta)\pi^*$. For small tariffs and for many functional forms (even with large tariffs) this correction factor is unity, and it is reasonable to assume that it will be close to unity in many applications.

Returning to (46), we need to express the derivatives of the balance of trade function in terms of the normalized substitution matrix S. Using equation (9) from chapter 4 and equation (3) above, we do this as follows:

$$B_\pi' = -t'E_{\pi\pi} = -T'\underline{\pi}E_{\pi\pi} = \bar{s}T'S\underline{\pi}^{-1}. \tag{48}$$

Substituting into (46) yields the proportional change in the TRI uniform tariff:

$$\frac{d\tau^\Delta}{1+\tau^\Delta} = \psi^\Delta \frac{T'S\,dT}{\bar{T}}. \tag{49}$$

This has a nice interpretation. From (11) any change in tariffs has a welfare cost that is proportional to $-T'S\,dT$, while from (12) a unit change in the generalized mean tariff has a welfare cost that is proportional to $-\bar{T}$. The resulting change in the TRI uniform tariff is proportional to the ratio of these two welfare costs. Finally, using (12) again, we can write the change in the TRI uniform tariff as a function of changes in the two generalized moments:

$$\frac{d\tau^\Delta}{1+\tau^\Delta} = \psi^\Delta \left(d\bar{T} + \frac{\frac{1}{2}dV}{\bar{T}} \right). \tag{50}$$

Thus τ^Δ is increasing in $\bar{T}$ and (provided that $\bar{T}$ is positive) in V.

Next consider the MTRI. From equation (5) in chapter 5, the proportional change in the MTRI uniform tariff can be written as follows:

$$\frac{d\tau^\mu}{1+\tau^\mu} = \frac{M_\pi \cdot d\pi}{M_\pi^\mu \cdot \pi^\mu} = \psi^\mu \frac{M_\pi \cdot d\pi}{M_\pi \cdot \pi}. \tag{51}$$

As before, ψ^μ is a correction factor that is needed because the derivatives of the import volume function are evaluated at two different points:

$$\psi^\mu \equiv \frac{M_\pi \cdot \pi}{M_\pi^\mu \cdot \pi^\mu}. \tag{52}$$

M_π is evaluated at the initial tariff-distorted price vector π, and M_π^μ is evaluated at the uniform-tariff-equivalent price vector $\pi^\mu \equiv (1+\tau^\mu)\pi^*$. The correction factor ψ^μ differs from ψ^Δ in (47), though both are likely to be close to unity.

To express (51) in terms of changes in generalized tariff moments, we make use of (27) and (29) above:

$$M_\pi' = (\pi^* + M_b t)' E_{\pi\pi} = [\iota - (1 - M_b)T]'\underline{\pi} E_{\pi\pi} = -\bar{s}[\iota - (1 - M_b)T]'S\underline{\pi}^{-1}. \tag{53}$$

Substituting into (51) gives

$$\frac{d\tau^\mu}{1+\tau^\mu} = \psi^\mu \frac{[\iota - (1 - M_b)T]'S\,dT}{1 - (1 - M_b)\bar{T}}. \tag{54}$$

As with the change in the TRI uniform tariff, we can use (30) and (31) to interpret this. The change in the MTRI uniform tariff is proportional to the ratio of the change in imports arising from the actual change in tariffs to the change in imports arising from a unit change in the generalized mean tariff $\bar{T}$. Finally, substituting from (31), we obtain

$$\frac{d\tau^\mu}{1+\tau^\mu} = \psi^\mu \left[d\bar{T} - \frac{\frac{1}{2}(1 - M_b)\,dV}{1 - (1 - M_b)\bar{T}} \right]. \tag{55}$$

Thus the MTRI uniform tariff is increasing in the generalized average tariff but *decreasing* in the generalized variance.

We can summarize the results of this section so far as follows:

Proposition 6.12   Both the TRI and the MTRI uniform tariffs are increasing in the generalized mean of the tariff schedule. The TRI uniform tariff is also increasing in the generalized variance of tariffs (provided $\overline{T}$ is positive), whereas the MTRI uniform tariff is decreasing in V (provided that both M_b and $(1 - M_b)\overline{T}$ are less than one).

Next consider the difference between the changes in the two indexes. Direct calculation shows that

$$\frac{d\tau^\Delta}{1 + \tau^\Delta} - \frac{d\tau^\mu}{1 + \tau^\mu} = \frac{\psi^\Delta - \psi^\mu}{\psi^\Delta}\frac{d\tau^\Delta}{1 + \tau^\Delta} + \psi^\Delta\frac{\frac{1}{2}dV}{\overline{T}[1 - (1 - M_b)\overline{T}]}. \tag{56}$$

Hence we may conclude:

Proposition 6.13   Assume that both $\overline{T}$ and $(1 - M_b)\overline{T}$ are positive and that the difference between ψ^Δ and ψ^μ can be ignored. Then a change in tariffs raises the TRI uniform tariff by more than the MTRI uniform tariff if and only if the generalized variance of tariffs rises.

The full relationship between changes in the TRI and MTRI uniform tariffs, on the one hand, and changes in the generalized tariff moments, on the other, is illustrated in figure 6.7, drawn in the space of $(dV, d\overline{T})$.

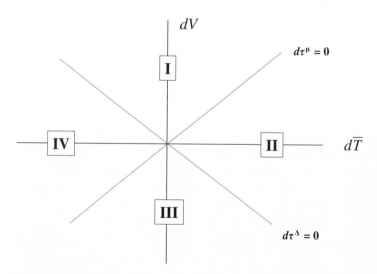

Figure 6.7
Changes in the TRI and MTRI expressed in terms of changes in generalized tariff moments

From equations (50) and (55) and proposition 6.12, both tariff indexes increase together in region II and fall together in region IV. In the other regions (denoted I and III) they move in opposite directions, with τ^Δ changing in the same direction as V and τ^μ changing in the opposite direction. A higher initial value of the generalized average tariff $\bar{T}$ reduces the algebraic slope of both loci, causing the four regimes to pivot in a clockwise direction. A higher marginal propensity to spend on imports M_b leaves the slope of the iso-τ^Δ locus unchanged but increases that of the iso-τ^μ locus, causing regions II and IV, in which the two uniform tariff indexes move together, to expand at the expense of the ambiguous regions I and III.[11] Note finally that a rise in τ^Δ is equivalent to a rise in welfare and a rise in τ^μ is equivalent to a rise in import volume. Hence figure 6.7 gives a complete characterization of the effects on welfare and import volume of arbitrary changes in the generalized tariff moments.

6.7 Relating Generalized to Observable Moments

So far we have shown how changes in welfare, market access and trade restrictiveness can be expressed in terms of the generalized mean and variance of the tariff schedule. These two generalized moments serve in effect as sufficient statistics for the whole n-by-1 vector of tariff rates. Of course, the generalized moments are not independent of the structure of the economy: on the contrary, they are defined in terms of the general-equilibrium substitution matrix. But there is clearly a huge economy of information from the fact that everything that is relevant to small changes in welfare and market access can be summarized in terms of changes in the two moments. However, there is no guarantee that the generalized moments are closely related to the standard moments, which can be calculated using only information on the tariff schedule and the levels of imports. In this section we show that the generalized moments coincide with the standard moments in a special but important case, where preferences take a homothetic constant-elasticity-of-substitution (CES) form, and where imports are imperfect substitutes for home-produced goods. The latter assumption follows Armington (1969) and is made in the vast majority of CGE models. Hence our result greatly enhances the usefulness of

---

11. From (50) and (55) the slope of the iso-τ^Δ locus is $-2\bar{T}$, while the slope of the iso-τ^μ locus is $2[1 - (1 - M_b)\bar{T}]/(1 - M_b)$.

the generalized moments and the results based on them presented in previous sections.[12]

The trade expenditure function in this case can be written as follows:

$$E(\pi_0, \pi, u) = e(\pi_0, \pi, u) - g(\pi_0) = u\Pi(\pi_0, \pi) - g(\pi_0). \tag{57}$$

Here we have made explicit the dependence of both the expenditure function e and the GDP function g on the prices of goods not subject to tariffs, which as always we aggregate into a composite numéraire good with price π_0. Expenditure is linear in u because preferences are homothetic, and it is a separable function of the prices of all $n + 1$ goods, mediated through Π, which is a constant-elasticity-of-substitution aggregate price index defined over both π_0 and π:

$$\Pi(\pi_0, \pi) = \left(\sum_{i=0}^{n} \beta_i \pi_i^{1-\sigma}\right)^{1/(1-\sigma)} , \quad \sum_{i=0}^{n} \beta_i = 1 \tag{58}$$

As for GDP, it is independent of π because of the assumption of noncompeting imports, though it does depend on π_0.

We proceed to explore the implications of the specification in (57) for the elements of the normalized substitution matrix S. Differentiating (57) with respect to π_i gives the Hicksian demand functions for all goods, which are also the import demand functions for goods 1 to n:

$$E_i = u\Pi_i = u\beta_i \left(\frac{\pi_i}{\Pi}\right)^{-\sigma}, \qquad i = 0, 1, \ldots, n. \tag{59}$$

Multiplying by prices and summing over all i gives total expenditure at domestic prices:

$$e = \sum_{i=0}^{} \pi_i E_i = u\Pi \frac{\sum_{i=0} \beta_i \pi_i^{1-\sigma}}{\Pi^{1-\sigma}} = u\Pi. \tag{60}$$

From this we can derive the share of good i in the value of imports:

$$\phi_i \equiv \frac{\pi_i m_i}{\pi \cdot m} = \frac{\pi_i E_i}{M} = \frac{\beta_i}{v} \left(\frac{\pi_i}{\Pi}\right)^{1-\sigma}, \tag{61}$$

where v is the share of imports in aggregate expenditure:

12. Anderson (1995) showed that generalized moments defined with respect to world prices coincide with standard moments when the trade expenditure function is Cobb-Douglas.

$$v \equiv \frac{M}{e} = \frac{\sum_{i=1} \pi_i E_i}{\sum_{i=0} \pi_i E_i}. \tag{62}$$

Differentiating (59) now yields

$$\pi_i E_{ij} \pi_j = -\sigma M \phi_i (\delta_{ij} - v\phi_j), \tag{63}$$

where δ_{ij} is the Kronecker delta (equal to one when $i = j$ and zero otherwise). Recalling the definition of the elements of the normalized substitution matrix from (4), we can now express them as

$$S_{ij} = \frac{\phi_i (\delta_{ij} - v\phi_j)}{1 - v}, \tag{64}$$

or in matrix form as

$$S = \frac{\phi - \phi v \phi'}{1 - v}. \tag{65}$$

Note that the column sums of the S matrix equal the import shares themselves,

$$\iota' S = \frac{\iota' \phi - \iota' \phi v \phi'}{1 - v} = \phi', \tag{66}$$

making use of the fact that the import shares sum to one: $\iota' \phi = \phi' \iota = 1$. This is the key implication of the CES specification: the generalized or marginal trade weights used in the construction of $\bar{T}$ and V equal average trade weights.

We can now state the main result of this section:

Proposition 6.14 When the trade expenditure function takes the form given by (57) and (58), the generalized average tariff is equal to the trade-weighted average tariff, and the generalized variance of tariffs is proportional to the trade-weighted variance, both evaluated at domestic prices.

The proof is immediate. The generalized average tariff becomes

$$\bar{T} \equiv \iota' S T = \phi' T = \frac{t \cdot m}{\pi \cdot m}, \tag{67}$$

which is simply the standard atheoretic trade-weighted average tariff at domestic prices. As for the generalized variance of tariffs, it becomes

$$V \equiv (T - \iota \bar{T})' S(T - \iota \bar{T}) = T'ST - \bar{T}^2$$

$$= \frac{T'(\underline{\phi} - \phi v \phi')T}{1 - v} - \bar{T}^2$$

$$= \frac{T'\underline{\phi}T - \bar{T}^2}{1 - v}. \tag{68}$$

The numerator of the final expression is simply the atheoretic trade-weighted variance of tariffs at domestic prices:

$$\tilde{V} \equiv (T - \iota \bar{T})'\underline{\phi}(T - \iota \bar{T}) = T'\underline{\phi}T - \bar{T}^2. \tag{69}$$

This proves the proposition.   ∎

6.8   Conclusion

In this chapter we have developed a new approach to characterizing the structure of tariff rates. Practical researchers have often attempted to summarize such structure in terms of the mean and variance of tariffs, but as we have seen at many points in this book, this approach has no theoretical justification. As with index numbers of trade restrictiveness, empirical measures that only use data on tariff levels and import shares fail to give an adequate picture because they ignore marginal responses. To deal with this problem, we drew on Anderson (1995) to introduce two generalized moments of the tariff structure. The generalization involves weighting actual tariff rates by the elements of the substitution matrix, so the generalized moments incorporate information on marginal responses by construction.

The first contribution of this chapter was to show that the effects of tariff changes on welfare and import volume can be fully characterized by their effects on the generalized mean and variance of the tariff distribution. We were thus able to use these tools to derive new results for welfare- and market-access-improving tariff changes. These imply significant generalizations of existing results, and can be conveniently illustrated in terms of two "cones of liberalization" in price space. The cones do not intersect, except along one boundary, because welfare is negatively but import volume positively related to the generalized variance. This is not to say that there are no reforms that meet both objectives, since the cones give only sufficient, not necessary, conditions for meeting one or other goal. However, without detailed information on the structure of the economy, we cannot characterize them. For practical policy-making, this suggests that negotiations on trade liberalization face a difficult choice between tariff-cutting formulas that guarantee an improvement in domestic welfare and formulas that ensure an increase in market access (and so are likely to be acceptable to foreign exporters).

Another contribution of the chapter was to relate the two generalized moments to the TRI and MTRI. The generalized moments can be thought of as a pair of index numbers that together provide a complete characterization of the structure of tariffs and that can in principle be used for many purposes. By contrast, both the TRI and MTRI provide a single index that is relevant for one purpose: measuring the restrictiveness of tariffs from the perspective of welfare or import volume respectively. Both approaches have their uses, and it is of interest to explore the links between them. Section 6.6 shows how local changes in the TRI and MTRI can be related to changes in the generalized moments of the tariff distribution. In particular, we show that under very general conditions small changes in tariffs raise the TRI uniform tariff τ^{Δ} by more than the MTRI uniform tariff τ^{μ} if and only if the generalized variance of tariffs rises. Given the practical interest in measures of tariff dispersion, these techniques seem likely to prove useful in many other contexts.

Just like the TRI and MTRI, the generalized tariff moments depend on the general-equilibrium substitution matrix, which at best is observable with a lot of error. Hence applying them in practice requires care and judgment. Of course, if a computable general-equilibrium model has been estimated for the economy, then they can be calculated explicitly. This is the approach that we will explore with the TRI and MTRI in later chapters. Alternatively, we can try to establish the properties of the generalized moments under special assumptions about the structure of the economy. This is the approach adopted in section 6.7, where we showed that if the trade expenditure function takes a CES form, the weights reduce to trade weights and the generalized moments are proportional to observable trade-weighted moments. The CES form is extremely special of course. Nevertheless, this result provides further insight into the role of intercommodity substitution in mediating the effects of tariff changes, and also provides a partial justification for the practical use of trade-weighted tariff moments.

7 Trade Reform with Tariffs and Quotas

So far we have assumed that tariffs are the only form of trade restrictions. We need to relax this assumption, since in recent decades tariffs have lost the importance they once had as barriers to international trade. Under the auspices of the General Agreement on Tariffs and Trade (since 1995 the World Trade Organization) and of regional free-trade groupings such as the European Community and the North American Free Trade Agreement, tariffs have been progressively reduced to fairly low levels, at least on trade between developed countries. This has not meant that protectionist instincts have been totally abandoned, of course. On the contrary, the reduction in average tariff levels has been accompanied by an explosion in the use of nontariff barriers, of which the most pervasive example is quantitative restrictions or quotas.

Evaluating trade reform and measuring trade restrictiveness in the presence of quotas is complicated by two features: quotas typically coexist with tariffs, and quota rents are commonly shared between exporting and importing countries. One extreme case, which we will call that of a "pure" quota, is where all the quota rents accrue to the importing country. The other extreme case, where none of the rents accrue to the importing country, is that of a "pure" voluntary export restraint (VER). In practice, real-world trade regimes typically lie between the two extremes, the case that poses the greatest problems for analysis.[1]

In this chapter we extend the theory of trade liberalization to incorporate quotas as well as tariffs and to allow for different degrees of rent

---

1. For example, the US markup on Japanese autos under the VER of 1981 to 1985 gave substantial rent to US dealers. Also in many cases (e.g., textiles and apparel) VERs coincide with substantial domestic import tariffs that retain a portion of the rent. Even apparently pure import quota systems such as the US cheese import control structure generate significant rent-sharing due to their allocation to very fine commodity-by-country categories, so bilateral monopoly is approximately the norm. (See Hornig, Boisvert, and Blandford 1990a,b, for evidence.)

retention by the importing country.[2] In the next chapter we show how the results may be applied to derive the general forms of the TRI and MTRI that measure the restrictiveness of a protective structure with both tariffs and quotas. Readers primarily interested in the latter topic need only look at sections 7.1 and 7.2 to familiarize themselves with the tools that will be applied in chapter 8.

7.1 The Distorted Trade Expenditure Function

We retain all the assumptions made in chapter 3, except that some goods are now assumed to be subject to quotas. Let q denote the vector of net imports of the quota-constrained goods, whose domestic and world prices are denoted by p and p^* respectively. As before, tariff-constrained goods are denoted by m, with domestic and world prices π and π^* respectively, and $\pi = \pi^* + t$. It will be convenient to refer to the two groups of goods as the q-goods and the t-goods. Finally exports and undistorted imports can be grouped together as a composite numéraire good, which we will mostly leave implicit throughout.

As we saw in chapter 3, the behavior of an economy in which tariffs are the only form of trade distortion is most conveniently summarized by the trade expenditure function. With two categories of tariff-constrained goods this is defined as

$$E(p, \pi, u) \equiv e(p, \pi, u) - g(p, \pi), \tag{1}$$

where $e(p, \pi, u)$ and $g(p, \pi)$ are the household expenditure and GDP functions respectively. The price derivatives of the trade expenditure function give the compensated net import demand functions for the q- and t-goods as functions of their domestic prices:

$$E_p(p, \pi, u) = q^c(p, \pi, u), \tag{2}$$

$$E_\pi(p, \pi, u) = m^c(p, \pi, u). \tag{3}$$

Since the trade expenditure function is concave in $\{p, \pi\}$, each of these import demand functions is nonincreasing in its own price. For convenience we will assume that they are strictly decreasing in their own price;

---

2. Hatta (1977b) and Fukushima (1979) extended the theory of trade liberalization to incorporate nontraded goods, which are formally equivalent to quotas set at prohibitive levels. Our presentation draws mostly on recent work on quotas by Corden and Falvey (1985), Falvey (1988), Neary (1988), Anderson and Neary (1992), and Neary (1995, 2003). See also Lahiri and Raimondos (1996).

with many goods in each category, this is equivalent to assuming that the matrices E_{pp} and $E_{\pi\pi}$ are negative definite.[3] The trade expenditure function may also be defined in an alternative way that will prove useful below. It equals the value at domestic prices of the cheapest import bundle that will yield a given level of utility:

$$E(p,\pi,u) \equiv \min_{m_0,q,m} [m_0 + p'q + \pi'm : U(m_0,q,m) = u], \tag{4}$$

where $U(m_0,q,m)$ is a Meade trade utility function defined over net imports (including those of the numéraire m_0) rather than final consumption.[4]

When the q-goods are restricted by quotas rather than tariffs, we need to adopt a different approach. We therefore introduce a new function, the *distorted trade expenditure function*. This equals net spending on the numéraire and the tariff-constrained goods conditional on the quota levels:

$$\tilde{E}(q,\pi,u) \equiv \min_{m_0,m} [m_0 + \pi'm : U(m_0,q,m) = u]. \tag{5}$$

Viewed as a function of π and u for given q, the distorted trade expenditure function behaves just like the standard trade expenditure function. Its derivative with respect to u is the marginal cost of utility e_u, and its derivatives with respect to π equal the compensated import demand functions for the t-goods conditional on the quotas:

$$\tilde{E}_\pi(q,\pi,u) = \tilde{m}^c(q,\pi,u). \tag{6}$$

These quota-constrained demand functions have properties with respect to π similar to those of the unconstrained demand functions (3) derived in chapter 3. In particular, since $\tilde{E}$ is concave in π, we have[5]

Lemma 7.1 The matrix of own-price derivatives of the quota-constrained demand functions for the t-goods, $\tilde{m}^c_\pi$, is negative definite.

Heuristically, the compensated net import demand functions for the t-goods slope downward.

---

3. As in chapter 3, for these matrices to be negative definite, as opposed to merely negative semidefinite, requires some substitutability in excess demand between the different groups of goods. We make this assumption throughout the chapter, without repeating the qualification.

4. See Chipman (1979), Woodland (1980), and Neary and Schweinberger (1986) for further details.

5. See Neary and Roberts (1980) and Keen (1989).

What about the properties of the distorted trade expenditure function as a function of the quota constraints? To derive these, note that the distorted and undistorted functions can be related provided the domestic prices of the quota-constrained goods are market clearing.[6] More precisely,

$$\tilde{E}(q, \pi, u) = E[p(q, \pi, u), \pi, u] - p(q, \pi, u)'q, \tag{7}$$

where the market-clearing price vector p is defined implicitly by

$$q = E_p(p, \pi, u). \tag{8}$$

Differentiating (7) with respect to q and using (8) to simplify gives an explicit expression for the prices p:

$$\tilde{E}_q(q, \pi, u) = -p(q, \pi, u). \tag{9}$$

Thus the derivatives of the distorted trade expenditure function with respect to the quotas give the *inverse* demand functions for the quota-constrained goods, expressing their market-clearing prices as functions of the exogenous variables. Finally, by totally differentiating (6), (8), and (9), we can relate the second derivatives of the distorted trade expenditure function to those of the undistorted trade expenditure function. In particular, we have the following:

Lemma 7.2   The matrix of derivatives of the inverse demand functions for the q-goods with respect to the quota levels, p_q, is negative definite.

Heuristically, the compensated inverse demand functions for the q-goods slope downward. This result is proved in the appendix, section 7A.1. The income derivatives of the *un*compensated import demand functions for the q- and t-goods, p_I and $\tilde{m}_I$, are also derived there.

7.2   Rent-Sharing and the Welfare Cost of Quotas

The distorted trade expenditure function summarizes the behavior of the private sector, and it only remains to specify public sector behavior, which is purely redistributive. As in earlier chapters we assume that all tariff revenue is redistributed in a lump-sum manner to the aggregate household. However, the same assumption is not plausible in the case of quota rents. Instead, we assume that a fraction ω_j of the quota rents on

---

6. This approach follows the analysis of household behavior under rationing by Neary and Roberts (1980), who called p the *virtual prices* of the rationed goods.

each good j is lost to the domestic economy. As noted in the Introduction, ω_j is zero in the case of a pure quota and unity in the case of a pure VER. Total quota rents retained at home and redistributed to households therefore equal $\sum_j (1 - \omega_j)(p_j - p_j^*)q_j$. In matrix form this can be written as $(p - p^*)'(I - \underline{\omega})q$, where I is the identity matrix and (as in chapter 6) a bar under a vector denotes the corresponding diagonal matrix (so $\underline{\omega}$ is a diagonal matrix with the rent-loss shares on the principal diagonal).

Armed with the properties of the distorted trade expenditure function and our assumptions about the disposition of quota rents, we are now ready to specify the general equilibrium of the economy. In equilibrium, net expenditure on the numéraire and on the tariff-constrained goods (5) plus net expenditure on the quota-constrained goods $p'q$ must equal retained quota rents $(p - p^*)'(I - \underline{\omega})q$ plus tariff revenue $t'm$:

$$\tilde{E}(q, \pi, u) + p'q = (p - p^*)'(I - \underline{\omega})q + t'm. \tag{10}$$

The first step toward deriving the welfare effects of trade policy reform is to totally differentiate equation (10). (We simplify by using (6), (9), and the fact that $d\pi = dt$. We also assume until section 7.8 that the rent-share parameters ω are constant, so we ignore terms in $d\omega$.) This gives

$$e_u \, du = (p - p^*)'(I - \underline{\omega}) \, dq - q'\underline{\omega} \, dp + t' \, dm. \tag{11}$$

As with equation (8) in chapter 3, this equation does not give the full effect of changes in trade policy because the terms in dp and dm are endogenous. Nevertheless, it is very helpful in providing intuition. Other things equal, welfare rises when quotas are relaxed (except for pure VERs where $\omega = \iota$, so all the rents are lost). Moreover welfare rises when the domestic prices of quota-constrained goods fall (except for pure quotas where $\omega = 0$), since this reduces total rents and hence reduces the amount transferred to foreigners. Finally, as in chapter 3, welfare also rises if the volume of tariff-constrained imports increases.

The second and final step is to use the differentials of (6) and (9) to eliminate dp and dm from (11). This yields the basic equation for the welfare effects of changes in trade policy in the presence of tariffs and quotas:

$$\mu^{-1} e_u \, du = \rho' \, dq + \chi' \, dt. \tag{12}$$

where ρ and χ are defined below. As in chapter 3 the coefficient of the change in real income $e_u \, du$ can be interpreted as the inverse of the shadow price of foreign exchange:

$$\mu \equiv (1 + q'\underline{\omega}p_I - t'\tilde{m}_I)^{-1}. \tag{13}$$

Any increase in real income has a multiplier effect that is greater to the extent that it raises demand for tariff-constrained imports, just as in chapter 3. In addition, when ω is positive, the multiplier effect is *dampened* to the extent that incipient increases in demand for quota-constrained goods push up their domestic prices and so increase the amount of rents lost. Because of the combined effect of these influences, μ may be either greater or less than unity. In any case, we assume throughout that it is positive, and this should be understood in all the propositions that follow in this chapter.[7]

The effect of trade reform, or the marginal cost of protection, therefore depends on the coefficients of changes in the policy variables, which we call the *shadow prices of quotas* and the *marginal cost of tariffs* respectively:

$$\rho' \equiv (p - p^*)'(I - \underline{\omega}) - q'\underline{\omega}p_q + t'\tilde{m}_q^c, \tag{14}$$

$$\chi' \equiv -q'\underline{\omega}p_\pi + t'\tilde{m}_\pi^c. \tag{15}$$

These formulas generalize the results of Anderson and Neary (1992) to allow for rent-share parameters that differ across commodities. They are the central equations of this chapter. Because of their complexity we consider their implications under a variety of simplifying assumptions about trade policy and the structure of the economy.

7.3   Trade Reform without Restrictions on the Trade Expenditure Function

The first group of results for trade policy reform are those that do not require any restrictions on tastes or technology. As in the tariffs-only case of chapter 3, the central result, proposition 7.4 below, relates to a uniform proportionate reduction in all distortions. However, because of the complexity of the model, it is useful to lead up to this result with some special cases.

Consider first quota reform. Setting $\omega = t = 0$ in the expression for ρ in (14) we have by inspection

---

7. As in chapter 3, the assumption that μ is positive may be rationalized on stability grounds or by invoking a minimal degree of rationality of government policy. Alternatively, we can look for sufficient conditions to sign the individual terms. The term in μ^{-1}, which did not appear in chapter 3, is $q'\underline{\omega}p_I$; from appendix 7A.1, it equals $-q'\underline{\omega}E_{pp}^{-1}q_I$. Alternative sufficient conditions for this to be positive are (1) from Hatta (1977a), that the q-goods are normal in demand and net substitutes, and (2) from Anderson and Neary (1992), that ω_j is the same for all goods and that the q-goods are homothetic in demand and have uniform import shares (so that $q_I = (\alpha/I)q$, where α is the common import share).

Proposition 7.1 (Corden and Falvey 1985)   With no tariffs and full rent retention, any quota relaxation must raise welfare.

In this case the shadow price of each quota is just the gap between home and world prices: the right-hand side of (14) reduces to: $\rho = p - p^*$. Hence there is no second-best problem: a relaxation of any quota is guaranteed to raise welfare irrespective of what happens to other quotas.

When some rents are lost to the domestic economy, an arbitrary quota relaxation need not raise welfare because the induced changes in the prices of the q-goods may lead to a transfer of rents which lowers welfare. From (14) with no tariffs, the shadow price of quotas ρ' is $(p - p^*)'(I - \underline{\omega}) - q'\underline{\omega}p_q$. This is the sum of the implicit tariffs $p - p^*$ (which measure the welfare gain on marginal imports of q-goods) and the change in rents $q'p_q$ (which measures the welfare gain on intra-marginal imports), both corrected for the share of rents accruing to home residents. The first term arises because the welfare gain on an additional unit of imports, $p_j - p_j^*$, is shared with foreigners, only $1 - \omega_j$ per cent being retained at home. The second term arises because lower domestic prices for q-goods reduce the quota rents transferred to foreign license holders. In the pure quota case ($\underline{\omega} = 0$) this term vanishes, since price changes merely transfer rents from domestic holders of import licenses to domestic consumers, and so are purely redistributive, with no effects on aggregate home welfare.

What can be said about the sign of the shadow prices of quotas in this case? For a single good the second term, $-q'\underline{\omega}p_q$, is necessarily positive. For more goods, p_q is negative definite from lemma 7.2, but this does not allow us to sign $-q'\underline{\omega}p_q$ for arbitrary quotas and preferences. Thus, with less than full rent retention, quota reform is just as prone to multicommodity complications as is tariff reform.[8] One approach to resolving the ambiguity is similar to that adopted in the discussion of tariff reform in chapter 3, to consider a uniform relaxation of quotas.[9] The only extra complication is that quotas should be relaxed in proportion to their initial levels *weighted* by the share of rents lost on each good: $dq_j = \omega_j q_j \, d\alpha$ or $dq = \underline{\omega}q \, d\alpha$. When quotas are relaxed in this way, (12) and (14) imply that the change in welfare is proportional to

$$du \propto \rho'\underline{\omega}q = (p - p^*)'(I - \underline{\omega})\underline{\omega}q - q'\underline{\omega}p_q\underline{\omega}q. \tag{16}$$

8. This was noted for the case of pure VERs ($\omega_j = 1$ for all i) in Neary (1988).

9. Heuristically, whereas equiproportionate tariff reform works if the reform permits a Hicksian composite commodity, equiproportionate quota reform requires that a composite Leontief commodity be constructed.

The first term on the right-hand side is positive, since all its elements are positive. The second term is minus a quadratic form in the matrix p_q, which from lemma 7.2 is negative definite. Hence we can be sure that total rents lost to foreigners do not rise, so the quota relaxation must raise welfare. This gives[10]

Proposition 7.2 With no tariffs and partial rent retention, a uniform proportionate relaxation of quotas, weighted by the share of rents lost on each quota-constrained good, must raise welfare.

It is intuitively plausible that the quotas that should be relaxed fastest are those that lose the most rent for the domestic economy. Of course, if the share of rents lost is the same for all quota-constrained goods (so ω is proportional to the unit vector $\imath$), an unweighted uniform relaxation of quotas $(dq = q\,d\alpha)$ raises welfare.

Consider next a reform of tariffs. From the expression for the marginal cost of tariffs in (15), we see that this has two effects. First, just as in the case of no quotas considered in chapter 3, there is a welfare effect arising from the induced change in tariff-constrained imports. The form of this expression, $t'\tilde{m}_\pi^c$, though not its magnitude, is unaffected by the presence of quotas (see Neary 1995). In addition, if any quota rents are lost, there is an extra effect arising from the induced changes in the prices of quota-constrained goods, whose magnitude depends on the cross-derivative matrix p_π. However, if all rents are retained (so $\omega = 0$), this complication vanishes and a uniform reduction result applies, where tariff changes satisfy $dt = -t\,d\alpha$. The change in welfare is then proportional to $-t'\tilde{m}_\pi^c t$, which is minus a quadratic form in a negative definite matrix (from lemma 7.1) and so is positive. This gives

Proposition 7.3 (Neary 1995) With full rent retention, a uniform proportionate reduction of tariffs must raise welfare.

Note that this result does not require any behavioural restrictions.[11] It also applies whether or not quotas are in force (provided that all rent is retained). Relative to proposition 3.1 in chapter 3, the only difference

---

10. This is theorem 2′ of Anderson and Neary (1992).

11. Proposition 7.3 has been stated by a number of authors, but with the unnecessary qualification that all goods are net substitutes. (See, for example, Hatta 1977b, Fukushima 1979, and Falvey 1988.) As noted in Neary (1995), lemma 7.1 implies that the matrix of own-price effects on the quota-constrained import demand functions for the t-goods is always negative definite, and so the qualification is unnecessary.

that quotas make is that they *reduce* the welfare gain from a given tariff reduction.[12]

All three propositions so far are of limited use, since they only apply when one set of trade policy instruments is either absent (no tariffs in propositions 7.1 and 7.2) or benign (full rent retention in proposition 7.3). However, a general result which applies in all cases can be devised by *combining* the policy rules of propositions 7.2 and 7.3: reduce tariffs and raise ω-weighted quotas by the same proportionate amount. Given $dt = -t\,d\alpha$ and $dq = \underline{\omega}q\,d\alpha$, the change in welfare is proportional to

$$du \propto p'\underline{\omega}q - \chi't$$

$$= (p - p^*)'(I - \underline{\omega})\underline{\omega}q - q'\underline{\omega}p_q\underline{\omega}q + t'\tilde{m}_q^c\underline{\omega}q + q'\underline{\omega}p_\pi t - t'\tilde{m}_\pi^c t. \qquad (17)$$

Inspecting this, we can see that the third and fourth terms, $t'\tilde{m}_q^c\underline{\omega}q$ and $q'\underline{\omega}p_\pi t$, cancel, since both are scalars and, from equations (6) and (9), $\tilde{m}_q^c$ is the transpose of $-p_\pi$. In words, the uniform quota relaxation lowers tariff revenue by exactly the same amount as the uniform tariff reduction raises lost quota rents. Equation (17) therefore simplifies to

$$du \propto (p - p^*)'(I - \underline{\omega})\underline{\omega}q - q'\underline{\omega}p_q\underline{\omega}q - t'\tilde{m}_\pi^c t. \qquad (18)$$

All three terms in this expression are positive, and hence a welfare gain is guaranteed. This gives the principal result of this section:

Proposition 7.4 (Neary 2003) A uniform proportionate relaxation of quotas, weighted by the share of rents lost on each quota-constrained good, combined with a uniform proportionate reduction of tariffs at the same rate, must raise welfare.

It is clear by inspection that proposition 7.4 nests the three preceding propositions, and so is the most general result available for simultaneous reform of quotas and tariffs.

7.4   Restricting the Trade Expenditure Function

The second group of results for trade policy reform requires restrictions on the structure of the economy. We consider two types of restriction.

---

12. From proposition 3.1, the welfare gain from a uniform tariff cut in the absence of quotas is $-t'E_{\pi\pi}t$. From proposition 7.3, the welfare gain from a uniform tariff cut in the presence of quotas is $-t'\tilde{E}_{\pi\pi}t$. Provided that they are evaluated at the same point, the first of these is greater: from equation (32) in appendix 7A.1, the difference between them is $-t'E_{\pi p}E_{pp}^{-1}E_{p\pi}t$, which is positive. See Neary and Roberts (1980).

Table 7.1
Restrictions on quota-constrained excess demand derivatives implied by net substitutability and implicit separability

In general	Net substitutability			Implicit separability
	q-Goods	t-Goods	Both	
p_q ND[a]	$\ll 0$[b]		$\ll 0$	$q'p_q < 0$[c]
$\tilde{m}_q^c = -p_\pi$			$\ll 0$[d]	$\ll 0$[e]
$\tilde{m}_\pi^c$ ND		$\left(\tilde{m}_\pi^c\right)^{-1} \ll 0$	$\left(\tilde{m}_\pi^c\right)^{-1} \ll 0$	

Sources: (a) Anderson and Neary (1992, p. 60) and lemma 7.2; (b) Hatta (1977b, p. 1866) and lemma 7.3; (c) Anderson and Neary (1992, p. 64) and lemma 7.5; (d) Hatta (1977b) and lemma 7.4; and (e) lemma 7.6.
Notes: ND: Negative definite. $\ll 0$ means that every element of the matrix in the first column is strictly negative. The restrictions in the fifth column require only that the q-goods are net substitutes for each other and for the t-goods. The t-goods need not be net substitutes for each other.

The first, which we have already encountered in the discussion of concertina tariff reform in chapter 3, is *net substitutability*, whereby cross-price effects are assumed to be positive. The second is *implicit separability* between the q-goods and the t-goods in the undistorted trade expenditure function. The discussion of these cases gets relatively technical, so it may be helpful to use table 7.1 as a road map in the remainder of this chapter.

Consider first the implications of net substitutability. With two groups of goods, we need to consider separately the implications of net substitutability *within* each group and *between* the two groups. Begin with the case where the q-goods are net substitutes for each other. Then we have the following result:

Lemma 7.3 Suppose that the q-goods are net substitutes for each other. Then all elements of the matrix p_q are strictly negative.

This comes from Hatta (1977b, p. 1866), and uses a result due to Debreu and Herstein (1953).[13] Net substitutability of the q-goods implies that all the off-diagonal elements of E_{pp} are positive. Of course, the diagonal elements are negative because E is concave in p. Hence the conditions of Debreu and Herstein's theorem are satisfied, and so all elements of the inverse matrix E_{pp}^{-1} are negative. From equation (32) in the appendix, this equals p_q, which proves the lemma. Intuitively this makes sense. If

13. Debreu and Herstein proved that if a matrix A has all diagonal elements positive and all off-diagonal elements negative, and if $Ax > 0$ for some vector $x > 0$, then all elements of A^{-1} are positive. Setting A equal to $-E_{pp}$, the result follows immediately.

good i is a substitute for all other quota-constrained goods, then relaxing the quota on good i reduces its own price and reduces the demand for the other quota-constrained goods, so reducing their prices too.

Next assume that the q-goods are net substitutes for the t-goods as well as for each other. This allows us to sign the cross-effects in demand:

Lemma 7.4 Suppose that the q-goods are net substitutes for each other and for the t-goods. Then all elements of the matrix $\tilde{m}_q^c$ are negative and all elements of p_π are positive.

It is intuitively plausible that when the two sets of goods are substitutes for each other, then relaxing the quotas on the q-goods should reduce imports of the t-goods, and raising the prices of the t-goods should raise the prices of the q-goods. However, it is necessary also that the q-goods themselves be substitutes. This follows immediately from the expression for $\tilde{m}_q^c$, which from equation (32) in the appendix, equals $E_{\pi p}E_{pp}^{-1}$. Net substitutability of the q-goods ensures that all the elements of E_{pp}^{-1} are negative, as we have seen in lemma 7.3, while net substitutability between the q-goods and the t-goods implies that all the elements of $E_{p\pi}$ are positive. Hence both restrictions are required to prove that all the elements of $\tilde{m}_q$ are negative. The final part of lemma 7.4, that all elements of the matrix p_π are positive, follows immediately because, as already noted, p_π is the transpose of $-\tilde{m}_q^c$. Note that lemma 7.4 requires only that the q-goods are net substitutes for each other and for the t-goods; the t-goods themselves need not be net substitutes for each other.

Consider next the restriction of implicit separability of the trade expenditure function between the q-goods and the t-goods. This restriction is less familiar in the theory of trade policy reform than net substitutability, but it is ubiquitous in empirical work. Hence it is of interest to explore its implications for the theory of trade policy, following Anderson and Neary (1992). Unlike net substitutability, separability imposes no restrictions on the relationships in demand *within* groups of goods: complementarities are allowed. However, it requires that every q-good must have the same cross-relationship with every t-good: either all substitutes or all complements.

Formally, implicit separability implies that the trade expenditure function can be written as follows:

$$E(p,\pi,u) = \xi[\phi(p,u),\eta(\pi,u),u], \tag{19}$$

The functions ϕ and η can be interpreted as price indexes for the q- and t-goods respectively. Implicit separability imposes some restrictions on

(19). The function ξ is concave and homogeneous of degree one in the subgroup price indexes ϕ and η, and each of them is concave and homogeneous of degree one in the appropriate price vector, so that[14]

$$\phi_p' p = \phi, \quad \eta_\pi' \pi = \eta. \tag{20}$$

The appendix to this chapter, section 7A.2, considers further the restrictions on behavior that rationalize (19).

Implicit separability allows us to sign many of the key terms in the expressions for ρ and χ, the shadow prices of quotas and the marginal costs of tariffs. The first implication of implicit separability concerns the critical term $q'\underline{\omega}p_q$ in expression (14) for ρ, which measures the change in rents on existing imports following a marginal relaxation of quota levels. This term is negative when q is a scalar but need not be so in general. However, at least when rent-sharing is uniform, implicit separability allows us to sign it:

Lemma 7.5 With implicit separability, the vector $q'p_q$ is strictly negative, equal to $-p'/\varepsilon$, where $\varepsilon \equiv -\phi\xi_{\phi\phi}/\xi_\phi > 0$, is the elasticity of demand for the quota-constrained group with respect to its aggregate price.

The proof is in the appendix. Intuitively this implies that while individual q-goods can be complements for each other, the group as a whole must exhibit substitutability in the aggregate.

The next result concerns the cross-relationships between the two groups of goods. Implicit separability implies that the two groups of goods are substitutes when consumers take all prices as given.[15] It turns out that this continues to be the case when the imports of the q-goods are fixed, so their prices are determined within the economy:

Lemma 7.6 With implicit separability, all elements of the matrix $\tilde{m}_q^c$ are negative and all elements of the matrix p_π are positive.

Once again, this is proved in the appendix. It implies that, while complementarities within the q-goods and t-goods are possible, each individual q-good is a substitute for each individual t-good in the quota-constrained

---

14. See Deaton and Muellbauer (1980, pp. 130–35) for further discussion.

15. To see this we need only evaluate the second cross-partial derivative of the expenditure function (19), which gives: $E_{p\pi} = \phi_p \xi_{\phi\eta} \eta_\pi'$. The vectors ϕ_p and η_π are proportional to the net import vectors q and m respectively. Hence all the cross effects have the same sign as the scalar $\xi_{\phi\eta}$, which must be positive from equation (41) in the Appendix. Hence an increase in the price of an imported q-good raises the demand for an imported t-good and lowers the demand for (i.e., increases the supply of) an exported t-good.

equilibrium. A relaxation of any quota reduces net imports of every t-good, and a rise in the price of any t-good increases the domestic price of every q-good.

Finally the relationships between the two sets of goods imply that the aggregate cross-effect in demand takes a particularly simple form:

Corollary 7.1   With implicit separability, the vector $t'\tilde{m}_q^c$ is negative and equals the import-weighted average tariff rate T^a times minus p'.

Here $T^a = t'm/\pi'm$ denotes the average tariff rate weighted by import shares valued at *domestic* prices. Since $t'\tilde{m}_q^c$ appears in the expression for the shadow prices of quotas, this result allows it to be simplified considerably.

7.5   Quota Reform

Armed with these results, we can now turn to consider what can be said about trade policy reform in the presence of both tariffs and quotas when we impose either of the restrictions considered in the last section on the structure of the trade expenditure function.

We begin with quota reform. In the general case with both tariffs and partial rent retention, quota changes have conflicting effects, so it is helpful to begin with special cases. Consider first the case with no tariffs. The shadow prices of quotas then simplify to

$$\rho' \equiv (p - p^*)'(I - \underline{\omega}) - q'\underline{\omega}p_q. \tag{21}$$

The first term shows that relaxing quotas yields a direct welfare gain provided some rents are retained, while the second shows that, if any rents are lost, then there is an additional welfare gain provided the domestic prices of q-goods fall. With only one quota-constrained good, its price must fall, but in the many-good case we need to impose one of the restrictions from the last section. Consider first the case of substitutability:[16]

Proposition 7.5   Assume that quota-constrained goods are net substitutes for each other. Then, with no tariffs and partial rent retention, all relaxations of quotas must raise welfare.

---

16. This is theorem 3 of Anderson and Neary (1992), extended (as indicated in footnote 21 of that paper) to nonuniform rent retention. Contrary to what is stated there, proposition 7.5 does not require that the q-goods be net substitutes for the t-goods.

This follows immediately from lemma 7.3: all the elements of p_q are negative, and so (21) is unambiguously positive. Notice that it requires *only* substitutability between the q-goods, and that any form of rent retention is allowed. By contrast, the corresponding result with implicit separability requires uniform rent retention:

Proposition 7.6 With uniform rent retention, zero tariffs, and implicit separability between the t- and q-goods, all relaxations of quotas must raise welfare.

Under these assumptions the diagonal matrix of rent retention shares $\underline{\omega}$ in equation (21) is replaced by a scalar ω, so lemma 7.5 can be used to justify a positive sign for ρ.

When quotas are relaxed in the presence of tariffs, there is a third effect (additional to the two terms in (21) we have just considered), given by the term $t'\tilde{m}_q^c$ in (14). This arises from the change in tariff revenue as changes in quota-constrained imports spill over to affect demands for tariff-constrained imports. If the two categories of goods are "constrained substitutes," in the sense that the elements of $\tilde{m}_q^c$ are negative, then this effect works in the opposite direction to the second term in (21), tending to reduce welfare. Different approaches to resolving the resulting ambiguity can be taken depending on whether we assume net substitutability or implicit separability.

In the case of net substitutability we can follow Falvey (1988), who derives a concertina reform result reminiscent of proposition 3.2 in chapter 3. The shadow price of the quota on good i, relative to the domestic market price of good i, becomes

$$\frac{\rho_i}{p_i} = (1 - \omega_i)T_i - \frac{q'\underline{\omega}p_{q_i}}{p_i} - \sum_j \theta_{ji}T_j. \tag{22}$$

The term p_{q_i} denotes the ith column of the matrix p_q, and gives the effects on the prices of all quota-constrained goods of an increase in the quota on good i. From lemma 7.3, we know that this term is negative under net substitutability. As for the final term, it is a weighted average of the explicit tariff rates on the tariff-constrained goods, where the weights θ_{ji} depend on the identity of the quota, i. Falvey shows that all these weights are positive under net substitutability. Hence we can state the result:[17]

---

17. Following Anderson and Neary (1992, p. 71), this extends Falvey's result to the case of rent-sharing.

Proposition 7.7 With uniform rent retention and all goods net substitutes, reducing the quota on good i is welfare-improving if the implicit tariff on good i is greater than any explicit tariff on the t-goods.

Note that the "implicit tariff" on good i should be understood as $(1 - \omega_i)\tau_i$, to take account of rents lost.

The alternative route to signing $\bar{m}_q^c$ is via implicit separability. From lemma 7.5 and corollary 7.1 in section 7.4, we have the shadow price of quotas with uniform rent retention and implicit separability

$$\rho = (1 - \omega)(p - p^*) + \left(\frac{\omega}{\varepsilon} - T^a\right)p. \tag{23}$$

The additional term $-T^a p$ acts in the "wrong" direction: quota reform causes a switch in spending away from tariff-ridden goods, so reducing their import levels still further below the first-best. Nevertheless, in plausible circumstances this is likely to be outweighed by the first two terms. We can state this formally as follows:

Proposition 7.8 With uniform rent retention and implicit separability, any quota relaxation improves welfare provided that $T^a \leq \omega/\varepsilon$; that is, the average tariff rate is not greater than the rent share deflated by the elasticity of quota-constrained goods with respect to their own average price.

Since the import-weighted average tariff T^a is readily observable, this result is likely to be important in practice. Average tariffs are very low in developed countries, elasticities of demand for quota-constrained goods such as textiles are typically below unity in absolute value, and some form of separability is almost always used in empirical work on the evaluation of trade reform. The implication is that the requirement of the proposition is met, since likely values of ω exceed εT^a. The result also suggests that an important task for empirical work is to develop information on ω.

An alternative condition, which avoids restricting the uniform rent-retention parameter ω, is available from manipulating (23):

$$\frac{\rho_i}{p_i} = (1 - \omega)(T_i - T^a) + \omega\left(\frac{1}{\varepsilon} - T^a\right). \tag{24}$$

This expresses the shadow price of the quota on good i relative to its market price as a weighted average of the implicit tariff on that good relative to the average tariff on the t-goods and of the inverse elasticity of import demand for the q-goods relative to the average tariff, where the weights depend on the rent-share parameter. This gives a sufficient condition for a welfare improvement:

Proposition 7.9 With a positive shadow price of foreign exchange, uniform rent retention and implicit separability, any quota relaxation improves welfare provided that the average tariff rate on the t-goods, T^a, is not greater than (i) the implicit tariff on every quota-constrained good, T_i, and (ii) the inverse of the elasticity of demand for quota-constrained goods with respect to their average price, ε.

Both conditions of proposition 7.9 appear to be met in developed countries, where average tariffs are below 5 percent while quota premia on actively negotiated categories such as textiles and steel are much higher.

It is also noteworthy that the ambiguity we have noted for the effects of quota relaxations vanishes if all quotas are *export* quotas. In that case the domestic price p_i is less than the world price p_i^*, and the quota levels are negative, $q_i < 0$, so ϕ_p and hence ε is negative. It follows that the shadow price of the quota, ρ, must be negative. An increase in an export quota is a reduction in q algebraically, so all export quota increases imply that $\rho'\,dq$ are positive. This result is of potential importance for less developed countries whose exports are subject to VERs. Under implicit separability all export quota increases are welfare improving.

7.6 Tariff Reform in the Presence of Quotas

We now turn to the evaluation of tariff reform. Recalling (15), the effect of a tariff change on welfare is

$$du \propto \chi'\,dt = (-q'\underline{\omega}p_\pi + t'\tilde{m}_\pi^c)\,dt. \tag{25}$$

The first term on the right-hand side reflects the welfare effect arising from the tariff-induced changes in the prices of quota-constrained goods. Loosely speaking, these are a cost if the goods are substitutes, since the presumption is that when tariffs increase the p's must rise: the prices of quota-constrained goods are driven up by substitution away from the tariff-ridden goods, which lowers welfare through the increased rent transfer to foreigners.

Falvey (1988) extended the two basic results on tariff reform to the presence of quotas with full rent retention: uniform radial cuts in tariffs and concertina cuts when all goods are net substitutes. Here we show that these continue to hold with less-than-full rent retention. Under net substitutability a rise in π will raise p, since $\tilde{m}_\pi^c$ is negative definite as noted earlier and since $\tilde{m}_q^c$ is equal to $-p_\pi'$. Hence we have, using lemmas 7.1 and 7.4,

Proposition 7.10 With net substitutability of the q-goods, a uniform proportionate reduction in tariffs is welfare-improving.

Similarly, using lemma 7.6, we obtain

Proposition 7.11 With implicit separability, a uniform proportionate reduction in tariffs is welfare-improving.

For completeness, we can add a concertina reform result due to Falvey (1988), though it only holds when no rents are lost ($\omega = 0$):

Proposition 7.12 (Falvey 1988) With full rent retention and net substitutability of the t-goods, a reduction in the highest tariff rate is welfare-improving.

For the case of implicit separability the p's also rise with a rise in tariffs. Specifically, from lemma 7.6,

$$\mu^{-1} e_u \, du = [-(q'\underline{\omega}p)\theta'\underline{\pi}^{-1} + t'\tilde{m}_\pi^c] \, dt, \tag{26}$$

Rearranging, we have

$$\mu^{-1} e_u \, du = \left[-\frac{q'\underline{\omega}p}{\pi'm} m' + t'\tilde{m}_\pi^c \right] dt. \tag{27}$$

For the case of a tariff reform in the presence of quotas, the new term arising from interaction with quotas thus tends to increase the set of welfare-improving reforms, *for practical purposes making further cuts in tariffs for developed countries welfare-increasing.* In addition, evaluating (25) at a zero tariff level, we obtain

Proposition 7.13 With uniform rent retention, tariff cuts below zero (i.e., import subsidies) on unconstrained goods are welfare-improving under either net substitutability or implicit separability.

The intuition of this proposition is that the import subsidy induces agents to shift away from quota-constrained imports, reducing the leakage to foreigners.[18] The second-best optimal ad valorem subsidy vector for the

18. A similar logic applies to exports.

case of implicit separability is, setting (27) equal to zero,

$$T^o = \frac{q'\underline{\omega}p}{\pi'm}[\underline{\pi}^{-1}(\tilde{m}_\pi^c)^{-1}\underline{m}]\iota, \tag{28}$$

where ι is a vector of ones, the underscore once again denotes a diagonal matrix and the term in brackets is the inverse elasticity matrix. If all unconstrained goods are net substitutes, by Hatta's (1977a) argument, the elasticities are negative for imports and positive for exports; and thus *every* unconstrained trade must be subsidized. Note, in particular, that this implies that countries with exports subject to VERs should subsidize their unconstrained exports.

7.7 Alternative Rent-Sharing Rules

So far the rent retention shares have been assumed to be invariant to the quota-setting process. Here we provide two alternative rationales for this assumption. The first is a Nash bargaining model of the determination of the rent share that guarantees invariance. The second is a model of endogenous rent share under which our previous results still obtain.

A Nash bargaining model of dividing the total rents is appropriate to situations of bilateral monopoly, which are likely to be prevalent in quota-constrained markets due to narrow quota definitions. Let R, equal to $(p - p^*)q$, denote the total quota rent on an individual import good (with subscripts i suppressed for convenience). Suppose that the division of R is determined by a Nash bargaining game between the importer and the exporter. If the parties do not agree, R is zero and hence both parties' utility is zero. This is the "threat point." If utility is a concave homogeneous function of income for each party, the Nash bargaining share ω is the solution to

$$\max_{\omega} \frac{[(1 - \omega)R]^{1-\alpha}(\omega R)^{1-\alpha^*}}{(1 - \alpha)(1 - \alpha^*)}, \tag{29}$$

where $1/\alpha$ and $1/\alpha^*$ are the home and foreign elasticities of intertemporal substitution. The first order condition yields the Nash bargaining value of ω as the solution to $(1 - \omega)(1 - \alpha^*) = \omega(1 - \alpha)$, which is independent of R and hence of the size of the quota. The more impatient party (the one with the lower elasticity of intertemporal substitution) receives the lower share of R (e.g., $\alpha > \alpha^*$ implies that ω is greater than $\frac{1}{2}$). With symmetry, the rent is divided equally. Hence this Nash bargaining model of dividing the total rents is sufficient for the rent share to be invariant to the size of the total rent.

Next consider the simplest case of endogenous rent retention, which arises when the government awards all licenses to competitive foreign exporters but taxes quota-constrained imports at a specific rate h_i to retain some rent.[19] The share of rents retained on good i, $1 - \omega_i$, is equal to $h_i q_i / (p_i - p_i^*) q_i$, which is generally a function of q. Nevertheless, the shadow price of the quota vector is essentially the same as in (14), with subsequent specializations applicable. To see this, note that the budget constraint in domestic prices becomes, instead of (10),

$$\tilde{E}(q, \pi, u) + p'q = h'q + t'm. \tag{30}$$

Following the same substitutions that led to (14), the shadow prices of quotas are

$$\rho' = h' - q'p_q + t'\tilde{m}_q^c. \tag{31}$$

By comparison with (14), the role of $(p - p^*)'(I - \underline{\omega})$ is taken by h', while the reverse transfer term $-q'p_q$ is independent of the rent retention shares ω. Equation (31) implies that when tariffs are the means of rent retention, we can use the uniform rent-retention special cases of the propositions above. This is true even though rent retention is in fact not uniform and its rate in each sector is endogenous. This is a useful result of considerable practical importance.

7.8 Conclusion

In this chapter we extended the theory of trade policy reform to allow for quotas as well as tariffs. The greater complexity of the policy regimes impose greater informational requirements on policy reform. Nevertheless, we showed that a number of important results can be obtained, including a general radial reduction result in the absence of any constraints on the structure of the economy (proposition 7.4) and further special results if either net substitutability or implicit separability is assumed. These results are of interest in themselves. In addition the technical tools we have introduced in the chapter, especially the distorted trade expenditure function and the restrictions implied by implicit separability, will prove useful

---

19. The ad valorem tariff case is essentially identical: the rent retention term in equation (30) becomes $\tau^{h'} \underline{\pi}^* q$.

later. In the next chapter we turn to consider how the TRI and MTRI can be evaluated when trade is distorted by quantitative restrictions as well as tariffs.

Appendix

7A.1   Properties of the Distorted Trade Expenditure Function

By totally differentiating (6), (8), and (9), we can relate the second derivatives of the distorted trade expenditure function to those of the undistorted trade expenditure function as follows:

$$
\begin{bmatrix} \tilde{E}_{qq} & \tilde{E}_{q\pi} & \tilde{E}_{qu} \\ \tilde{E}_{\pi q} & \tilde{E}_{\pi\pi} & \tilde{E}_{\pi u} \end{bmatrix} = \begin{bmatrix} -E_{pp}^{-1} & E_{pp}^{-1}E_{p\pi} & E_{pp}^{-1}q_I e_u \\ E_{\pi p}E_{pp}^{-1} & E_{\pi\pi} - E_{\pi p}E_{pp}^{-1}E_{p\pi} & (m_I - E_{\pi p}E_{pp}^{-1}q_I)e_u \end{bmatrix}.
$$
$$(32)$$

For reference, these derivatives correspond to the derivatives of the virtual price and import demand functions as follows:

$$
\begin{bmatrix} \tilde{E}_{qq} & \tilde{E}_{q\pi} & \tilde{E}_{qu} \\ \tilde{E}_{\pi q} & \tilde{E}_{\pi\pi} & \tilde{E}_{\pi u} \end{bmatrix} = \begin{bmatrix} -p_q & -p_\pi & -p_u \\ \tilde{m}_q^c & \tilde{m}_\pi^c & \tilde{m}_u^c \end{bmatrix}.
$$
$$(33)$$

Looking at the first entry in each of these matrices, we can immediately deduce that $\tilde{E}$ is convex in q. Since E is concave in p, the matrix E_{pp} is negative definite; hence $\tilde{E}_{qq}$, which equals $-E_{pp}^{-1}$, must be positive definite. (This result may also be shown directly, following Anderson and Neary 1992, by noting that $\tilde{E}(q, \pi, u)$ is the solution to the problem of maximizing $\{E(p, \pi, u) - p'q\}$ with respect to p, and so it must be convex in q.) Since E_{pp} equals $-p_q$, it follows that p_q is negative definite, which proves lemma 7.2. Finally the income effects on the prices of the q-goods and the imports of the t-goods are implied by the last column of (32):

$$
p_I = -E_{pp}^{-1}q_I = -p_q q_I \quad \text{and} \quad \tilde{m}_I = m_I - E_{\pi p}E_{pp}^{-1}q_I = m_I + m_p p_I. \quad (34)
$$

7A.2   Rationalizing Implicit Separability

Assumptions sufficient to yield implicit separability of the trade expenditure function are (1) implicit separability of the expenditure and GDP functions and (2) the Armington assumption. The Armington assumption is that imports and domestically produced goods are imperfect substitutes in consumption or production. Also exports are imperfect substitutes for domestically consumed goods. Such differentiation is empirically well founded and is rationalized as due to packaging, safety requirements, and so on. The Armington structure may be seen as the general case, with perfect substitutes emerging as its limiting specialization.

Any trade expenditure function is a reduced form, with nontraded goods in the background, contributing to the substitution and real income effect structure. Nontraded goods prices are determined by a reduced form function of traded goods prices. In the present context the reduced form is implicitly separable if the structural expenditure and GDP functions are implicitly separable with respect to the partition between traded and nontraded goods.

Formally, let the expenditure function be $e[\phi^1(p^1, u), \eta^1(\pi^1, u), h, u]$ and the GDP function be $g[\phi^2(p^2), \eta^2(\pi^2), h]$, where h is the nontraded goods price vector; p^1 and p^2 are disjoint price vectors, as are π^1 and π^2. Market clearance implies $e_h = g_h$, and the equilibrium price has a reduced form solution $h(\phi^1, \phi^2, \eta^1, \eta^2, u)$. The implicitly separable trade expenditure function is

$$\xi(\phi^1, \phi^2, \eta^1, \eta^2, u) \equiv e[\phi^1, \eta^1, h(\phi^1, \phi^2, \eta^1, \eta^2, u), u]$$
$$- g[\phi^2, \eta^2, h(\phi^1, \phi^2, \eta^1, \eta^2, u)]. \tag{35}$$

Equation (19) follows under the further simplifying assumption that either ϕ^1 or ϕ^2 is null; that is, quota constraints are placed either on intermediate inputs or on final consumption, but not both.

The (mild) consequence of relaxing the last assumption is that lemma 7.4 must be replaced by

$$p_q q = \begin{bmatrix} p^1/\varepsilon^1 \\ p^2/\varepsilon^2 \end{bmatrix}, \tag{36}$$

while corollary 7.1 becomes

$$t'\tilde{m}_q = \begin{bmatrix} -\tilde{T}^1 p^1 \\ -\tilde{T}^2 p^2 \end{bmatrix}. \tag{37}$$

In (36) the inverse elasticities ε^i are specific to the quota-constrained groups, and in (37) the average ad valorem tariffs $\tilde{T}^i$ are trade-weighted average final consumption and intermediate input tariffs respectively. These collapse to lemma 7.5 and corollary 7.1 in the special case of $\tilde{T}^1 = \tilde{T}^2$ and $\varepsilon^1 = \varepsilon^2$. Generally, in the applications that follow, the propositions can be restated in terms of an average inverse elasticity and an average of the two tariffs.

7A.3   Proof of Lemma 7.5

From (19) the import demand functions for the quota-constrained goods are

$$q = E_p = \xi_\phi \phi_p. \tag{38}$$

Differentiating with respect to π yields

$$E_{p\pi} = \phi_p \xi_{\phi\eta} \eta_\pi'. \tag{39}$$

Moreover E_p is homogeneous of degree zero in p and π,

$$E_{pp} p + E_{p\pi} \pi = 0, \tag{40}$$

and ξ_ϕ is homogeneous of degree zero in ϕ and η,

$$\xi_{\phi\phi} \phi + \xi_{\phi\eta} \eta = 0. \tag{41}$$

Because ξ is concave in ϕ, the scalar $\xi_{\phi\phi}$ is negative. Hence the scalar $\xi_{\phi\eta}$ must be positive, which from (39) implies that each one of the q-goods must be a net substitute for each one of the t-goods.

With these preliminaries over, we can now prove lemma 7.5. We first use (40) to write p as follows:

$$p = -E_{pp}^{-1} E_{p\pi} \pi. \tag{42}$$

From (32) we can replace E_{pp}^{-1} by p_q, and from (39) we can eliminate $E_{p\pi}$:

$$p = -p_q \phi_p \xi_{\phi\eta} \eta_\pi' \pi. \tag{43}$$

Next we use (20) to eliminate $\eta_\pi' \pi$,

$$p = -p_q \phi_p \xi_{\phi\eta} \eta, \tag{44}$$

and use (41) to eliminate $\xi_{\phi\eta}$,

$$p = p_q \phi_p \xi_{\phi\phi} \phi. \tag{45}$$

Finally from (38) this becomes

$$p = p_q q \frac{\phi \xi_{\phi\phi}}{\xi_\phi}. \tag{46}$$

Inverting this gives lemma 7.5.

7A.4   Proof of Lemma 7.6

From equation (32) the derivatives of the demand functions for the t-goods with respect to the quota levels are

$$\tilde{m}_q^c = \tilde{E}_{\pi q} = E_{\pi p} E_{pp}^{-1}. \tag{47}$$

Substituting from (39) for $E_{\pi p}$ and recalling from (32) that E_{pp}^{-1} equals p_q, this becomes

$$\tilde{m}_q^c = \eta_\pi \xi_{\eta \phi} \phi_p' p_q. \tag{48}$$

This equation can be simplified by replacing η_π and ϕ_p by m/ξ_η and q/ξ_ϕ respectively:

$$\tilde{m}_q^c = m \frac{\xi_{\eta \phi}}{\xi_\eta \xi_\phi} q' p_q \tag{49}$$

Now use lemma 7.5 to substitute for $q'p_q$, and (41) to eliminate $\xi_{\eta \phi}$:

$$\tilde{m}_q^c = -\frac{mp'}{\eta \xi_\eta} = -\frac{mp'}{\pi'm} \tag{50}$$

where the denominator is simply the value of imports of t-goods at domestic prices. Equation (50) shows that all the elements of $\tilde{m}_q^c$ are negative. Finally, since $\tilde{m}_q^c$ and $-p_\pi$ are transposes of one another, it follows that p_π equals $pm'/\pi'm$, all of whose elements are positive. This proves lemma 7.6.

7A.5 Proof of Corollary 7.1

Premultiply (50) by the tariff vector t to obtain

$$t'\tilde{m}_q^c = -T^a p', \tag{51}$$

where $T^a = t'm/\pi'm$ denotes the average tariff rate weighted by import shares valued at *domestic* prices.

8 The TRI and MTRI with Quotas

Ad hoc studies of trade restrictiveness are forced to present separate indexes to measure the average height of tariffs and the pervasiveness of quotas. Such indexes have no common metric, so it is not possible to combine them in a meaningful way. What is required for this is, first, a theoretical framework that encompasses both tariffs and quotas and, second, the application of this framework to generate an appropriate index of the overall stance of commercial policy. Chapter 7 implemented the first of these tasks, and this chapter proceeds to the second.

Section 8.1 extends the approach of chapter 4 to derive the TRI in the presence of tariffs and quotas. The steps in the derivation are similar to those in the case of tariffs only, with the key additional feature that quotas are characterized in terms of their equivalent or "virtual" prices in order to make them comparable with tariffs. Section 8.2 deals with the issue of how to control for changes in exogenous variables, which make quotas more restrictive even when trade policy does not change. Finally section 8.3 shows how the MTRI can also be extended to allow for both kinds of trade intervention.

8.1 The TRI with Tariffs and Quotas

As in the last chapter let q denote the vector of quota-constrained imports, with domestic prices p and world prices p^*, while m, π and π^* continue to denote the quantity and prices of tariff-constrained imports. As we saw there, the equilibrium of a small open economy subject to tariffs and quotas is conveniently represented using the distorted trade expenditure function $\tilde{E}(q, \pi, u)$. This equals net spending on imports of goods not subject to quotas, $m_0 + \pi'm$, conditional on the quota levels q.

Such an equilibrium is our benchmark in this chapter, and it is very convenient to be able to summarize it in a compact way. Hence we define a new function, the *distorted balance of trade function*, as the deviation from such an equilibrium:

$$\tilde{B}(q, \pi, u) \equiv \tilde{E}(q, \pi, u) + p'q - (p - p^*)'(I - \underline{\omega})q - (\pi - \pi^*)'m. \tag{1}$$

This is a natural extension of the undistorted function introduced in chapter 4. As always, p^*, π^*, ω and the other exogenous variables characterizing the equilibrium are subsumed into the $\tilde{B}$ function. By contrast, the variables p and m on the right-hand side, denoting respectively the equilibrium domestic prices of quota-constrained goods and the equilibrium imports of tariff-constrained goods, are endogenous. As discussed in chapter 7, they equal the derivatives of $\tilde{E}$ with respect to $-q$ and π respectively. As for the rents generated by the two types of trade restrictions, we continue to assume that they are disbursed differently. The domestic aggregate household receives all the tariff revenue, $(\pi - \pi^*)'m$, but only some of the quota revenue, with the elements of the ω vector $(0 \leq \omega_i \leq 1)$ denoting the share of quota rents on good i lost to foreigners.

The problem of measuring trade restrictiveness can now be stated compactly: we wish to find a scalar index of the restrictiveness of trade policy in period 0 relative to period 1, in each of which equilibrium prevails such that

$$\tilde{B}(q^0, \pi^0, u^0) = \tilde{B}(q^1, \pi^1, u^1) = b^0. \tag{2}$$

Clearly, this raises a new problem relative to the case with tariffs only which was considered in chapter 4. It makes little sense to apply a common deflator to all the trade policy instruments, since they comprise quantities for quota-constrained goods and prices for tariff-constrained goods. There are two alternative routes to avoiding this problem: we can express all trade policy instruments in terms of either quantity equivalents or price equivalents. The former approach is a natural extension of the case where quotas are the only form of trade policy, and it builds on a tradition of quantity indexes in the theory of index numbers and aggregate efficiency, stemming from Malmquist and Debreu. We explore this approach in chapter 14 below. The latter approach is more intuitively appealing, and builds naturally on the treatment of the tariffs-only case considered in earlier chapters. We therefore use it as the basis for our most general specification of the TRI and MTRI in the remaining chapters of this book, other than chapter 14.

To allow us to work with prices for both classes of goods, we define the *undistorted balance of trade function*:[1]

$$B(p, \pi, u) \equiv E(p, \pi, u) - (p - p^*)'(I - \underline{\omega})q - (\pi - \pi^*)'m. \tag{3}$$

This is essentially the standard balance-of-trade function introduced in chapter 3, appropriate to the case where tariffs (on *both* q- and t-goods) are the only form of trade intervention. (The only difference is that it allows for the loss of tariff revenue on the q-goods.) However, it also describes the equilibrium where the q-goods are subject to quotas, if p equals their market-clearing price vector. Thus we have two alternative ways of characterizing any quota-constrained equilibrium: the distorted and undistorted balance-of-trade functions coincide when the quota vector on which the distorted function depends is consistent with the price vector on which the undistorted function depends. From chapter 7, we know that consistency in this sense implies that the prices equal the quota derivatives of the distorted trade expenditure function:[2]

$$\tilde{B}(q, \pi, u) = B[p(q, \pi, u), \pi, u] \quad \text{when} \quad p(q, \pi, u) = -\tilde{E}_q(q, \pi, u). \tag{4}$$

These prices are the actual domestic market-clearing prices in the quota-constrained equilibrium; following the tradition of rationing theory, they can also be called the virtual prices corresponding to the quotas.

We can now define the TRI as the factor of proportionality Δ by which period-1 prices (i.e., the domestic prices for *both* tariff- and quota-constrained goods) must be deflated to ensure that equilibrium prevails when utility is at its period-0 level:

$$\Delta(q^0, \pi^0, u^0, q^1, \pi^1, u^1) : B\left[\frac{p(q^1, \pi^1, u^1)}{\Delta}, \frac{\pi^1}{\Delta}, u^0\right] = \tilde{B}(q^0, \pi^0, u^0). \tag{5}$$

For comparisons with free trade, the notation is greatly simplified. Domestic prices in the new equilibrium are now simply world prices, p^* and π^*, and as usual, they can be omitted from the list of arguments of Δ:

---

1. This function characterizes the economy's behavior when the q-goods are subject to tariffs rather than quotas. Hence "tariffs-only" or "price-taking" might be more appropriate labels than "undistorted." We prefer the latter, since it seems natural to begin with the price-taking case and to view quantitative restrictions as departures from or distortions of that approach.

2. We follow the convention of Anderson and Neary (2003) in evaluating the virtual prices at $\{q^1, \pi^1, u^1\}$, rather than at $\{q^1, \pi^1, u^0\}$, as in Anderson and Neary (1996). Both approaches are valid, but the former has a number of advantages. It is conceptually much neater, since the virtual prices are the *actual* market-clearing prices in the new equilibrium, it converges more often in CGE applications, and as equation (6) below shows, it is well-defined for comparisons with free trade, whereas the earlier specification is not.

$$\Delta(q^0, \pi^0, u^0) : B\left(\frac{p^*}{\Delta}, \frac{\pi^*}{\Delta}, u^0\right) = \tilde{B}(q^0, \pi^0, u^0).$$ (6)

Finally, just as in the tariffs-only case of chapter 4, note that Δ deflates period-1 prices to attain period-0 utility. Hence it is a compensating variation type of measure, an increase in Δ corresponding to a *fall* in trade restrictiveness. Especially for comparisons with free trade, it is easier to interpret the results when we express them in terms of the TRI uniform tariff, which is defined by $\tau^\Delta = (1 - \Delta)/\Delta$:

$$\tau^\Delta(q^0, \pi^0, u^0) : B[(1 + \tau^\Delta)p^*, (1 + \tau^\Delta)\pi^*, u^0] = \tilde{B}(q^0, \pi^0, u^0).$$ (7)

This extends in a natural way the tariffs-only TRI uniform tariff defined in chapter 4: the uniform tariff rate τ^Δ, if applied to all imported goods, would yield balance-of-trade equilibrium at the same level of welfare as the trade policy vector $\{q^0, \pi^0\}$.

As in chapter 4, the interpretation of the TRI uniform tariff is enhanced by considering small changes in the period-0 instruments $\{q^0, \pi^0\}$. Totally differentiating the equation that implicitly defines τ^Δ in (7), holding world prices p^* and π^* constant, yields

$$(B_p^\Delta \cdot p^* + B_\pi^\Delta \cdot \pi^*) \, d\tau^\Delta + B_u^\Delta \, du^0 = \tilde{B}_q \cdot dq^0 + \tilde{B}_\pi \cdot d\pi^0 + \tilde{B}_u \, du^0.$$ (8)

Once again, the derivatives of the balance-of-trade function are evaluated at two different points: those without superscripts are evaluated at the initial policy-distorted vector $\{q^0, \pi^0\}$, while those with superscript Δ are evaluated at the uniform-tariff price vector $\{p^\Delta, \pi^\Delta\} \equiv \{(1 + \tau^\Delta)p^*, (1 + \tau^\Delta)\pi^*\}$. To eliminate the change in utility, we can use the fact that it varies only because of the change in trade policy, so equation (8) is zero. This yields the proportional change in the TRI uniform tariff:

$$\frac{d\tau^\Delta}{1 + \tau^\Delta} = \psi^\Delta \frac{\tilde{B}_q \cdot dq^0 + \tilde{B}_\pi \cdot d\pi^0}{B_p \cdot p^0 + B_\pi \cdot \pi^0},$$ (9)

where

$$\psi^\Delta \equiv \frac{B_u^\Delta}{\tilde{B}_u} \frac{B_p \cdot p^0 + B_\pi \cdot \pi^0}{B_p^\Delta \cdot p^\Delta + B_\pi^\Delta \cdot \pi^\Delta}.$$

As in chapter 4, ψ^Δ is a correction factor needed because the balance-of-trade function is evaluated at two different points.

Equation (9) has a straightforward interpretation. The numerator is the change in foreign exchange required to support the initial utility level following a change in trade policy, while the denominator is the additional foreign exchange needed to support the initial utility level when all domestic prices of quota- and tariff-constrained goods rise by 1 percent. Thus the proportional change in τ^Δ, when trade policy changes, equals the conventional measure of the welfare cost of the change, normalized by the marginal cost of a uniform change in protection.

8.2 Equi-restrictive Quotas Following Changes in Exogenous Variables

So far we have left implicit the exogenous variables on which both the initial and the new equilibrium depend. This is appropriate for a hypothetical cross-sectional comparison with an equilibrium that has identical values of all exogenous variables other than trade policy. It is also correct in principle for time-series comparisons. If we use the TRI to evaluate a change in protection over time, then the balance of trade function in the uniform-tariff equilibrium should be evaluated at the initial values of all exogenous variables other than trade policy, since otherwise some of the effects of changes in these variables would be attributed to changes in trade policy.

However, in the presence of quotas, we need to be careful in interpreting the phrase "changes in trade policy" when other exogenous variables are also changing. For example, if real growth takes place in the economy, constant quota levels imply an increased restrictiveness of trade policy. These considerations are familiar to policy makers, who frequently build in automatic adjustments to quotas in line with economic growth. Note that this problem is peculiar to quotas. Growth also alters the welfare cost of tariff protection, but we would not wish to say that it makes given tariffs *more* restrictive.

All this suggests that, in evaluating the trade restrictiveness of changes in trade policy, our benchmark should be, not the case of constant quotas, but that of an *equi-restrictive quota policy*. The natural way to define such a policy is by the quota vector that would maintain the initial prices of the quota-constrained goods following the change in trade policy.

To formalize these ideas, we first restate the definition of the TRI from the last section, making explicit for the first time the values of the exogenous variables γ. In the initial equilibrium these take the value γ^0, while in the new equilibrium they take the value γ^1. Now consider the TRI uniform tariff factor:

$$\tau^\Delta : B[(1 + \tau^\Delta)p^1, (1 + \tau^\Delta)\pi^1, u^0, \gamma^0] = \tilde{B}(q^0, \pi^0, u^0, \gamma^0). \tag{10}$$

This is similar to the TRI uniform tariff in equation (7), except that it compares the initial equilibrium, denoted by 0, with an arbitrary new equilibrium, denoted by 1, which need not coincide with free trade. Since the prices p^1 are the *actual* market-clearing prices in the new equilibrium, they depend on the levels of utility and of the exogenous variables in that equilibrium:

$$p^1 = p(q^1, \pi^1, u^1, \gamma^1) = -\tilde{E}_q(q^1, \pi^1, u^1, \gamma^1). \tag{11}$$

Now we can define the equi-restrictive or "compensated" quota vector q^c as the vector which would yield the new market-clearing prices at the *old* levels of utility and of the exogenous variables:

$$q^c : p(q^c, \pi^1, u^0, \gamma^0) = p(q^1, \pi^1, u^1, \gamma^1). \tag{12}$$

To see the implications of this equation, totally differentiate it and evaluate it for small changes in trade policy and in the exogenous variables:[3]

$$dq^c = dq^1 - q_I e_u \, du^1 - q_\gamma \, d\gamma^1. \tag{13}$$

Consider, for example, the case where actual quotas do not change, so $dq^1 = 0$. Equation (13) then shows that growth implies a tightening of the equi-restrictive quotas whenever it raises the net demand for quota-constrained goods, either directly (so q_γ is positive) or indirectly via the income effect q_I.

Equation (13) can be calculated in any particular case given assumptions about the nature of growth. One simple set of assumptions that proves extremely convenient in empirical work is that of "neutral growth": homothetic tastes plus "balanced" technical progress, in the sense that all sectors would grow at the same rate if prices were constant. It is shown in the appendix that under these assumptions the distorted balance of trade function is homogeneous of degree one in $\{q, u, \gamma\}$. Thus, in this case, compensating for the increased restrictiveness of quotas as a result of growth at *given* quota levels would require that the quotas be relaxed at *exactly* the rate of growth.

Finally note that compensating for growth in the presence of quotas does not imply a different value of the TRI when quotas are expressed in terms of their implied domestic prices. By contrast, in chapter 14 we consider a quantity-based TRI, and this must be adjusted for growth in the presence of quotas, using an approach based on this section.

---

3. The derivations make use of the properties of the p function given in appendix 7A.1.

8.3   Quotas and the MTRI

The final contribution of this chapter is to extend the MTRI of chapter 5 to the case where some goods are subject to quotas. We saw in section 8.2 that calculating the TRI in the presence of quotas and tariffs requires that we express all trade policy instruments in terms of prices, using the distorted balance of trade function. In the same way, to calculate the MTRI in the presence of quotas and tariffs, we must work with a "distorted" import volume function.

We have already encountered in chapter 5 the Marshallian import volume function in the absence of quotas. This equals the sum, at world prices, of the Marshallian import demand functions for individual goods, which in general equilibrium depend on domestic prices and on the trade balance b (since b plays the role of the economy's exogenous income). In the case of two classes of imports this can be written as follows:

$$M(p, \pi, b) = p^* \cdot q(p, \pi, b) + \pi^* \cdot m(p, \pi, b). \tag{14}$$

The Marshallian import demand functions are related to the Hicksian ones via a Slutsky identity. For example, for the tariff-constrained goods this is given by the following:

$$m^c(p, \pi, u) = m[p, \pi, B(p, \pi, u)]. \tag{15}$$

We can define the quota-distorted Marshallian import demand functions in exactly the same way:

$$\tilde{m}^c(q, \pi, u) = \tilde{m}[q, \pi, \tilde{B}(q, \pi, u)]. \tag{16}$$

Hence the total volume of imports at world prices in the presence of quotas is given by the *quota-constrained* import volume function:

$$\tilde{M}(q, \pi, b) = p^* \cdot q + \pi^* \cdot \tilde{m}(q, \pi, b). \tag{17}$$

We saw in equation (4) that the distorted and undistorted balance of trade functions coincide when the quota and price vectors q and p are mutually consistent. Exactly the same is true of the distorted and undistorted import volume functions

$$\tilde{M}(q, \pi, b) = M[p(q, \pi, u), \pi, b] \tag{18}$$

when

$$p(q, \pi, u) = -\tilde{E}_q(q, \pi, u) \tag{19}$$

and

$$\tilde{B}(q, \pi, u) = b. \tag{20}$$

In words, the prices at which the undistorted import volume function is evaluated must be the equilibrium domestic prices for the quota-constrained goods, and the trade balance at which both functions are evaluated must be the equilibrium trade balance corresponding to the utility level at which the prices are evaluated.

We are now ready to define the MTRI in the presence of quotas. As before, we seek the uniform tariff that would yield the same import volume M^0 as the initial distortions $\{q^0, \pi^0\}$. Of course, it would not make sense to deflate the quota vector directly. Instead, we apply the uniform tariff to the free-trade prices of the quota-constrained goods. This leads directly to a generalization of the MTRI uniform tariff, equation (2) in chapter 5, to the case where trade is distorted by both tariffs and quotas:

$$\tau^{\mu}(q^0, \pi^0, b^0) : M[(1 + \tau^{\mu})p^*, (1 + \tau^{\mu})\pi^*, b^0] = \tilde{M}(q^0, \pi^0, b^0). \tag{21}$$

With the quotas reduced to their price equivalents, the interpretation of the MTRI uniform tariff now proceeds in exactly the same way as in the case of tariffs only.

8.4 Conclusion

The conceptual framework needed to allow consistent aggregation of both tariffs and quotas was developed in the last chapter. In this chapter we used it to extend both the TRI and the MTRI to cases where trade is restricted by quotas as well as tariffs. The key idea in both cases is to ask what uniform tariff applied to *all* imports will yield the same trade balance or import volume as the *actual* trade instruments. This yields a single index that is easily interpretable and that aggregates both price and quantity distortions in a consistent way.

Appendix A: Neutral Growth and the Restrictiveness of Quotas

If tastes are homothetic, the expenditure function $e(p, \pi, u)$ may be written, without loss of generality, as $u\bar{e}(p, \pi)$. Similarly, if technical progress is "balanced" (in the sense that all sectors grow at the same rate when prices are given), then the GDP function $g(p, \pi, \gamma)$ can be written, without loss of generality, as $\gamma\bar{g}(p, \pi)$, where γ is a scalar. With these assumptions combined, the trade expenditure function becomes

$$E(p, \pi, u, \gamma) \equiv u\bar{e}(p, \pi) - \gamma\bar{g}(p, \pi). \tag{22}$$

This is clearly homogeneous of degree one in (u, γ), and hence so are its derivatives E_p and E_π. Thus the (undistorted) balance of trade function, (3), is homogeneous of degree one in $\{u, \gamma\}$.

The next step is to show that the distorted trade expenditure function is homogeneous of degree one in $\{q, u, \gamma\}$. To show this, consider the domestic price function $p(q, \pi, u, \gamma)$, which, from (22), is defined implicitly by

$$q = u\bar{e}_p(p, \pi) - \gamma\bar{g}_p(p, \pi). \tag{23}$$

Since the left-hand side is homogeneous of degree one in q and the right-hand side is homogeneous of degree one in $\{u, \gamma\}$, it follows that $p(q, \pi, u, \gamma)$ must be homogeneous of degree zero in $\{q, u, \gamma\}$. Hence the distorted trade expenditure function $\tilde{E}(q, \pi, u, \gamma)$ must be homogeneous of degree one in $\{q, u, \gamma\}$.

Finally, what does this imply for the distorted balance of trade function, (52)? From Shephard's lemma, $\tilde{m}(q, \pi, u, \gamma)$ equals $\tilde{E}_\pi(q, \pi, u, \gamma)$ and so is homogeneous of degree one in $\{q, u, \gamma\}$. It follows that each individual term on the right-hand side of (52), and hence the expression as a whole, is homogeneous of degree one in $\{q, u, \gamma\}$:

$$\tilde{B}'_q q + \tilde{B}_u u + \tilde{B}'_\gamma \gamma = \tilde{B}. \tag{24}$$

But $\tilde{B}$ itself is zero, since the exogenous trade balance b is subsumed into the γ vector. Hence the utility and quota levels must satisfy:

$$\hat{u}^1 = \hat{\gamma}^1 = \hat{q}^c_j \qquad \text{for all } j. \tag{25}$$

In words, "compensating" for neutral growth requires that all quota levels, and the utility level itself, rise at exactly the rate of growth.

Appendix B: Partial Equilibrium Antecedents of the TRI and MTRI

Having examined both the TRI and MTRI in the presence of both tariffs and quotas, this is an appropriate point at which to consider in detail some antecedents of our work. Partial-equilibrium indexes have been proposed as solutions to the welfare equivalence or volume equivalence problems in at least three contributions, two of which precede our work. It is useful to review all three of these other indexes here, both to connect our work to the literature and to make clear the importance of appropriate general equilibrium methods. All three indexes are presented as if they were true general-equilibrium methods, but we will show that they are not.

In practice, all index numbers must be calculated with some assumed structure and parameter values. It is thus possible that a particular approximation to an inappropriate index may come closer to the true index of interest than does the particular approximation utilized to calculate the true index. Nevertheless, a taste for scientific consistency leads us to advocate approximations to true indexes over other alternatives. The only "model-free" index numbers are mere descriptive statistics such as arithmetic means and standard deviations, with no necessary connection to any economically relevant concern.

The distinction we draw between partial- and general-equilibrium index numbers hinges on the treatment of government revenue. The partial-equilibrium basis for index numbers of trade policy is the trade expenditure function. The general-equilibrium basis for index numbers of trade policy is the balance-of-trade function, the difference between the trade expenditure function and the government's net revenue from trade distortion. Since holding constant trade expenditure with an index procedure based on partial equilibrium will generally not hold constant the trade distortion revenue, the balance of trade will generally not be at its equilibrium value in such a hypothetical experiment. This typically means that there must be some additional implicit lump-sum transfer taking place in order to meet all constraints. The partial-equilibrium index numbers we review implicitly evaluate the combined effect of the trade policy change *and* the lump-sum transfer. Hence the two approaches are not equivalent.

We review partial-equilibrium indexes for the evaluation of trade policy systems proposed by Boorstein and Feenstra (1991), Corden (1966), and Leamer (1974). These various indexes also illustrate the construction of different index numbers based on different *independent variables*, different *reference points* and different *aggregates*, a convenient taxonomic scheme that we pursue further in part III.

8B.1 The Boorstein and Feenstra Index

Boorstein and Feenstra (1991), reviewed in Feenstra (1996), propose what amounts to a partial-equilibrium version of the TRI. Their index may usefully be fitted into the taxonomy of part III in that the independent variables are *quotas*, the reference point is *welfare*, and the index is a *price aggregate*.

Quota systems in practice typically give rise to dispersion in ad valorem tariff equivalents. Under a foreign exchange constraint (see Anderson 1988) this is inefficient relative to a uniform ad valorem tariff equal to the trade-weighted average of the tariff equivalents.[4] Boorstein and Feenstra propose a measure of this inefficiency using index number methods as follows:

First, assume that total domestic expenditure on the product group subject to quotas is fixed.[5] This is a partial equilibrium assumption: the link between the distortion revenue or production income and the domestic prices of quota-constrained goods is broken. When the quotas bind, household expenditure is $e(p^0, \pi^0, u^0)$ and the quota constrained quantity vector is $e_p(p^0, \pi^0, u^0) = q^0$. Then the ad valorem tariff equivalent of the quota system is defined by[6]

$$\tau = \frac{p^{0\prime} q^0}{p^{*\prime} q^0} - 1. \tag{26}$$

Under "free trade" (the quotation marks denoting that trade is only free in the quota-constrained category), the level of expenditure is $e(p^*, \pi^0, u^*)$. Under a uniform tariff equal to τ, expenditure is equal to $e[p^*(1 + \tau), \pi^0, u^0]$. All three expenditure levels are equal by assumption.

Second, assume that preferences are homothetic so that

$$e(p^0, \pi^0, u^0) = \bar{e}(p^0, \pi^0) u^0.$$

Then

$$\frac{u^0}{u^*} = \frac{\bar{e}(p^*, \pi^0)}{\bar{e}[p^0, \pi^0]} \quad \text{and} \quad \frac{u^1}{u^*} = \frac{\bar{e}(p^*, \pi^0)}{\bar{e}[p^*(1 + \tau), \pi^0]}.$$

Third, assume that the expenditure function is separable with respect to the partition between the quota-constrained and unconstrained product groups. Then

$$\bar{e}(p, \pi) = \bar{e}[\phi(p), \eta(\pi)].$$

---

4. Boorstein and Feenstra associate the inefficiency with *quality upgrading*, the change in the composition of trade due to relative price changes. This seems misleading, as the inefficiency is due to the inefficient instruments (given the assumed constraint). The composition change given the instruments is efficient; welfare would be still lower if it were not allowed. This in fact happens with US cheese quotas, as shown in Anderson (1985, 1988).

5. The foreign exchange value of the quota-constrained product group is constant by construction, since the goal is to compare alternative allocation systems that satisfy the constraint.

6. This follows from solving $(1 + \tau) p^{*\prime} e_p = p^{0\prime} e_p$ for τ.

Moreover suppose that expenditure on the quota-constrained group $\bar{e}_\phi(\phi, \eta)\phi u$ is only negligibly affected by changes in p, a more restrictive type of partial-equilibrium assumption than usual. Then

$$\frac{u^1}{u^*} = \frac{\phi(p^*)}{\phi(p^*)(1+\tau)} = \frac{1}{1+\tau}.$$

The efficiency gain of the uniform tariff over the existing system with dispersed license prices, expressed as a percentage of the initial level of real income is, using the formula for τ,

$$\frac{u^1 - u^0}{u^*} = \frac{p^{*\prime}q^0}{p^{0\prime}q^0} - \frac{\phi(p^*)}{\phi(p^0)} = BF.$$

In interpreting the BF index by the middle formula, we find that the first term is the inverse of the Paasche price index for the move from the quota to free trade while the second term is the inverse of a true price index for the same move.

Feenstra advocates using the BF index rather than the TRI on the ground that it is simpler, as the first term is based on the observable trade-weighted average tariff equivalent while the second term can be approximated with standard share-weighted relative price differences. By contrast, even a local approximation to the TRI requires elasticities or slopes to yield terms like E_{pp}. However, this simplicity is obtained only at the cost of inconsistency with general equilibrium. For quota systems that loom large in resource misallocation, this will vitiate the purpose of the analysis. Fixing the inconsistency leads straight to the TRI.

To see this clearly, we reformulate the Boorstein and Feenstra index as a compensated efficiency measure akin to the TRI. In doing so, we can relax the homotheticity and separability assumptions used by Boorstein and Feenstra, though at some cost in operationality. The first term of the relative efficiency measure BF is always $1/(1+\tau)$, where τ is chosen to satisfy the foreign exchange constraint on the product group (in the present case, however, at constant utility). The second term of the BF index may be replaced with a distance function measure derived using the methods of this book as

$$d(p^*, p^0, \pi^0, u^0) : e\left(\frac{p^*}{d}, \pi^0, u^0\right) = e(p^0, \pi^0, u^0).$$

Thus we define the relative inefficiency of dispersed quota license premia as

$$BF' = \frac{1}{1+\tau} - d(p^*, p^0, \pi^0, u^0). \tag{27}$$

Without separable categories in the special sense above, the Paasche index interpretation of $1/(1+\tau)$ is removed, but its operationality remains. With even weak or implicit separability between p and π it remains true that

$$\frac{1}{1+\tau} - d(p^*, p^0, \pi^0, u^0) \geq 0.$$

This follows from

$$\frac{1}{1+\tau} = \frac{p^{*\prime}q^0}{p^{0\prime}q^0} \geq \frac{\phi(p^*, u^0)}{\phi(p^0, u^0)}$$

for the subexpenditure function ϕ, due to expenditure minimization.

Note that the Boorstein and Feenstra index is a partial-equilibrium index in the sense that it does not account for changes in government revenue. Satisfying the social budget constraint means that there must be a lump-sum transfer from outside the system equal to the difference between the actual revenue with a uniform tax, $(p^1 - p^*)'e_p(p^1, \pi^0, u^1)$, and the initial revenue, $(p^0 - p^*)'e_p(p^0, \pi^0, u^0)$, where $p^1 = (1+\tau)p^*$. The substitution effect together with the dispersion of initial tariffs will tend to change tariff revenue significantly, which is not accounted for in the Boorstein and Feenstra measure.[7]

The general equilibrium analysis of the Boorstein and Feenstra problem, the inefficiency of a quota system with dispersion in tariff equivalents, runs as follows: The uniform tariff τ efficiently meets the constant foreign exchange constraint in the quota-restricted group. The (partial) TRI uniform tariff yields balance-of-trade equilibrium at the same level of utility as the non-uniform tariffs in the distorted equilibrium. It is defined by

$$\tau^\Delta : B[p^*(1+\tau^\Delta), \pi^0, u^0] = B(p^0, \pi^0, u^0) = 0.$$

(Here the argument p^0 is made explicit to connect the analysis to that of Boorstein and Feenstra.)

---

7. Our methods avoid the income effect directly, by working with compensated measures that use the tariff system itself to compensate. For Boorstein and Feenstra's uncompensated measure, in cases where tariffs are very low the income effects will be small, so differences in u will not matter to revenue. Otherwise, this too is a problem for their approach.

The relative efficiency measure of dispersion in quota license premia is the difference between the TRI deflator for the efficient uniform tariff and the TRI deflator for the dispersed license premia:

$$BF^* = \frac{1}{1+\tau} - \frac{1}{1+\tau^\Delta(p^*, \pi^0, u^0; p^0)}. \tag{28}$$

Comparing BF (in its compensated form, without the assumptions of separability and homotheticity) and BF*, the difference lies in replacing the partial equilibrium deflator $d(.)$, based on the expenditure function $e(.)$, with the general equilibrium deflator $\Delta(.)$, based on the balance-of-trade function $B(.)$.

8B.2   The Corden Index

Corden (1966) proposes a uniform tariff equivalent index to measure tariffs as independent variables and he uses the *balance of distorted trade* as a reference point. Although he does not make explicit whether his import demand functions are in general equilibrium or not, it is clear that they cannot include the revenue feedback, which is the essence of the difference between what we call general-equilibrium and partial-equilibrium methods. Both Corden's and our import demand functions include endogenous factor prices so that the supply response in the Corden index is in general equilibrium.

As usual, π^0 is the initial distorted price, π^* is the free trade price, and u^0 is the initial level of utility. The initial vector of distorted imports is $E_\pi(\pi^0, u^0)$, equal to m^0, and the compensated "free-trade" vector is $E_\pi(\pi^*, u^0)$ equal to m^*. We interpret Corden's index to be a simple transform of the compensated MTRI:

$$\tau^c = \frac{1}{\mu^c} - 1,$$

where

$$\mu^c(\pi^1, u^0, M^0) : \pi^{*\prime} E_\pi\left(\frac{\pi^1}{\mu^c}, u^0\right) = M^0.$$

The general equilibrium version of the Corden index is the uniform tariff implied by the MTRI. Using the decomposition of chapter 5, and solving for the compensated MTRI, we can write the proportionate rate of change of the Corden index as the weighted average of the rates of change of the MTRI and the TRI:

$$\hat{\mu}^c = \left(\frac{1}{\lambda}\right)\hat{\mu} + \left(1 - \frac{1}{\lambda}\right)\hat{\Delta}. \tag{29}$$

Here the coefficient $1/\lambda$ is the ratio of the uncompensated to the compensated response of restricted trade volume to a 1 percent rise in domestic prices.

8B.3 The Leamer Index

Leamer (1974) also uses partial equilibrium as a basis for a tariff measure. This serves as a *quantity aggregate* example of an index of *tariffs* as independent variables, with the *balance of distorted trade* as a reference point. We develop the Leamer index and offer a general equilibrium version. In its general equilibrium form it is a quantity aggregate, like our coefficient of trade utilization (see chapter 14), while referencing a balance of restricted trade, like our Mercantilist TRI. Leamer evaluates the full system of trade distortions with tariffs only.

Leamer's indexes are not based on a trade expenditure function, and the ceteris paribus assumption of his "free-trade" experiment is not clear. However, we may interpret his index as a compensated index, as it clearly does not include the feedback from revenue into income. The new volume of tariff-restricted trade is $\pi^{*\prime}E_{\pi\pi}(\pi^1, u^0)$, evaluating each trade quantity at external prices where the quantity is that which would be demanded at the new prices and the initial level of utility. Leamer concentrates on the case where the new prices are equal to the free trade prices. The initial volume of tariff-restricted trade is equal to $\pi^{*\prime}E_\pi(\pi^0, u^0) = M^0$. Leamer's index L is defined as

$$\frac{1}{\mu^L} - 1, \tag{30}$$

where

$$\mu^L(\pi^1, u^0, M^0) : \frac{\pi^{*\prime}E_\pi(\pi^1, u^0)}{\mu^L} = M^o.$$

Leamer's index is based on the uniform quantity deflator which contracts the "new" vector of trade at the old utility such that the initial external value of restricted trade is maintained. The Leamer index is related to the Corden index by a simple formula. In proportional rates of change it is equal to the Corden index times the aggregate compensated price elasticity of M:

$$\hat{\mu}^L = \hat{\mu}^c \left(M_\pi^c \cdot \frac{\pi}{M} \right). \tag{31}$$

The term in parentheses is the aggregate price elasticity, the response of M to a 1 percent rise in all restricted prices. We may immediately apply the decomposition of chapter 5 to (31) in order to relate the Leamer index to the MTRI and the TRI:

$$\hat{\mu}^L = \left[\frac{1}{\lambda} \hat{\mu} + \left(1 - \frac{1}{\lambda} \right) \hat{\Delta} \right] \frac{M_\pi^c \pi}{M}. \tag{32}$$

Leamer approximates μ^L using what we interpret as a system of compensated demand functions, holding real income constant. If the "new" quantity must be defined with reference to the new equilibrium utility u^1 rather than initial utility u^0, we have a trivial quantity version of the MTRI where $\delta^{LU} = M^0/\pi^* \cdot E_\pi(\pi^*, u^*)$.

9 Alternative Economic Environments

Our methods apply to a wide range of economic structures. Elsewhere we assume a small open economy with convex technology and perfectly competitive behavior. This chapter illustrates the extension of our methods to structures in which world prices are endogenous, in which external economies of scale obtain, and in which a monopolistically competitive sector is present. The analysis is meant to guide the use of the TRI and MTRI in future applied work that includes these or similar complications.

Familiar elements of the theory of distortions are treated here with the compact structure of the balance of trade function. In our own applications we have found the analytic setup of the balance of trade function and its derivatives to be invaluable as a guide to interpreting the results, and to eliminating the errors which arise in the process of arriving at the results. A by-product of our analysis is a synthesis of some results of the trade policy literature of the past twenty years.

Our modeling strategy below is to take what was in earlier chapters an explicit or implicit parameter in the balance of trade function (e.g., the world price vector) and then develop the added structure required to determine the "parameter" as a reduced form function of the trade policy and the real income of the representative agent of the home country. The reduced form balance-of-trade function can then be utilized along the lines of the preceding chapters to define the TRI and MTRI.

Each of the extended environments implies a distortion (a departure from Pareto efficiency on some margin) additional to the marginal deadweight loss of tariffs. When world prices are endogenous with respect to trade volume, the marginal social cost of imports is greater than the private marginal cost, equal to the external price. External economies of scale imply that price exceeds marginal cost. Monopolistic competition means that trade policy affects the number of varieties available, where the number is not generally optimal.[1]

Free trade is no longer the optimal trade policy due to the distortion, in contrast to the simple environment of earlier chapters. This raises a key conceptual question: Should the benchmark against which to evaluate any given trade policy be free trade or the optimal policy? We argue that it remains natural to define trade restrictiveness by comparing the current instrument levels to free trade, but the alternative comparison to optimal levels may also be attractive. We provide a full discussion of this issue below in the context of endogenous world prices, but the discussion applies to the other distortions as well.

In section 9.1, we analyze the TRI with endogenous world prices in the two-country case (appendix A contains further details, and appendix B describes the TRI and MTRI for the many-country case). In section 9.2, we analyze an environment with external scale economies. In section 9.3, we analyze a model with monopolistic competition. We maintain the assumption of a representative agent subject to a static external payments constraint. In the concluding section 9.4, we argue that the simplification is relatively harmless.

9.1   Trade Restrictiveness in a Large Country

Consider a simple model with just two countries. The key issue explored here is that since it pays to exploit market power over world prices, should the index be calculated relative to free trade or to the optimal trade policy?

To isolate this issue, only one country has an active trade policy in this section. The real-world setting of two or more countries with active trade policies poses a second conceptual issue. We must choose between a unilateral approach (only one country's trade policy is altered to form its index) and a multilateral approach (all countries' indexes are calculated simultaneously). We develop both approaches to the many country case in appendix B. The unilateral approach appears to be sensible in applica-

---

1. Short-run equilibrium involves pure economic profits as an additional distortion, and brings in the potential complications of oligopoly models. We stick to long-run zero-profit equilibrium analysis in this chapter to avoid treating imperfect competition generally. We conjecture that oligopoly can be fitted into the framework of this book. But there is no generally accepted general equilibrium trade model with oligopoly. Extensions of index number theory to this environment must wait on better models.

tions where the purpose is to evaluate a unilateral move, such as World Bank Structural Adjustment Loan auditing. The multilateral TRI that shifts all countries to a uniform welfare equivalent tariff simultaneously would be appropriate for cross-country analysis that requires indexes of trade policy for a set of countries, such as in investigations of openness and growth.

Returning to the two-country world, assume that the foreign country (denoted with an asterisk) trades freely. Free-trade equilibrium is not optimal for the home country (a "distortion" in the sense of the theory of distortions) because, while the private marginal cost of imports is equal to the world price, the social marginal cost of imports is equal to the world price plus the world price increasing effect of another unit of imports on inframarginal trade volume.

In the background there is a numéraire commodity which by convention is not taxed in any country, so all explicitly listed prices are understood to be relative prices. There is also a price vector p of undistorted prices that changes with policy. Typically these would be exported goods. In earlier chapters all the undistorted prices were constant with respect to trade policy and could be subsumed into the composite commodity numéraire. Since changes in p have welfare consequences, we must now keep track of them.

World prices are solved as functions of the policy instruments and the domestic reference utility using the conditions of world general equilibrium. World equilibrium requires international market clearance for distorted and undistorted goods:

$$E_p(p, \pi, u) + E_p^*(p, \pi^*, u^*) = 0,$$
$$E_\pi(p, \pi, u) + E_{\pi^*}^*(p, \pi^*, u^*) = 0. \tag{1}$$

Here we extend the notation to cover the foreign economy in an obvious way, with trade expenditure function E^* and utility u^*. The budget constraint for the foreign economy requires that

$$B^*(p, \pi^*, u^*) = b^{*0}. \tag{2}$$

Together the system of equations (1) and (2) solves for the endogenous variables (p, π^*, u^*) as functions of the instruments π and the reference utility u: $p(\pi, u)$, $\pi^*(\pi, u)$ and $u^*(\pi, u)$.

The solution exists under standard conditions. Appendix A contains details on the derivative properties of the reduced form price and foreign utility functions. The tariff vector is equal to $\pi - \pi^*(\pi, u)$ when domestic utility is at its equilibrium level, provided that π is feasible as an equilibrium of the tariff-distorted trading world.

The domestic balance-of-trade function $B(p, \pi, \pi^*, u)$ is directly a function of the instrument vector π, but it is also a function of π indirectly through the influence of the instrument vector on π^* and p. It is convenient to define the reduced form domestic balance-of-trade function, a function of the instrument vector π and the reference utility u:

$$\bar{B}(\pi, u) \equiv B[p(\pi, u), \pi, \pi^*(\pi, u), u].$$

The equilibrium level of utility is defined by $\bar{B}(\pi, u) = b^0$.

Now consider measuring the trade restrictiveness of policy in the home economy. The Trade Restrictiveness Index is defined by

$$\tau^\Delta : \bar{B}[\pi^*(1 + \tau^\Delta), u^0] = \bar{B}(\pi^0, u^0) = b^0. \tag{3}$$

Here π^* is the equilibrium value with the uniform tariff, solved jointly with p, u^* from

$$E_\pi[p, \pi^*(1 + \tau^\Delta), u^0] + E_{\pi^*}^*(p, \pi^*, u^*) = 0,$$

$$E_p[p, \pi^*(1 + \tau^\Delta), u^0] + E_p^*(p, \pi^*, u^*) = 0,$$

$$E^*(p, \pi^*, u^*) = 0.$$

The interpretation of (3) is exactly as in the small country case: for any arbitrary policy vector it gives the uniform tariff that is equivalent in welfare to the initial tariff vector. Compared to the small-country case, the key difference buried in the compact structure of $\bar{B}(\cdot)$ is that the world prices of tariffed and untariffed goods are endogenous. Changes in the instruments drive terms of trade changes that are consequential for welfare. Behind the scenes proper account is being taken of these changes.

A significant complication is that the TRI as defined in (3) may not exist because the initial tariff vector may yield a higher level of utility than the best uniform tariff vector. We illustrate with figure 9.1. Note that the free trade point at F is where the tariffs are both equal to zero. The space of tariff factors is filled with iso-utility loci. The initial utility level u^0 is associated with the point T^0, also attainable with other tariffs along the locus labeled u^0. The optimal tariff is located at H. See the appendix A for details. The best uniform tariff is located at E, where another iso-utility locus is tangent to ray OF.[2] The TRI is constructed by

2. The equilibrium foreign price vector is assumed for illustrative purposes not to change in the move from U to the optimal uniform tariff. Normally the assumption would not hold.

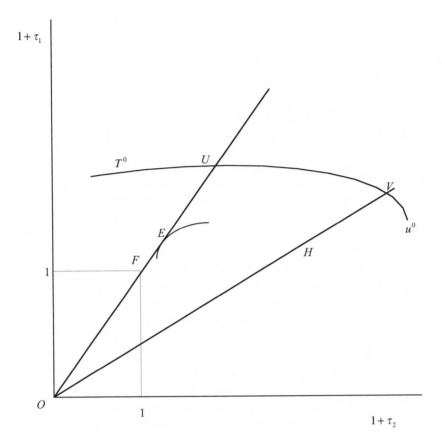

Figure 9.1
Tariff space analysis

traveling on the initial utility locus to the intersection of the locus with the ray through OF, point U. The TRI uniform-tariff factor is given by the ratio OU/OF. The existence problem arises because the initial tariff vector may be located closer to H than is E, in the sense that the locus u^0 yields higher utility than does the policy at E. Specifically, for any initial tariff yielding utility greater than the utility achieved by the optimal uniform tariff, the TRI as defined by (3) does not exist. The existence problem does not arise in the small country case where H and F coincide.

We could alternatively measure the trade restrictiveness of the initial policy relative to the *optimal* policy. This procedure evades the existence problem. The optimal policy is defined as

$$\tilde{\pi} \equiv \arg\min_{\pi} \bar{B}(\pi, \tilde{u}),$$

where

$$\tilde{u} = u : \bar{B}(\tilde{\pi}, u) = b^0.$$

Then the analogue to the TRI is

$$\tilde{\tau} : \bar{B}[\tilde{\pi}(1 + \tilde{\tau}), u^0] = \bar{B}(\pi^0, u^0).$$

The tariff vector in the hypothetical new situation is given by $\tilde{\pi}(1 + \tilde{\tau}) - \pi^*[\tilde{\pi}(1 + \tilde{\tau}), u^0]$. Thus $\tilde{\tau}$ is interpreted as a uniform-tariff surcharge that, levied on the optimal price, yields welfare equal to the given tariff structure. The alternative procedure of measuring trade restrictiveness comes at a cost in the ease of use of the index and in sensitivity to specification and measurement error in defining the optimal tariff, as we discuss below. This index always exists when distorted trade equilibrium exists, though it is not necessarily unique. Graphically the alternative index is defined by traveling on the locus u^0 to its intersection V with the ray from the origin through H. The uniform tariff factor surcharge is OV/OH.

The existence problem is likely to be a theoretical quibble in many applications because most actual tariff vectors appear to be far from what we imagine from back-of-the-envelope calculations to be the optimal tariffs. For example, for developed countries the optimal tariffs are very low on textiles/apparel and food based on high export supply elasticities and the usual inverse elasticity reasoning, whereas actual barriers are high. This creates the situation of the figure where the "wrong" tariffs are high. We also note that existence has not been a practical problem in any of the applications we have carried out.

As for uniqueness, the diagram suggests that we have the formal possibility of a uniform subsidy generated by the lower intersection of u^0 with OF.[3] This can be discarded as economically irrelevant: subsidizing trade destroys welfare just as tariffs do, but it increases rather than restricts trade. Nevertheless, the alternative intersection suggests a more serious problem if the set of tariff factors superior to the initial one is not convex. Not much can be said about the shape of the iso-utility contours in general, so the positive protection level indexes need not be unique. See Neary (1995) and the appendix to chapter 3 above for more discussion.

---

3. This possibility also arises with the small open economy case.

We think that users of the TRI should ordinarily use free trade as the reference alternative policy in constructing the TRI for the large-country case, as indeed we do in the Multi-Fibre Arrangement application of chapter 12 where the quota policy of Hong Kong, a large supplier, is evaluated. Two reasons suggest this practice.

First, several prominent potential uses of the TRI seem to indicate the desirability of an index that measures distance from free trade rather than from the optimal tariff. For example, in investigations of the link from openness to growth, a tariff index as an independent variable is meant to indicate the stance of policy toward the size of trade, thinking of trade as a channel through which technological transfer may occur, inter alia. Also in World Bank loan conditionality investigations, a tariff index is desired because it is assumed that openness is good for growth, in addition to its static effects on real income.

Second, the value of the optimal tariff factor will be very sensitive to measurement error and specification error. Specifically, the inverse elasticity formula that defines the optimal tariff vector requires a computable general equilibrium model based on specifications and elasticity parameterizations that are subject to considerable uncertainty. While specification error is a concern for any measure of the TRI, our applications of part III show that our TRI and MTRI estimates are insensitive to variations in elasticities.

9.2 External Scale Economies

External scale economies have long been incorporated into standard general equilibrium trade models. They are especially tractable when the scale effects in an industry are multiplicative, a strategy followed here. We follow Helpman (1984), who showed that the GDP function can still be defined as a maximum value function by replacing the producer prices with marginal costs. This permits the use of dual structures as in the rest of this book.

Competitive equilibrium is inefficient because private marginal cost, equal to price due to perfect competition, is greater than social marginal cost because the scale economy external to the firm implies that a marginal increase in one firm's output lowers the costs of all firms in the industry. Trade policy has an effect beyond those of preceding chapters since it affects the undersupply of goods with external scale economies. Naturally the evaluation of trade policy must account for the effect of marginal changes in trade policy on the production distortion. In this section we lay out the proper accounting method in a simple case.

For simplicity only one sector is characterized by external scale economies, entering multiplicatively. An industry of n identical firms operating at volume of activity y has cost functions defined by selecting an input bundle v^i to minimize costs while using production process $g(v^i)$ to satisfy the required activity level y. Thus

$$c(y, w) \equiv \min_{v^i} \{w \cdot v^i \mid y = g(v^i)\}.$$

Activity y is assumed to generate output of $z = f(Y)y$, where $Y = ny$ is the industry total activity. We assume f has elasticity greater than zero, reflecting external scale economies. Also the scale elasticity must be less than one or behavior is explosive and the marginal cost of output is nonsensically negative. The marginal cost of a unit of activity is c_y, while the marginal cost of a unit of output is $c_y/f(Y)$. Zero profit firms operate where price is equal to unit cost $c/f(Y)y$ and competitive firms operate where private marginal cost $c_z = c_y/f(Y)$ facing the firm is equal to price. The social marginal cost of a unit of output is given by

$$mc = \frac{c_y}{f}\left[1 - \frac{Yf_Y}{f}\right] < \frac{c_y}{f} = p.$$

Note that $Yf_Y/f = (p - mc)/p$, the scale elasticity is equal to the percentage excess of price over social marginal cost.

The implicit price of activity y is $pf(Y)$. Denoting the aggregate restricted profit function of all firms in the increasing returns sector as Π, we define the GDP function as

$$g[pf(Y), \pi, v] = \min_{w}\{\Pi[pf(Y), \pi, w] + w \cdot v\}.$$

By Hotelling's lemma, $\partial g/\partial p = g_1 f = Yf(Y) = Z$, where Z is the aggregate output of the increasing returns sector. As usual, g_π gives the output vector of the constant returns sectors. Hotelling's lemma implies that the scale of activity of the increasing returns industry is an implicit function of prices of the goods and of factor endowments: $Y(p, \pi, v)$ is the solution to

$$g_p[pf(Y), \pi, v] = Yf(Y).$$

The supply curve of output is $Z(p, \pi, v) = Y(p, \pi, v)f[Y(p, \pi, v)]$. The supply curve can easily slope downward, $[f + Yf_Y]Y_p < 0$ whenever

$Y_p < 0$. This is more likely as external scale effects are strong or the sources of increasing opportunity cost of resources are weak. Substituting $Y(p, \pi, v)$ into the GDP function, we form the reduced form function

$$G(p, \pi, v) = g\{pf[Y(p, \pi, v)], \pi, v\}.$$

The properties of the reduced form GDP function differ in important ways from the usual GDP function due to the embedded inefficiency of output. Based on previous results,

$$G_p = Z + (p - mc)fY_p,$$

$$G_\pi = g_\pi + (p - mc)fY_\pi.$$

The balance-of-trade function for an economy with tariffs only and an increasing returns sector is defined as

$$B(p, \pi, u; p^*, \pi^*) = e(p, \pi, u) - G(p, \pi) - (p - p^*) \cdot [e_p - f(Y(\cdot))Y(p, \pi)]$$
$$- (\pi - \pi^*) \cdot [e_\pi - g_\pi].$$

Here we suppress the irrelevant argument v along with, as usual, the undistorted external prices.

The implications for the analysis of trade policy introduced by scale economies are most easily seen in the case where only the increasing returns sector has a tariff. The marginal cost of tariffs is given by

$$B_p = -(p - p^*)m_p - (p - mc)fY_p,$$

where

$$m_p = e_p - (f + Yf_Y)Y_p.$$

At zero initial tariffs ($p = p^*$), a small tariff is welfare increasing (reduces the foreign exchange required to support the initial utility) because the implied production subsidy acts to correct a domestic production distortion. The subsidy increases the output of the increasing returns industry where price is greater than social marginal cost. As $f_Y \to 0$, then $p \to mc$, and we return to the constant returns case where the optimal tariff is equal to zero.

With tariffs on the constant returns sectors, changes in the tariff of the increasing returns sector have a cross-effect $-(\pi - \pi^*)'E_{\pi p}$. Moreover changes in the tariffs of constant returns sectors have an effect on the undersupply of the increasing returns sectors, $-(p - mc)Y_\pi$ as well as the cross-effect on $-(p - p^*)[e_p - f(Y)Y]$.

The TRI for an economy with external economies of scale is defined as before:

$$\tau^\Delta : B[p^*(1 + \tau^\Delta), \pi^*(1 + \tau^\Delta), u^0] = 0.$$

Embedded in the balance-of-trade function for this economy are the second-best aspects of tariffs due to the domestic distortion from the output of the increasing returns industry being too low.

9.3 Monopolistic Competition

Simple versions of monopolistic competition in long run equilibrium (Helpman and Krugman 1985) are quite similar to competitive models. Our method of measuring trade restrictiveness extends to this environment. Monopolisitic competition adds a new element—endogeneity of the number of goods—to the considerations of endogenous world price and endogenous inefficiency of scale. A proper accounting requires additional conceptual work. We show that the Dixit-Stiglitz model can be represented with a balance-of-trade function with properties that we analyze. Then the TRI can be defined and analyzed as before.

The Dixit-Stiglitz symmetric differentiated products model used by Helpman and Krugman and many others has the advantage of great tractability. Two key conceptual elements are introduced: scale economies are internal to the firm, and the number of varieties is endogenous. Because price exceeds marginal cost due to scale economies, it is possible that a tariff improves welfare via its production-subsidizing role. Because the number of varieties changes, it is possible that a tariff can improve welfare by increasing the range of varieties. Finally it is possible that a tariff can improve the terms of trade, a natural possibility in a model in which each firm has monopoly power in its own variety but the firm may not internalize its market power in a socially optimal manner.

Helpman and Krugman (1989, ch. 7) analyze trade policy in a series of monopolistically competitive structures designed to highlight the production efficiency and terms of trade possibilities in turn, removing the other possibilities by careful choice of assumptions. All of their models can be cast in terms of balance of trade functions. Rather than repeat their work, we illustrate the application of our methods in just one rather comprehensive monopolistically competitive model that includes the variety effect they suppress.

We assume that one sector is monopolistically competitive, producing symmetric varieties both at home and abroad in long-run zero-profit equilibrium. All varieties sell at price p^* in the foreign market, but home tariffs raise the home price of foreign varieties to $p > p^*$.

The GDP function is defined using competitive factor markets as in the preceding section. GDP is given by $g(p, \pi, v, y)$, where p is the uniform price of the symmetric monopolistically competitive goods produced at home (eventually set by the markup decision of the firm but treated for analytic convenience now as if it were a parameter), y is the scale of output of the monopolistically competitive good produced by each symmetric home firm, and π is the price of competitive goods subject to distortion. The internal scale economies associated with y have an effect similar to the external scale economies effect $f(Y)$ of the preceding section. Therefore $g_y > 0$, and GDP is raised by increases in the scale of output of monopolistically competitive firms because price exceeds marginal cost. Hotelling's lemma continues to apply so that the aggregate output of monopolistically competitive goods is given by g_p. We restrict the scale effect to be multiplicative. Then the GDP function has the special form $g[pf(y), \pi, v]$. With this specification, increases in y act on the competitive parts of the production structure (competitive supply and factor returns) like increases in the price of monopolistically competitive output.

The expenditure function for the Dixit-Stiglitz economy is written

$$e(p, p^*, \pi, n, n^*, u) = e[(n + n^*)^{1/(1-\sigma)} P, \pi, u],$$

where

$$P \equiv \left[\frac{n}{n + n^*} p^{1-\sigma} + \frac{n^*}{n + n^*} (p^*)^{1-\sigma} \right]^{1/(1-\sigma)}, \qquad \sigma > 1.$$

The parameter σ is the elasticity of substitution between varieties, and the condition that it exceed one is required for marginal revenue of the firms to be positive; n and n^* are the number of home and foreign varieties consumed, p is the price of home varieties, and p^* is the home price of foreign varieties. The form of the price index emphasizes two separate aspects of entry and exit of firms—change in the total number of varieties (more is better) and change in the proportion of high- and low-priced varieties. The love of variety implied by the Dixit-Stiglitz framework implies that expenditure is falling in the number of varieties. Thus

$$\frac{e_n n}{e} = \frac{s}{1 - \sigma} < 0,$$

where s is the share of home expenditure falling on home monopolistically competitive goods. Shephard's lemma holds for the expenditure function. Hence, for example, $e_p p/e = s$.

The description of the economy is completed by determining y and n from the monopolistic firm's markup condition, and the aggregation of firms condition in the monopolistically competitive sector. Under the multiplicative form for economies of scale, the unit cost of output is specified as $c(w)/f(y)$, where $f/y > f_y > 0$. Here $c(w)$ is increasing and homogeneous of degree one in the factor price vector w. The standard properties of the GDP function imply $w = g_v$. The first-order condition of the monopolistic firm implies for the Dixit-Stiglitz economy that

$$p\frac{\sigma - 1}{\sigma} = \frac{c(w)}{f(y)}\left[1 - \frac{y f_y(y)}{f(y)}\right].$$

In long-run equilibrium, price is equal to unit cost. Hence the first-order condition is solved for the scale of output independently of prices:[4]

$$\bar{y} = \left\{y \left| \frac{y f_y(y)}{f(y)} = \frac{1}{\sigma}\right.\right\}.$$

Then we use Hotelling's lemma to determine the number of firms as a function of the prices and factor endowments:

$$n(p, \pi, v) = \frac{g_p[pf(\bar{y}), \pi, v]}{\bar{y}}.$$

Various special cases of production structure yield restrictions on the second derivatives of the GDP function. These can be used to sign the derivatives of the reduced form $n(p, \pi, v)$ function. But we note that in general, as is intuitive, the number of varieties is increasing in the equilibrium price (equal to unit cost):

$$n_p = \frac{g_{pp}}{\bar{y}} > 0.$$

Note also that the home number of varieties is independent of the home price of foreign varieties.

A parallel set of calculations yields the foreign scale of output $\bar{y}^*$ and number of varieties $n^*(p^*, \pi^*, v^*)$. It is convenient to simplify notation by

---

4. For example, consider $f(y) = a + by$. The equilibrium scale is $\bar{y} = a/b(\sigma - 1)$.

making the foreign economy inactive in trade policy, so its domestic prices are equal to the world prices for the homogeneous goods and for the varieties of differentiated goods that it produces.

Now we are ready to consider equilibrium. It is convenient to assume that all homogeneous traded goods prices except for the numéraire are potentially distorted, thereby avoiding the need to separately account for the movement of prices of untaxed homogeneous traded goods. We also simplify by assuming that the foreign varieties of the differentiated goods are all taxed at the same rate τ.

The balance-of-trade function for a long run Dixit-Stiglitz economy with trade taxes only[5] is written as

$$B(p, p^*, \tau, \pi, \pi^*, n, n^*, u) = e[p, p^*(1 + \tau), \pi, n, n^*, u] - g[pf(\bar{y}), \pi, v]$$
$$- \tau p^* \cdot e_{p^*(1+\tau)} - (\pi - \pi^*) \cdot (e_\pi - g_\pi).$$

For simplicity, we suppress the inactive variables v and $\bar{y}$ from the argument list on the left. We can rewrite the balance-of-trade function as a reduced form function of the trade instruments, the endogenous prices and the levels of utility by substituting for n and n^* the reduced form functions $n(p, \pi, v)$, $n^*(p^*, \pi^*, v^*)$:

$$\bar{B}(p, p^*, \tau, \pi, \pi^*, u) = B[p, p^*, \tau, \pi, \pi^*, n(p, \pi, v), n^*(p^*, \pi^*, v^*), u].$$

This treatment parallels that of the first section, adding the elements of scale economies parallel to the second section and incorporating the aspect of endogenous varieties unique to this section. The foreign economy is inactive in trade policy, so its reduced form balance-of-trade function is written as

$$\bar{B}^*(p, p^*, \pi, \pi^*, u^*) = e^*[p, p^*, \pi, \pi^*, n(p, \pi, v), n^*(p^*, \pi^*, v^*), u^*]$$
$$- g[p^*f(\bar{y}^*), \pi^*, v^*].$$

General equilibrium of the world economy is reached when the endogenous levels of utility (u, u^*) and the endogenous prices of traded goods (p, p^*, π^*) satisfy under given trade policy instrument levels (τ, π)[6] both the balance-of-trade constraints,

---

5. We suppress for simplicity the possibility of export subsidies or taxes on the differentiated export goods.

6. The tax $\pi - \pi^*$ is the instrument but can be replaced by the domestic price, using the arbitrage condition: $\pi = \pi^* + (\pi - \pi^*)$.

$$\bar{B}(p, p^*, \tau, \pi, \pi^*, u) = b^0,$$

$$\bar{B}^*(p, p^*, \pi, \pi^*, u^*) = b^{*0},$$

and the market clearance relations,

$$\bar{e}_p - g_p + \bar{e}_p^* = 0,$$

$$\bar{e}_{p^*(1+\tau)} + \bar{e}_{p^*}^* - g_{p^*}^* = 0,$$

$$\bar{e}_\pi - g_\pi + \bar{e}_{\pi^*}^* - g_{\pi^*}^* = 0.$$

Here the bar over the expenditure function and its partial derivatives with respect to prices has the same meaning as with the balance-of-trade function: it denotes the reduced form where the number of varieties depends explicitly on the domestic prices.

Now consider the effect of trade policy acting through the price changes it drives in general equilibrium. The monopolistic competition structure implies that the variety effect of trade policy operates through the terms of trade. The potential scale effect of trade policy is suppressed since scale is determined independently of prices for large n.[7] Thus, for example,

$$B_p = (e_p - y) - \tau p^* e_{p^*(1+\tau),p} - (\pi - \pi^*) \cdot (e_{\pi p} - g_{\pi p}),$$

where the first negative term represents the conventional terms of trade effect for an export sector and the second negative term represents the cross-effects of the change in p on tariff revenue. Combining this with the variety effect yields

$$\bar{B}_p = B_p + B_n n_p,$$

where $B_n = e_n < 0$ and $n_p > 0$. Thus a rise in the price of a differentiated product export sector is beneficial for the usual terms of trade reason and for an additional reason: it increases the number of varieties. Tariff increases on homogeneous goods will normally raise domestic prices and reduce the number of varieties, since $n_\pi = g_{p\pi}/\bar{y}$ is negative in most production structures. Finally tariff increases on imported varieties will normally reduce their number through worsening the terms of trade of the exporter $dn^*/d\tau = (g_{p^*p^*}^*/\bar{y}^*) dp^*/d\tau$, where $dp^*/d\tau$ is the terms of trade

---

7. The scale effect would operate in short-run monopolistic competition, acting very much like the external economies case but with the important distinction that scale operates at the firm level. A rise in industry output due to more firms which reduced scale would by the latter effect raise inefficiency.

effect, and should normally be negative. A full analysis is quite complex because any tariff changes all endogenous prices. Normally a tariff on differentiated product imports might be expected to raise the scale and number of varieties at home while shrinking those abroad and improving home terms of trade.

The TRI uniform tariff for a monopolistically competitive economy is now defined as the solution for τ^Δ simultaneously with (p, p^*, π^*, u^*) in

$$\bar{B}[p, p^*, 1 + \tau^\Delta, \pi^*(1 + \tau^\Delta), \pi^*, u^0] = b^0,$$

$$\bar{B}^*[p, p^*, \pi^*(1 + \tau^\Delta), \pi^*, u^*] = b^{*0},$$

$$\bar{e}_p[p, p^*(1 + \tau^\Delta), \pi^*(1 + \tau^\Delta), p^*, \pi^*, u^0] - g_p[p, \pi^*(1 + \tau^\Delta)]$$

$$\quad + \bar{e}_p^*[p, p^*, \pi^*(1 + \tau^\Delta), \pi^*, u^*] = 0,$$

$$\bar{e}_{p^*(1+\tau)}[\cdot] + \bar{e}_{p^*}^*[\cdot] - g_{p^*}^*(p^*, \pi^*) = 0,$$

$$\bar{e}_\pi[\cdot] - g_\pi[\cdot] + \bar{e}_{\pi^*}^*[\cdot] - g_{\pi^*}^*(\cdot) = 0.$$

As with the simpler environments of preceding chapters, we replace the actual differentiated tariff vector with the uniform tariff that maintains real income u^0 along with the external budget constraint and all the other requirements, in this case, the world market-clearing conditions and the foreign budget constraint. Embedded in the reduced form functions are the effects of trade policy on the scale of output and number of varieties of monopolistically produced goods, as delineated above. Analysis of the TRI and its key elements in local changes can be developed as needed based on our framework using the vector of marginal cost of tariffs $(\bar{B}_\tau, \bar{B}_\pi)$.

The MTRI is generated following similar steps to those we have taken before. The new element is the volume-of-trade function. The compensated volume-of-trade function defined for a set of base world prices is

$$M^c(p, p^*, \tau, \pi, \pi^*, u) = \pi^{*0} \cdot (\bar{e}_\pi - g_\pi) + p^{*0} \cdot \bar{e}_{p^*(1+\tau)},$$

where the derivative functions on the right-hand side, the compensated import demand functions, are evaluated at the current policy levels. The MTRI uniform tariff is determined as the solution for τ^μ simultaneously with (p, p^*, π^*, u, u^*) in

$$M^c[p, p^*, 1 + \tau^\mu, \pi^*(1 + \tau^\mu), \pi^*, u] = M^0,$$

$$\bar{B}[p, p^*, 1 + \tau^\mu, \pi^*(1 + \tau^\mu), \pi^*, u] = b^0,$$

$$\bar{B}^*[p, p^*, \pi^*(1 + \tau^\mu), \pi^*, u^*] = b^{*0},$$

$$\bar{e}_p[p, p^*(1 + \tau^\mu), \pi^*(1 + \tau^\mu), p^*, \pi^*, u^0] - g_p[p, \pi^*(1 + \tau^\mu)]$$

$$+ \bar{e}_p^*[p, p^*, \pi^*(1 + \tau^\mu), \pi^*, u^*] = 0,$$

$$\bar{e}_{p^*(1+\tau)}[\cdot] + \bar{e}_{p^*}^*[\cdot] - g_{p^*}^*(p^*, \pi^*) = 0,$$

$$\bar{e}_\pi[\cdot] - g_\pi[\cdot] + \bar{e}_{\pi^*}^*[\cdot] - g_{\pi^*}^*(\cdot) = 0.$$

9.4 Conclusion

We have shown that the TRI and MTRI can be defined for a wide range of economic environments. Many other environments that we do not explicitly cover can be easily fitted into our framework.

We have simplified by focusing on a static model of a representative agent facing an external payments constraint. These restrictions are relatively harmless. Description of a many household economy requires additional structure to describe household expenditure patterns and the distribution of factoral income and government transfers. In this setting it is straightforward to calculate the MTRI. As for the TRI, we can calculate the uniform tariff that maintains the foreign exchange required to support the original vector of household utilities. The actual maintenance of the vector of household utilities under such a tariff change is feasible with lump-sum redistribution. In the absence of such redistribution, the aggregate surplus equivalent uniform tariff is a useful measure of trade restrictiveness.[8]

The static budget constraint can also be partially relaxed. The static model easily extends to an intertemporal Arrow-Debreu model, simply through labeling goods and policies by date and imposing a single intertemporal budget constraint which implicitly allows unconstrained international borrowing and lending. More complex intertemporal models are characterized by a sequence of constraints that may or may not bind, and raise new issues beyond the scope of this book.

---

8. If a social welfare function is available to aggregate household utilities (with the government making efficient lump-sum transfers that are endogenous to the trade policy), the environment is essentially what it was in the single-household case. But with a social welfare function in the absence of lump-sum redistribution, the interesting issue arises of characterizing a uniform tariff that is social welfare equivalent to the status quo, understanding that a key part of the action is compensating for changes in income distribution. This requires analysis outside the scope of this book.

Appendix A: Details of the Two-Country Model

The two-country case of the text uses the reduced form balance-of-trade function. Its properties determine the properties of the TRI. Here we lay out the reduced form properties in terms of the trade expenditure function.

The balance-of-trade function is defined as

$$B(p, \pi, \pi^*, u) = E(p, \pi, u) - (\pi - \pi^*) \cdot E_\pi(p, \pi, u).$$

Substituting the reduced form prices into the balance-of-trade function and differentiating we have

$$\bar{B}_\pi = B_p \cdot p_\pi + B_\pi + B_{\pi^*} \cdot \pi_\pi^*,$$

where

$$B_p = E_p - (\pi - \pi^*) \cdot E_{\pi p},$$

$$B_\pi = -(\pi - \pi^*) \cdot E_{\pi\pi},$$

$$B_{\pi^*} = E_\pi.$$

The price derivatives p_π and π_π^* come from market clearance and the foreign balance-of-payments constraint. Market clearance implies:

$$\begin{pmatrix} E_{pp} + E_{pp}^* & E_{p\pi^*}^* \\ E_{\pi^* p}^* & E_{\pi^*\pi^*}^* \end{pmatrix} \begin{pmatrix} dp \\ d\pi^* \end{pmatrix} + \begin{pmatrix} E_{pu^*}^* \\ E_{\pi^* u^*}^* \end{pmatrix} du^* = -\begin{pmatrix} E_{p\pi} \\ E_{\pi\pi} \end{pmatrix} d\pi.$$

With foreign free trade, $B^*(p, \pi^*, u^*) = E^*(p, \pi^*, u^*)$. Then foreign utility changes with prices according to $du^* = -[E_p^* \, dp + E_{\pi^*}^* \, d\pi^*]/E_{u^*}^*$. Substituting into the market clearance relations and solving yields the implicit derivatives p_π, π_π^*. The price derivatives with respect to domestic real income u are defined exactly analogously.

The existence of distorted trade equilibrium is assumed above. Of course, not all possible domestic price vectors can be generated as trading equilibria distorted by tariffs. Our treatment implicitly uses only feasible domestic price vectors.

The optimal domestic price vector discussed in the text is characterized using the model above. To simplify in order to focus on essentials, assume that all but the numéraire commodity are subject to tax. The optimal price (and hence the optimal tariff) vector is defined by $\bar{B}_\pi = 0 = B_\pi + B_{\pi^*} \cdot \pi_\pi^*$. See the appendix to chapter 3 for details.

Appendix B: Multicountry Trade Policy

The analysis of the text is considerably simplified by its focus on the trade policy of the home country only. With many countries having active trade policies, it is useful to allow for both unilateral and multilateral indexes of trade restrictiveness. Unilateral TRI and MTRI measures evaluate the restrictiveness of one country's policy while holding all other countries' policies fixed. Multilateral measures evaluate the trade restrictiveness of all countries' policies simultaneously. Each country's trade restrictions affect the restrictiveness of policy of each other country in this setting. Following description of both variants of the TRI, we analyze the MTRI.

Generalizing our setup to a trading world with an arbitrary number of countries, each with active trade policy, we start from an arbitrary set of tariffs for every country at an equilibrium denoted with superscript 0. Each country k distorts some traded goods prices $\pi^*(k)$. Prices distorted by other countries but not by k are denoted $\pi^*[\bar{k}(k)]$. We specify the tariff factor diagonal matrix of country k as $\underline{T}^{k0}$ in the initial equilibrium. We set the balance of trade for each country equal to zero for simplicity.

We first calculate the unilateral uniform tariff equivalent τ^{Δ^k} for country k. It is solved along with the world prices and the utilities of all countries other than k from

$$B^k[p^*, \pi^*(k)(1+\tau^{\Delta^k}), \pi^*[\bar{k}(k)], u^{k0}] = 0,$$

$$B^{k'}(p^*, \pi^*, \underline{T}^{0k'}, u^{k'}) = 0, \qquad \forall k' \neq k,$$

$$\sum_{k' \neq k} E_p^{k'}[p^*, \pi^*(k') \cdot \underline{T}^{0k'}, \pi^*[\bar{k}(k')], u^{k'}]$$

$$+ E_p^k[p^*, \pi^*(k)(1+\tau^{\Delta^k}), \pi^*[\bar{k}(k)], u^k] = 0, \tag{4}$$

$$\sum_{k' \neq k} E_\pi^{k'}[p^*, \pi^*(k') \cdot \underline{T}^{0k'}, \pi^*[\bar{k}(k')], u^{k'}]$$

$$+ E_\pi^k[p^*, \pi^*(k)(1+\tau^{\Delta^k}), \pi^*[\bar{k}(k)], u^k] = 0.$$

The calculation in (4) can be performed for each country k separately. It is the natural extension of our analysis of the two-country case, in which the foreign economy was assumed to be passive in its trade policy.[9]

---

9. The reduced form method of the two-country case is impossible for the multilateral case, so our analysis of the many country model is in terms of the regular balance-of-trade function.

The multilateral TRI is based on the uniform tariff vector, one element for each country, which maintains the reference utility of each country and satisfies the market-clearing conditions of the world economy. The uniform-tariff equivalent vector is calculated from simultaneous solution for $\{\tau^{\Delta^k}, p^*, \pi^*\}$ from the system

$$B^k[p^*, \pi^*(k)(1 + \tau^{\Delta^k}), \pi^*[\bar{k}(k)], u^{k0}] = 0 \qquad \forall k,$$

$$\sum_k E_p^k[p^*, \pi^*(k)(1 + \tau^{\Delta^k}), \pi^*[\bar{k}(k)], u^{k0}] = 0, \tag{5}$$

$$\sum_k E_\pi^k[p^*, \pi^*(k)(1 + \tau^{\Delta^k}), \pi^*[\bar{k}(k)], u^{k0}] = 0.$$

Here we assume that a set of uniform tariffs can achieve the same vector of utilities as the initial distorted equilibrium. The issues raised by its existence are similar to those already considered in the case of the unilateral TRI.

Notice that terms of trade effects link the measurement of the restrictiveness of trade policies across countries. Thus, moving to the hypothetical set of uniform-tariff equivalents induces shifts in real incomes that must be offset by further changes in the uniform-tariff equivalents. It is conceptually helpful to think of the analysis in stages—first calculate the TRI uniform-tariff for each country given the world prices from the first equation system in (5) and then calculate the change in world prices from the next two systems of equations in (5). Plug in the new world prices and recalculate the uniform tariff equivalents. Keep on repeating the sequence until convergence.

Description of the MTRI for many countries parallels the treatment of the TRI. It is straightforward to define a unilateral MTRI, as in the first subsection. We then set out the multilateral MTRI. This appears most likely to be useful as a background to trade negotiations, and for panel data investigations of implicit trade barriers using the gravity model (Anderson and Marcouiller 2002).

The unilateral MTRI is solved by finding the uniform-volume equivalent tariff of country k along with the real income levels $\{u^k\}$ and the world prices of distorted and undistorted goods (p^*, π^*) in

$$B^k[p^*, \pi^*(k)(1 + \tau^{\mu^k}), \pi^*[\bar{k}(k)], u^k] = 0,$$

$$B^{k'}(p^*, \pi^*(k'), \underline{T}^{0k'}, \pi^*[\bar{k}(k')], u^{k'}) = 0 \qquad \forall k' \neq k,$$

$$M^{c^k}[p^*, \pi^*(k)(1+\tau^{\mu^k}), \pi^*[\bar{k}(k)], u^k] = M^{0k},$$

$$E_p^k[p^*, \pi^*(k)(1+\tau^{\mu^k}), \pi^*[\bar{k}(k)], u^k] \qquad\qquad (6)$$

$$+ \sum_{k' \neq k} E_p^{k'}[p^*, \pi^*(k') \cdot \underline{T}^{0k'}, \pi^*[\bar{k}(k)], u^{k'}] = 0,$$

$$E_\pi^k[p^*, \pi^*(k)(1+\tau^{\mu^k}), \pi^*[\bar{k}(k)], u^k]$$

$$+ \sum_{k'} E_\pi^{k'}[p^*, \pi^*(k') \cdot \underline{T}^{0k'}, \pi^*[\bar{k}(k)], u^{k'}] = 0.$$

Existence of the unilateral MTRI is not a problem; the trade increasing implications of moving to uniformity can always be offset by a sufficiently high uniform tariff regardless of terms of trade movements. Uniqueness cannot be guaranteed. The trade volume function is defined with reference to initial world prices.[10]

The multilateral MTRI is the vector of uniform-volume equivalents that preserves each country's distorted trade volume. It is solved along with the vector of utilities from

$$B^k[p^*, \pi^*(k)(1+\tau^{\mu^k}), \pi^*[\bar{k}(k)], u^k] = 0 \qquad \forall k,$$

$$M^{c^k}[p^*, \pi^*(k)(1+\tau^{\mu^k}), \pi^*[\bar{k}(k)], u^k] = M^{0k} \qquad \forall k,$$

$$\sum_k E_p^k[p^*, \pi^*(k)(1+\tau^{\mu^k}), \pi^*[\bar{k}(k)], u^k] = 0, \qquad\qquad (7)$$

$$\sum_k E_\pi^k[p^*, \pi^*(k)(1+\tau^{\mu^k}), \pi^*[\bar{k}(k)], u^k] = 0.$$

The multilateral MTRI forces the analysis to deal with an important extra dimension of interdependence among the measures of trade restrictiveness. As with the TRI, interdependence travels through the changes in endogenous world prices to affect the volumes of distorted trade. In addition real income effects shift the volume of distorted trade. These shifts must be offset by further shifts in the uniform trade tax equivalents. For example, suppose that there are only import tariffs. The uniform tariff that is equivalent in volume for country i is affected by the movement in

10. Trade volume defined with reference to endogenous world prices does not appear to correspond to the Mercantilist concerns that motivate it.

world prices due to replacing initial tariffs with the uniform tariff equivalent for j, even though j does not distort the goods it sells to i.

A little more analysis suggests that the terms of trade movements induced by movement from the initial tariffs to the volume equivalent uniform tariff may often have modest effects on real income, at least when the distortions are sufficiently symmetric. Preserving the external price value of distorted trade for each country restricts the terms of trade effect to a channel that operates through the tariff revenue in each country. To see the argument, suppress the undistorted good with price p. Let $m(k)$, $m[\bar{k}(k)]$, $\pi^*(k)$, $\pi^*[\bar{k}(k)]$ denote the vectors of restricted and unrestricted trade of country k, together with their world price vectors. Let $\pi(k)$ denote the domestic price vector of distorted trade. Finally $m^0(k)$ is the amount of the numéraire good traded by country k. Totally differentiate the external budget constraint. This yields

$$[\pi(k) - \pi^*(k)] \cdot dm(k) = m(k) \cdot d\pi^*(k) + m[\bar{k}(k)] \cdot d\pi^*[\bar{k}(k)],$$

which means that the terms of trade effect is equal to the change in tariff revenue, subject to the constant volume constraint, which implies $\pi^*(k) \cdot dm(k) = 0$. Moreover the right hand side, summed across all countries in the world, is equal to zero due to market clearance; real income changes due to terms of trade changes average out to zero.

10 Aggregating Trade Restrictions in Modeling

Both econometric and simulation modeling inevitably confront the issue of the appropriate aggregation of sectoral trade barriers. Thousands of tariff lines must be aggregated into a computationally manageable number of imported goods. Each application has a purpose that ideally should frame its approach to aggregation. All appropriate indexes are members of a family defined using the general method of this book: a uniform-tariff equivalent is defined for a relevant set of trade barriers such that some relevant-to-the-purpose constraint is met, all in the setting of a relevant-to-the-purpose economic equilibrium model.

This chapter considers aggregation in four basic contexts: the estimation of demand and supply elasticities, general-equilibrium simulation modeling, the inference of unobservable trade costs, and inference of links between policy openness and economic growth. We relate ideal aggregates to the TRI and MTRI, and to atheoretic aggregates.

10.1 Demand Estimation

Appropriate aggregation in the context of demand and supply estimation is straightforward under a separability assumption. Since expenditure is a dependent variable, it is desirable to aggregate such that expenditure on the product group is preserved. The uniform tariff that preserves expenditure on the group of tariffed goods being aggregated is equal to the true average tariff for that group of goods, as defined in chapter 5.

Formally, the group to be aggregated is the set of goods with price vector π on the one hand while all other traded goods have price vector p on the other hand. The true average tariff index for the group is defined by $E(p^0, \pi^0, u^0) = E(p^0, \pi^*(1 + \tau^\delta), u^0)$. The true average tariff τ^δ is a function of p^0, π^0 and u^0 with such a complex structure that consistent aggregation does not really achieve simplification after all.

Consistent aggregation achieves simplicity if the trade expenditure function is implicitly separable with respect to the partition between the members of the group to be aggregated and all other goods: $E(p, \pi, u) = F[p, \eta(\pi, u), u]$. (See chapter 6 for extensive analysis of the implications of separability in general equilibrium structure.) Shephard's lemma implies that F_η is a natural aggregate quantity demanded, and $\eta(\pi, u)$ is its natural price index. Aggregation prior to estimation requires applying the properties of η to the data on $\pi - \pi^*$.

The subexpenditure function $\eta(\pi, u)$ for the goods to be aggregated has the standard properties in the price vector: it is homogeneous of degree one and concave in π. Consistent aggregation of the tariff vector $\pi^0 - \pi^*$ is based on preserving the expenditure on the group:

$$F_\eta \eta(\pi^0, u^0) = F_\eta \eta[\pi^*(1 + \tau^\delta), u^0]$$

$$\Rightarrow \tau^\delta = \frac{\eta(\pi^0, u^0)}{\eta(\pi^*, u^0)} - 1.$$

The second step follows from the homogeneity of degree one of η in π. Under the separability assumption the tariff aggregate defined in this way (1) preserves the aggregate trade expenditure, $E(p^0, \pi^0, u^0) = F(p^0, \eta[\pi^*(1 + \tau^\delta)], u^0)$, and (2) preserves the pattern of expenditure on each item, $F_p(p^0, \eta[\pi^*(1 + \tau^\delta)], u^0)$, and group expenditure, $F_\eta \eta[\pi^*(1 + \tau^\delta)]$.

Consistent aggregation of this type is entirely appropriate for econometric estimation of the demand system defined by E_p and E_η. Normally the econometrician is concerned with just the aggregate domestic price η. But in the trade context, where the domestic price of the import is often not directly observable, it is necessary to construct it from world prices, tariffs, exchange rates, transport margins, and the like. Theory and empirical practice suggest that different margins have different effects on the domestic price in the short run. Then for time-series estimation it is useful to have a series for the aggregate tariff in periods when it is changing, and similarly for other margins. Provided that the separability condition holds and the true η function is used, the aggregation in τ^δ is exact. Various approximations to the exact aggregator can be used, of which the standard trade weighted average tariff is one.

10.2   Simulation Models

Consistent aggregation as defined in τ^δ is in contrast not appropriate for use in general equilibrium simulation models. For example, Cox and

Harris (1984) have employed "consistent" aggregation in their CGE model. When the simulation analysis is focused on the welfare effects of trade policy changes, as is most frequently the case, the appropriate sectoral tariff aggregator is the sectoral TRI uniform tariff. When the analysis is concerned with sectoral trade volumes measured in terms of external prices, the appropriate aggregator is the sectoral MTRI uniform tariff. We have shown in chapter 5 that under the separability assumption which justifies consistent aggregation, the trade-weighted average tariff is less than the "consistent" aggregate tariff, which in turn is less than the MTRI sectoral uniform tariff which is less than the TRI uniform tariff.

The inconsistency of "consistent" aggregation is due to the general-equilibrium budget constraint. The tariff revenue implied by the uniform tariff τ^δ is not equal to the tariff revenue that would be collected with the actual tariff vector. The balance of trade function for the economy is written under separability as

$$B(p^0, \pi^0, u^0) = F[p^0, \eta(\pi^0, u^0), u^0] - F_p \cdot (p^0 - p^*) - F_\eta(\pi^0 - \pi^*) \cdot \eta_\pi.$$

In preserving the sectoral price index η when the tariff vector $\pi^0 - \pi^*$ is replaced with the uniform tariff $\tau^\delta \pi^*$, the values of η, F_η, and F_p are preserved in the preceding expression for the balance of trade. But $(\pi^0 - \pi^*) \cdot \eta_\pi(\pi^0, u^0)$ is not preserved.

The analyst has two natural choices for constructing an expression for the tariff revenue received from the aggregated category, both of which must give an overestimate of the actual revenue. The first choice for fixing the revenue is to calibrate the model using the actual external value of distorted imports in the aggregate category. Then the imputed tariff revenue using "consistent" aggregation will be taken as $F_\eta \tau^\delta \pi^* \cdot \eta_\pi(\pi^0, u^0)$. The actual tariff revenue from the category to be aggregated is $F_\eta(\pi^0 - \pi^*)\eta_\pi(\pi^0, u^0)$. The difference in the balance of trade due to the difference in tariff revenue is positively proportional to

$$\tau^\delta \pi^* \cdot \eta_\pi(\pi^0, u^0) - (\pi^0 - \pi^*) \cdot \eta_\pi(\pi^0, u^0).$$

Dividing both sides by $\pi^* \cdot \eta_\pi$, the difference in revenue is positively proportional to

$$\tau^\delta - \frac{\eta(\pi^0, u^0)}{\pi^* \cdot \eta_\pi(\pi^0, u^0)} = \eta(\pi^0, u^0) \left[\frac{1}{\eta(\pi^*, u^0)} - \frac{1}{\pi^* \cdot \eta_\pi(\pi^0, u^0)} \right] \geq 0.$$

The inequality follows from the properties of expenditure minimization.

The second natural choice for constructing tariff revenue from the aggregated category is to evaluate the distorted trade quantities using prices $\pi^*(1 + \tau_\pi^\delta)$. Then the imputed tariff revenue is equal to $F_\eta \tau^\delta \pi^* \cdot \eta_\pi[\pi^*(1 + \tau_\pi^\delta), u^0]$. In this case the difference in the balance of trade due to the difference in revenue is given by

$$B(p^0, \pi^0, u^0) - B[p^0, \pi^*(1 + \tau^\delta), u^0]$$

$$= F_\eta\{\tau^\delta \pi^* \cdot \eta_\pi[\pi^*(1 + \tau^\delta), u^0] - (\pi^0 - \pi^*) \cdot \eta_\pi(\pi^0, u^0)\}.$$

Using $\tau^\delta = \eta(\pi^0, u^0)/\eta(\pi^*, u^0) - 1$ and $\pi^0 \cdot \eta_\pi(\pi^0, u^0) = \eta(\pi^0, u^0)$, we have

$$B(p^0, \pi^0, u^0) - B[p^0, \pi^{0*}, (1 + \tau^\delta), u^0]$$

$$= F_\eta\{\pi^* \cdot \eta_\pi(\pi^0, u^0) - \eta(\pi^*, u^0)\} \geq 0.$$

The implication of either choice is that the "consistent" aggregate tariff index imputes too much revenue and thus too high a level of utility (given a positive shadow price of foreign exchange) to any given tariff vector. Put in the context of the standard trade liberalization experiment, removal of the tariff vector causes too low a gain in utility when the CGE model is based on "consistent" aggregation.

Aggregation that is consistent with the general equilibrium budget constraint can be defined with the (partial) TRI. Specifically, we define the consistent general-equilibrium tariff aggregator as

$$\tau^\Delta : B[p^0, \pi^*(1 + \tau^\Delta), u^0] = B(p^0, \pi^0, u^0).$$

Based on the preceding analysis, in the separable case we can guarantee $\tau^\Delta \geq \tau^\delta$. Formally,

Proposition 10.1 The consistent tariff aggregator for an implicitly separable group of imports τ^δ is less than or equal to the welfare equivalent uniform tariff aggregator for that group.

In general cases of substitutability, no such ranking is possible, as chapter 4 reveals.

Aggregation may sometimes be desired which is consistent with constant trade volume measured in external prices. The partial MTRI is appropriate for this purpose:

$$\tau^\mu : M[p^0, \pi^*(1 + \tau^\mu)] = M(p^0, \pi^0).$$

Evidently the "consistent" aggregator τ^δ will not generally be equal to the constant volume aggregator. What can be said about the difference?

The compensated MTRI and the consistent aggregator are equal under our separability assumption. The latter preserves group expenditure in domestic prices at constant real income. The compensated MTRI preserves group expenditure in foreign prices at constant real income, which turns out to be equivalent under separability. Group expenditure at domestic prices with the "consistent" aggregator is equal to $F_\eta(p^0, \eta^0, u^0)(1 + \tau^\delta)\eta(\pi^*, u^0)$. Group expenditure at external prices and constant real income under the "consistent" aggregator is equal to

$$F_\eta(p^0, \eta^0, u^0)\pi^* \cdot \eta_\pi[\pi^*(1 + \tau^\delta), u^0] = F_\eta \eta(\pi^*, u^0).$$

Replacing the differentiated initial tariff vector with the uniform tariff τ^δ that preserves expenditure at domestic prices thus preserves expenditure at external prices.

Turning to the income effects, we have from the discussion of the TRI in chapter 5 that $\tau^\Delta \geq \tau^\delta$. With a positive shadow price of foreign exchange, this implies that utility with uniform tariff τ_π^δ is higher than with the initial tariffs. By lemma 3, under our assumptions about the trade volume function $M(p, \pi, b)$, $M_u^c > 0$, so

$$M^c[p^0, \pi^*(1 + \tau^\delta), u^a] > M^c[p^0, \pi^*(1 + \tau^\delta), u^0] = M^0.$$

Therefore we can state

Proposition 10.2   The consistent tariff aggregator for an implicitly separable group of imports τ^δ is less than or equal to the volume equivalent uniform tariff, $\tau^\mu \geq \tau^\delta$ under our assumptions about the trade volume function.

The trade-weighted average sectoral tariff is always less than or equal to the consistent or true average sectoral tariff, as shown in chapter 4. So for sectoral aggregation based on implicit separability, under the added assumptions of normality and a composite elasticity of import demand greater than one, by propositions 5.1 and 5.2, we have a complete ranking of the natural tariff indexes:

$$\tau^\Delta \geq \tau^\mu \geq \tau^\delta \geq \tau^a.$$

The differences among the various indexes become large when substitution possibilities grow large, when income effects are important, and when tariff dispersion is important. The results of chapter 14 suggest that at least in the context of that chapter's simple general-equilibrium model, the assumptions of the ranking hold up almost always.

What advice can be given to policy analysis modelers based on this discussion? Avoid aggregation is the simplest answer—the only consistent aggregator must use all the detail of protection and the general-equilibrium model required by the disaggregated approach. But the information requirements of disaggregated modeling often make this impractical advice.

Aggregate smarter is a more useful answer. The error in consistent aggregation arises from the tariff revenue term. The revenue can be corrected as follows. Rewrite the balance-of-trade function with "consistent" aggregation as

$$B(p, \pi, u) = F[p, (1 + \tau^\delta)\eta(\pi^*, u), u] - (p - p^*) \cdot F_p(\cdot) - F_\eta(\cdot)(\pi - \pi^*) \cdot \eta_\pi$$

$$= F(\cdot) - (p - p^*) \cdot F_p(\cdot) - F_\eta(\cdot)\tau^\delta \eta(\pi^*, u)$$

$$- F_\eta(\cdot)[\eta(\pi^*, u) - \pi^* \cdot \eta_\pi(\pi, u)].$$

The last term on the third line is the error correction, which adjusts the imputed revenue $F_\eta \eta(\pi^*, u)\tau^\delta$ so that for any vector of tariffs $\pi - \pi^*$ the sum of the imputed term plus the correction term gives the correct revenue. The model builder can undertake some experimentation to establish a plausible error correction factor by using detailed tariff information, combined with plausible elasticity assumptions for CES subexpenditure functions nested inside the higher level CES structures typically used in applied general-equilibrium modeling. As this becomes common practice in applied modeling, and error correction factors appear not to differ much across different tariff structures or economic structures, it may be plausible to draw on error correction factors produced by others. It is possible, though not likely, that the error corrections uncovered by experimentation will be quite small. The results of chapter 14 show that in economywide tariff aggregation, $\tau^\Delta > \tau^\mu > \tau^a$ generally, with the first inequality quantitatively quite significant.

Apart from the error correction, the elements of the balance-of-trade function are analyzed just as if the consistent aggregation were exact. Thus the rest of the structure of the CGE model can use the consistent aggregate tariff while the error correction is applied to calculate the tariff revenue. The error correction is feasible because it uses only the information assumed to be available for consistent aggregation in the first place.

10.3   Inference of Trade Costs

Recent interest in implicit trade costs has been generated by the importance of trade costs to economic geography and to macroeconomics.

The basic idea is to infer trade costs from trade volume, controlling statistically for all factors that increase or decrease the volume of trade independently of implicit trade costs. The trade costs themselves are assumed to be a reduced form function of observables suggested by various theories. Estimated models can also be used for simulation.

This literature is based on the gravity model. There are two distinct aggregation issues that arise in this research: aggregation across trading partners and aggregation across distinct commodity groups. As to aggregation over partners, it seems obvious from general equilibrium considerations that trade flows between any pair of partners will be affected by trade costs between partners and third parties or even between parties not directly involved in the bilateral trade. How is this to be feasibly aggregated? As to aggregation over distinct commodities, the advantages and disadvantages of aggregation are essentially the same as in the two preceding sections, but the analysis in the specific context of gravity is quite useful.

Our overall approach to construction of ideal index numbers provides the appropriate aggregators and some insight into the approximation error and estimation bias that may arise with typical procedures. We restrict attention in the text to the structural gravity model implied by CES structure because of the importance of this form in empirical work done on trade cost inference. The appendix treats gravity more generally.

The gravity model is theoretically derived in a general-equilibrium exchange setting by Anderson (1979). It is extended by Anderson and van Wincoop (2003, 2004) to a setting in which the allocation of production and expenditure is assumed to occur separably from the allocation of trade across countries conditional on the production and expenditure allocations. For a given product line, each trading partner is assumed to produce a distinct variety, priced differently in various destinations due to varying bilateral trade costs. CES preferences over varieties provide the structure of demand (final or intermediate) while the structure of trade costs is an ad hoc loglinear function of directly measurable costs and implicit costs as a function of bilateral distance and other plausible exogenous variables.

Higher bilateral trade costs from origin i to destination j reduce trade, but the volume of trade obviously also depends on the price of alternatives to i available at j and on the alternative benefits at other destinations to the sellers at i. In Anderson and van Wincoop (2003), the multilateral resistance index (one each for inward and outward trade) is proposed as the appropriate aggregator of the price of alternatives. In Anderson and van Wincoop (2004), the multilateral resistance index is shown to be the ideal index in the sense of this book, a simultaneously solved vector of uniform trade costs across partners which preserves the initial value of aggregate trade (so that markets clear at original prices). We expand on the argument below and relate multilateral resistance to the MTRI.

The second aggregation issue arises because when estimating the gravity model, thousands of individual tariff and import lines are inevitably aggregated, quite often to a single aggregate import from each trading partner. The individual commodity level bilateral tariffs must be aggregated with a tariff index. Where tariff indexes are used in the gravity literature, the trade-weighted average tariff is the typical index (see Anderson and Marcouiller 2002 for an example where the bilateral tariff is removed with membership in a regional trade agreement). Sometimes a production-weighted average tariff is used. Harrigan (1993) uses bilateral trade (and alternatively production) weights to control for differential composition of imports across trading partners within a given product line. The ideal index is a uniform tariff across the product lines being aggregated. We set out the appropriate analysis below and draw some bias inferences in special cases.

Aggregation over Trading Partners

It is very natural to define trade cost indexes that aggregate over trading partners for a given commodity class. For example, in the context of the key questions of location theory and regional economics we might wish to know by how much, on average, are shipments from one region to all destinations disadvantaged relative to shipments to all destinations from other regions. Alternatively, in the inward direction, we might wish to know by how much are shipments to one destination from all origins disadvantaged relative to shipments to other destinations from all origins. An ideal index for this purpose is multilateral resistance, defined below. Another important issue in the context of trade negotiations is to compare by how much, in each region, are shipments to the region from other regions impeded relative to shipments from within the region. An ideal index for this purpose is the uniform border barrier, defined below.

Multilateral Resistance
Applying the methods of this book to the present context, the natural reference point for the construction of trade cost aggregates is the requirement that the initial equilibrium total value of shipments be preserved. This constraint preserves the set of initial supply prices and thus is consis-

tent with the conditioning production and expenditure allocations of the initial equilibrium. Trade cost aggregates in this context must be defined simultaneously, as with the many country versions of the MTRI and TRI analyzed in chapter 8.

Consistent aggregation gains real simplification under the assumption of *trade separability* the allocation of production and expenditure across commodity lines occurs separably (at a different budgeting stage) from the allocation of trade across origins or destinations given the allocations of production and expenditure. Assuming something like separability is close to an empirical necessity. As Paul Armington long ago emphasized, models of trade with homogeneous goods predict far too much specialization to be empirically relevant. The obvious solution is to assume products which differ by place of origin within a class of goods. It is natural to suppose that products within a class are better substitutes for each other than for other goods. Introducing the extra dimensionality of products differing by place of origin is sufficiently burdensome that further simplification is close to inevitable. The assumption of separability satisfies both objectives.

The gravity model is a special case of trade separable general-equilibrium models. In a particular commodity line k (e.g., clothing), each country is assumed to produce a unique variety. All varieties are demanded by users according to a CES preference (for final goods) or technology (for intermediate goods) system that is common to all countries. The allocation of expenditure across product lines and the allocation of resources to production of national varieties in each product line are taken as given for the analysis of conditional general equilibrium. The full general equilibrium, of course, requires prices that clear world markets in the conditional analysis to coincide with the prices that support the allocation of expenditure and production within each trading country. It is important to emphasize here that gravity need make no particular assumption about the nature of the upper level general-equilibrium allocation mechanism. Earlier expositions of gravity theory made very restrictive assumptions that are unnecessary. The appendix shows that the basic logic of gravity extends to a much more general class of preferences over traded goods.

Trade costs (represented as factors $T_{ij}^k = 1 + \tau_{ij}^k$ on trade from i to j in product line k) augment factory gate prices p_i^k to yield domestic prices $p_{ij}^k = p_i^k T_{ij}^k$. This setup excludes the dependence of costs on trade volume. The objective of gravity analysis is first of all to measure trade costs that are not directly observable based on attributes which are observable, such as tariffs, transport costs, distance, common language, and common borders. Underlying this is some implicit reduced form in which the observable attributes are related to the costs and assumed to be exogenous to trade flows.

The CES subexpenditure function for product line k is $e_j^k = P_j^k u^{jk}$ where the CES price index is $P_j^k = [\sum_i (p_i^k \beta_i^k)^{1-\sigma_k} (T_{ij}^k)^{1-\sigma_k}]^{1/(1-\sigma_k)}$ and the subutility indicator is u^{jk}. Also σ_k is the elasticity of substitution parameter between varieties in product line k, while β_i^k is a distribution parameter. The expenditure by country j on line k from country i is given by

$$x_{ij}^k = \left(\frac{\beta_i^k p_i^k T_{ij}^k}{P_j^k}\right)^{1-\sigma_k}.$$

General equilibrium requires market clearance. Let the nominal landed value of shipments (inclusive of payments which cover trade costs) from origin i in line k be given by y_i^k. Then

$$y_i^k = \sum_j x_{ij}^k = (\beta_i^k p_i^k)^{1-\sigma_k} \sum_j \left(\frac{T_{ij}^k}{P_j^k}\right)^{1-\sigma_k} e_j^k.$$

The gravity model of trade flows follows by solving the market clearance equations for $(\beta_i^k p_i^k)^{1-\sigma_k}$ and substituting into the expenditure expression. Let world receipts for good k from country i, equal to expenditure, be denoted Y^k. Then the gravity model is

$$x_{ij}^k = \frac{y_i^k e_j^k}{Y^k} \left(\frac{T_{ij}^k}{P_j^k \Pi_i^k}\right)^{1-\sigma_k},$$

$$(P_j^k)^{1-\sigma_k} = \sum_i \left(\frac{T_{ij}^k}{\Pi_i^k}\right)^{1-\sigma_k} \left(\frac{y_i^k}{Y^k}\right),$$

$$(\Pi_i^k)^{1-\sigma_k} = \sum_j \left(\frac{T_{ij}^k}{P_j^k}\right)^{1-\sigma_k} \left(\frac{e_j^k}{Y^k}\right).$$

The CES price index definition and the market clearance equations implicitly determine the import P_j^k and export Π_i^k price indexes in the simultaneous equation system. The additional assumptions of symmetry in trade costs and a single good economy so that $e_j^k = y_j^k$ yields $P_i^k = \Pi_i^k$. Anderson and van Wincoop (2003) dub the solution price index "multilateral resistance." With asymmetry or with e not necessarily equal to y, we interpret P_j^k as the inward multilateral resistance that users in country

j face on average on shipments from all sources, while Π_j^k is the outward multilateral resistance that sellers face on shipments to all destinations.

The gravity model of trade flows implies that bilateral trade is a function of the bilateral resistance relative to the product of inward and outward multilateral resistance. Trade is decreasing in relative resistance with elasticity $\sigma_k > 1$, a condition met in all empirical estimates (see Anderson and van Wincoop 2004). It is intuitive that bilateral resistance should be assessed relative to both inward resistance to imports at j from all sources, P_j, and to outward resistance to shipments from i to all destinations, Π_i.

Multilateral resistance obviously aggregates trade costs facing buyer j and seller i while embedding costs over the trade other than that between i and j. But multilateral resistance has a much more elegant and remarkable property—it is an ideal aggregate in the sense of this book. The reference point is the initial full general-equilibrium volume of trade. Suppose that the differentiated matrix of trade costs $\{T_{ij}^k\}$ is replaced by a set of uniform trade costs (including trade within a country), $\{T_j^k\}$ for inward trade and $\{X_i^k\}$ for outward trade, such that the market for each variety continued to clear (aggregate expenditure continued to equal the original value of receipts) and the original factory gate price continued to hold. The set of ideal price indexes in this sense are the multilateral resistance indexes: $T_j^k = P_j^k$, $X_i^k = \Pi_i^k$. The proof is simple. Under the uniform-trade–cost-equivalent vectors of trade costs, $T_{ij}^k = T_j^k X_i^k$ and $x_{ij}^k = y_i^k e_j^k / Y^k$; hence the value of aggregate demand is equal to y_i^k as required. The individual bilateral trades are different in this hypothetical equilibrium, $\tilde{x}_{ij}^k = y_i^k e_j^k / Y^k$, but their sum is the same.

The hypothetical equilibrium is a very natural reference point because it is equivalent to a frictionless equilibrium in which the endowments of each origin are reduced to resistance-equivalent levels y_i^k / Π_i^k, the expenditures at each destination are reduced to resistance-equivalent levels e_j^k / P_j^k, and the frictionless equivalent bilateral trade is given by $\tilde{x}_{ij}^k / (\Pi_i^k P_j^k) = (y_i^k / \Pi_i^k)(e_j^k / P_j^k)(1/Y)$.

A qualification to this interpretation of multilateral resistance must be entered when the trade costs include taxes or quota premia (or other sources of rent such as monopoly power). In this case, the shift to a hypothetical equilibrium will shift the total rent in each location j. If the rent is returned to the expenditure stream it will shift the conditioning pattern of expenditures. Our interpretation of the hypothetical equilibrium associated with multilateral resistance rules this shift out, so it is a rent-constant hypothetical equilibrium.

Multilateral resistance (MR) is a uniform-volume-equivalent tax factor where the volume in question is measured at domestic prices. It differs from the MTRI in its definition of volume by including internal trade and also by using domestic prices rather than external prices. Moreover, being based on a conditional general-equilibrium structure, MR suppresses the potential income effect as changes in revenues from tariffs and quotas due to the shift to the hypothetical uniform barriers would shift the expenditure in various regions. In this it is like the compensated MTRI. We emphasize again that the MR indexes are multilaterally solved, simultaneously indexing the trade costs of all countries. Every bilateral trade cost affects every multilateral resistance index so that P_j^k depends on trade costs not directly involving j. In this property, MR resembles our treatment of the multilateral MTRI in chapter 8.

Multilateral resistance is also interpreted as a general equilibrium multilateral analogue to what we have called the True Average Tariff (only in this case including trade costs on internal shipments). In this context it is useful to provide a ranking:

Proposition 10.3   The trade-weighted average trade cost on all shipments is less than or equal to the multilateral resistance index.

The ranking is due to the substitution effect. The proof is simple. The multilateral resistance index is formed by hypothetically replacing all the existing trade costs with uniform trade costs, one for each country's imports and another for its exports. The supply (factory gate) prices do not change and are conveniently normalized to one. Then multilateral resistance is given by $P(p_j^k) = (1 + \tau_j^k)P(\iota) = 1 + \tau_j^k$. The trade-weighted average trade cost is given by $P(p_j^k)/P_p(p_j^k) \cdot \iota - 1 \leq \tau_j^k$ where the inequality follows from the expenditure-minimizing property of P.

Anderson and van Wincoop (2003) argued that the older gravity model literature was subject to omitted variable bias in the estimation of implicit trade costs. That literature failed to allow for the effect of multilateral resistance in the trade flow regression equation. Thus the error term of the stochastic version of the trade flow equation must be correlated with the variables that proxy trade costs. Appropriate aggregation thus allows consistent estimation. Anderson and van Wincoop use a full information approach that imposes the market clearance and price index definition equations simultaneously with estimation. A computationally simpler approach to estimation (of the trade cost function parameters) is to control for the multilateral resistance terms with fixed effects, as Feenstra (2003) notes. But fixed effects estimation does not provide the value of the multilateral resistance indexes, which we argue here are very useful as a summary of trade costs across all trading partners. Analysts intending to compute MR might wish to use the full information approach.[1]

In comparative static experiments, the changes in the multilateral resistance terms are crucial. Anderson and van Wincoop show that the famous border puzzle posed by McCallum (1995) is solved by analyzing the implications of multilateral resistance. McCallum ran a gravity regression for aggregate trade flows over US states and Canadian provinces that included in the trade cost function a dummy variable for trade among Canadian provinces. The implication of his estimated coefficient was that trade between Canadian provinces was, all else equal, a factor 22 times trade between Canadian provinces and US states. The appropriate comparative static experiment (based on an assumed endowment model with one good in each region) incorporates the property that the removal of the border, besides lowering bilateral resistance between formerly separated regions, lowers multilateral resistance in Canada by far more than in the United States. The upshot of a proper general equilibrium comparative static experiment is that the border effect lowers international trade by 40 percent—still substantial but no longer wildly implausible.

Uniform Border Barrier

A second concept developed by Anderson and van Wincoop is also very useful in the context of structural gravity: the uniform border barrier. Replace the costs on all trade that crosses borders (i.e., excluding internal trade) with a border barrier for each country that is uniform across its trading partners subject to a constant value of the domestic value of international trade. The uniform border barrier, like MR, maintains the initial equilibrium demand and hence the initial world prices. It is a bit closer to the MTRI in being focused on international trade but it uses domestic as opposed to world prices to form the volume constraint. Like MR, it is a conditional general equilibrium concept that therefore does not account for the effect on expenditure of changes in tariff revenue in going to the hypothetical uniform barrier. Thus the uniform border barrier is a compensated MTRI concept with trade volume defined on the domestic price

---

1. It is possible to calculate MR based on the results of fixed effects regressions. Just combine parameter estimates from fixed effects regressions with the constraints of market clearance and the price index definitions. The additional software needed to calculate MR is a substantial part of that needed for the full information estimation, so the latter approach is preferable.

base. In the context of evaluating total trade costs, of which trade policy is a small part, abstraction from redistribution of tariff revenue and quota rent is a perhaps justifiable simplifying assumption.

The uniform border barrier is defined by replacing the differentiated trade costs with uniform barriers such that the domestic price value of trade remains constant. The conditional general equilibrium of gravity potentially implies a new set of MR's, denoted with a tilde ($\sim$). However, the preservation of domestic value of trade along with the conditional general equilibrium implies that the value of domestic shipments is constant, implying that MR's do not change:

$$\left(\frac{T_{jj}^k}{P_j^k \Pi_j^k}\right)^{1-\sigma} \frac{e_j^k y_j^k}{Y^k} = \left(\frac{T_{jj}^k}{\tilde{P}_j^k \tilde{\Pi}_j^k}\right)^{1-\sigma} \frac{e_j y_j}{Y}.$$

Using the preceding result and the CES price index definition, we can solve for the uniform border barriers in each importing country:

$$v_j^k = \left[\sum_{i \neq j} (T_{ij}^k)^{1-\sigma_k} \omega_{ij}^k\right]^{1/(1-\sigma_k)},$$

where

$$\omega_{ij}^k \equiv \frac{(\Pi_i^k)^{\sigma_k-1} y_i^k / Y}{\sum_{i \neq j} (\Pi_i^k)^{\sigma_k-1} y_i^k / Y}.$$

It remains to rank the uniform border barrier relative to the trade weighted average tariff. We show that:

Proposition 10.4   The uniform border barrier exceeds the trade weighted average trade cost.

Our development abstracts from nonborder costs such as transport (which naturally does vary by trading partner); the extension to calculation of uniform border barriers in their presence is straightforward.

The proof is quite simple in contrast to the ranking proofs of chapter 5, because the uniform border barrier, like the MR index, is defined in terms of the domestic value of shipments. There is thus no need for elasticity conditions and the ranking follows from the minimum value property of expenditure functions. A potential complication is with cross-effects among goods traded across borders and those shipped internally, which required an added separability assumption in the ranking proposition of chapter 5. The cross-effect is eliminated in the gravity model because the CES form is *strongly separable*, no additional assumption is required.

The CES form thus implies (due to its strongly separable structure) that total expenditure, on border crossing goods plus domestic shipments, is the same with the uniform border barrier as with the initial differentiated trade cost vector. Let the CES cost or price index function be denoted $c(T, 1)$, where the 1 argument stands for domestic shipments with internal costs normalized at unity for simplicity and T is the vector of trade cost factors. Formally, $c(v, 1) = c(T, 1)$. By definition of the trade-weighted average trade cost (adapting the notation for the trade-weighted average tariff),

$$c_i[\iota(1 + \tau^a), 1] \cdot \iota(1 + \tau^a) + c_1(T, 1) \cdot 1 = c(T, 1)$$

$$= c(v, 1) \quad \text{as shown}$$

$$\geq c_i[\iota(1 + \tau^a), 1] \cdot \iota(1 + \tau^a)$$

$$+ c_1[\iota(1 + \tau^a), 1] \cdot 1$$

by the minimum value property. Therefore the trade weighted average trade cost is lower than the uniform border barrier, due to the operation of the substitution effect.

Aggregating over Products

Aggregation over products is inevitable. Convenience and ease of interpretation often dictate an aggregate approach, but even the most determined insistence on detailed estimation can never come close to the granularity of nature. This leads to the question of appropriate aggregation and the bias due to standard practices such as trade-weighted aggregation of trade costs.

There are actually two separate problems of aggregation: the ideal aggregate when the economic structure of trade costs and elasticities is known, and the problem of the appropriate procedure to use on aggregate data in the estimation of the parameters of gravity equations. In either case we analyze bias from inappropriate procedures.

Ideal Indexes

In terms of the gravity model setup above, summing over k yields an aggregate bilateral trade flow vector that is to be modeled with an aggregate trade cost to replace the complex sum that results from mechanically summing both sides of the gravity system over k. Anderson and van Wincoop (2004) offer some insight into a complex problem based on simplification to two symmetric countries.

Let there be two equally sized countries and N sectors. Each country produces half the world's output. Each country spends θ_k of its income on the output of sector k (due to Cobb-Douglas preferences over goods classes). The value share of sector k in the world economy is thus equal to θ_k in equilibrium. The only trade cost is a border barrier v_k that differs by sector k. The price index and market-clearing equations for each sector imply a convenient closed form solution $P^k = \Pi^k = (0.5 + 0.5 v_k^{1-\sigma_k})^{1/2(1-\sigma_k)}$. Then the uniform trade cost that leads to the same value of aggregate trade can be solved from

$$\sum_k \theta_k \frac{v_k^{1-\sigma_k}}{1 - v_k^{1-\sigma_k}} = \sum_k \theta_k \frac{v^{1-\sigma_k}}{1 - v^{1-\sigma_k}}.$$

The properties of the ideal index relative to a natural production-weighted average can be established by analyzing the preceding simple equation. Starting from a benchmark where the border barriers are all equal and the elasticities are all equal, we introduce variation in the barriers and in the elasticities such that the industry size weighted averages remain constant, $\bar{v} = \sum_k \theta_k v_k$ and $\bar{\sigma} = \sum_k \theta_k \sigma_k$ are maintained. First, note that the function $U(v, \sigma) \equiv v^{1-\sigma}/(1 - v^{1-\sigma})$ is decreasing and convex in v. Then Jensen's inequality implies that for a mean-preserving spread in the distribution of the $\{v_k\}$, $v < \bar{v}$. Second, variation in σ for uniform v has no effect. So, third, consider covariation in v and σ. We consider marginal variation holding constant $\lambda = \text{var}(\sigma)/\text{var}(v)$. We can use a second order Taylor's series expansion to show that

$$\frac{\partial v}{\partial \, \text{var}(v)} = -\alpha_1 + \alpha_2 \lambda \, \text{corr}(v, \sigma), \qquad \alpha_1, \alpha_2 > 0.$$

Anderson and van Wincoop cite evidence that negative correlation of v and σ is realistic. This reinforces the implication that the uniform v is less than the size-weighted average $\bar{v}$.

The trade-weighted average trade cost, in contrast, cannot be clearly ranked relative to the uniform v. It will be less than the production-weighted average trade cost, due to the substitution effect.[2]

Estimation Bias

The simple two country example also illuminates aggregation bias in estimation. Although there are N sectors with differing border barriers,

---

2. The trade-weighted average trade cost is given by $\sum_k \theta_k v_k (v_k^{-\sigma_k} P_k^{\sigma_k - 1})/\sum_k \theta_k (v_k^{-\sigma_k} P_k^{\sigma_k - 1})$. Compared to the production-weighted average trade cost, lower weights are associated with higher trade costs.

the aggregate estimation pretends there is only one border barrier and one elasticity. The aggregate equation is written

$$\ln(x_{ij}) = \alpha_i + \alpha_j + (\sigma - 1) \ln(v) \delta_{ij},$$

where α_i, α_j are country-specific constants that depend on the multilateral resistance indexes and δ_{ij} is the Kronecker delta.

The parameters of the two country symmetric example are exactly identified with OLS estimation. Thus

$$\hat{v}^{1-\sigma} = \frac{x_{12}}{x_{11}^{0.5} x_{22}^{0.5}}.$$

Substitution of the theoretical expressions for x_{12}, x_{11}, x_{22} into the preceding expression yields

$$\frac{\hat{v}^{1-\sigma}}{1 + \hat{v}^{1-\sigma}} = \sum_k \theta_k \frac{v_k^{1-\sigma_k}}{1 + v_k^{1-\sigma_k}}.$$

It follows that the estimate $\hat{v}$ based on the aggregate gravity equation is equal to the ideal index when all the price elasticities are equal and we set σ at the correct level. When (realistically) the price elasticities differ across sectors, we should choose σ below the average in order for the estimate $\hat{v}$ to be equal to the ideal index v. If we choose σ to be equal to its average, then the inference of $\hat{v}$ will be lower than the ideal uniform barrier v.

10.4 Openness and Growth Regressions

The plausible hypothesis that openness fosters economic growth has been the intellectual basis in the 1980s and 1990s for one of the greatest policy shifts in history—the adoption of liberal trade by the developing and formerly communist countries. Yet the main evidence for the hypothesis is casual, such as the success of a number of East Asian economies with apparently outward orientations in economic policy. Attempts to do more serious empirical work have had to make do with what all practitioners agree are inadequate measures of trade policy (Edwards 1992). We argue below that the TRI is the natural index for such studies and contrast the TRI with the alternatives which have been proposed or used in the literature.

Much recent empirical work has looked at regressions of growth rates on a set of right-hand side variables that include openness. The basic structure behind empirical investigations of openness and growth is given by Barro and Sala-i-Martin (1995; see also Lee 1993 and Edwards 1993). Their analysis is based on local perturbations about a steady state growth path in a neoclassical growth model. The observations of the regression are countries in a cross section for the time period. Theory shows that initial GDP matters, as do savings rates and the parameters of the production function. Then a list of other variables which might affect the process are tried as right-hand side variables in a series of regressions. Some attempts are made to control for the possible endogeneity of suspicious right-hand side variables. The initial level of openness and the rate of change of openness are both potentially interesting in this exploration. We take as given the state of the theory, such as it is, and ask how to sensibly measure openness in this context by embedding its consideration in our model.

Formally, the general-equilibrium model of the open economy at each point in time satisfies the balance-of-trade equilibrium condition:

$$B(\pi^t, u^t, \gamma^t) - b^t = 0.$$

Provided intertemporal separability holds, the argument list of $B(.)$ includes only variables at time t. The vector γ^t includes a list of factor endowments as well as technology parameters, while b^t denotes external borrowing or lending at time t. This static model can be embedded in intertemporal optimizing behavior by determining the level of borrowing (which now includes both domestic and external borrowing) as a function of the entire sequence of anticipated exogenous variables. At the steady state, borrowing is equal to zero and the steady state real income level is a function of the tariff structure, the terms of trade, the steady state levels of various types of capital and the other exogenous variables. The investigator does not observe any steady state variable but assumes that the initial conditions represent small deviations from the steady state. Then growth theory implies that the growth rate over some interval following the initial period depends on the initial income and the arguments that determine steady state real income. These include the tariff structure.

The trade policy openness measure must for practical degrees of freedom reasons be a scalar index, or at most a few indexes for each country at each point in time. In the absence of a complete theory of how openness affects growth, it is impossible to specify a complete theory of aggregation of trade policy as a justification for any one index number. However, in replacing a vector of trade policies with a single index number in this context it seems desirable that the index be consistent with the same real income as the vector it replaces. The TRI uniform tariff uniquely fits the requirement. Using the TRI uniform tariff as an exogenous variable in a regression that attempts to explain real income or its growth can pick up the influence of trade policy on income without introducing a spurious relationship that reflects aggregation bias. This would not be true of any other tariff index, such as, for example, the trade-weighted average tariff.

We conclude with a survey of alternative measures used in the growth literature from the perspective of the TRI. Alternative measures of trade policy may be divided into direct and indirect measures.

Direct Measures

Direct measures of policy all aggregate the primary data, tariffs, and non-tariff barriers. A commonly used measure of tariff policy is the trade-weighted average tariff t^a. Sometimes analysts also report the arithmetic average tariff. No one believes either one is a good measure, but trade-weighted tariff averages are readily available because they can be calculated without line item data as the ratio of tariff revenue to the world price value of imports.

Other tariff measures focus on dispersion, on the hypothesis that dispersion is welfare-reducing, ceteris paribus. The coefficient of variation of tariffs can be calculated, as with the average tariff, with either trade weights or arithmetic weights. Other measures of tariff dispersion, such as the maximum tariff and the percentage of dutiable items in the total import list are sometimes reported. Calculating these indexes faces the difficulty of obtaining line item detail on tariffs. (See Anderson and van Wincoop 2004 for a report on the paucity of coverage of even the most comprehensive database on commodity line tariffs.)

Nontariff measures present much greater difficulties for the analyst, even before aggregation. Some quantitative restrictions are accompanied by license markets that provide data on the "tariff equivalent" of the quota. Some other cases permit the analyst to make international price comparisons that can be used to construct tariff equivalents. In most cases the best the analyst can expect is a simple indication of whether or not there is a nontariff barrier present. Based on the latter the most commonly used aggregate is the percentage of items in the import list which are covered by nontariff barriers, the NTB coverage ratio.

Faced with the plethora of tariff and nontariff indexes, some analysts have constructed subjective indexes of trade policy (Papageorgiu et al. 1991) that include the average tariff, the coefficient of variation of tariffs, the NTB coverage ratio, and other more purely subjective elements as inputs to the various atheoretic indexes.

These indexes, separately or in combination, have been used in some of the openness and growth regression literature. Based on the theory of this book, we believe our index offers a much better way to evaluate trade policy in the context of examining openness and growth. Based on the empirical work discussed in part III, we are confident it will give fundamentally different empirical results because our TRI estimates differ from all the standard indexes, often very dramatically. The chief difficulty is the paucity of commodity line detail on tariff and nontariff barriers, but this is a difficulty faced by all work in the area.

Indirect Measures

Faced with the inadequacies of existing data, especially with respect to nontariff barriers, some analysts have tried to get at policy openness indirectly. The most obvious idea is to take the share of trade in national income as an indicator of trade policy. This approach immediately is confounded by the problem that some countries are more naturally open than others. The next step is to attempt to control for the natural openness of countries so that trade policy is inferred by the deviation of the actual trade pattern from that predicted for a country with the same situation in terms of endowments. Lawrence (1987), Leamer (1988a, b, 1990) are early examples while a recent example is Harrigan (1996).

In any of these examples the results are very sensitive to the assumed structure of the model being estimated. If we were confident in the model, this sensitivity would perhaps not be a problem, but our confidence is justifiably low. In the cited papers the model is usually a form of the Heckscher-Ohlin-Vanek (HOV) model. Recent work of Trefler (1995) indicates that while some form of the HOV model may fit the data well, it is not the simple one used in these studies. Moreover Trefler's work still leaves a number of important puzzles unexplained and gives an important perspective on the magnitude of the ignorance we have. Gravity models are also sometimes used to infer trade barriers (e.g., Harrigan 1996). Anderson and van Wincoop (2003b) argue that there can be little confidence in such estimates.

In the context of concern with trade policy evaluation, it is also extremely important to note that the regression approach is always very highly aggregated, while with trade distortions the details are very important—protection dispersion at very fine levels of disaggregation is significant in both tariffs and tariff equivalents. Thus aggregation tends to wash out the most important examples of distortion.

If believable versions of the indirect approach eventually appear, they could be used in conjunction with our methods. Essentially the indirect method implies a vector of industry specific "free-trade" quantities, m^*. The current trade vector m^0 is observable. An index of openness must aggregate these vectors. The TRI or its quantity version, the CTU give a consistent method of aggregating the quantity vectors such that real income equivalence is maintained. (It requires some additional information and simplifying assumptions, as illustrated by the applications in part III.) Other aggregation methods will not be consistent with the purpose of an analysis that should preserve real income.

In contrast, the quantity version of the MTRI can be calculated directly as $\pi^{*\prime}m^0/\pi^{*\prime}m^*$, assuming that free-trade imports are known (which essentially requires all the information of a general equilibrium model). This is Leamer's (1990) procedure. The price version of the MTRI requires the same sort of additional information and simplifying assumptions as does the TRI.

Appendix: Multilateral Resistance in the Generalized Gravity Model

Multilateral resistance indexes are defined here for the class of homothetic preferences over the relevant varieties. This setup yields a generalized gravity model. The validity and usefulness of multilateral resistance in this more general context gives further insight into its properties.

Consider conditional general equilibrium in a particular goods class (to suppress notational clutter, we omit indication of the index of goods class). All countries or regions share a common subexpenditure or subcost function for the representative goods. For simplicity we impose homotheticity: $e(p, u) = e(p)u$. The expenditure share on goods from origin i at destination j is given by

$$s_i\left(\frac{p_1 t_{1j}}{P_j}, \ldots, \frac{p_n t_{nj}}{P_j}\right) = \frac{p_i t_{ij} e_i(p^j)}{e(p^j)},$$

$$P_j \equiv e(p^j), \quad p^j \equiv \{p_1 t_{1j}, \ldots, p_n t_{nj}\}.$$

The share function is obtained using Shephard's lemma and the homogeneity of degree zero of demand systems. It can be shown that the assumption of homotheticity is an irrelevant simplification, since maintaining the conditional equilibrium prices allows the hypothetical equilibrium to support the initial subutilities, nullifying the nonneutral income effects that might otherwise operate.

Market clearance for each good implies that

$$y_i = \sum_j s_i \left(\frac{p_1 t_{1j}}{P_j}, \ldots, \frac{p_n t_{nj}}{P_j} \right) e_j \qquad \forall i.$$

The initial equilibrium is solved for $\{p_i\}$ conditional on the exogenous variables $\{Y_i, E_i, t_{ij}\}$, with the solution obtained from market clearance using the price indexes $\{P_j\} = \{e(p^j)\}$.

For the purpose of anatomizing the structure of trade costs, it is convenient to treat $\{P_j\}$ as an endogenous variable in the market clearance equations, with the extra structure needed to solve for equilibrium provided by the budget constraints for each country. The budget constraint for each location implies that

$$1 = \sum_i s_i \left(\frac{p_1 t_{1j}}{P_j}, \ldots, \frac{p_n t_{nj}}{P_j} \right) \qquad \forall j.$$

Now consider the implications of replacing the actual set of trade costs of dimension n^2 with a hypothetical set of bilateral trade costs $\tilde{t}_{ij} = \Pi_i P_j$ of dimension $2n$, constructed to satisfy the market clearance constraints and the budget constraints at the initial supply prices. The inward portion of each bilateral trade cost is equal to P, which is already given from the initial equilibrium. The outward portion of each bilateral trade cost $\{\Pi_i\}$ is calculated from

$$y_i = \sum_j s_i (p_1 \Pi_1, \ldots, p_n \Pi_n) e_j = s_i(\bullet) y, \qquad \forall i.$$

On the right-hand side of the equation, $p_i \tilde{t}_{ij}/P_j = p_i \Pi_i$ is used to evaluate the shares at the hypothetical trade cost structure. Solving this system yields a unique vector of outward trade cost indexes $\{\Pi_i\}$ as a function of the endowments $\{z_i\}$ and the equilibrium supply prices. It is convenient to choose units such that the equilibrium supply prices are all equal to unity. Then multilateral resistance is solved from

$$\frac{z_i}{\sum_i z_i} = s_i(\Pi_1, \ldots, \Pi_n) \equiv D_i(\Pi).$$

For each country or region the inward multilateral resistance P_j summarizes the trade costs faced on its purchases while the outward multilateral resistance Π_j summarizes the trade costs it faces on its sales. Both indexes have the ideal index property that they are consistent with conditional general equilibrium at the initial prices, and hence with the full general equilibrium.

It is very useful to lay out how the setup here yields a generalized gravity model. First, form an outward trade cost deflator for i:

$$D_i = s_i(\Pi) \qquad \forall i.$$

These price deflator functions are homogeneous of degree one in $\{\Pi_i\}$. Next note that in the hypothetical equilibrium, every destination has the same budget share for good i, equal in equilibrium (by market clearance) to y_i/y, the world spending share on good i. Divide both sides of the market-clearing equations by y, and then the left side by y_i/y and the right side by D_i to obtain

$$1 = \sum_j \frac{s_i(t_{1j}/D_iP_j, \ldots, t_{nj}/D_iP_j)e_j}{y}.$$

Here we use the homogeneity of degree one of the share function to take D_i into the share function. The budget constraints can be rewritten as

$$1 = \sum_i \frac{s_i(t_{1j}/D_iP_j, \ldots, t_{nj}/D_iP_j)y_i}{y}.$$

Finally, the expenditure system can be rewritten as

$$x_{ij} = \frac{s_i(t_{1j}/D_iP_j, \ldots, p_nt_{nj}/D_iP_j)e_jy_i}{y}.$$

The generalized gravity model consists of the expenditure equations subject to the preceding two equation systems that serve to generate $\{D_i, P_i\}$. Then the system $D_i = s_i(\Pi_1, \ldots, \Pi_n)$ generates the vector of implied outward multilateral resistances.

In the CES case, $s_i(p^j) = (\beta_i p_i t_{ij}/P_j)^{1-\sigma}$ and $D_i = (\beta_i p_i \Pi_i)^{1-\sigma}$; hence the generalized system reduces to the simple form of the text. It appears that the suppression of p_i in the CES version of gravity is significant, but this is deceptive. In the conditional equilibrium the vector of supply prices is given and plays no useful role in the cross-sectional structure that is used to estimate trade costs or calculate multilateral resistance. But in comparative static analysis the changes in p_i cause changes in Y_i and thus in multilateral resistance and trade flows. This is so in either the special or general case.

For some important purposes it is legitimate as well as convenient to choose units such that the supply prices (which are constant in the equilibrium and otherwise uninteresting) are all equal to one. One example is empirical work which is oriented toward exploiting the pure cross-sectional variation of trade flows to infer unobservable trade costs based on observables. The unit price simplification is also useful for understanding and reporting results on the anatomy of trade costs in a multicountry system.

As in the special case the hypothetical equilibrium with uniform inward and outward trade costs is equivalent to a frictionless equilibrium in which resistance equivalent endowments y_i/Π_i are shipped to destinations that can then utilize only $1/P_j$ of each unit embarked. This property follows because

$$p_i\Pi_i\left(\frac{z_i}{\Pi_i}\right) = s_i(p_1\Pi_1, \ldots, p_n\Pi_n)\,y$$

and the frictionless prices $\{p_i\Pi_i\}$ clear the markets with the resistance equivalent endowments $\{z_i/\Pi_i\}$.

The generalized gravity model reveals how inward and outward multilateral resistance play a key role in summarizing the structure of trade costs. Inward multilateral resistance is bound up with bilateral resistance and interdependence operating through the system of budget constraints. Outward multilateral resistance is bound up with bilateral resistance and interdependence operating through the system of market clearing relations. And the two systems are linked.

Since the multilateral resistance concepts operate in a full general equilibrium, it is not surprising that they are dependent on *all* the bilateral trade costs in the system, not just those that, for example, directly affect inward trade to country j. The size of these summary measures of trade costs is also dependent on the distribution of expenditure and of production, not just those directly involved. For example, the outward multilateral resistance of country j is affected by outputs in other countries as well as its own output and the set of expenditure levels in each destination.

Estimation is focused on inference of the parameters of the demand system (implicit in the share functions) together with the parameters of the trade cost function relating t_{ij} to observables. For this purpose it may or may not be useful to utilize multilateral resistance with full information methods. See Anderson and van Wincoop (2004) for discussion of this issue in the CES case. For the purpose of reporting results on trade costs and conducting comparative static experiments, it appears that multilateral resistance should play a central role.

III APPLICATIONS

11 A General Framework for Measuring Policy Restrictiveness

The applications in part III of the book illustrate the very wide applicability of our method by showing how the restrictiveness of economic policy can be evaluated in a variety of contexts. Our method permits us to set all the applications in a general framework that encompasses a family of index numbers. Welfare and trade volume are natural concerns in a trade context, and have motivated the analysis in previous chapters, but other concerns are also relevant and fit into the framework. As we will see, our methods can be applied to sectoral or national employment levels, to effective rates of protection, or to domestic tax and subsidy policies. Our methods could also be applied to other domestic policy issues, such as measuring competitiveness or comparing the height of tax or regulatory barriers across jurisdictions. To keep a tight focus in this book, we do not develop these applications.

Much of the focus in part III is on the practical issues that arise in empirically estimating our indexes. In addition all the applications make use of a general method for constructing policy index numbers that can be explained in principle as follows. In each application we define a scalar aggregate of a set of economic policies by evaluating their restrictiveness with reference to a naturally interesting economic variable. For example, the TRI starts from a vector of *independent variables*, the trade policy instruments q and π; it fixes a *reference point*, the level of utility u; and it uses a variant of the distance function to map the instruments into a scalar *price aggregate*, the TRI. Different choices of independent variables, reference points or aggregates generate other members of a broad family of index numbers. For example, by changing the reference point from the level of utility to the volume of trade while maintaining the instruments q and π and continuing to map them to a price aggregate, we generate the MTRI.

The subsequent chapters of this part develop members of the family of index numbers generated by different choices in each of the three categories. Each index is chosen for its natural importance to economic policy making. Our treatment by no means exhausts the set of useful applications of our methods.

Alternative choices of independent variables result in several useful index numbers. Considering only trade distortions, we can construct a partial index of some of the distortions that would be appropriate in sectoral or bilateral trade negotiations, or a full index of all of them, that would be appropriate in comprehensive or multilateral trade negotiations. We can extend the index to include distortions on exports.[1] The most comprehensive trade distortion index likely to be practically useful in international comparisons is one that includes all imports (since all are potentially restricted and nearly all are restricted by at least some countries) as well as those exports subject to restriction in at least some countries. In the application of chapter 15 we estimate the TRI and MTRI indexes of all import restrictions for a set of countries. We find considerable difference between the theoretically consistent indexes and the standard atheoretic indexes.

Domestic taxes and subsidies affect trade, and hence are often the subject of trade negotiations. These alternative independent variables introduce some new conceptual issues for our methods that are considered in chapter 12. It is natural to think of the uniform trade tax equivalent of domestic policies, and numerous authors have done so with atheoretic methods. To construct the TRI appropriate to domestic distortions we fix real income as a reference point and apply the distance function to the domestic price distortions affecting traded goods, yielding the uniform trade tax which is welfare equivalent to the domestic policies. In chapter 12 we also aggregate domestic price distortions into a uniform domestic tax that is welfare equivalent to the consumption or production policies. These theoretically consistent indexes are related to atheoretic indexes used in the literature. Moreover the trade tax equivalent of domestic distortions can be decomposed into a function of the domestic tax equivalents. The application of chapter 12 estimates the TRI for Mexican agricultural policy from 1985 to 1989. It shows that the real income-

---

1. Naturally the scope of the index cannot include *all* traded goods, since distortion rests on relative price wedges. Formally, the homogeneity of degree zero of the economy with respect to prices implies that the distance function price deflator is undefined for an index comprising all prices. The analyst must select a natural numéraire.

equivalent measures of domestic consumer and producer subsidies differ substantially from the usual atheoretic measures. We note that the MTRI for domestic distortions is readily defined and may be useful in some contexts.

Sectoral reference points for trade policy often arise in policy making, as politically active firms or producer associations seek to protect profits, unions seek to protect high wages or employment, and industry coalitions target the outputs of "strategic" industries. These pressures often result in trade policy changes in the United States and its trading partners. It is natural in this context to compare sectors by how much protection is given. As for profits, a political economy perspective suggests that sector-specific income in politically active sectors is an appropriate reference point. Conceptual issues that arise when factor income is taken as a reference point are analyzed in chapter 13, where we develop a theoretically consistent index of trade policy with reference to sector-specific income. In terms of our scheme, we fix sector-specific income as a reference point and apply the distance function to the existing trade policy vector. The resulting index of effective protection is a proper generalization of Corden's (1966) original concept, reducing to it in a very special case. The application of chapter 13 shows that the "true" effective rate of protection schedule is not at all closely related to the effective rate schedule calculated with the Corden formula.

Alternatively, sectoral employment often becomes a target, in association with fixed wage premia. If we think of the sector-specific factor as the specialized labor that enjoys the premium, the preceding structure applies isomorphically: the sector-specific employment target is the dual of the specific-factor income target, and the effective rate of protection applies to the employment reference point as well. As to output as a target, production volume in politically sensitive sectors or in politically sensitive bilateral relationships is sometimes critical to negotiations. In chapter 13 we sketch how our methods apply when the reference points of policy are the various production volumes of interest.

Sometimes policy makers may be interested in quantity indexes of policy rather than the price indexes that have been our focus heretofore. This may be especially true if the policy instruments are mainly quantitative and are imposed with trade volume in mind. Where price instruments are used in such contexts, they have quantity equivalents. In chapter 14 we develop a *quantity aggregate* alternative to the TRI in which the distance function is applied to quantity instruments as the independent variables and real income is taken as a reference point. The concept is applied to the evaluation of US policy toward textiles and clothing imports under the Multi-Fibre Arrangement (MFA), and to the dairy import quota system of the United States. There are important differences between the two applications in how quota rents are shared. The MFA allocates rents to the exporters (above that retained by a tariff) while the dairy import quota system results in rent sharing between US licensees and foreign marketing boards. Both applications show that the theoretically consistent quantitative policy index is nearly uncorrelated with the atheoretic trade-weighted average tariff-equivalent measure.

A principal implication of all the applications in part III is that the results of theoretically consistent index number computations differ significantly from the usual atheoretic index computations in a wide variety of contexts. We believe this result is robust. Our applications implement our methods by making particular model choices which we find plausible, but other choices could implement our methods with different results.

12 Other Policy Distortions

A variety of policy distortions affect trade and are commonly aggregated. We first go beyond tariffs in this chapter to consider subsidies on imports and taxes or subsidies on exports. The main business of the chapter takes up domestic distortions, considering taxes or subsidies on consumption and production and their implications for trade restrictiveness. All these domestic and trade tax and subsidy policies are frequently to be found in agricultural trade, as we illustrate with an application of our methods to Mexican agricultural policy. Appendix B treats trade restrictions more complex than either tariffs or quotas, notably antidumping duties.

We choose as independent variables the consumer and producer prices either separately or together, and for each choice of independent variable we create a price aggregate to maintain real income. We are interested in the *trade* implications of domestic policies here, so we form a uniform *trade* tax equivalent of the domestic policies. It decomposes neatly into a combination of the "true" consumer and producer subsidy equivalents, where these are theoretically consistent versions of atheoretic indexes used in the literature in response to articulated policy concerns. Thus in treating a vector of subsidies to production (agricultural fuel and fertilizer subsidies, land use subsidies) we can form a uniform "true" producer subsidy equivalent while in treating a vector of subsidies to consumption we can form a uniform "true" consumer subsidy equivalent. We put quote marks around "true" to emphasize that while we define conceptually ideal index numbers here, the operational implementation of these index numbers may be flawed.

12.1 Import Subsidies and Export Distortions

Subsidies to trade are common, especially in agriculture. Import subsidies are handled within our previous treatment of the TRI simply by noting that a subsidy is a negative tax, reducing the domestic price of imports and thus reducing the restrictiveness of trade policy. On the export side, in contrast, subsidies *raise* the domestic price of exports, while reducing the restrictiveness of trade policy. Export taxes are common outside the United States (where they are unconstitutional), and export taxes *reduce* domestic prices, leading to a rise in trade restrictiveness. Fixed exchange rate regimes with misaligned rates and various instruments of exchange controls combine aspects of import and export taxation/subsidization (with issues of the distribution of rents similar to quotas). How should we construct an index of trade restrictiveness that combines all four types of distortions—import taxes and subsidies and export taxes and subsidies?

In tackling this question we need only to keep track of import and export prices separately, as the intuitive discussion makes clear. A fall in the price of an import reduces restrictiveness whether it comes from a tariff cut or an increase in an import subsidy. In contrast, a *rise* in the price of an export reduces restrictiveness, whether coming from a fall in an export tax or from an increase in an export subsidy. Although export policies now enter the model, it is never sensible to consider an index of restrictiveness on *all* traded goods prices. By convention, there is always at least one undistorted good that we may as well think of as an export.

It makes sense to construct partial indexes of trade restrictiveness for import and export distortions separately and then to combine them in an overall index. Thus consider the index of the trade restrictiveness of import distortions only (including import subsidies) in the presence of distortions on exports. Distorted export prices are now separately denoted p_x^0 while import prices are denoted p_m. In the background the undistorted traded good is the numéraire. The partial index of trade restrictiveness of import distortions is implicitly defined as

$$\tau^m : B[p_m^*(1 + \tau^m), p_x^0, u^0] = B(p_m^0, p_x^0, u^0). \tag{1}$$

Note that if all (or a sufficient proportion of) import distortions were subsidies, $\tau^m < 0$, imports are on balance subsidized.

Symmetrically we define the partial index of the trade restrictiveness of export distortions by[1]

$$\tau^x : B(p_m^0, p_x^*/(1 + \tau^x), u^0) = B(p_m^0, p_x^0, u^0). \tag{2}$$

---

1. In Anderson and Neary (1996) we defined an index with the form of equation (2) and called it the trade subsidization index. The present discussion generalizes this to include export taxes and recognizes that it is just a partial TRI for exports.

In contrast to the case of imports, the export tax equivalent is defined by a scalar that divides rather than multiplies the free-trade prices in the index. The partial index of trade restrictiveness of exports is defined in this way so that a positive τ^x implies restriction of trade, lowering the domestic price of exports. The interpretation of each trade distortion index is clear: the uniform ad valorem import tax (export tax) is welfare equivalent to the existing set of import distortions (export distortions).

Finally the combined index of trade restrictiveness incorporates both import and export distortions. Combining the partial TRI's for import distortions and export distortions above, we define the full Trade Restrictiveness Index as

$$\tau^\Delta : B\left[p_m^*(1 + \tau^\Delta), \frac{p_x^*}{1 + \tau^\Delta}, u^0 \right] = B(p_m^0, p_x^0, u^0) = 0. \tag{3}$$

The interpretation of (3) is straightforward along the lines laid down in chapter 4.[2]

Further insight is gained from the local proportionate rate of change of the uniform tariff factor:

$$\frac{d\tau^\Delta}{1 + \tau^\Delta} = \frac{B_u^1}{B_u^0} \left[\lambda \frac{B_{p_m}^0}{B_{p_m}^1} \frac{dp_m^0}{p_m^1} - (1 - \lambda) \frac{B_{p_x}^0}{B_{p_x}^1} \frac{dp_x^0}{p_x^1} \right], \tag{4}$$

where

$$\lambda = \frac{B_{p_m}^1 p_m^1}{B_{p_m}^1 p_m^1 - B_{p_x}^1 p_x^1}.$$

The two terms inside the square brackets represent the separate effects of the partial import and export distortion indexes. Disregarding differences in the shadow price of foreign exchange in three different equilibria, which are each labeled 1 (uniform import tax equivalent, uniform export tax equivalent and the combined uniform trade tax equivalent), the square bracket term gives a decomposition into the separate contributions of the contribution of rises in the import tax and the export tax (which lowers domestic prices of exports). The decomposition indicates that the combined index is an intuitive weighted average of the two partial indexes of trade restrictiveness for imports and exports separately. (λ is ordinarily

---

2. For completeness, consider what happens if we attempt to define an index that covers *all* traded goods so that there is no numéraire left out of the base. The balance-of-trade function $B(p_m^*, p_x^*, u)$ is in this case homogeneous of degree zero in prices and hence τ, implying that there is no uniform tax on imports and on exports that can reduce utility to the distorted level, as required in the definition of the index (3).

positive and less than one.[3]) The weights reflect the relative importance of import distortions and export distortions in the welfare cost of the distortions.

For practical purposes we sometimes evaluate local changes about initial prices in (3). Then $B_u^1/B_u^0 = 1$ and $p^1 = p^0(1 + \tau^\Delta)$. This procedure is applied in some of our CGE applications in the presence of quota-constrained goods, where the free-trade price is typically unobservable. In our partial-equilibrium applications, supply and demand elasticities might be used to extrapolate to a distant equilibrium, but it seems safer to use local approximation techniques.

Having shown how export distortions can be handled, we return for the rest of the book to the case where trade distortions are import distortions only, except where specifically noted in our study of exporters subject to Multi-Fibre Arrangement quotas in chapter 13.

12.2 The Trade Restrictiveness of Domestic Distortions

Domestic relative price distortions are particularly prominent in agriculture, and have long been understood to affect international trade. The Uruguay Round of multilateral trade negotiations resulted in agreements that initiated constraints on domestic policies such as production subsidies in agriculture. In this context it is useful to ask what index gives the trade restrictiveness equivalent of a set of domestic distortions. Previous researchers who have considered indexes of domestic policies as they may affect trade have constructed fixed weight *producer subsidy* and *consumer subsidy equivalents* (see Cahill and Legg 1990). These are open to all the objections raised for the fixed weight average tariffs considered in part II. We set out "true" index counterparts and combine them in the TRI of domestic distortions.

We now distinguish between domestic consumer prices r and producer prices p. Where consumption and production of tradable goods are treated differently, we start with the standard textbook insight that a tariff is equivalent to a tax on consumption plus an equal rate subsidy on production. This insight suggests defining the TRI for domestic distortions as

$$\tau^\Delta : B[\pi^*(1 + \tau^\Delta), \pi^*(1 + \tau^\Delta), u^0] = B(p^0, r^0, u^0). \tag{5}$$

---

3. This cannot be guaranteed for all patterns of distortions and substitution effects. It certainly holds in the neighborhood of free trade and should hold quite broadly elsewhere.

Separate production and consumption taxation/subsidization are allowed for by recognizing that $r^0 \neq p^0$. The interpretation of τ^Δ follows familiar lines: it is the uniform tariff which is equivalent in welfare to the existing differentiated structure of domestic distortions of consumption and production.

The index τ^Δ can be decomposed into its consumer and producer price effects along the lines of our decomposition of import and export distortions, as follows from inspecting (5). The consumer and producer price components lead to a comparison of our approach with the commonly used ad hoc measures of producer and consumer subsidy equivalents.

Ad hoc versus True Consumer and Producer Subsidy Equivalents

As a preliminary step to a full analysis of true consumer and producer distortion indexes, we develop the properties of the balance-of-trade function when consumers and producers face different prices for imported goods. For simplicity, these are the only distortions. We define

$$B(p, r, u) \equiv e(r, u) - g(p) - (r - p^*)' e_r(r, u) + (p - p^*)' g_p(p), \qquad (6)$$

where we suppress the dependence of B on the exogenous variables, including the world price p^*. Recall from chapter 3 that the terms e_r and g_p are equal to the consumption vector x and the production vector y respectively, by Shephard's lemma and Hotelling's lemma. The marginal welfare effects of changes in the policy variables p and r are given by

$$-B_r = (r - p^*)' e_{rr} = (r - p^*)' x_r \qquad (7)$$

and

$$-B_p = -(p - p^*)' g_{pp} = -(p - p^*)' y_p. \qquad (8)$$

A rise in a single consumption tax will lower welfare by (7) since compensated demand functions slope downward, while a rise in a single production subsidy will lower welfare by (8) since supply functions slope upward. A pure tariff is the case of $r = p$.

The Producer Distortion Index

The true producer subsidy equivalent index is defined as

$$\tau^p : B(p^*(1 + \tau^p), r^0, u^0) = B(p^0, r^0, u^0) = 0. \qquad (9)$$

Here τ^p is the uniform production subsidy that is welfare equivalent to the initial set of production subsidies. The proportionate rate of change of this index is calculated as

$$\frac{d\tau^p}{1 + \tau^p} = -\frac{B_u^1}{B_u^0} \frac{B_p^0 \cdot dp^0}{B_p^1 \cdot p^1}. \tag{10}$$

The elements of this rate of change are the marginal welfare weights given by (8).

When our concern is the effect of production distortions on overall efficiency or welfare, it is best to use the true producer subsidy equivalent. But, in contrast, if our concern is the effect of producer subsidies on productive efficiency, we should use the true GDP deflator defined as

$$\tau^{Ap} : g[p^*(1 + \tau^{Ap})] = g(p).$$

The proportional change in the GDP deflator is

$$\frac{d\tau^{Ap}}{1 + \tau^{Ap}} = \frac{y^0 \cdot dp}{y^1 \cdot p^1}.$$

Here we use Hotelling's lemma and use superscript 1 to denote evaluation at prices $p^1(1 + \tau^{Ap})$. Each index is appropriate for its chosen purpose. They differ because the true producer subsidy equivalent index incorporates the effect of output changes on the social budget via subsidy payments while the GDP deflator does not.

The commonly used producer subsidy equivalent (PSE) defined on the domestic price base is an approximation to the GDP deflator:

$$\text{PSE} = \frac{\sum_i y_i^0 (p_i^0 - p_i^*)}{y^0 \cdot p^0}. \tag{11}$$

Its proportional change is defined as

$$\hat{\text{PSE}} = \frac{y^0 \cdot dp}{y^0 \cdot p^0}. \tag{12}$$

The true GDP deflator stands in the same relation to the PSE as the true average tariff stands to the trade-weighted average tariff. Comparing (10) and (12) and recalling (8), we see that the difference in the two indexes hinges on the use of average production shares as weights in (12) as opposed to marginal welfare shares in (10).

The Consumer Distortion Index

The consumption distortion index is derived with a parallel set of derivations. First, we can define the *true consumer subsidy equivalent index*:

$$\tau^r : B[p^0, p^*(1 + \tau^r), u^0] = B(p^0, r^0, u^0) = 0. \tag{13}$$

The proportionate change in this index is a weighted average of the distortion changes, where the weights are the marginal welfare weights:

$$\frac{d\tau^r}{1 + \tau^r} = \frac{B_u^1}{B_u^0} \frac{B_r^0 \cdot dr}{B_r^1 \cdot r^1}. \tag{14}$$

In contrast, the change in the ad hoc consumer subsidy equivalent (CSE) index is

$$\hat{\mathrm{CSE}} = \frac{x^0 \cdot dr}{x^0 \cdot r^0}, \tag{15}$$

where initial consumption shares are used as weights. The CSE approximates a true consumer cost of living deflator defined by τ^{Ar}: $e[p^*(1 + \tau^{Ar}), u^0] = e(r^0, u^0)$. The true consumer subsidy equivalent incorporates the effect of consumption changes on the social budget, whereas the true cost of living index does not.

In practice, applications that make use of local rates of change will utilize the expedient of evaluating about the initial equilibrium. In this case the difference disappears between the changes in the true GDP deflator, and the true consumer cost of living deflator, on the one hand, and the changes in the PSE and CSE, on the other hand. But differences between the true producer and consumer subsidy equivalents and the atheoretic PSE and CSE remain—the former are based on marginal welfare weights and the latter are not.

The TRI of Domestic Distortions

The TRI is defined by the uniform tariff that is welfare equivalent to the initial producer and consumer distortions:

$$\tau^\Delta : B[p^*(1 + \tau^\Delta), p^*(1 + \tau^\Delta), u^0] = B(p^0, r^0, u^0).$$

Bringing together these results, the change in the overall TRI can be expressed as a "weighted average" of the changes in the true producer and consumer subsidy equivalent indexes:[4]

$$\hat{\Delta} \equiv \frac{d\tau^\Delta}{1 + \tau^\Delta} = \frac{B_u^1}{B_u^0} [\lambda \hat{\Delta}^p + (1 - \lambda)\hat{\Delta}^r], \tag{16}$$

---

4. This result is an approximation only, because the changes in the three indexes are evaluated at different points.

where

$$\hat{\Delta}^i \equiv \frac{d\tau^i}{1 + \tau^i}, \qquad i = p, r, \quad \text{and} \quad \lambda \equiv \frac{B_p^1 \cdot p^1}{B_p^1 \cdot p^1 + B_r^1 \cdot r^1}.$$

The weight λ is the ratio of the marginal welfare cost of a 1 percent rise in producer prices (via a subsidy) to the marginal welfare cost of a 1 percent rise in producer and consumer prices (via a tariff). λ is less than one in the one-good case when consumption is taxed and production is subsidized, while it is greater than one when consumption and production are both subsidized. In the latter case, rises in r are welfare increasing, and by (16), rises in r reduce the TRI, indicating that a reduction in consumer subsidization is welfare equivalent to a cut in trade restriction.

The MTRI of Domestic Distortions

When trade negotiations motivate the evaluation of trade policy, the volume-equivalent uniform tariff is a useful index of domestic distortions. Combining the methods above with those of chapter 5, we can readily define the MTRI for domestic policy distortions as

$$\tau^\mu : M[p^*(1 + \tau^\mu), p^*(1 + \tau^\mu)] = M[p^0, r^0].$$

Here we write the trade volume function $M[\cdot]$ as a function of consumer and producer prices. The detailed structure of this function can be generated using the trade balance function (6) for the domestic distortions case and combining it with the definition of the distorted trade volume as in chapter 5. As with the TRI in (16), the effects of domestic subsidies can be decomposed into their producer and consumer subsidy volume equivalents. Details are left to the reader. The MTRI for domestic distortions ought to be of great practical importance as a background for future agricultural trade negotiations and we hope to see applications on these lines.

The preceding discussion serves to place in perspective the advantages of our approach to trade policy evaluation of domestic distortions over the commonly used alternative: it uses appropriate weights, it correctly aggregates the effects of changes in the two types of distortions, and it maps domestic distortions into an intuitive border tax equivalent.

Nontraded Goods Market Distortions

It is relatively straightforward to incorporate distortions in nontraded goods markets into the framework used so far. Let h and c denote respectively the consumer and producer prices of nontraded goods, distorted by a tax, $t^h = h - c$. Adding the nontraded goods prices to the list of arguments of the expenditure and GDP functions, the condition for equilibrium in the nontraded goods markets may be written as

$$e_h(r, h, u) = g_c(p, c). \tag{17}$$

Substituting for h in (17), the equation is solved for the equilibrium producer price vector, c, which depends on all the exogenous variables. Then

$$c = c(t^h, r, p, u), \quad h(t^h, r, p, u) = c(\cdot) + t^h. \tag{18}$$

The derivatives of this function are easily derived from (17); for example, the effect of changes in the distortion levels t^h on the producer prices c (at given u) equals

$$c_{t^h} = (g_{cc} - e_{hh})^{-1} e_{hh}. \tag{19}$$

Incorporating the endogenous determination of c (and hence of h), the reduced form balance-of-trade function is

$$B(p, r, t^h, u) \equiv e[r, h(\cdot), u] - g[p, c(\cdot)] - (r - p^*) \cdot x[r, h(\cdot), u]$$
$$+ (p - p^*) \cdot y[p, c(\cdot)] - t^h \cdot e_h[r, h(\cdot), u]. \tag{20}$$

Consumer demands x now depend on the producer prices of traded goods p indirectly through their dependence on nontraded goods prices h, and similarly supplies depend indirectly on consumer prices r.

The TRI may now be extended to the case where some distorted goods are nontraded.[5] Equation (5) becomes

$$\tau^\Delta : B[p^*(1 + \tau^\Delta), r^*(1 + \tau^\Delta), 0, u^0] = B(p^0, r^0, t^h, u^0). \tag{21}$$

Note that the TRI is defined by inflating free-trade prices of tradable goods, not including a distortion on the home goods; the third argument of $B[\cdot]$ on the left-hand side of the equation is equal to 0. This is because we define an index of *trade* restrictiveness: the uniform tariff that would compensate for the changes in distortions in *both* traded and nontraded sectors. Differentiating (21) to obtain the change in the TRI yields, instead of (16),

$$\hat{\Delta} \equiv \frac{d\tau^\Delta}{1 + \tau^\Delta} = \frac{B_u^1}{B_u^0} \left[\lambda \frac{d\tau^p}{1 + \tau^p} + (1 - \lambda) \frac{d\tau^r}{1 + \tau^r} + \frac{B_{t^h}^0 \, dt^h}{B_p^1 \cdot p^1 + B_r^1 \cdot r^1} \right], \tag{22}$$

---

5. Undistorted nontraded goods are easily understood to be implicitly in the background.

where λ is defined as before. The first two terms on the right-hand side, relating $\hat{\Delta}$ to distortion changes in traded goods markets, are identical to (16) except that the derivatives of B must now take account of changes in the prices of nontraded goods. The third term, which incorporates the effects of distortion changes in nontraded goods markets, is also estimable in principle.

Factor Market Distortions

So far we have assumed that the only forms of distortions are in final goods markets and that production is carried out efficiently within and between sectors. However, a significant number of distortions occur in factor markets rather than goods markets, and it is desirable to have a method of quantifying their trade equivalents also when they are significantly related to trade. For example, sectorally targeted capital subsidies or labor policies are often a key concern in trade policy discussions. To provide a framework for trade restrictiveness indexes of factor market distortions, we must go behind the economywide production structure given by the GDP function and allow for inefficiencies arising from differences in factor prices between sectors.[6]

To illustrate how this may be done, suppose that the economy can be divided into two sectors, 1 and 2, such that factors are allocated efficiently within but not between the two sectors. Each of these sectors may itself be made up of a number of distinct subsectors. We assume that the only form of goods market distortions are tariffs (so that r equals p) and that import-competing goods are produced in sector 1 only. (These assumptions are made solely to simplify the exposition; the appendix shows how they may be relaxed.) We now make the factor endowment argument v explicit in the gross domestic product function. The assumption that factors are allocated efficiently within sectors 1 and 2 allows us to specify sectoral product functions $g^1(p, v^1)$ and $g^2(v^2)$ for each. The allocations of the factors to the sectors, represented by the vectors v^1 and v^2, are not given but adjust endogenously to meet the full employment constraint

$$v^1 + v^2 = v \tag{23}$$

and the factor price constraint.

6. A substantial literature developed in the 1970s dealing with factor market distortions, although it paid relatively little attention to their implications for international trade; for example, see Jones (1971), Magee (1973), and Neary (1978). Our approach here is closest to Dixit and Norman (1980, sec. 6.3) and to Jones and Neary (1991).

A general way of specifying factor distortions, following Jones and Neary (1991), is to write the factor price vector in sector 1, denoted by w^1, as a function of the factor price vector in sector 2, w^2, and of a vector of distortion parameters, denoted by α:

$$w^1 = f(w^2, \alpha). \tag{24}$$

This specification encompasses as special cases many important forms of factor market distortions. To see this, differentiate (24) totally:

$$dw^1 = f_w \, dw^2 + f_\alpha \, d\alpha. \tag{25}$$

Different types of factor market distortion may now be expressed in terms of restrictions on the elements of the two square matrices, f_w and f_α. For example, absolute differentials imply that f_w and f_α both equal the identity matrix, I; proportional differentials ($w^1 = Aw^2$, where A is the diagonal matrix formed from the vector α) imply that f_w equals A and f_a equals $\underline{w}^2$, the diagonal matrix formed from the vector w^2; and sector-specific factor price rigidities can be represented by setting all the elements in the corresponding rows of f_w equal to zero.

The production side of the model is completed by the assumption that factors are allocated efficiently within sectors, so that factor prices are equal to sectoral value marginal products:

$$w^1 = g_v^1(p, v^1) \quad \text{and} \quad w^2 = g_v^2(v^2). \tag{26}$$

The economy's total product is then the sum of outputs from the two sectors:

$$g(p, v, \alpha) = g^1[p, v^1(\cdot)] + g^2[v^2(\cdot)], \tag{27}$$

where v^1 and v^2 are determined endogenously by (23), (24), and (26). (The derivatives of equation 27 are given in the appendix.)

The remaining steps in deriving the TRI in the presence of factor market distortions are familiar. The balance-of-trade function in this model becomes

$$B(p, \alpha, u) \equiv e(p, u) - g(p, v, \alpha) - (p - p^*)'\{e_p(\cdot) - g_p^1[p, v^1(\cdot)]\}. \tag{28}$$

Following now familiar steps, we have the TRI equal to the uniform tariff factor that would compensate for the removal of both tariffs and factor market distortions:

$$\tau^\Delta : B[p^*(1 + \tau^\Delta), 0, u^0] = B(p^0, \alpha^0, u^0). \tag{29}$$

12.3 An Application: The Trade Restrictiveness of Mexican Agricultural Policy

To illustrate the application of the TRI to domestic distortions, we turn finally to a case study of an important phase in the liberalization of the Mexican economy: the reforms of agricultural policy in the late 1980s. We calculate the change in the TRI for ten crops, taking account also of subsidies to fertilizer input use, over the five years 1985 to 1989. (Further details may be found in a background paper by Anderson and Bannister 1992.)

As in most countries the pattern of government intervention in Mexican agriculture is extremely complicated: most commodities are subsidized at both the consumer and producer levels and also benefit from input subsidies, especially to fertilizer use. Additional subsidies apply in the market for the single most important crop, maize (which accounts for over half of Mexican agricultural production and about a quarter of its agricultural imports). In particular, whole maize, which is a traded good, is the principal input into milled maize, which is a nontraded good and benefits from a subsidy. Table 12.1 shows the extent of the changes, over the period we consider, in the rates of subsidy to maize and to fertilizer usage. The pattern of policy change revealed is a complicated one, with no clear inferences possible without the construction of some overall index number of policy restrictiveness. The standard producer and consumer subsidy equivalent indexes can be constructed for this model and the picture they reveal is discussed below. However, their theoretical shortcomings have already been outlined above. So it is desirable to apply the new measure we have introduced above.

For the application to Mexican data we evaluate the effect of year-on-year changes in policy relative to an initial set of policies. We thus use for the "new" prices the most recent prices rather than the free trade prices. Formally, we obtain the TRI in the form

Table 12.1
Primary distortions in maize and fertilizer

	1985	1986	1987	1988	1989
Producer subsidy $(p - p^*)/p^*$	0.32	0.28	0.63	0.39	0.01
Consumer subsidy $(p^* - r)/p^*$	0.31	0.4	0.08	0.2	0.35
Nontraded good subsidy $(c - h)/c$	0.71	0.39	0.24	0.27	0.27
Fertilizer input subsidy $(f^* - f)/f^*$	0.69	0.68	0.64	0.59	0.55

$$\Delta : B(p^1\Delta, r^1\Delta, \tau^1, u^0) = B(p^0, r^0, \tau^0, u^0) = 0.$$

Specializing to the details of the Mexican case, we obtain local percentage rates of change:

$$\hat{\Delta} = -\frac{\sum_i (B_i p_i)\hat{p}_i + \sum_j (B_j r_j)\hat{r}_j + (B_f f)\hat{f} + (1/\Delta)B_\tau \, d\tau}{B_p \cdot p + B_r \cdot r + B_f f}, \qquad (30)$$

where p and r denote producer and consumer prices of traded goods as before, f denotes the domestic price of the traded input, fertilizer, and τ denotes the subsidy to milled maize usage. It is p^1 that is assumed to change now and hence all derivatives are evaluated at the "new" point in (30).

Compared to (22), the scale term B_u^1/B_u^0 disappears, allowing a simpler structure. To operationalize this equation, we require estimates of the supply and demand responses that underlie the derivatives of the balance-of-trade function, as given in equations (7) and (8). Ideally these should come from a computable general-equilibrium model, but as is typically the case in applied work such a model, with a commodity disaggregation compatible with the set of policy instruments in which we are interested, has not been estimated for the Mexican agricultural sector. We must therefore have recourse to partial equilibrium estimates. For the present study, we assume that all cross-price elasticities are zero and take estimates of own-price elasticities of output supply and input demand from Nathan Associates (1990). We use a discrete form of (30) to calculate the TRI and thus form welfare weights that are arithmetic averages of the local weights at each data point. Specifically, multiply both sides of (30) by Δ to obtain the form of a first-order linear differential equation. The discrete analogue of it has the form $\Delta(t) = (1 + a)\Delta(t - 1) + b$. This formula is applied to each year-on-year interval of change (with different coefficients a and b for each interval), along with the normalization condition $\Delta(0) = 1$.

The results of our procedure are given in the first row of table 12.2. The pattern of changes in trade restrictiveness revealed by the overall TRI is clearcut. The TRI shows a large increase in restrictiveness in 1986 and especially 1987 followed by major reductions in restrictiveness in 1988 and 1989. The cumulative effect of these changes is a 40.9 percent fall in trade restrictiveness over the four-year period.

As we noted in (16), it is possible to decompose the overall change in the TRI in order to pinpoint the sources of change. First we consider the decomposition by type of agricultural commodity. The next eleven rows

Table 12.2
The TRI and its components (% changes per annum)

	1986	1987	1988	1989	Cumulative 1985–1989
TRI	7.5	40.2	−40.3	−34.3	−40.9
Decomposition by commodity					
Maize	−3.9	38.8	−23.4	−29.3	
Sorghum	17.5	−7.9	0.7	−3.3	
Wheat	−1.3	0.4	1.0	−3.6	
Soy bean	−2.0	5.1	−6.2	4.4	
Dry bean	−2.9	−0.1	0.3	−0.3	
Barley	0.2	−0.3	0.3	−0.2	
Cottonseed	0.3	5.4	−11.1	−0.8	
Sesame seed	0.0	0.3	−0.1	0.4	
Sunflower seed	0.0	0.0	0.0	0.0	
Coffee	0.1	0.0	0.4	−0.1	
Fertilizer	−0.5	−1.5	−2.0	−1.4	
Decomposition by policy instrument					
Production subsidy	7.1	43.4	−41.4	−28.7	
Consumption subsidy	0.9	−1.6	3.2	−4.2	
Input (fertilizer) subsidy	−0.5	−1.5	−2.0	−1.4	
Comparison of true and ad hoc subindexes					
PSE	−7.4	2.4	−4.9	−5.9	−15.1
Δ^p	7.1	34.4	−31.6	−30.1	−31.2
CSE	−6.4	15.3	32.5	−31.0	−1.3
Δ^q	−79.8	−11.4	69.7	−7.9	−72.0

of the table show that the dominant influence on the overall TRI has been policy toward maize. However, it has not always been decisive: in 1986, for example, a significant tightening of policy in the sorghum market dominates a mild liberalization in maize policy to yield an overall rise in restrictiveness.

The next three rows in table 12.2 present an alternative decomposition of the overall change in the TRI: this time by type of instrument rather than by commodity group. Referring to equation (16), we see that the first of these rows gives the calculated values of λ^p, and analogously for the remaining two rows. This reveals that by far the bulk of the change in the overall TRI is accounted for by changes in production subsidies. Changes in consumption and fertilizer subsidies, by contrast, account for extremely small changes in the overall stance of policy.

Finally, it is of interest to compare the pattern of policy change revealed by the TRI with that suggested by the ad hoc producer and consumer subsidy equivalent indexes. This is done in the final four rows of table 12.2. The decomposition of changes in overall restrictiveness revealed by the "true" indexes, Δ^p and Δ^r, is similar to that revealed by the earlier decomposition by policy instrument. By contrast, the pattern of changes in the ad hoc PSE and CSE indexes is completely different. Comparing first the PSE with Δ^p, the movements in the two are in the same direction in only three of the four years and in those three years the magnitude of the change in Δ^p ranges from five to fourteen times that in the PSE. While the cumulative changes in the two indexes are comparable, it is clear that the PSE is a totally inadequate guide to changes in the true index Δ^p. Similar discrepancies between changes in the CSE and in the true consumer subsidy equivalent index Δ^r show that here too the ad hoc measure cannot be relied upon to provide an accurate reflection of the change in the restrictiveness of consumer price policies. Recalling that there is no consistent method of aggregating the PSE and CSE suggests that despite the limitations of the TRI enforced by the need to use crude elasticity estimates, there is no alternative to using it if we seek an index of the overall impact on trade of policy in domestic markets.

12.4 Conclusion

In this chapter we showed how the simple TRI may be extended to incorporate distortions other than tariffs. Import subsidies, export taxes and subsidies and domestic policy distortions can all be taken into account, with their effect on real income or other reference variables such as trade volume summarized in terms of a uniform trade policy equivalent.

Appendix A: Effects of Factor-Market Distortions

In this appendix we provide further details on the behavior of the economy in the presence of factor-market distortions. Sections 12A.1 and 12A.2 show how to calculate the price and distortion derivatives of the GNP function and the output supply functions respectively. These are a necessary step in calculating the derivatives of the balance-of-trade function (28) that are needed to evaluate the expression for $d\Delta$ implied by (29). Section 12A.3 then shows how the approach to modeling factor-market distortions adopted in section 12.5 can be generalized to allow for any number of sectors, all of which may produce the import-competing goods.

12A.1   Derivatives of the GDP Function: $g(p,v,a)$

The GDP function was defined in (27). Totally differentiating this, making use of (23) and (26), gives

$$dg = g_p^1 \cdot dp + (w^1 - w^2) \cdot dv^1. \tag{31}$$

To eliminate the changes in factor allocations from this, differentiate (26) and combine with (25) to obtain

$$dv^1 = (g_{vv}^1 + f_w g_{vv}^2)^{-1} (-g_{vp}^1 \, dp + f_\alpha \, d\alpha). \tag{32}$$

Substituting into (31) and collecting terms gives the expressions we seek for the effects of price and distortion changes on GDP:

$$g_p = g_p^1 - (w^1 - w^2) \cdot (g_{vv}^1 + f_w g_{vv}^2)^{-1} g_{vp}^1. \tag{33}$$

$$g_\alpha = (w^1 - w^2) \cdot (g_{vv}^1 + f_w g_{vv}^2)^{-1} f_\alpha. \tag{34}$$

In both these equations, a key matrix is $(g_{vv}^1 + f_w g_{vv}^2)^{-1}$, which gives the effects of higher factor prices in sector 1, w^1, on employment levels there, v^1. In the case of absolute factor-price differentials, f_w collapses to the identity matrix and the key matrix is negative definite. But nothing can be said about its properties in general. In equation (33), the first term on the right-hand side, g_p^1, is the vector of outputs of import-competing goods, y^1. In the presence of distortions, this differs from the price derivative of GNP by the second term: if the matrix $(g_{vv}^1 + f_w g_{vv}^2)^{-1}$ is negative definite, this term tends to encourage a further increase in GNP whenever a price increase tends to raise the returns in sector 1 of those factors that are paid higher premia there (i.e., whenever the vectors $(w^1 - w^2)$ and g_p are positively correlated). As for equation (34), its interpretation is straightforward when the distortions take the form of absolute price differentials, implying that a proportionate reduction in distortions will raise GNP.

12A.2   Derivatives of the Output Supply Functions: $y^1(p,v,a) = g_p^1\{p,v^1(.)\}$

Differentiating totally the equation for the output supply functions, making use of (32), gives the required derivatives

$$y_p^1 = g_{pp}^1 - g_{pv}^1 (g_{vv}^1 + f_w g_{vv}^2)^{-1} g_{vp}^1, \tag{35}$$

where the second term takes account of the induced factor reallocation between sectors and

$$y_\alpha^1 = g_{pv}^1 (g_{vv}^1 + f_w g_{vv}^2)^{-1} f_\alpha. \tag{36}$$

Once again, these derivatives have a straightforward interpretation with absolute intersectoral factor-price differentials. But, more generally, as is well known from the literature on factor-market distortions in the two-sector model, perverse price–output and distortion–output responses are possible.

12A.3   The GDP Function with Many Sectors

Suppose now that there are more than two production sectors. The assumption that factors are allocated efficiently within each sector allows us to specify sectoral product functions for each sector i:

$$g^i(p^i, v^i) \equiv \max_{y^i} \{p^i \cdot y^i : F^i(y^i, v^i) = 0\}, \tag{37}$$

where $F^i(y^i, v^i) = 0$ is the production constraint for sector i, summarizing the technology there, which is assumed to be convex. As for the distortions themselves, following Jones and Neary (1991), we can extend equation (24) from two to n sectors by writing the factor-price vector in sector i, denoted by w^i, as a function of a vector of "free" or undistorted factor prices, denoted by w, and of a vector of sector-specific distortion parameters, denoted by α^i:

$$w^i = f^i(w, \alpha^i), \qquad i = 1, \dots, n. \tag{38}$$

The free factor prices w will typically be associated with the actual factor prices in at least one sector of the economy; nevertheless, the symmetric specification is more convenient.

The production side of the general model is completed by adding the marginal productivity conditions:

$$w^i = g_v^i(p, v^i), \qquad i = 1, \dots, n, \tag{39}$$

the full-employment constraint,

$$\sum v^i = v, \tag{40}$$

and the fact that GDP equals the sum of sectoral products,

$$g(p, v, \{\alpha^i\}) = \sum g^i(p, v^i). \tag{41}$$

The $2n + 1$ vector equations (37), (39), and (40) can now be solved for the $2n + 1$ vector unknowns, $\{w^i\}$, $\{v^i\}$, and w; and substituting the results into (41) allows us to proceed as in the text.

Appendix B: Complex Trade Policies

We conclude with analysis of complex trade policies that do not reduce to a quota or tariff equivalent. Two types of complexity are treated here, one relating the tariff to other endogenous economic variables and the other relating to international discrimination.

12B.1   Endogenous Trade Policy

Endogenous trade policy is typified by contingent protection, in which protection is delivered according to a rule based on endogenous economic variables. Contingent protection usually boils down to making the tariff a function of the volume of trade.

We analyze tariff quotas and antidumping duties to show how the TRI is calculated in an environment where the tariff is a function of the trade volume. Tariff quotas are a fairly common instrument which sets a tariff that is an increasing step function of trade volume. A similar but much more widely used policy is antidumping duties, which deliver protection equal to the calculated dumping margin, where the dumping margin is a function of the trade volume. A complete catalog of endogenous trade policy is beyond the scope of this book, but these examples illustrate a broad class of nontariff distortions.

Political economy has also provided a rich description of endogenous trade policy featuring dependence on trade volume. Our treatment can be understood to cover political economy, but a full analysis should utilize all the elements of political economy structure and would take us beyond the scope of this book.

The technical issue posed by endogenous tariffs is that the equilibrium tariff and associated volume, prices, and welfare are all determined simultaneously as a function of the policy parameters (along with the economic parameters). We describe the basic setup and then the equilibrium determination for our two examples. In this environment we show how to calculate the TRI and MTRI.

12B.2   Tariff Quotas

In the tariff quota case the tariff rate steps upward with volume. The parameter vector contains the tariff rates on each step and the volume break points where the tariff steps upward. Formalizing the idea of volume dependent tariffs, let the diagonal matrix of ad valorem tariffs be $\underline{\tau}(m, \gamma)$, where m is the vector of trade volumes and γ is the vector of exogenous trade policy parameters. For each element on the diagonal, the tariff factor is increasing in "own" trade, and we allow for cross-effects without tying them down. By construction, $\underline{\tau}(m^*, \gamma^*) = 0$, where γ^* represents the free-trade level of the policy parameters and $m^* = E_\pi(\pi^*, u^*)$, and free-trade utility is determined by $E(\pi^*, u^*) = b$.

Now consider the determination of equilibrium under a tariff quota. The domestic price vector is given by $\pi = \pi^* \cdot [I + \underline{\tau}(m, \gamma)]$. The vector of trade volumes is given by $m = E_\pi(\pi, u)$. Then the vector of volumes in equilibrium is an implicit function of exogenous variables and the utility of the representative agent, defined by $\tilde{m}(\pi^*, u, \gamma)$, which is the solution to $m = E_\pi\{\pi^* \cdot [I + \underline{\tau}(m, \gamma)], u\}$. We assume here that a unique solution exists for the fixed point problem, as indeed it should for the simple examples that motivated our tariff function. Substituting into the arbitrage condition for domestic prices we obtain the reduced form price function

$$\tilde{\pi}(\pi^*, u, \gamma) = \pi^* \cdot \{I + \underline{\tau}[\tilde{m}(\pi^*, u, \gamma), \gamma]\}.$$

12B.3 Antidumping Duties

The second and much more prominent example of volume dependent tariffs is antidumping duties. A simple illustration stands in for many other variants that depend on the specification of export firm behavior and the details of antidumping rules. Suppose that a monopoly export firm sells into a market where the antidumping authority will penalize sales at prices below a reference price a, taken to be exogenous to the firm's decisions.[7] The exporter's profits are given by $pm(p) - C[m(p)] - (a - p)m(p)$ for $p \le a$. Here C is the total cost of the exporting firm. The second term imposes an antidumping duty for sales below the reference price a. In the absence of antidumping, the firm prices such that $p + m/m_p = c = C'$, while for sufficiently high values of a the firm will choose not to dump and simply sell at price equal to a (effectively

---

7. An important variant of the antidumping law sets a equal to the exporting firm's price on sales in its home market. While the antidumping authority must estimate this price, giving it some degree of control, the exporting firm also has influence over a. A full model of this process is not necessary for the purpose of measuring trade restrictiveness, although understanding it is important for tracing the effect of antidumping rules changes on outcomes.

Consider the case where the exporter sells at monopoly price p^* in his home market. Substitute p^* for a in the analysis of this chapter, and the qualitative analysis is unchanged. Changes in antidumping rules and economic conditions will change p^* in predictable ways, which a full analysis of antidumping should develop.

returning to a competitive environment). Under an active antidumping penalty the firm prices such that $p + m/m_p = (a + c)/2$. The implied rate of specific tax is $t = (a - c)/2$ while the ad valorem rate will be $\tau = (a - c)/2c$. If marginal cost c is constant, the implied tariff is constant. But if we consider the standard U-shaped average cost curve diagram, it is plausible that dumping occurs in the region to the left of the bottom of the average cost curve, where marginal cost is first falling and then rising. (The reference price a might be interpreted as an estimate of the average cost at the bottom of the average cost curve. This interpretation is consistent with the logic of current US antidumping law.) The implied tariff function $\tau(m, \gamma)$ is in this case first rising and then falling in trade volume. The parameter vector includes a and the parameters of import demand and marginal cost.

A slightly more elaborate version of antidumping accounts for the probabilistic nature of the antidumping duty during a period of investigation (a well-studied feature of antidumping policy).[8] The profit function of the exporting firm is given by

$$pm(p) - C[m(p)] - \pi[m(p)](a - p).$$

Here the probability of an antidumping duty is given by π, which may be a function of trade volume. The first-order condition implies an implicit tax equal to

$$\tau = \frac{\pi}{1 + \pi}\left[\frac{a - c}{c} + \left(m\frac{\pi_m}{\pi}\right)\frac{a - p}{c}\right].$$

To complete the specification of τ as a function of volume, p is replaced on the right-hand side with the inverse import demand function. Clearly, the larger the threat π, the larger is the implicit tax. The parameter list γ expands to include the parameters of the probability function.

Important intertemporal aspects of antidumping (and other forms of contingent protection) that link pricing through time to current values of γ are suppressed with this static model description. The suppression is inessential for purposes of analyzing tariff aggregates at a point in time. A full dynamic model is required to treat intertemporal distortions and the aggregation of them into proper index numbers. The extension is in

8. US trade law requires that an antidumping duty can be levied only if the International Trade Commission finds that there has been material injury to domestic firms by means of dumped imports. The ITC often turns down petitions which fail this test. Presumably, affirmative findings are more likely with higher import market shares.

most respects straightforward, but it takes us beyond the subject of this book.

Proceeding to analyze equilibrium in the antidumping case, we obtain the reduced form domestic price function $\tilde{p}(\gamma, u)$ from the first-order condition of the monopoly exporter. In general equilibrium the perceived demand function $m(p)$ must equal $E_p(p, u)$. In the case where the monopolist chooses to price below a and pay the antidumping duty, changes in a are usually less than fully passed through to domestic prices.[9] In the case where the monopolist's best move is to refrain from dumping, the domestic price is equal to a, and the analysis reverts to the standard small country analysis with a fixed price a set by the government, effectively the same as when it is set by the world markets. Higher a inflicts a terms of trade loss on the economy. The free-trade reference point is $p^* = p : m + pm_p = c$.

12B.4 The TRI and MTRI with Complex Trade Policies

The balance of trade for the distorted economy is $B(\pi, u)$. In the background it is necessary to stipulate the distribution of the rents associated with the complex distortion. The issues are similar to those that arise with quota rents, so we suppress details here. In the case of the tariff quota, substituting the reduced form price function for π, we define the reduced form balance-of-trade function $\bar{B}(\pi^*, u, \gamma) \equiv B[\tilde{\pi}(\pi^*, u, \gamma), u]$. In the background the complex trade policy operates on the structure of $\bar{B}$. The equilibrium utility is implicitly solved from $\bar{B}(\tilde{\pi}, u, \gamma) = 0$. For the antidumping case, the analogous steps lead to $\bar{B}[\tilde{p}(\gamma, u), u]$. Let γ^1 represent the "new" trade policy and γ^0 represent the old policy. The equilibrium utility with the new policy is given by u^1. The TRI in this environment is defined as

$$\tau^\Delta : \bar{B}[\pi^1(1 + \tau^\Delta), u^0, \gamma^*] = \bar{B}(\pi^0, u^0, \gamma^0) = 0.$$

For the antidumping case, exactly similar steps define the TRI. Thus

$$B[p^*(1 + \tau^\Delta), u^0] = B[\tilde{p}(\gamma, u^0), u^0].$$

For comparisons with alternative trade policies not equal to free trade, we substitute the equilibrium new domestic price vector π^1 for π^* in the

9. Dynamic considerations can push dp/da outside the unit interval. When market-sharing arrangements settle antidumping cases, negative pass-through is possible (Anderson 1992). When considering administrative review of existing antidumping duties under US trade law, $dp/da > 1$ is possible (Blonigen and Haynes, 2002).

definition of τ^Δ. We thus define the TRI by first creating the price equivalent of the new policy, then applying a uniform price deflator that restores the initial level of utility.

The interested reader can derive the properties of the TRI as a function of the parameters of the tariff function, imposing structure on the latter to reflect the particular features of tariff endogeneity that are of interest.[10]

The MTRI can be similarly defined for complex trade policies. The compensated trade volume function is $\overline{M}^c(\pi^*, u, \gamma) \equiv \pi^* \cdot \tilde{m}(\pi^*, u, \gamma)$. Equilibrium utility is the solution to $\overline{B}(\pi^*, u, \gamma) = b$. The uncompensated trade volume function is defined through the Slutsky relation $\overline{M}^c(\pi^*, u, \gamma) = \overline{M}[\pi^*, \overline{B}(\pi^*, u, \gamma), \gamma]$. The MTRI is defined by τ^μ: $\overline{M}[\pi^*(1 + \tau^\mu), b^0, \gamma^*] = \overline{M}(\pi^*, b^0, \gamma^0)$.

12B.5 Discriminatory Trade Policies

In the bulk of this book we treat trade policies toward a single world source of imports, almost always selling at fixed prices. In reality, countries practice discrimination, most prominently by regional trade agreements but also by voluntary export restraints (notably the recently expired Multi-Fibre Arrangement). Properly measuring trade restrictiveness in such an environment presents no new analytic issues for the importing country. At the application level, however, there is an important aggregation problem.

Simple models of trade suggest that detailed product line trade should be highly specialized: an importer should buy from only one source. Bilateral trade patterns are far less specialized than this. The response of empirical trade modelers has been to treat goods in detailed product lines from different sources as different goods, albeit close substitutes. Applying the framework of the earlier part of the book, the index of goods is

---

10. It is interesting to note that under antidumping with a certain duty,

$$B_a = [2E_p - (a - p)E_{pp}]\frac{dp}{da} - E_p$$

$$= \left(2\frac{dp}{da} - 1\right)E_p - \frac{dp}{da}tE_{pp}.$$

The second term represents the standard marginal deadweight loss effect utilized throughout the book, modified here by the imperfect passthrough coefficient dp/da. The first term aggregates two separate effects of the change in a. First, a rise in a will raise tariff revenue, all else equal, which is beneficial. In contrast, the rise in a will raise the "world" price paid by importers, a negative terms of trade effect. The first term represents the net of these offsetting effects.

understood to range over both product lines and countries of origin. Differentiation of tariffs ranges over both product lines and national discriminatory policies (regional trade preferences, VER's, etc.).

The TRI and MTRI replace the differentiated tariff structure with a uniform tariff which implicitly ends the discriminatory dimension. Our application to the Multi-Fibre Arrangement in chapter 14 provides an example. Since discrimination imparts a large amount of dispersion to the tariff structure, and since dispersion increases the TRI uniform tariff, it is likely that a full analysis at a sufficiently detailed level to encompass discriminatory trade policy will result in much higher measures of overall trade restrictiveness than those provided in chapter 15.

13 Alternative Reference Points

Alternative reference points give rise to different indexes and hence different results when deflating the same price or policy vector. Part II of this book defines two ideal indexes of trade policy, the TRI with reference to real income and the MTRI with reference to trade volume.

This chapter focuses on indexes based on sectoral reference points, motivated by political economy.

The political economy of trade policy usually emphasizes that trade policy is driven by protection to sector specific factor income. It is thus natural to seek a measure of the height of tariffs with reference to a fixed sector specific income. We develop the implied index formally and relate it to the theoretically dubious older concept of effective protection, showing that the latter is a very special case of the former. Our treatment in section 13.1 condenses that of Anderson (1998a). Section 13.2 provides an application to the evaluation of redefined effective protection in the United States.

Political arguments for protection are often made with reference to sectoral output or employment, so these are legitimate alternative sectoral reference points. We conclude with a sketch in section 13.3 of the implied alternative sectoral indexes of trade policy. These have no previous counterpart in the literature but may prove useful in political economy analysis.

13.1 Sector-Specific Income[1]

Effective protection is the ranch house of trade policy construction—ugly but apparently too useful to disappear. Building to the blueprint of

---

1. This section and section 13.2 appeared in somewhat different form in Anderson (1998a).

theorists such as Corden (1966), a generation of applied economists have calculated effective rates of protection in cheerful disregard of the design critique best summarized by Ethier (1977). Academics surveying the theory of protection (e.g., Dixit 1985 and Anderson 1994) cover effective protection since the volume of its applications make it too practically important to ignore; but awkwardly, since the critique of the concept is so convincing (see also Anderson 1970, Ethier 1971, and Tan 1970).

In this section we rehabilitate effective protection by carefully defining the question the resulting index number is supposed to answer. The usual definition of the effective rate of protection is the percentage change in value added per unit induced by the tariff structure. The effective rate of protection breaks down in general equilibrium (see the critique cited above): it predicts neither changes in output nor any other economically interesting variable. In contrast, the effective rate of protection for sector j is defined here as the uniform tariff (on distorted goods), which is equivalent to the actual differentiated tariff structure in its effect on the rents to residual claimants in sector j. This definition of effective protection applies to general as well as partial equilibrium economic structures, though resulting in a different formula in each structure. The redefined effective protection concept applies to all economic structures in which sectoral residual claims exist.

The new definition should be useful for operationalizing the measurement of the height of protection in testing political economy models. Political economy seems to be an important reason for both the development of the early effective protection literature and the continued use of effective protection by applied economists despite the critique. For example, Baldwin's authoritative survey (1984) of trade policy in developed countries states that effective rates of protection should be used as the measure of protection in political economy models. The new definition of effective protection gives a precise measure of how much protection is given on a comparable basis across sectors. The height of protection defined in this way reflects the power of the interest group to compel sacrifices of general welfare for its sector specific rents. Higher effective rates of protection imply higher sacrifices of welfare and so more powerful lobbies. (See section 13.1.3 below for more details.)

As we have emphasized throughout the book, the two questions, how much protection is given? and how much does the objective (sector-specific factor income in this case) change as a result? are distinct. Differences in the rent changes across sectors reflect both the structure of protection and differences in the importance and substitutability of the sectoral factor in the technology. This chapter redefines the effective protection measure to avoid, by definition, the problems that complicate the link between specific factor returns, on the one hand, and measures of effective protection, on the other hand. For complete clarity the new definition might be called the *distributional effective rate of protection*. However, since the new definition implies the old formula in a special case, it seems preferable to retain the old title.

Several antecedents in the literature emphasize the possible usefulness of the standard measure of effective protection in analyzing sector specific factor returns. Jones (1975) characterized the loose but still useful relationship between the set of specific factor returns and the set of effective rates of protection in the Ricardo-Viner (one mobile factor and many sector-specific factors) case. The theme that effective protection might usefully be linked to distribution and hence political economy was echoed by Ethier (1977) in his conclusion. More recently Kohler (1991) applied this idea in a study of Austrian tariff structure. Nevertheless, only in very special cases can the ranking (or sign) of the usual measure of effective protection replicate the ranking (or sign) of sector-specific factor income changes.

Alternatively to distributional concerns, the old effective rate of protection literature also attempted to link the sectoral effective rates of protection to the changes in sectoral output. Ethier (1971) showed this was impossible in general, as even without intermediate inputs there is no presumption that tariff and output changes are perfectly positively correlated. Output prices and outputs are associated through the gross domestic product function. The output vector is equal to the derivative of the gross domestic product function with respect to the output price vector. The maximum value property of the gross domestic product function guarantees only that the correlation of price changes and output changes is positive. With intermediates it is necessary to distinguish between gross and net outputs. The gross domestic product function in this case subsumes intermediates and its derivatives give net outputs. With intermediate inputs under fixed coefficients, Ethier showed that gross outputs could similarly be associated with "value-added prices" so that a pseudomaximum value function could be constructed with changes in gross outputs positively correlated with changes in value-added prices, or effective rates of protection. Without fixed coefficients no such association is possible. In addition the effective protection literature produced counterexamples of simple economies in which the rankings of gross output changes and effective rates of protection were reversed (e.g., Tan 1970). This chapter is concerned with distribution rather than output changes, as the motivation for a focus on output is not apparent. However, we note in passing that the methods of this book can be used to construct *output effective rates of protection*, based on the uniform tariff on all distorted sectors that produces the same level of (either gross or net) output, sector by sector, as does the initial differentiated tariff structure. Thus this old concern of the effective protection literature can likewise be rigorously addressed using modern index number theory.

The main business of the chapter is to characterize the new concept and relate it to the old one. In a special case, that of partial equilibrium with fixed coefficients of production, the formula implied by the new definition is identical to the usual effective rate of protection formula. With variable coefficients but still in partial equilibrium, the formula is a simple variant on the usual formula that can be treated as an approximation. In general equilibrium the usual formula is a component of a decomposition of the formula implied by the new definition. In general, the ranking of sectors by the usual formula and the new formula will differ, though a special case is offered in which the ranking is identical. With the decomposition the trail leading from the general-equilibrium formula to the partial-equilibrium formula is clear and straight.

Like the earlier effective rate of protection, the new definition is operational. In the last generation computable general-equilibrium (CGE) models became fairly widely available, and such models can be readily adapted to calculate the effective rate of protection on each sector. An example is provided in section 13.2 using the USDA/ERS agricultural CGE model distributed in the GAMS (general algebraic modeling system) library. The results show that the effective rates calculated with the new and old definitions are not significantly correlated. Most important from a practical view, in three of ten sectors the sign of protection is reversed, including three of five of the agricultural sectors that are the focus of the USDA/ERS model.

Section 13.1.1 gives the partial-equilibrium version of the effective protection index. The special case of fixed coefficients gives the standard formula, while substitution possibilities imply a simple variant. Section 13.1.2 gives the general-equilibrium version of the effective protection index and shows how it is related to the partial-equilibrium index. Section 13.1.3 contrasts the effective protection index to the sector-specific factor income change. See Anderson (1998a) for a number of extensions of economic structure (imperfect competition, scale economies, nontraded goods) and of the type of distortions (quotas, domestic taxes and subsidies) admitted. In each case the set of distortions is mapped to a uniform tariff equivalent.

13.1.1 Partial-Equilibrium Effective Protection

The competitive neoclassical small open economy model of this book is assumed, save that we now explicitly allow for intermediate goods. There are no distortions save for tariffs on a set of final and intermediate goods. In keeping with the partial-equilibrium setting, nonproduced input prices are fixed in this section but are endogenous in section 13.1.2. Save for endogenous prices, all the essential issues with the new definition of effective protection arise in this setting.

The task is to evaluate the given tariff structure relative to some alternative structure with equivalent effect on rents earned in sector j. The residual payments or rents to owners of specific factors in sector j can be aggregated in a sectoral profit function $\Pi^j(\pi, w)$ with the standard properties. Π^j should be thought of as including firm and sector-specific payments to human capital.[2] Here π is the vector of goods prices, including both those for the output of sector j and the outputs of sectors from which sector j buys inputs. Since domestic distortions are absent, supply and demand prices for intermediate goods are the same. Sector j can produce a set of outputs for w, the vector of nonproduced input prices.

Definition of Effective Protection
The idea is to find the uniform tariff on all *distorted* goods that has an effect on profits of j equivalent to that of the initial tariff structure. Some goods prices are normally not distorted (e.g., those of export sectors), so this qualification matters. The undistorted prices are subsumed into the background with prices equal to one. Let the initial price vector for distorted goods be denoted π^0 and the free-trade price vector be denoted π^*. Let the price vector for nontraded inputs be denoted w^0 which by assumption of partial equilibrium is invariant to the change in π. The effective protection index $\tilde{\tau}_j^e$ for sector j in partial equilibrium is defined implicitly as

$$\tilde{\tau}_j^e = \frac{1}{d^j(\pi^*; w^0, \pi^0)} - 1, \tag{1}$$

2. The profit function is usually justified by appeal to the maximization activity of an actual firm. However, the hypothesis of competition implies that the collection of interests in specific factors within each sector can be modeled as if maximizing rent.

where

$$d^j(\pi^*; w^0, \pi^0) = \Pi^j\left(\frac{\pi^*}{d}, w^0\right) = \Pi^j(\pi^0, w^0).$$

Working backward, d^j is the uniform input and output price deflator that maintains profits in j. (Conditions under which d exists and is unique are deferred to section 13.1.3.) In the simplest case where all distortions are tariffs, π^* is lower than π^0, d^j is less than one, and is equal to the inverse of a uniform tariff factor. Then $\tilde{\tau}_j^e$ is equal to the uniform tariff on distorted goods, which has the same effect on the profits of sector j as the initial tariff vector.

The effective rate of protection defined in (1) can also be applied to comparing any two distortion structures. If π^* represents a partial tariff reform price vector rather than the free-trade price vector, the effective rate defined by (1) is interpreted as the uniform tariff *surcharge* that is required to make the new protection structure equivalent to the initial structure in its effect on profits of sector j. Of course, the surcharge could be negative if π^* represents an increase in protection. This extension is practically significant, since many comparisons are in practice between one distortion structure and another. Moreover the formal definition in (1) is readily understood to include distorted exports, and both taxes and subsidies are admitted. The restriction of discussion to imports and taxes is for ease of discussion only.

Should currently *undistorted* traded goods prices be included in the index? At a formal level an alternative normalization for the effective rate of protection can certainly include currently undistorted traded goods in the base; d^j may be used to deflate both distorted and undistorted traded goods prices. The rationale for restricting the index to distorted prices is that for political economy analysis of the sectoral pattern of protection within a nation, it seems more useful to come as close as possible to an index for each sector akin to a tariff for that sector: a relative price wedge between the protected sector's price and all the undistorted prices. However, for purposes of making comparisons of the height of protection across nations as well as sectors, it may be useful to use the alternative normalization, including all traded goods prices in the index.[3]

---

3. This multiplicity of purposes is reflected in the common current practice of reporting national average tariffs on both the tariff-ridden goods and on all goods.

Relation to the Old Definition of Effective Protection

In the special case of (1) nonjoint outputs, (2) all intermediate goods prices distorted, and (3) fixed coefficients, the formula for $\tilde{\tau}_j^e$ is identical to the usual formula for the effective rate of protection. Elsewhere it has a simple relationship to the usual formula. To see this, it is helpful to begin with the case of small changes in the prices due to small tariffs. (Alternatively, π^* need not be interpreted as the free-trade price vector, just a price vector π^1 that is close to π^0.) The proportional rate of change of $\tilde{\tau}_j^e$ is equal to minus the proportional rate of change of d^j. The latter is equal to

$$-\hat{d}_j = \frac{\Pi_\pi^{j\prime} \, d\pi}{\Pi_\pi^{j\prime} \pi}. \tag{2}$$

Here the derivatives are understood to be evaluated at $(\pi^1/d, w^0)$. To evaluate this expression, first use Hotelling's lemma[4] and then impose nonjoint production (only one output price) and also the condition that all intermediate input prices are distorted, hence included in π. Next divide the numerator and denominator by the value of total output of j to obtain

$$-\hat{d}^j = -\frac{\hat{\pi}_j - \sum_i \alpha_{ij} \hat{\pi}_i}{1 - \sum_i \alpha_{ij}}, \tag{2'}$$

where the α_{ij}'s are the intermediate input cost shares in the jth sector, evaluated at the point π^1/d, the deflated "new" (possibly free) trade price vector. In the case of fixed intermediate input coefficients, equation (2) applies to discrete changes in price. The discrete form of $\hat{\pi}_j$ is equal to $-\tau_j$, the negative of the ad valorem tariff applied to imports of j. Then

$$\tilde{\tau}_j^e = \frac{\tau_j - \sum \alpha_{ij} \tau_i}{1 - \sum \alpha_{ij}}, \tag{3}$$

the usual formula for the effective rate of protection.

For more general protection structures, in which some intermediate inputs are not distorted or an output price may be undistorted, the denominator in (2) and hence (3) becomes "the contribution of protected prices to profits." For more general production structures the "own

---

4. The derivatives of the profit function with respect to output prices are equal to the vector of outputs and with respect to input prices are equal to minus the vector of inputs. The lemma only holds for differentiable profit functions, which is well known to rule out certain types of flatness in the technology.

price" becomes a price index for jointly produced products. For discrete protection with substitution the discrete form of (2) can be evaluated exactly using an intermediate value of the derivatives (the shares) in the formula. The Törnqvist form of the effective protection index averages the shares at π^0 and π^1/d as an approximation, provided that these are observable. Index number theory gives other approximations which nod at substitution effects in the absence of information about shares at the two prices.[5] But (1) is fundamental and can be calculated directly with an explicit functional form for the profit function, or an implicit form such as the translog, or even supply structures for which the profit function must be evaluated with numerical integration.

Existence and Uniqueness of the Effective Rate of Protection

A technical but important issue with the new definition of effective protection is its existence and uniqueness. It is implicitly defined in (1), based on the deflator d, despite Π being assumed to be a well-behaved differentiable and strictly (due to specific factors) convex function of prices, d, and hence $\tilde{\tau}^e$ may not exist or may exist but not be unique.

In the definition of d, the function $\Pi(\pi^*/d, w^0)$ may be considered as a function of d alone, $f(d)$. Since Π is differentiable under mild conditions, it is convenient to assume it is twice differentiable as well. Then the first derivative of $f(d)$ is

$$f' = -\frac{\Pi_\pi \cdot \pi^*}{d^2},$$

and its second derivative is

$$f'' = \frac{2\Pi_\pi \cdot \pi^*}{d^3} + \frac{\pi^* \cdot \Pi_{\pi\pi} \cdot \pi^*}{d^4}.$$

Note that $f'(0)$ is unbounded, so f approaches $d = 0$ asymptotically. The first derivative has the sign of minus the contribution of protected prices to profits. Ordinarily $\Pi_\pi \cdot \pi^*$ may be positive, since protection to output usually exceeds protection to inputs. While $f(d)$ should thus ordinarily be a decreasing convex function, the sign of f' cannot be guaranteed everywhere. First, inessentially, in a sector that receives no output protection but faces protection on its inputs, the contribution of protected prices to profits is negative throughout its range.[6] Second, even an initially positive contribution of protected prices to profits can turn negative, $\Pi_\pi \cdot \pi^* < 0$.[7] If the derivative changes sign at $f_{\min}$ it may change sign again (the two terms of f'' differ in sign when f' is positive), but this is not essential. The sign change of f' is the cause of both the existence problem shown in figure 13.1 and the uniqueness problem shown in figure 13.2. Let Π^0 denote $\Pi(\pi^0, w^0)$. Examining figure 13.1 and recalling that f approaches the vertical axis asymptotically, *d does not exist if and only if* $\Pi^0 < f_{\min}$. Note that the *existence problem only arises when protection is negative*; $\Pi^0 < \Pi^1 = f(1)$, in which case it can happen that no value of d is large enough to deflate free-trade prices and obtain the original level of sector specific rent.

The uniqueness problem is illustrated by figure 13.2. Assuming existence, we have Π^0 at a level where it intersects f. But $f(d)$ could have multiple solutions in d if there are multiple intersections. Nonuniqueness is, however, of no economic relevance. At d equal to one, the sign of $f'(d)$ together with the sign of $\pi^* - \pi^0$ can be applied to determine the sensible direction in which to move d. In the example shown, with $\pi^1 < \pi^0$, there is initial protection and the sensible value of d is less than one, implying $\tilde{\tau}^e > 0$. The alternate solution value of $d > 1$ implies negative protection and makes no economic sense. The general rule is to use the value of d that lies in the region where f' has the same sign as at $d = 1$.

In some cases it is possible to restrict $f'(d)$ to one sign and hence prove both existence and uniqueness for all prices π^* in the positive orthant. One case is that of nonjoint output under the restriction that the initial profit is nonnegative. Figure 13.3 illustrates. With nonnegative initial profit, the convex isoprofit contour must hit the nonnegative portion of the vertical axis. Then any point π^* in the positive quadrant of prices

---

6. With distorted input prices only, f must be monotonic due to Hotelling's lemma and the formula for f'. There could be a possible sign change of f' from an initial negative value due to the counteracting influence of the two terms of f''. This case is less likely and presents no issues not covered with the initially positive f' case in the text, so it is not further discussed.

7. Intuitively this may be associated with "negative value added" if all traded goods prices are in the index. The problem of negative value added at free-trade prices was emphasized in the old effective protection literature (Tan 1970). In terms of figure 13.1, this occurs if $f(1)$ lies on the upward sloping part of $f(d)$. For such an interpretation, the upward sloping portion of f should also lie below the horizontal axis: profits at d equal to one should be negative. This guarantees that existence is not a problem for the case where value added is negative at free-trade prices, provided (as is reasonable) that the initial profits are nonnegative.

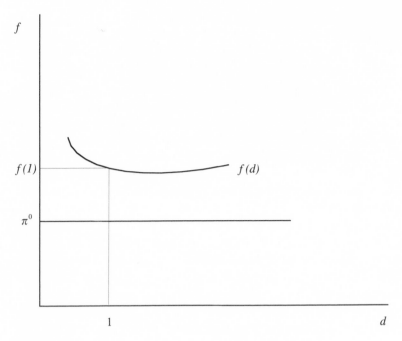

Figure 13.1
Existence problem

defines a ray from the origin that cuts the contour Π^0; hence d exists and is unique.

The discussion here is in terms of the partial-equilibrium profit function. However, the logic uses only the convex structure of the profit function, which carries over to the general equilibrium structure of section 13.1.2.

13.1.2 General-Equilibrium Effective Protection

In general equilibrium the primary (nonproduced) factors of production have factor prices that are endogenous, and nontraded goods may have prices that change as well. Nontraded goods are suppressed as inessential (see Anderson 1998a for a treatment). The sum of all profits is defined as $\bar{\Pi} = \sum_j \Pi^j$. The payments to all factors (including residual claimants) is equal to gross domestic product. Let v denote the fixed supply of primary factors which are mobile between sectors at price w, and let k denote the vector of sector-specific factors. The vector k is a convention, not necessarily associated with any measurable factor, that accounts for diminishing returns and thus positive profits that go to residual claimants. A

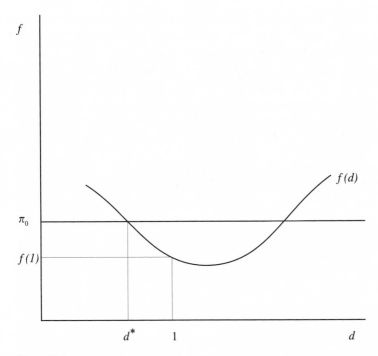

Figure 13.2
Uniqueness problem

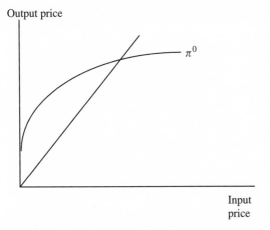

Figure 13.3
A special case

sectoral profits structure is required for a meaningful definition of the interests of a "sector" in general equilibrium, which seems to be the motivation for the effective protection literature.

The gross domestic product function of a competitive economy has well-known properties (Dixit and Norman 1980). It is useful here to derive it in an alternative fashion. Gross domestic product is defined by

$$g(\pi, v, k) = \min_{w}\{w'v + \bar{\Pi}(\pi, w, k)\}. \tag{4}$$

Here k is inserted as an explicit argument of the profit function, having been previously implicit. The first-order condition of program (4) implies factor market clearance. Program (4) has a unique global minimum, since $\bar{\Pi}$ is strictly convex.[8] g_π is equal to the vector of general-equilibrium net (final) supply functions of the economy. g_v is equal to the vector of competitive factor prices for intersectorally mobile factors. g_k is equal to the vector of the sector-specific competitive factor returns. If k is paid this competitive return, $\bar{\Pi}'_k k$ is equal to $\bar{\Pi}$, and similarly each sectoral profit Π^j is equal to $k_j \Pi^j_{k_j}$. Choosing units such that k is equal to one, g_k is equal to $\{\Pi^j\}$.

The effective rate of protection of sector j in general equilibrium is defined as the uniform tariff which has an effect on the return to specific factor j equivalent to the initial tariff structure. Equivalently, the sectoral profit Π^j is held constant in the switch from the initial tariff structure to a uniform tariff structure, since constant g^j_k implies constant Π^j. Thus

$$E^j = \frac{1}{D^j} - 1, \tag{5}$$

where

$$D^j(\pi^*; \pi^0, v, k) : g^j_k\left(\frac{\pi^*}{D}, v, k\right) = g^j_k(\pi^0, v, k), \tag{6}$$

or

$$D^j(\pi^*; \pi^0, v, k) : \Pi^j\left[\frac{\pi^*}{D}, w\left(\frac{\pi^*}{D}, v, k\right), k\right] = \Pi^j(\pi^0, w^0, k). \tag{6'}$$

The existence and uniqueness of D are guaranteed if $\left[\Pi'_\pi + \Pi'_w w_\pi\right]\pi$ is one signed, following the discussion in section 12.1.3. This is a more restric-

---

8. Strict convexity follows from the sector-specific factors imposed on convex technology.

tive condition than in the partial-equilibrium case, since $w_{\pi\pi}$ is subject to magnification effects in the sense of Jones (1965).

The properties of E are intuitively characterized by local proportional rates of change. With (6) as the output price deflator, the proportional rate of change of g_k with respect to π forms the weights in the index, parallel to the role played by Π_π in equation (2). The proportional rate of change of g_k with respect to output prices is a rich general-equilibrium construct with strong properties: own output price elasticities are greater than one and all others are negative (Dixit and Norman 1980). The value of these general-equilibrium inverse elasticities has no simple connection to the input–output coefficients, and involves all the other share and substitution parameters of the production structure in a highly nonlinear form. However, the alternative form of the gross domestic product function developed here permits an intuitive decomposition of the rate of change of E^j into partial- and general-equilibrium components. From definition $(6')$ for the output price deflator, we have the proportional rate of change of D^j equal to

$$-\hat{D}^j = -\frac{\Pi_\pi^{j\prime} \, d\pi + \Pi_w^{j\prime} w_\pi \, d\pi}{\Pi_\pi^{j\prime} \pi + \Pi_w^{j\prime} w_\pi \pi}. \tag{7}$$

The numerator of (7) gives the change in profits of sector j. The normalization term in the denominator of (7) is the effect on sector j profits of a uniform proportionate 1 percent rise in distorted prices π. If all outputs have distorted prices, Π^j is homogeneous of degree one in π and w, implying further that w is homogeneous of degree one in π by properties of (4); hence $\Pi_\pi \pi + \Pi_w w_\pi \pi = \Pi$. Then the normalization in (7) is simply profits and the effective rate of protection is equal to the proportional rate of change of profits. With only some output prices distorted, the change in profits is normalized by the contribution to profits of directly and indirectly distorted prices. This term need not be positive. (The simplest case arises when a sector receives no protection directly.)

Now consider a decomposition of (7) into partial- and general-equilibrium terms. The first terms in both numerator and denominator are the partial-equilibrium terms. As before, minus the proportional rate of change of D^j is equal to the proportional rate of change of E^j. Equation (7) can then be decomposed as

$$\hat{E}^j = \hat{e}^j v^j - \sum_l s_{jl} \hat{w}_l (1 - v^j), \tag{8}$$

where

$$v^j = \frac{\Pi_\pi^j \cdot \pi}{\Pi_\pi^j \cdot \pi + \Pi_w^j \cdot w_\pi \pi},$$

while s_{jl} is the share of mobile primary factor payments paid to the lth factor in sector j. v is ordinarily positive (when the numerator is negative the denominator is likely to be negative as well). However, v may well exceed one. Equation (8) gives ample reason to suspect that the ranking of E and e will differ, both due to general equilibrium effects on factor markets and due to the influence of the term v. Not much can be said in general about the factor price change term, as is well known.

Sharper results are available by specializing the model. Consider the special case in which all output prices are distorted. Then, using the homogeneity properties of Π, we obtain

$$\mu^j = \frac{\Pi_\pi^{j\prime}\pi}{\Pi^j} = \frac{1}{\theta_{Kj}},$$

where θ_{Kj} is the share of the specific factor in value added, or "capital's share" in the usual trade-theoretic model. Specializing still further, in the pure Ricardo-Viner model there is one intersectorally mobile factor, labor. The weighted average of factor price changes $\sum_l s_{jl}\hat{w}_l$ collapses to $\hat{w}$ in (8), leaving for the Ricardo-Viner case:[9]

$$\hat{E}^j = \frac{\hat{e}^j + \hat{w}}{\theta_{Kj}} - \hat{w}. \tag{9}$$

The term $\hat{w}$ is equal to a weighted average of the rates of change of π implied by reverting to free trade, the ith weight being equal to $w_{\pi_i}\pi_i/w$.[10] Thus $\hat{w}$ is negative for the reversion to free trade and equal to the negative of an "average" tariff. Now suppose without loss of generality that sectors are ordered from low capital share to high. In the

9. Equation (9) is equivalent to equation (24) of Jones (1975). In Jones's equation the right-hand side is identical to (9) when all intermediate input prices are distorted. The left-hand side for Jones is the proportionate rate of change in the return to the sector-specific factor, which is locally equal to the effective rate of protection under the current definition with all output prices distorted.

10. For the Ricardo-Viner model the elasticity of w with respect to each element of π is trapped between 0 and 1, while the homogeneity of degree one of w in π means that the sum of elasticities is equal to one.

Ricardo-Viner case, if the highest effective rates of protection are coincident with the lowest specific factor shares, then E^j and e^j give the same rank of effective protection. The condition that the effective rates of protection be perfectly negatively correlated with specific factor shares is not a plausible restriction, showing the nature of the general difficulty in relating the usual measure to the new measure.

How operational is the effective rate of protection defined above? The early effective protection literature was confused by the apparent general-equilibrium nature of the partial-equilibrium measure d. Effective protection attracted applied economists because it appeared to be an operational tool that at least captured an element of general equilibrium. Equation (8) makes clear the sense in which the partial-equilibrium measure is indeed part of a general-equilibrium measure. Equation (8) thus partially legitimizes the applied economists' approach. However, the boundary of operationality has moved on in the last twenty-five years. For any specific factor computable general equilibrium (CGE) model the effective rate of protection can be calculated for each sector j. Section 13.2 provides an example.

An extension in Anderson (1998a) develops the effective protection index for a variety of models, including increasing returns and imperfect competition. In this class of models too the profit function plays a key role, and entry is treated explicitly in somewhat the manner implied by the specific factor k. Recent CGE models of this type make such effective protection measures operational as well.

13.1.3 Political Economy, Effective Protection, and Rent

The two questions are distinct. How much protection is given? And how much does income change as a result? Sector-specific factor income changes are a product of the level of protection given the sector (which the old effective protection concept tried to measure) and the rate at which the level of protection is translated into sector-specific factoral income. Differences in income changes across sectors arise due to differences in both elements of the product, and the new concept gives a precise measure of the "level" of protection in this context. Modern political economy makes the usefulness of a measure of the level of protection clear. In the influential model of Grossman and Helpman (1994) lobbies buy protection with contributions to a politician who trades off aggregate contributions against the aggregate welfare. The equilibrium generally yields a differentiated structure of protection. In this type of model the level of protection to each sector may usefully be defined as here[11] to be the level of a uniform tariff on the distorted goods that achieves equal income (hence an equal contribution for the politician) for the sector-specific factor. The higher is the uniform tariff equivalent, the higher is the general welfare loss associated (hypothetically) with compensating the specific factor interest.[12] Thus the new concept gives a precise meaning to the idea of a sector's buying a greater or lesser level of protection in an observed equilibrium.

With a CGE model the analyst can straightforwardly measure the proportionate income change for specific factors implied by the existing structure of protection as compared to free trade. This indeed is the theoretical tack of Jones (1975) and the main concern of the application of Kohler (1991). The alternative measure, sectoral income changes due to the tariff structure is of course appropriate for other purposes of analysis. In the classic public economics view of the state, a rational benevolent planner potentially can alter policies. If the main concern of the analysis is income distribution, the income metric is useful despite use of an infeasible instrument—lump-sum taxation or subsidization—to render the implications of the fiscal system comparable across sectors. With a CGE model, analysts can easily compute either index.

The distinction between the two metrics would not matter if the ranking of sectoral protection by the two measures were always the same. In some special cases they are. For example, in the limiting case of all producer prices distorted, the two measures coincide. This follows from the homogeneity of the profit function and the definition of D:

$$\Pi\left[\frac{\pi^*}{D}, w\left(\frac{\pi^*}{D}\right)\right] = \frac{\Pi[\pi^*, w(\pi^*)]}{D} = \Pi(p^0, w(p^0)).$$

Hence

$$D = \frac{\Pi[\pi^*, w(\pi^*)]}{\Pi[p^0, w(p^0)]}.$$

But, in general, a ranking of sectors by the proportionate change in income reflects both the level of the price changes and the sectoral conver-

11. In Grossman and Helpman's model the general equilibrium is so specialized that the nominal tariff is equal to the effective rate of protection under the new definition; the index number problem of this paper does not arise. However, Grossman and Helpman assume redistribution of the tariff revenue is incorporated in the lobby's objective function, which leads to an interest in lower tariffs for sectors other than the lobby's own.
12. Welfare is assumed to be monotonic in the uniform tariff for simplicity.

sion of given price changes into rent changes. This conversion depends on the share of the specific factor in value added and on various substitution parameters, as equation (8) makes clear. A simple counterexample provided in the appendix to Anderson (1998a) shows that the two metrics can be perfectly negatively correlated in the usual case when only some producer prices are distorted. Generally, the two metrics must give different rankings.

13.2 Effective Protection in the United States: An Application

Effective protection of US agriculture in 1982 is analyzed here with the use of the USDA/ERS computable general equilibrium model (Robinson et al. 1990), available from the GAMS library. The main purpose of the exercise is to illustrate the ease with which the concepts of this paper can be operationalized, given the availability of a CGE model. Secondarily the results show that the old and new measures of effective protection are weakly correlated, with the calculated correlation coefficient not significantly different from zero. It is interesting to note that the largest deviations between the old and new measures are found among the agricultural sectors which the CGE model is designed to analyze.

The first subsection briefly summarizes the USDA/ERS model. For more details, see Robinson et al. (1990). The second subsection presents the results. The third subsection presents a sensitivity analysis.

13.2.1 The USDA/ERS Model

Computable general equilibrium (CGE) models are by now familiar to many readers, so the explanation that follows is brief. The USDA/ERS model is a small-scale Walrasian model designed to focus on agriculture while achieving a consistency with general equilibrium. The model has five agricultural sectors out of ten total sectors.

Demand is of the Armington variety, so that products are differentiated by place of origin. The demand structure is represented by a two-level CES expenditure function, the lower level splitting demand between home and imported goods according to a CES subexpenditure function while the upper level allocates expenditure across the ten sectors according to a Cobb-Douglas expenditure function. Three different types of households are distinguished (property owners, wage earners, and transfer recipients), the differences in behavior between them coming through expenditure shares at the upper level. There is also parametric government consumption.

Production requires intermediate inputs according to a Leontief technology, and primary inputs of capital, labor, and land according to a Cobb-Douglas value-added production function. We assume that "capital" is fixed in each sector with labor and land being freely mobile between sectors (the original USDA/ERS model has capital mobile as well). Production in each sector is allocated between home sales and exports according to a CET transformation function, with an elasticity that differs across sectors.

Trade is treated simply. The United States is assumed to be a price taker for its imports, but to face downward-sloping import demand functions for its exports, with a parametric elasticity.

Distortions of trade include tariffs only, despite the prominence of nontariff barriers in agriculture. There are, however, also factor taxes, commodity taxes, and several types of government transfer allowed in the model.

The model is initialized on 1982 data. This includes consistent data on the input–output table, sectoral factor allocations, tariffs, factor taxes, commodity taxes, several types of government transfer, and government consumption.

13.2.2 Effective Protection of US Agriculture

The basis results of the analysis are presented in table 13.1. The cell entries are nominal and effective rates of protection (ERPs). The old ERP is the usual concept; the new ERP is the uniform tariff equivalent that holds constant the real income of the specific capital of the sector

Table 13.1
Three measures of protection of US agriculture

Sector	Nominal tariff	Old ERP	New ERP
Dairy and meat	0.014*	−0.011*	0.016*
Grains and oilseeds	0.029	0.030	0.038
Other agriculture	0.037*	0.034*	−0.059*
Agricultural processing	0.115	0.127	0.010
Agricultural inputs	0.003*	−0.084*	0.014*
Intermediate manufacturing	0.018	0.04	0.052
Final demand manufacturing	0.027	0.025	0.008
Trade and transport	0.027	0.018	0.011
Services	0	−1.938	−0.024
Real estate	0	−0.010	−0.008

Note: The asterisk (*) denotes sectors that have different signs for old ERP and new ERP.

denoted by the row heading. The first five sectors are agricultural. They all receive nominal protection, though agricultural inputs are nearly unprotected. According to the old ERP concept, dairy and meat as well as agricultural inputs receive negative effective protection. According to the new concept, both receive positive effective protection, while other agriculture receives the most negative effective protection of nearly 6 percent. Note that agricultural inputs, despite a trivial nominal tariff (0.3 percent), leading to a −8.4 percent ERP under the old concept, receive new ERP protection of nearly 1.4 percent. Note also that under the old concept, agricultural processing receives the highest effective rate of protection (12.7 percent), while under the new concept it falls to the middle at just under 1 percent.

As might be expected with these results, the correlation between the old and new ERPs is low, 0.334, which is not significantly different from zero. The correlation between the nominal tariff and the new ERP is nearly zero (0.022). The most dramatic aspect of the difference between the two concepts is seen in sign changes, however. In the agricultural sectors that are the focus of the model, three out of five ERPs (marked *) change sign with the change in concept.

13.2.3 Sensitivity Analysis

An important potential difficulty with the use of CGE models is that elasticity parameters are not known with precision. To assess the significance of errors in the elasticities it is therefore customary to conduct sensitivity analysis. In practice, results are usually not sensitive to elasticity values, a finding replicated here for the most part. However, there are some notable exceptions to this rule.

The sensitivity analysis is based on varying the base case elasticity parameter by 50 percent upward and downward. There are a total of 23 elasticities to study: one substitution elasticity in consumption and production for each sector (20) plus 3 foreign import demand elasticities (for US exports), the remainder of US exports being assumed to face infinitely elastic demand. Most variations in elasticities result in changes in ERPs of much less than 50 percent. Tables 13.2 and 13.3 below concentrate on the exceptions. As above, the cell entries are (new) ERPs. The row labels refer to tariffs designed to hold constant the rental of the sector-specific factor in sectors 1 through 10, which have the same definitions as the names in table 13.1. The column headings refer to the consumption elasticity parameter ρ_C, the transformation elasticity parameter ρ_T, and the demand for exports elasticity ρ_E. The variation factor of 0.5 and

Table 13.2
ERP sensitivity to selected agricultural elasticities

	Consumption elasticity		Transformation elasticity		Export demand elasticity		Base level
Grains and oilseeds elasticities							
Variation	0.500	1.500	0.500	1.500	0.500	1.500	
ERP1	0.016	0.017	−0.012*	0.030*	−0.016*	0.033*	0.016*
ERP2	0.038	0.037	0.084	0.021	0.134*	0.007*	0.038*
ERP3	−0.059	−0.058	−0.063	−0.056	−0.067	−0.054	−0.059
ERP4	0.010	0.010	0.016	0.016	−0.006	0.018	0.010
ERP5	0.014	0.014	0.012	0.015	0.011	0.015	0.014
ERP6	0.052	0.051	0.048	0.053	0.042	0.056	0.052
ERP7	0.008	0.008	0.007	0.009	0.002	0.011	0.008
ERP8	0.011	0.011	0.010	0.011	0.009	0.012	0.011
ERP9	−0.024	−0.024	−0.025	−0.023	−0.026	−0.023	−0.024
ERP10	−0.008	−0.008	−0.008	−0.009	−0.007	−0.009	−0.008
Other agriculture elasticities							
Variation	0.500	1.500	0.500	1.500	0.500	1.500	
ERP1	0.007*	0.002*	0.016	0.017	0.015	0.017	0.016*
ERP2	0.040*	0.036*	0.038	0.038	0.039	0.038	0.038*
ERP3	0.333	0.020	−0.061	−0.058	−0.072	−0.051	−0.059
ERP4	0.005	0.014	0.009	0.010	0.009	0.010	0.010
ERP5	0.013	0.014	0.014	0.014	0.014	0.014	0.014
ERP6	0.050	0.052	0.051	0.052	0.051	0.052	0.052
ERP7	0.006	0.010	0.008	0.008	0.008	0.009	0.008
ERP8	0.010	0.011	0.011	0.011	0.011	0.011	0.011
ERP9	−0.024	−0.039	−0.024	−0.024	−0.024	−0.024	−0.024
ERP10	−0.010	−0.007	−0.008	−0.008	−0.009	−0.008	−0.008

Note: The asterisk (*) denotes significant sensitivity to elasticity changes.

1.5 is applied to the base value of these. In tables 13.2 and 13.3 the asterisked cases are those for which the variation of the ERP due to elasticity changes is significant. Table 13.3 differs from table 13.2 because sectors 4 through 10 do not have finite demand elasticities facing US exports.

The first row of table 13.2 has an example of a sign change due to a shift in both the demand elasticity and the supply elasticity in sector 2, Grains and Oilseeds. The second panel of table 13.2 refers to the effect of changes in elasticities in sector 3, other agriculture, and here there are two examples of nonmonotonic relationships between the consumption

Table 13.3
ERP sensitivity analysis to other selected elasticities

	Consumption elasticities		Transformation elasticities		Base level
Agricultural processing elasticities					
Variation	0.500	1.500	0.500	1.500	
ERP1	0.009*	0.041*	0.018	0.015	0.016*
ERP2	0.036	0.041	0.041	0.037	0.038
ERP3	−0.062	−0.056	−0.057	−0.060	−0.059
ERP4	0.007	0.012	0.010	0.010	0.010
ERP5	0.014	0.014	0.014	0.014	0.014
ERP6	0.056	0.047	0.050	0.053	0.052
ERP7	0.010	0.007	0.008	0.008	0.008
ERP8	0.011	0.011	0.011	0.011	0.011
ERP9	−0.024	−0.024	−0.024	−0.024	−0.024
ERP10	−0.009	−0.008	−0.008	−0.009	−0.008
Agricultural inputs elasticities					
Variation	0.500	1.500	0.500	1.500	
ERP1	0.017	0.016	0.017	0.016	0.016
ERP2	0.037	0.037	0.038	0.038	0.038
ERP3	−0.058	−0.060	−0.064	−0.054	−0.059
ERP4	0.010	0.010	0.010	0.010	0.010
ERP5	0.009	0.019	0.009	0.016	0.014
ERP6	0.049	0.054	0.052*	0.166*	0.052*
ERP7	0.010	0.007	0.009	0.007	0.008
ERP8	0.011	0.011	0.011	0.011	0.011
ERP9	−0.024	−0.024	−0.024	−0.024	−0.024
ERP10	−0.008	−0.008	−0.008	−0.008	−0.008
Intermediate manufacturing elasticities					
Variation	0.500	1.500	0.500	1.500	
ERP1	0.019	0.014	0.018	0.015	0.016
ERP2	0.044	0.030	0.038	0.038	0.038
ERP3	−0.054	−0.063	−0.071	−0.050	−0.059
ERP4	0.011	0.009	0.011	0.009	0.010
ERP5	0.016*	0.122*	0.015	0.013	0.014*
ERP6	0.029*	0.105*	0.059	0.048	0.052*
ERP7	0.014	0.009	0.012	0.007	0.008
ERP8	0.011	0.010	0.011	0.010	0.011
ERP9	−0.024	−0.024	−0.023	−0.025	−0.024
ERP10	−0.009	−0.008	−0.008	−0.008	−0.008

Note: The asterisk (*) denotes significant sensitivity to change in elasticities.

elasticity in sector 3 and the ERP in sectors 1 and 3. For the latter the ERP changes sign in the interval between the high and low values. Other values marked with asterisks (*) here and in table 13.3 merely have large monotonic sign-preserving changes. The asterisked cases are not confined to "own" effects; six of the nine are cross-effects. Also the asterisked cases are due to variation in all three classes of elasticity. The problematic cases number 9 out of 230 that might be interpreted as a trivial incidence. But even a small incidence of sign changes and nonmonotonicity is trouble-some. It is difficult to avoid the conclusion that elasticities may matter in calculating the new version of ERPs. Thus sensitivity analysis will always be needed in any application.[13]

In contrast to the rather negative results of the sensitivity analysis, the simulation results showed that existence and uniqueness were not practical problems. Forcing a wide range of starting values always produced the same equilibrium. This point is particularly worth noting because the nonmonotonicity reported above might otherwise reflect multiple equilibria.

13.3 Other Sectoral Reference Points

Occasionally the political rationale for trade policy involves protecting a level of sectoral production or employment. For example, political pres-sure was expressed in employer association targets for semiconductor out-put in the United States in the 1980s or in trade union employment targets by sector in the same period. Moreover the theory of distortions literature suggested that such targets might arise as "noneconomic" objectives, possibly justified on the basis of embedded distortions in product markets (technological externalities) or labor markets (wage rigidities). In either case it is of interest to compare sectors in terms of the height of protection given by the overall design of trade policy.

The method applied in each case is to form a tariff index sector by sector that uses as a reference point alternately sectoral production and sectoral employment. We revert to a production structure that suppresses intermediate inputs.

---

13. It is possible to manipulate a simplified version of the specific factors general-equilibrium model to gain some insight into why the ERP may not be one-signed as the elas-ticities vary. However, the limited analytic results do not hold with any generality so they are not reported here. The relationships reflected in the numbers of tables 13.2 and 13.3 are inherently highly nonlinear and complex, and require simulation.

13.3.1 Production

Suppose that a set of sectors receive protection and that it is desirable to compare the level of protection across the sectors.[14] For the set of protected sectors we imagine that there is a target level of output for each member of the set, such as the value of shipments of steel or electronic components in some base prices.

Formally, we first form an expression for the domestic value of shipments $y_i(\pi) \equiv g_{\pi_i}(\pi, v)$ in sector i. We suppress inactive arguments of the GDP function here. So long as nontraded goods price changes are suppressed, we can define the output price deflator without reference to the level of u and hence the tariff revenue. In this case, straightforwardly, the ideal tariff index is defined as

$$\tau_i^y = \frac{1}{d^i(\pi^0, \pi^*, v)} - 1,$$

where

$$d^i(\pi^0, \pi^*, v) : g_{\pi_i}\left(\frac{\pi^*}{d}, v\right) = g_{\pi_i}(\pi^0, v).$$

In local approximation

$$\hat{\tau}_i^y = -\hat{d}^i = \frac{g_{\pi_i\pi}(\pi^0, v) \cdot d\pi^0}{g_{\pi_i\pi}(\pi^*/d, v) \cdot (\pi^*/d)}.$$

Intuitively price changes are weighted by their marginal significance to output in sector i.

13.3.2 Employment

Employment constraints in a sector may be rationalized by a sectoral wage rigidity coupled with barriers to mobility in the labor market such that unemployment is possible. Then trade policy intervention is designed to meet an employment target. Such employment targets seem to more or less explain the US auto VERs of the early 1980s, the reference price system in steel shortly thereafter, and the persistence and spread of the textile and apparel VER arrangements.

The formal model of uniform sectoral employment equivalent tariffs can rely on duality if we suppose that the sector-specific factoral income

---

14. Each sector may produce a group of goods. But the index problem is straightforward, so we suppress it.

analyzed in section 13.1 is paid to sector-specific labor. Then the effective rate of protection as redefined there is also the uniform sectoral employment equivalent.

A familiar metric in the context of employment protection is the welfare cost per job created by the restriction. When efficiency is the primary concern, this method is appropriate, but when political economy is the concern, the effective rate of protection is the proper concept.

13.4 Conclusion

In this chapter we showed that our method can be applied and operationalized for a number of plausible alternative sectoral reference points. We detail one and sketch two others in this chapter. We may also note that our methods readily extend to reference points for intersectorally mobile factors of production, allowing indexes of how much trade protection is given to skilled labor, unskilled labor, and capital, for example. Our readers may think of more useful reference points and policy evaluations as they bring new perspectives on policy issues of the future to the text.

14 Quantity Aggregates

Trade restriction distorts both price and quantity, so aggregation of restrictions can be done in terms of either price or quantity distortion. The quantity analog to the CTU is the uniform reduction in the vector of distorted trade quantities which is welfare equivalent to free trade.

This quantity aggregate was indeed our initial approach to the evaluation of trade policy in Anderson and Neary (1990), where we called it the coefficient of trade utilization (CTU). We developed the CTU for the case of quotas only (though in the presence of tariffs). This is the most natural use of our quantity aggregate, but the extension to a quantity index of the effect of both tariffs and quotas is provided here. In addition we note that a quantity analogue to the MTRI may be defined and related to its price analogue, the MTRI.

We next explore the connection between the TRI (a price measure) and its quantity analogue, the CTU.[1] They are not duals, in contrast to similar distance function indexes in price and quantity space for undistorted economies.[2] Nevertheless, there is a close connection between them. It is further useful to relate our quantity index to Debreu's seminal quantity measure of resource efficiency, the coefficient of resource utilization.

Two applications evaluating annual changes in quota systems with the CTU are presented in the concluding empirical part of this chapter. The applications differ in their treatment of quota rent retention. In the case of Multi-Fibre Arrangement quotas, all rent goes to the exporter save

---

1. The CTU could equally logically be called the "quantity" TRI, and indeed, our early application of our methods (1994) to Multi-Fibre Arrangement quotas called it the "TRI." A separate label for the quantity analogue of the TRI is preferable, however, given our current perspective with experience of a much wider range of applications of our methods.

2. For example, as is well known, the cost and production function based methods of measuring total factor productivity are duals.

for that retained by rent-retaining tariffs. In the case of the US dairy quota system, due to the bilateral monopoly structure of the industry, rent is shared and the rent-retaining tariff of the US serves as a lump-sum tax on the import licensee. Both cases incorporate the effect of changes in quota policy on the tariff revenue from unconstrained goods. The quantity indexes in each case imply a very different evolution of the restrictiveness of quota policy than that given by trade-weighted averages of tariff equivalents. Together the applications illustrate the flexibility and usefulness of our quantity aggregate in evaluating quota policy.

14.1   The Quantity Analogue of the TRI

The initial vector of quotas is q^0, the new or alternative vector is q^1, the vector of unconstrained but distorted imports is $\tilde{m}$, and we denote the free-trade quantity of imports as q^*.

The coefficient of trade utilization (CTU), the quantity version of the TRI, is defined for an index of quota policy (though possibly in the presence of tariffs), as

$$D(q^0, \pi^0, u^0; q^1) : \tilde{B}(q^1 D, \pi^0, u^0) = \tilde{B}(q^0, \pi^0, u^0). \tag{1}$$

Note that D multiplies the new quantity rather than dividing it, indicating that a value of D less than one means that trade is restricted. For simplicity we now temporarily drop the inactive π argument. (Of course, trade distortions on unconstrained goods affect the balance-of-trade function and hence the evaluation of quota policy.) In comparisons to free trade $q^1 = q^*$.

Figure 14.1 illustrates. The net foreign exchange expenditure required to support u^0 is less the further out on any ray from the origin is the quota vector. (This is a plausible simplifying assumption, qualified by cross-effect factors which have previously been discussed.) For some initial quota vector q^0, the associated value of the balance of trade that supports utility u^0 in equilibrium (which for simplicity may be equal to zero) is equal to $B^0 = B(q^0, u^0)$, after dropping the inactive domestic price argument π^0. The iso-expenditure locus $B(q, u^0) = B^0$ is plotted in the diagram. (It need not always have the concave shape illustrated.) The initial quota vector q^0 must lie on it somewhere but is not drawn. The free-trade quota vector is q^*. D is the uniform radial quota reduction factor that is as inefficient as the initial quota vector. The CTU is equal to the ratio OA/Oq^*.

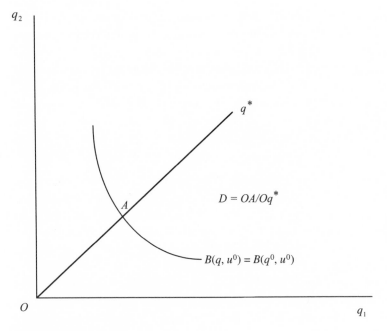

Figure 14.1
Coefficient of trade utilization

The properties of D are readily derived based on those of $B(q, u)$. D is homogeneous of degree one in q. The local proportional rate of change of the CTU is[3]

$$\hat{D} = \psi \frac{\tilde{B}_q^0 \cdot dq^0}{\tilde{B}_q^0 \cdot q^0},$$

where

$$\psi \equiv \frac{\tilde{B}_u^D}{\tilde{B}_u^0} \frac{\tilde{B}_q^0 \cdot q^0}{\tilde{B}_q^D \cdot q^D},$$

$$q^D \equiv q^1 D,$$

3. A change in the quota dq^0 will change the initial utility by du^0. With reference to maintaining this new level of utility, the quantity index must change according to

$$\tilde{B}_q^0 \, dq^0 + \tilde{B}_u^0 \, du^0 = 0 = \tilde{B}_q^D q^1 \, dD + \tilde{B}_u^D \, du^0.$$

We solve the first equation for du^0 and substitute into the second, and then solve for dD/D.

and the D superscript denotes evaluation of derivatives at $(q^1 D, u^0)$. Here the vector $\tilde{B}_q$ is minus the shadow price of quotas vector (given in chapter 8).

The notation emphasizes that the quota-constrained balance-of-trade function is evaluated at two different points in (2). With the initial point q^0 close to the alternative point q^1 the formula collapses to

$$\hat{D} = \sum_j \frac{B_j q_j}{\sum B_j q_j} \hat{q}_j. \tag{2}$$

Based on (2), a rise in an element of the quota vector will ordinarily raise the CTU, meaning trade restrictiveness falls. The various institutional details of rent-retaining tariffs, other rent-sharing devices, and tariffs on other goods will alter the calculation of the shadow price of quotas. The various economic structural details will likewise alter the elasticities needed to calculate the shadow price of quotas.

The alternative trade policy q^1 and the meaning of the change in trade policy dq^0 both require special attention in the context of measuring changes in trade restrictiveness based on actual changes in trade flows. In a changing economy, as noted in chapter 8, an unchanged quota vector implies changing trade restrictiveness. The preferred alternative is to compare actual quota policy to an equi-restrictive quota policy that maintains a constant domestic price of quota-constrained goods.

The equi-restrictive quota $\bar{q}^1$ is implicitly defined by $-\tilde{E}_q(\bar{q}^1, u^0, \gamma^0) = -\tilde{E}_q(q^1, u^1, \gamma^1)$, where the parameter vector γ shifts to reflect economic growth or other fundamental change. To evaluate trade restrictiveness or its change, the setup of (1) and (2) applies with q^1 understood to be equal to $\bar{q}^1$ and $dq^0 = \bar{q}^1 - q^0$. The latter is a growth-compensated change in quota policy, and the corresponding change in the CTU is a compensated change in trade restrictiveness. The CTU based on actual changes in quota policy is correspondingly an uncompensated measure. The difference between them is just the effect of growth on the restrictiveness of trade policy.

We apply a discrete form of (2) with $dq^0 = \bar{q}^1 - q^0$ below to the evaluation of the Multi-Fibre Arrangement and of the US dairy quota system. Here q^1 is based on the next year's value in year-on-year evaluation, adjusted for the influence of growth on the restrictiveness of quotas. Making the assumption of neutral growth, we impose $\bar{q}^1 = q^1/(1 + \hat{\gamma})$, where $\hat{\gamma}$ is the growth rate. Using local rates of change, the growth compensated change in quota policy for good i is calculated as $(q_i^1 - q_i^0)/q_i^0 - \hat{\gamma}$. The rate of change of the compensated CTU is equal to the rate of change of the uncompensated CTU minus the rate of growth. For clarity in presenting the results below, D^c represents the growth-compensated CTU and D represents the uncompensated CTU. (In our earlier applications we arrived at essentially the same operational method with a different rationale, and calculated a compensated CTU which is the negative of the concept calculated here.)

For the evaluation of both quotas and tariffs simultaneously with a quantity index we denote the free-trade quantities of both categories of distorted trade as (q^*, m^*). The CTU for the entire trade distortion system is defined by

$$D(q^0, \pi^0, u^0; q^*, m^*) : \tilde{B}(q^* D, m^* D, u^0) = \tilde{B}(q^0, \pi^0, u^0). \tag{3}$$

The CTU is interpreted as in the case of quotas only. It is the quantity analogue to the TRI for tariffs and quotas previously defined. Usually the price version of the TRI will be more intuitively useful in the analysis of trade policy involving tariffs.

14.2 The Quantity Analogue of the MTRI

The quantity analogue of the MTRI is quite straightforward. It is the uniform contraction factor applied to all distorted goods that reduces free-trade volume (measured at external prices) by the same proportion as the initial trade distortion schedule. That is, the contraction factor δ^μ is defined by $\pi^* \cdot [\delta^\mu m(\pi^*, b)] = M^0$.

The definition implies a neat relationship between the MTRI and its quantity analogue:

$$\delta^\mu = \frac{M[\pi^*(1 + \tau^\mu), b]}{M(\pi^*, b)}.$$

Evidently $\partial \delta^\mu / \partial \tau^\mu < 0$.

14.3 Duality and Policy Distance Functions

It is useful to develop the parallels between the connection of the price and quantity trade policy variants of the distance function we use here, on the one hand, and the well-known duality between the expenditure and distance functions in standard consumer theory, on the other hand.

It is natural to think that the TRI and the CTU are duals. In fact they are not, although there is a close connection between the two. We return to the case of a partial index of quotas, but in the presence of possible tariffs on unconstrained goods.

The diagram above closely resembles the standard consumer theory analysis (Deaton and Muellbauer 1982) in which the contour is an isoutility locus. Indeed, the trade analysis can be reinterpreted so that B measures money metric utility and the contours are iso-utility contours with greater u associated with moving northeast from the origin. In consumer theory the quantity space must include all commodities rather than a subset as in the trade policy analysis.[4] In the consumer analysis the distance function as developed by Deaton (1979) is denoted $d(q^1, u^0)$ and is defined implicitly by

$$d(q^1, u^0) : U\left(\frac{q^1}{d}\right) - u^0 = 0.$$

Note the parallel with (1). The expenditure function can be defined using the indirect utility function as

$$e(p^1, u^0) : V\left(\frac{p^1}{e}, 1\right) - u^0 = 0,$$

where the indirect utility function is defined by

$$V(p, e) = \max_q \{U(q) : p \cdot q = e\}.$$

Note the parallel between this definition of the expenditure function and the definition of the TRI: $\Delta(p^1, u^0) : B(p^1/\Delta, \pi^0, u^0) = 0$. Here we use the TRI in its deflator form $\Delta \equiv 1/(1 + \tau^\Delta)$ for convenience in making connections in this chapter. Notice that in the standard consumer analysis, the expenditure and distance functions are defined over all prices and quantities, whereas the policy indexes are defined for only some prices and quantities.

Further properties of the expenditure and distance functions of consumer theory reveal a second and even more important connection between them: they are minimum value functions and are duals. The distance function may be defined explicitly as

---

4. Usually in consumer theory the quantities are all positive, but for the case of household supply of labor and other resources there are negative quantities that represent household exports.

$$d(q^1, u^0) \equiv \min_p \{p \cdot q^1 : e(p, u^0) = 1\}.$$

In the latter form, d is interpreted as the ratio of the value of q^1 relative to the minimum value of q required to support u^0, all based on using the normalized shadow prices p to evaluate the quantities. The expenditure function has a dual definition:

$$e(p^1, u^0) \equiv \min_q \{p^1 \cdot q : d(q, u^0) = 1\}.$$

The use of the term "distance function" (Deaton 1979) strictly applies only to situations where duality may be invoked. We describe our general approach as using a variant of the distance function because we define our distance function implicitly on a subset of arguments of a function that is not a minimum value function. Thus duality does not obtain. Specifically, we apply a scalar to a subset of arguments of the balance-of-trade function that is not a minimum value function. Moreover the quantity derivatives of the balance-of-trade function are not proportional to prices nor are its price derivatives proportional to quantities.

Nevertheless, there is a close connection between the CTU, the quantity analogue to the TRI, and the TRI, the price analogue of the CTU, as alternative ways of expressing the trade restrictiveness of the same policy system. The two are ordinarily monotonically related, just as in the scalar case the tariff equivalent of a quota is monotonically related to the quota. Moreover the two indexes evaluate marginal changes in trade quantities with alternative normalizations. This follows from considering local changes about free trade where the virtual price is equal to the external price, $\tilde{p} = p^*$:

$$\frac{1}{D} D_{q_i} = \frac{\tilde{B}_{q_i}}{\tilde{B}'_q q D},$$

$$\frac{1}{\Delta} \Delta_{q_i} = \frac{B'_{\tilde{p}} \tilde{p}_{q_i}}{B'_{\tilde{p}} \tilde{p} / \Delta}.$$

The numerators of the two ratios are equal by construction. The denominators are ordinarily opposite in sign but not equal in absolute value, save in the special case where

$$-\tilde{p}_q q = \tilde{p}.$$

The qualification on monotonicity and on the sign of the denominator is needed when not all elements of $B_{\tilde{p}}$ and $\tilde{B}_q$ are the same sign or when not all elements of $\tilde{p}_q q$ have the same sign.[5]

14.4   Relation to the Coefficient of Resource Utilization

Debreu (1951) developed the seminal idea of evaluating the actual consumption bundle for a closed economy relative to the most efficient set of bundles available with the technology and the resources of the economy using what, following Deaton, we now call the distance function. He called it the coefficient of resource utilization (CRU). We give added perspective to the TRI and the CTU, by relating them to this concept in our context of a small open economy.

As Debreu showed, the CRU has the minimum value property, and so it has a dual. We have established that the TRI and its quantity analogue, the CTU, are not minimum value functions and thus do not have duals. Nevertheless, there are connections between the CRU, on the one hand, and the TRI and CTU, on the other hand. The CRU is a measure of the efficiency of the trading economy as a whole, a welfare measure, while the TRI and CTU are measures of the restrictiveness of the trade policy.

Debreu did not explicitly develop an open economy version of his model (though, by considering trade as a technology, we may interpret him to encompass a trading economy), while his treatment included many consumers and great generality with respect to production sets and consumer preferences. We interpret his CRU in modern terms for our small open economy. We develop the cases of price distortions only and of quota distortions only and relate the CRU to the TRI for the former case and to its quantity analogue the CTU for the latter case.

Debreu's coefficient of resource utilization is implicitly defined as

$$\kappa(\pi^0, \pi^*, u^0, v^0) : B(\pi^*, u^0, \kappa v^0) = B(\pi^0, u^0, v^0).$$

Here we make explicit the resource (factor) endowment vector v^0 and consider tariffs only. The CRU, κ, gives the scalar amount by which all resources (factor endowments) can be shrunk while delivering the original

---

5. In the scalar case the monotonic relation of the tariff equivalent and the quota is automatically guaranteed by the concavity of the trade expenditure function in prices, and the problem of aggregating distinct components does not arise.

level of utility at free-trade prices. It is a measure of the overall inefficiency of the economy, a compensating variation type of welfare measure. For a small trading economy with no distortions but those of trade, the efficient price vector is the free-trade price vector; hence $\pi^0 \neq \pi^* \Rightarrow \kappa < 1$. With constant returns to scale in production we can solve explicitly for the CRU as

$$\kappa = \frac{e(\pi^*, u^0)}{g(\pi^*, v^0)} = \frac{e(\pi^*, u^0)}{e(\pi^*, u^*)}.$$

Now consider the TRI for the same economy. It is defined by

$$\tau^\Delta : B[\pi^*(1 + \tau^\Delta), u^0, v^0] = B(\pi^0, u^0, v^0) = 0.$$

Even if the technology is homogeneous of degree one, it is impossible to solve explicitly for the uniform tariff equivalent. This is because the vector of distorted prices does not include the undistorted prices; hence none of the underlying functions is homogeneous in π.

A more significant difference between the TRI and the CRU is that the CRU has the minimum value property[6] while the TRI does not. Nevertheless, the TRI $(\Delta = 1/(1 + \tau^\Delta))$ is equal to one, as is the CRU, when a small economy trades freely $(\tau^\Delta = 0)$, and ordinarily the CRU falls monotonically as the TRI rises.

Now consider the CTU and CRU measures in economies with quotas. The CTU is defined by

$$D : \tilde{B}(Dq^*, \pi^*, u^0, v^0) = \tilde{B}(q^0, \pi^*, u^0, v^0) = 0.$$

Here the constraining quotas act essentially like "resource" constraints and we denote the free trade quantities as q^*. The CRU in an economy with quotas is defined by

$$\kappa(q^0, q^*, u^0, v^0) : \tilde{B}(q^*, \pi^*, u^0, \kappa v^0) = \tilde{B}(q^0, \pi^*, u^0, v^0) = 0.$$

Again, the CRU is a measure of the inefficiency of the trading economy as a whole. The CTU is a measure of the degree to which trade is restricted. Both are equal to one at free trade and the CRU ordinarily falls monotonically as the CTU falls.

---

6. Define the vector of shadow prices of resources as $w = B_v(\pi, u, v)$. Invert to obtain the resource demand vector as $v = \varphi(\pi, u, w)$. Substitute into the balance-of-trade function to define $G(\pi, u, w) = B[\pi, u, \varphi(\pi, u, w)]$. Then the explicit definition of the CRU is

$$\kappa(\pi, u, v^0) = \min_w \{w'v^0 : G(\pi, u, w) = 0\}.$$

14.5   Application 1: The Multi-Fibre Arrangement

We apply the methods of this chapter to the evaluation of two quota
systems with distinct institutional features: textiles and apparel, and dairy
products. Taken together they illustrate the adaptability of our method to
different forms of rent-sharing and different economic structural details.
In both the MFA and dairy cases we construct annual rates of change of
trade restrictiveness. These are compared to the implications of annual
average tariff equivalents of the quotas. In both cases we find that the
quantity version of the TRI, or CTU, is nearly uncorrelated with the
atheoretic trade-weighted average of tariff equivalents.

The most important quota system in the world is that for textiles and
apparel (the Multi-Fibre Arrangement), affecting the trade of most developed importing nations and a host of developing exporting nations.
In form it is a voluntary export restraint (VER) system, in which the
exporters negotiate quotas with the importers under threat of possible tariffs. The importers' tariffs on textiles and apparel serve to retain some
quota rent, with the remainder going to the license holders. The restrictiveness of this system shifts about through time as demand shifts and
negotiated quota changes take effect. Key evidence of such shifts is provided by data on the price of quota licenses on the Hong Kong and
Jakarta markets, which reveal both time-series and cross-sectional variation in the underlying scarcity of licenses. Our methods permit a rigorous
evaluation of the restrictiveness of policy for both importer and exporter
based on a proper index making use of this data.

We analyze the US imports of MFA-constrained goods from a set of
exporters. An interesting feature of this system is that Hong Kong has
substantial monopoly power in trade for MFA-constrained exports to
the United States. Quota relaxation then has a negative terms-of-trade
effect for Hong Kong, and for sufficiently low elasticities, Hong Kong
loses from relaxation. Our study shows this occurs at the low end of a
plausible range of elasticities.

Not all of the VER rents accrue to license holders since the United
States levies ad valorem tariffs on such imports.[7] This implies that the
share of rents accruing to the United States varies both with q and across
commodities within the quota-constrained group. The basis of our study
is data on license transfer prices from the Hong Kong market. While

---

7. Since the quotas always bind, the goods are quota-constrained throughout and so these
tariffs serve solely as a rent-sharing mechanism.

there are restrictions on transfer that act rather like a tax, we treat the license price as equal to the rent going to license holders. We also have a limited amount of data on Indonesian license prices, treated similarly. For other exporters, we follow Carl Hamilton in generating imputed quota rents from extrapolating from the Hong Kong database. Because of its greater reliability we report US–HK results first, from both countries' points of view. Then we report changes in the restrictiveness of the MFA for other exporters.

The first task is to construct an expression for the shadow price of quotas. We assume that for any individual quota-constrained import, indexed by j, international arbitrage equates the US import price p_j to the Hong Kong export price p^*, plus the price of a Hong Kong export license ρ_j, grossed up by the ad valorem US tariff rate τ_j:[8]

$$p_j = (1 + \tau_j)(p_j^* + \rho_j). \tag{4}$$

The effect of US tariff policy is thus to divide up the total rent per unit import, $p_j - p_j^*$, such that only the license price ρ_j accrues to Hong Kong and the balance, $p_j - p_j^* - \rho_j$, accrues to the United States. Summing over all the quota-constrained goods, the rents accruing to the United States equal the total rents $(p - p^*)'q$ less Hong Kong license revenue $\rho'q$. Using (4) to simplify and substituting into the distorted balance-of-trade function using $\underline{x}$ to denote the diagonal matrix with the elements of vector x on the principal diagonal, we obtain[9]

$$[\tilde{B}(q, \pi, u, \gamma)]_{US} \equiv \tilde{E}(q, \pi, u, \gamma) + p'(I + \underline{\tau})^{-1}q - t'm - \beta.$$

Differentiating with respect to q and simplifying yields the following expression for the shadow price of quotas from the US point of view:

$$[-\tilde{B}_q']_{US} = p'\underline{\tau}(I + \underline{\tau})^{-1} - q'(I + \underline{\tau})^{-1}p_q + t'\tilde{m}_q. \tag{5}$$

Our assumptions about partial rent-sharing are seen to affect the expression for the shadow price of quotas in two ways. First, relaxing the quota on good j by one unit yields a direct gain that in the general case equals the price differential, $p_j - p_j^*$, dampened by the fraction of rents lost ω_j and by any change in ω_j. Under the present specification this gain simplifies to the price differential less the rent ρ_j that accrues to the

---

8. We follow other researchers in assuming that the license price is included in the FOB price and so is subject to the tariff. Estimates based on the alternative assumption, $p_j = (1 + \tau_j)p^* + \rho_j$, are available on request.

9. In this case, the share of rents lost is: $\omega_j = \{p_j - (1 + \tau_j)p^*\}/\{(1 + \tau_j)(p_j - p^*)\}$.

exporter; from (4), this equals $\tau_j p_j / (1 + \tau_j)$. Second, such a relaxation tends to alter the domestic prices p of all quota-constrained goods, so altering the fraction $1/(1 + \tau_j)$ of rents on each good j that is lost to foreigners.

The economic structure appropriate to applications where we are interested in only a few markets is naturally one of partial equilibrium. This implies that changes in trade policy do not affect the prices of nontraded goods and factors and that the goods to be considered are *separable* from others in excess demand. In our application to Hong Kong–US trade, all the goods examined were subject to binding export quotas, so separability is a restriction on the cross relationships between quota-constrained and other goods. This imposes a specific structure on the trade expenditure function:

$$E(p, \pi, u) = \xi[\mu(p, u), \psi(\pi, u), u].$$

The implications of this specification have been examined in chapter 7. In particular, two complicated matrix terms in the expression for the shadow price of quotas, equation (5), are greatly simplified. First, the term $-q'p_q$ (measuring the change in total rents arising from the effect of a quota relaxation on home prices) is replaced by $-p'/\varepsilon$, where ε (a negative scalar) is the aggregate elasticity of demand for quota-constrained goods. We impose for convenience the simplifying assumption that US tariffs on textile imports are uniform: $\tau_j = \tau$, all j.[10] This implies that the term $-q'(I + \underline{\tau})^{-1} p_q$ in (5) is replaced by $-[(1 + \tau)\varepsilon]^{-1} p'$. Second, the term $t'm_q$ (measuring the change in tariff revenue arising from a quota relaxation) is replaced by $-\tau^m p'$, where τ^m is the import-weighted average ad valorem tariff on the tariff-constrained m goods. With these simplifications, equation (5) for a single good j becomes

$$[-B_j]_{US} = \left[\frac{1}{1 + \tau} \left\{ \tau - \frac{1}{\varepsilon} \right\} - \tau^m \right] p_j.$$

Since the US tariffs on Hong Kong exports of textiles and apparel (τ_j) are of the order of 20 percent, but the US average tariff on other goods (τ^m) is only about 4 percent, the shadow prices of quotas are likely to be positive for the United States.

---

10. This assumption avoids the requirement for detailed estimates of the substitution matrix p_q. An alternative approach, adopted in Anderson and Neary (1994), is to assume a particular structure of demand, allowing the term $-q'(I + \underline{\tau})^{-1} p_q$ to be calculated explicitly.

In this application we assume plausibly that the United States is a small open economy: it faces constant marginal costs of Hong Kong textiles and apparel, so p^* is fixed in the relevant range of exports. The same cannot be assumed of Hong Kong, since it faces downward-sloping demand curves in the United States. Strictly speaking, this should be taken into account in our theoretical derivation.[11] However, a simpler approach that is appropriate in this partial equilibrium application is to subtract from the expression for the shadow price of quotas (now taking the Hong Kong rather than the US point of view) the effect on quota rents retained of changes in the quota licenses arising from a change in quota levels: $q'(d\rho/dq)$. From equation (4) this equals $q'(1 + \underline{\tau})^{-1}p_q$. Since this is also the second term in (5), our procedure amounts to treating the terms of trade *gain* to the United States of a quota relaxation as equaling the *loss* to Hong Kong. The other two terms in the expression for the shadow price of quotas are easily modified. Since Hong Kong exporters receive only the license price, the first term is simply ρ, and since Hong Kong does not impose tariffs on other goods, the t vector is zero and the third term vanishes.

The vector of quota shadow prices from Hong Kong's perspective is therefore

$$[-\tilde{B}'_q]_{HK} = \rho' + q'(I + \underline{\tau})^{-1}p_q. \tag{6}$$

As in the US case, assuming separability and uniform US tariffs yields for good j:

$$[-\tilde{B}_j]_{HK} = \rho_j + \frac{1}{(1 + \tau)\varepsilon}p_j.$$

Depending on the size of ε these shadow prices may be positive or negative.

We turn finally to our empirical application, which calculates a partial index for the restrictiveness of voluntary export restraints on US imports from Hong Kong under the MFA. Our sample consists of exports of twenty-seven categories of textiles and apparel from Hong Kong to the United States over the six years 1983 to 1988. The choice of coverage was determined by the availability of data on Hong Kong export quota licence prices, ρ; for these we used data collected by Carl Hamilton supplemented by World Bank estimates. (Our data are of average license

---

11. See Anderson and Neary (1992, sec. II.4), and Neary (1995) for further details.

prices, so implicitly assuming that quota allocations are fully utilized.) Data on export prices and quantities and US tariffs in each category were extracted from the World Bank's MFA database, and changes in real income for the two countries were measured by the growth rates in real disposable income.

Estimates of ε, the price elasticity of US demand for Hong Kong imports, were not available, so table 14.1 presents results for three alternative values -2.5, -5.0, and -10.0.[12] For each year and each value of ε, we give the changes in the uncompensated and compensated (for neutral growth) CTU's from the US and Hong Kong points of view. Our estimates for the change in the uncompensated CTU are calculated from equation (2), using the expressions for the shadow prices of quotas in equations (5) and (6) for the United States and Hong Kong respectively.[13] We also estimate the change in the compensated CTU, assuming that growth is neutral. In this case the rate of growth is subtracted from the rate of change of the uncompensated CTU. The changes in D and D^c are compared with the changes in the average tariff equivalent, calculated in the conventional manner as a trade-weighted average of the implicit tariffs, $p - p^*$.

Consider first the results from the US point of view. Our measure suggests that over the period there was a marked increase in the protectiveness of the trade regime. Although the uncompensated index D rose slightly in all years except 1984, it did so by less than the growth rate of real income. Therefore the value of the compensated index D^c fell in five of the six years, with a cumulative fall (representing an effective tightening of the quotas) of 15.7 percent. By contrast, the traditional measure, the average tariff equivalent, fluctuated widely over the same period, with a cumulative fall of 22.9 percent, apparently implying a lessening of restrictiveness. The year-to-year variability of this measure is highly implausible. Moreover in four out of six years and over the period as a whole, the average tariff equivalent has the opposite implication for the change in trade restrictiveness as our index. This dramatic

12. These values reflect the fact that imports from Hong Kong are relatively close substitutes for other textile imports. If the two categories of imports are additively separable in US demand, then ε equals the elasticity of US demand for all textile imports, ε', divided by the Hong Kong import share. The latter equaled 20 percent in 1983, so our chosen values for ε correspond to values for ε' of -0.5, -1.0, and -2.0, with the unitary case being the literature's consensus. See Trela and Whalley (1990).

13. The formula for changes in the CTU refers to local changes whereas the data refer to discrete intervals. To allow for this, the changes given are Törnqvist indexes, calculated using the arithmetic averages of the parameters in two successive periods.

Table 14.1
Changes in the CTU: Hong Kong textiles and apparel exports to the United States, 1982 to 1988

	US point of view, changes in:			Hong Kong point of view, changes in:			Change in average tariff equivalent
	D	Real income	D^c	D	Real income	D^c	
ε: −2.5							
1983*	2.6	3.9	−1.3	4.1	5.4	−1.3	84.4
1984*	−4.1	6.8	−10.9	−3.7	10.6	−14.3	−8.1
1985*	1.9	3.2	−1.3	0.5	2.5	−2.0	−39.2
1986	6.5	2.8	3.7	0.0	8.6	−8.6	42.2
1987	1.1	2.9	−1.8	−8.0	12.7	−20.7	12.0
1988*	0.8	4.5	−3.7	−0.9	6.4	−7.3	−53.0
1983–1988	8.8	26.6	−15.7	7.8	55.6	−66.1	−22.9
ε: −5.0							
1983	2.8	3.9	−1.1	2.4	5.4	−3.0	84.4
1984	−4.2	6.8	−11.0	−5.4	10.6	−16.0	−8.1
1985	1.7	3.2	−1.5	3.9	2.5	1.4	−39.2
1986	6.6	2.8	3.8	3.9	8.6	−4.7	42.2
1987	1.0	2.9	−1.9	0.9	12.7	−11.8	12.0
1988	0.9	4.5	−3.6	−0.1	6.4	−6.5	−53.0
1983–1988	8.8	26.6	−15.7	5.8	55.6	−46.9	−22.9
ε: −10.0							
1983	3.0	3.9	−0.9	−2.7	5.4	−8.1	84.4
1984	−4.3	6.8	−11.1	−4.6	10.6	−15.2	−8.1
1985	1.6	3.2	−1.6	3.0	2.5	0.5	−39.2
1986	6.7	2.8	3.9	5.1	8.6	−3.5	42.2
1987	0.9	2.9	−2.0	1.1	12.7	−11.6	12.0
1988	1.1	4.5	−3.4	0.1	6.4	−6.3	−53.0
1983–1988	9.0	26.6	−15.4	2.3	55.6	−52.1	−22.9

Notes: All figures are percentage changes; the asterisk (*) denotes cases in which the marginal quota deflator was negative from Hong Kong's point of view.

finding, similar to that in our next case of US dairy quotas, reveals the serious practical inadequacy of the standard measure of trade restrictiveness. Note that our US estimates are not at all sensitive to different assumptions about the elasticity of demand, ε. Although from equation (5) all shadow prices rise as the elasticity falls, this tends to affect all categories uniformly in both the numerator and denominator of the expression for the change in D and so does not significantly alter the estimated change.

Turning to the results from the Hong Kong point of view, they reveal further interesting properties of the CTU approach. The estimates are much more sensitive to the value of the elasticity than were those for the United States. Moreover in four years when ε is at its low value, most or all of the estimated quota shadow prices are negative, with the result that the marginal quota deflator, $B'_q q$, is itself negative. This implies that a fall in D is welfare-*improving*, namely that in those cases Hong Kong's monopoly power in trade is so great that the actual quota levels are *above* their optimal values.[14] If we confine attention to the central case ($\varepsilon = -5$), D^c fell in five of the six years, implying that Hong Kong as well as the United States has been experiencing policy changes in the direction of greater restrictiveness. Once again, the implications of our measure are very different from those of the crude change in the average tariff equivalent.

We can draw inferences about the restrictiveness of the MFA with regard to other exporters by filling in missing license price data using a technique of Carl Hamilton. By assuming perfect substitutability and perfect arbitrage, it can be inferred that the export price must be the same in each category:

$$p^{*EX} + \rho^{EX} = p^{*HK} + \rho^{HK} \qquad \text{for any exporter } EX. \tag{7}$$

The right-hand side is given, so the left-hand side can be split into its two components if the variable p^{*EX} can be identified. Hamilton's method is to construct marginal costs of exporters based on relative wage data adjusted for labor productivity. For Taiwan he reports that the implied estimates of ρ do not differ much from the limited license price information available. (See Hamilton 1988 for details.) In Krishna, Erzan, and Tan (1992), Hamilton's method was checked against two years of Indonesian license price data and found to give a large overestimate of the value

14. Trela and Whalley (1990) also find that the terms-of-trade loss from a reversion to free trade hurts Hong Kong, although their results are not fully comparable with ours.

of a license. A prime explanation of this is that the cost projection method is in error.[15]

Fortunately, the CTU results are insensitive to across-the-board adjustments of the type implied by the productivity story, as noted below. (A more problematic reason for the divergence of the inferred from the direct license data is quality differences, which implies that the arbitrage equation is not applicable. If this were important, it would mean that the results for exporters other than Hong Kong are suspect.)

The level of commodity aggregation within textiles and apparel is to the 27 categories for which license price data are available, and the years studied (1982–1988) are similarly those for which complete license price data are available. Not all exporters ship in all categories, of course, and Bangladesh is subject to constraint only for 1986 to 1988 (after MFA-IV). Panel A of table 14.2 presents the results for the base case of US demand elasticity equal to one. Panels B and C of the table report the results for elasticity equal to 0.5 and 2 respectively. The change in trade restrictiveness of US policy for all exporters (including Hong Kong for reference) from both the exporter and US point of view is compared to the level and percentage change in average tariff equivalent.

The results are quite striking in their implications for the use of the CTU. First, in the base case, *the yearly changes in the tariff equivalent of the quota have the opposite implication from the rate of change of the CTU in 21 out of the 38 observations.* The correlation between the two series is equal to -0.01, which is not significantly different from zero.

Second, the results are not very sensitive to changes in the assumed elasticity of demand. In table 14.2 sensitivity appears only in the results for Hong Kong from the Hong Kong point of view. This arises because Hong Kong has significant monopoly power in the low-elasticity case.

Third, the results are not sensitive to variations in the method used to impute the license prices for exporters other than Hong Kong. A simple test of sensitivity to the method arises if relative unit costs are inferred from relative wages without adjusting for productivity. The imputed license prices rise by several hundred percent. Nevertheless, the CTU rates of change from this experiment (not shown) are altered by less than 5 percent of the values in table 14.2.

Finally, a natural use of the CTU is to compare the evolution of trade policy across countries. The relative treatment of exporters in the MFA is

---

15. Effectively, a Cobb-Douglas framework is assumed. See Krishna, Erzan, and Tan (1994) for details.

Table 14.2
CTU and tariff-equivalent indexes

	Year	Change in export D^c	Average tariff equivalent	Average tariff equivalent change	Change in US D^c
Panel A: Base case $\varepsilon' = -1.0$					
Bangladesh	1987	10.9	189.9	−3.8	14.1
	1988	17.0	182.8	−3.8	13.1
Hong Kong	1983	−3.0	30.9	84.4	−1.1
	1984	−16.2	28.5	−8.1	−11.0
	1985	1.4	19.2	−39.2	−1.5
	1986	−4.7	29.4	42.2	3.8
	1987	−11.8	33.2	12.0	−1.9
	1988	−6.5	19.3	−53.0	−3.6
India	1983	31.6	80.0	−14.6	28.8
	1984	−9.3	73.2	−8.8	−12.2
	1985	6.4	127.1	53.8	9.5
	1986	−31.1	225.3	55.7	−30.4
	1987	62.3	140.6	−46.3	70.1
	1988	−5.8	154.2	9.2	−1.0
Indonesia	1983	−0.5	23.4	225.4	4.4
	1984	3.0	65.5	94.8	6.0
	1985	4.6	71.8	9.1	5.1
	1986	18.5	127.1	55.7	22.5
	1987	−3.2	168.3	27.9	1.2
	1988	5.6	175.6	4.2	8.6
South Korea	1983	−8.4	90.8	40.1	−0.1
	1984	−11.2	67.9	−28.9	−9.4
	1985	14.8	96.0	34.3	13.5
	1986	−6.1	74.7	−24.9	1.9
	1987	−10.9	56.1	−28.5	−2.3
	1988	−13.5	27.3	−69.1	−7.4
Mexico	1983	26.9	67.7	218.9	21.5
	1984	19.4	40.5	−50.3	15.5
	1985	−53.9	52.7	26.2	−38.1
	1986	78.4	56.2	6.3	58.5
	1987	36.8	80.0	35.0	29.0
	1988	8.3	77.9	−2.7	5.1
Thailand	1983	11.5	72.8	−16.7	16.4
	1984	−1.1	38.3	−62.2	2.5
	1985	−36.3	67.5	55.2	−38.1
	1986	33.4	48.7	−32.3	28.2
	1987	−17.7	50.9	4.4	−15.3
	1988	−9.4	45.5	−11.2	−4.5

Table 14.2
(continued)

Year	Change in export D^c	Average tariff equivalent	Average tariff equivalent change	Change in US D^c
Panel B: $\varepsilon' = -0.50$				
Bangladesh	1987	10.9	189.9	-3.8	13.9
	1988	17.0	182.8	-3.8	13.0
Hong Kong	1983*	-1.3	30.9	84.4	-1.3
	1984*	-14.3	28.5	-8.1	-10.9
	1985*	-2.0	19.2	-39.2	-1.3
	1986	-8.6	29.4	42.2	3.7
	1987	-20.7	33.2	12.0	-1.8
	1988*	-7.3	19.3	-53.0	-3.7
India	1983	31.7	80.0	-14.6	30.0
	1984	-9.3	73.2	-8.8	-12.0
	1985	6.4	127.1	53.8	9.3
	1986	-31.1	225.3	55.7	-29.9
	1987	62.3	140.6	-46.3	68.1
	1988	-5.8	154.2	9.2	-1.0
Indonesia	1983	-0.2	23.4	225.4	4.4
	1984	2.9	65.5	94.8	6.2
	1985	4.7	71.8	9.1	4.8
	1986	18.4	127.1	55.7	22.7
	1987	-3.2	168.3	27.9	1.1
	1988	5.6	175.6	4.2	8.6
South Korea	1983	-8.4	90.8	40.1	0.0
	1984	-11.2	67.9	-28.9	-9.4
	1985	16.4	96.0	34.3	13.3
	1986	-5.8	74.7	-24.9	2.0
	1987	-10.8	56.1	-28.5	-2.3
	1988	-19.1	27.3	-69.1	-7.4
Mexico	1983	27.9	67.7	218.9	21.8
	1984	19.5	40.5	-50.3	15.6
	1985	-54.6	52.7	26.2	-39.3
	1986	78.8	56.2	6.3	59.6
	1987	37.1	80.0	35.0	29.4
	1988	8.4	77.9	-2.7	5.3
Thailand	1983	11.5	72.8	-16.7	16.6
	1984	-1.2	38.3	-62.2	2.0
	1985	-36.3	67.5	55.2	-38.1
	1986	33.6	48.7	-32.3	28.9
	1987	-17.6	50.9	4.4	-15.3
	1988	-9.3	45.5	-11.2	-4.3

Table 14.2
(continued)

	Year	Change in export D^c	Average tariff equivalent	Average tariff equivalent change	Change in US D^c
Panel C: $\varepsilon' = -2.0$					
Bangladesh	1987	10.9	189.9	−3.8	14.5
	1988	17.0	182.8	−3.8	13.3
Hong Kong	1983	−8.1	30.9	84.4	0.9
	1984	−15.2	28.5	−8.1	−11.1
	1985	0.5	19.2	−39.2	−1.6
	1986	−3.5	29.4	42.0	3.9
	1987	−11.6	33.2	12.0	−2.0
	1988	−6.3	19.3	−53.0	−3.4
India	1983	31.5	80.0	−14.6	26.9
	1984	−9.3	73.2	−8.8	−12.5
	1985	6.4	127.1	53.8	9.9
	1986	−31.1	225.3	55.7	−31.2
	1987	62.4	140.6	−46.3	73.5
	1988	−5.8	154.2	9.2	−1.1
Indonesia	1983	−0.8	23.4	225.4	4.4
	1984	3.1	65.5	94.8	5.8
	1985	4.6	71.8	9.1	5.5
	1986	18.5	127.1	55.7	22.1
	1987	−3.1	168.3	27.9	1.3
	1988	5.6	175.6	4.2	8.6
South Korea	1983	−8.4	90.8	40.1	−0.1
	1984	−11.2	67.9	−28.9	−9.5
	1985	14.3	96.0	34.3	13.7
	1986	−6.2	74.7	−24.9	1.8
	1987	−11.0	56.1	−28.5	−2.4
	1988	−13.9	27.3	−69.1	−7.4
Mexico	1983	26.0	67.7	218.9	21.0
	1984	19.4	40.5	−50.3	15.3
	1985	−53.6	52.7	26.2	−36.3
	1986	78.2	56.2	6.3	56.7
	1987	36.7	80.0	35.0	28.4
	1988	8.3	77.9	−2.7	4.8
Thailand	1983	11.5	72.8	−16.7	16.0
	1984	−1.0	38.3	−62.2	3.2
	1985	−36.4	67.5	55.2	−38.0
	1986	33.3	48.7	−32.3	27.2
	1987	−17.8	50.9	4.4	−15.2
	1988	−9.4	45.5	−11.2	−4.8

Note: All figures in the table give annual percentage changes except for the level of the average tariff equivalent, in percent. See the text for details of calculations. The asterisk (*) denotes negative shadow value of distorted trade.

a subject of considerable international political interest and pressure, peaking at negotiation times. The results show that there is a large degree of nonuniformity across exporters in the evolution of MFA policy, broadly in favor of the lower cost exporters. Table 14.2 shows that MFA trade policy became more restrictive toward Korea and Thailand as well as Hong Kong. By contrast, policy became less restrictive toward Indonesia, Mexico, and Bangladesh. Toward India, policy evolved more ambiguously, but on balance became somewhat less restrictive. Significantly this policy difference across exporters is not well described by the evolution of the average tariff equivalent index due to the zero correlation between imputed average tariff equivalents and the CTU.

Each bilateral policy might naturally be evaluated from either the exporter's or the importer's point of view. The main emphasis here is on the exporter's point of view, but political pressure by exporters on importers might well be countered with use of a CTU based on the importers point of view. In this case adjustment of quota policy for growth makes a significant difference to the policy conclusion. With high-growth exporters and low-growth importers, the change in point of view is enough to make the evaluation of quota policy using the compensated CTU reverse sign in five cases of small monopoly power (2 for Indonesia, 1 for Korea, and 1 for Thailand), besides two cases for Hong Kong that mix this effect with the effect of monopoly power. In such cases a more appropriate index is the uncompensated CTU for the exporter or importer. The uncompensated CTUs differ in sign in only one observation in the base case, that of Hong Kong for 1988.

We conclude our discussion of results with some speculation as to why the CTU and average tariff equivalent results are uncorrelated. The trade-weighted average tariff equivalent has no theoretical foundation of course, but its common use (along with the even more common use of average tariffs for non–quota-constrained goods) makes it a natural benchmark. The lack of correlation is perplexing in light of intuition based on only one quota-constrained good. In this case the rate of change of the license price and minus the rate of change of the quota necessarily have the same sign.[16] Where does the difference in the two indexes come from?

---

16. The rate of change of the domestic price is equal to the elasticity of demand times minus the rate of change of the quota. The rate of change of the license price is equal to the rate of change of the domestic price times the ratio of the domestic price to the license price.

First, license prices change for many reasons other than shifts in the quota. This can explain the absence of strong negative correlation between changes in license prices and changes in quotas over time for each element of the indexes. On the supply side of the market, the export prices change over time independently of the level of the importer's quotas. On the demand side of the market, the domestic prices p_j are changed over time by changes in national income and changes in unconstrained goods prices as well as changes in quotas. It should also be noted that the generalized law of demand, even for the separable case, does not guarantee perfect negative correlation of price and quantity, ceteris paribus.

Second, there is a difference in practice between the CTU weights and the trade weights used to form the indexes. For the importer this difference disappears in the separable case under the restriction that the rent-retaining tariff is uniform over quota-constrained goods. For the exporter, extreme false assumptions are required to reduce CTU weights to trade weights. It is possible to construct an argument that the weights of the CTU and the tariff equivalent tend to be negatively correlated in the cross section of quota-constrained goods due to the dispersion of rent-retaining tariffs and of ad valorem license prices.

We conclude that theory gives no reason to expect that the average tariff equivalent will behave similarly to the CTU. Where it diverges, the CTU is a properly weighted index of changes in the actual policy, the vector of quotas, while the average tariff equivalent is an atheoretically weighted index of changes in the license prices (or price differentials) that can be the result of changes in many factors other than policy.

14.6   The Trade Restrictiveness of US Dairy Quotas

The US restricts the imports of a large number of cheeses and other dairy products as an adjunct to the milk price support system. (See Anderson 1985 for a full description.) Arbitrage of quota licenses is prevented by regulation backed by an apparently effective audit. Small numbers of license holders for narrowly defined products (Danish blue cheese) face small numbers of exporters (the Danish cheese marketing board). In these circumstances economic theory predicts bargaining over the quota rents, and indeed Hornig, Boisvert, and Blandford (1990a,b) develop data on European factory cost and US wholesale price that reveal that across a number of cheese categories the rent is evenly split, with little variation over categories. Direct comparison of US wholesale prices for imported cheese with the corresponding f.o.b. export prices makes it possible to infer quota rents which flow to US license holders. The restrictiveness of US quota policy implied by this data varies substantially across cheese varieties and shifts about substantially through time. We apply our methods to construct an index of the overall restrictiveness of dairy quota policy.

Based on this description we specialize the general expression for the shadow price of quotas as follows. We assume that the rent share is constant across categories (and in the application equal to $\frac{1}{2}$ as in the Nash bargaining solution). We interpret this as a solution to Rubinstein's (1982) alternating offers game with bargaining power determined by equal discount rates for the two partners. The United States levies an ad valorem tariff on cheese imports, but the tariff serves only to redistribute rent between the importer and the government. So it acts as a lump-sum tax on licensees, with no effect on the bargaining solution and no effect on the shadow price of quotas. The shadow price of quotas is taken to be $-B'_q = (1 - \omega)(p - p^*)' - \omega q' p_q + t' \tilde{m}_q$. Applying implicit separability, the shadow price becomes (see chapter 6)

$$-B'_q = (1 - \omega)(p - p^*) + \left(\frac{\omega}{\varepsilon}\right) p' - \tau^m p'.$$

The model is implemented for US cheese data from 1964 to 1979. We first construct the shadow price of quotas for each category in each year. The aggregate elasticity ε is built up from the detailed elasticity system estimated by Anderson (1985) using Deaton and Muellbauer's AIDS (almost ideal demand system), which is a flexible functional form. At the point of means, the elasticity of US aggregate demand for cheese (6 domestic and 9 imported categories) was calculated to be -3.54. The rent share ω is equal to $\frac{1}{2}$ based on Boisvert et al. The trade-weighted average tariff on all other goods than cheese is calculated for each year in the sample to provide the value of τ^m. Finally the data on US wholesale prices of imported cheese and on the f.o.b. export price (the bargained price) are used to provide estimates of $(1 - \omega)(p - p^*)$ as the remaining element of the shadow price. The average annual percentage change in each category of imported cheese is then calculated. We then calculate the discrete form of equation (2) with a Törnqvist index. (See Anderson 1991 for more details, and applications to evaluation of quota reform.)

Table 14.3 presents the annual percentage changes in the CTU for cheese imports from 1965 to 1979 in the right column. Notice the very restrictive policies followed in the mid- and late 1970s, with a break in

Table 14.3
Rate of change of cheese trade efficiency, 1965 to 1979

Year	Tariff equivalent	CTU
1965	0.10	−0.12
1966	**0.26**	**0.10**
1967	0.05	−0.03
1968	**0.40**	**0.05**
1969	**− 0.47**	**− 0.09**
1970	**− 0.02**	**− 0.12**
1971	**0.13**	**− 0.15**
1972	**− 0.04**	**− 0.08**
1973	**− 0.08**	**− 0.06**
1974	**− 0.05**	**− 0.27**
1975	**− 0.03**	**− 0.32**
1976	−0.01	0.03
1977	0.12	−0.21
1978	0.06	−0.15
1979	0.15	−0.22
Average	0.04	−0.11

1976, a year in which a temporary relaxation of the quota was permitted to help in the political struggle against food price inflation.

The annual percentage change in the trade-weighted average tariff equivalent of the quotas is presented in the middle column. The average change over the fifteen years is 4 percent, doubling the average tariff rate every eighteen years, and similarly implying a sharp rise in restrictions. In contrast, the observations for which the two measures have the same sign (diverge in implication) are printed in boldface. This occurs in eight of fifteen cases. Another way to describe the result is with correlation analysis. One might expect the two series to be perfectly negatively correlated in a rank sense. Spearman's rank correlation coefficient for the two series is 0.34, which does not permit rejection of the null hypothesis of no relation between the series.

The level of restrictiveness on average in the sample period is high according to either measure. The average level of the ad valorem tariff equivalent is around 25 percent (the basis for the changes in table 14.1). It should be noted that this figure is related to the retained rent concept used in forming the shadow price of quotas, with an average "tariff equivalent of retained rent" equal to $(1 - \omega)(p - p^*) \cdot q/p^* \cdot q$. The coefficient of trade utilization for the move to free trade is 2.3, meaning a 130 percent average rise in quantity can be achieved. The two percentages are very roughly connected via the aggregate elasticity of -3.5.

We conclude with a brief discussion of sensitivity to specification assumptions. Since all time series are substantially driven by cyclical phenomena, it is worth noting that cyclic disturbances are purged by the device of using trade quantities calculated to lie on the demand functions, which should take care of much of the problem. A complete accounting of cyclic versus other reasons for the behavior of effective trade policy is beyond the scope of this analysis, but something like 1966 to 1976 is a complete cycle, and the data do not suggest the dominance of cyclic phenomena in cheese policy.

The underlying data for the analysis includes detail on by-commodity by-country prices and quantities of cheese—New Zealand cheddar is different from Canadian cheddar. Feasibility of demand system estimation dictated aggregation, so the cheddar from various sources was treated as homogeneous. This implied large variation in imputed quota rents across source countries. (See Anderson 1985 for details.) This feasibility-driven compromise has an unknown influence on the quantitative results, but it is unlikely to alter the qualitative conclusion that the CTU and the trade-weighted tariff equivalent give very different implications.

15 Measuring Trade Restrictiveness in a Simple CGE Model

Which country's trade barriers are highest? Which countries have liberalized the most? The theory of part II shows that the appropriate measure of trade restrictiveness depends on the purpose of the analysis, defining the TRI with reference to welfare equivalence and the MTRI with reference to trade volume constancy. This chapter uses the TRI and MTRI to evaluate the overall trade restrictiveness of trade policy for a set of twenty-five countries. We implement the model with a common simple computable general-equilibrium model. The results show that traditional atheoretic measures of trade restrictiveness provide answers that are different from those obtained with the application of our methods. This conclusion should hold up under refinements of our methods and improvements in the data.

The evidence presented here is not as comprehensive as we would like, because systematic detailed panel data for trade policies are not available.[1] We present estimates of the trade restrictiveness of the overall trade policies of a set of twenty-five countries, using the TRI and the MTRI to provide a set of internationally comparable measures of the height of trade barriers. The sample includes both developed and developing countries, and high- and low-protection countries.

The uniform welfare equivalent tariff exceeds the uniform volume equivalent tariff and both usually exceed the trade-weighted average tariff. Our results show that using the average tariff can seriously distort the measure of trade restrictiveness. We provide additional measures of the

---

1. Detailed data for trade flows, tariffs, and nontariff barriers are needed on a comparable classification basis, which requires the detailed data and a concordance effort. Recently the TRAINS data set of UNCTAD provides such information for a subset of countries for recent years. While the best available, it is limited and incomplete. See Anderson and van Wincoop (2004) for discussion of its limitations.

change over time of trade restrictiveness for five countries. This provides a reference point for evaluation of yearly trade policy changes. The differences between the TRI and MTRI and between them, on the one hand, and the standard measures, on the other hand, are much larger for yearly changes. This is intuitive because in the move to free trade, all measures of trade restrictiveness fall, whereas with partial reform this need not be the case. The results for both levels and changes in trade restrictiveness suggest that there are errors in variables problems with the large body of empirical work which uses standard atheoretic measures of policy openness to control for the effect of trade policy as an independent variable in regression analysis.

We apply a common simple computable general-equilibrium (CGE) model specification to calculate our indexes, naturally changing the share parameters to reflect each country's economic structure and changing the distortion parameters to reflect each country's distortion structure.[2] The common model approach holds constant the effect of model specification in evaluating trade policy, a useful property that is purchased at the possible cost of raising the approximation error for some economies. The effect of different CGE common model specifications on the ranking of trade restrictiveness awaits further work.[3] Within the common model specification, sensitivity analysis reveals that the ranking of countries' trade restrictiveness is not much affected by variation in the elasticity parameters. The specification imposes simplicity in production to make feasible the calculation of almost any country's TRI and MTRI without requiring detailed production data of the kind needed in typical CGE models. The model nevertheless preserves the detailed structure of protection in each country to the maximum extent that is feasible.

The treatment of nontariff barriers (NTB's) is critical to the evaluation of trade distortions. Here too extremely simple assumptions are imposed to permit analysis in the face of missing information, particularly on free-trade prices. We test for sensitivity to assumptions, confirming our expectation that the analyst's treatment of the trade distortions (both tariff and nontariff) makes a big difference.

Our applications demonstrate that it is feasible to apply general-equilibrium models to calculate index numbers of trade policy. Detailed

2. In contrast, most CGE models are quite expensive to assemble and have specifications which are not common across countries because they are built by different scholars with different purposes in mind.

3. O'Rourke (1997) suggests that specification matters, at least for a special case of high dispersion.

trade and tariff information for many countries and years is now available on the World Bank's Trade and Production Database Web site (http://www1.worldbank.org/wbiep/trade/tradeandproduction.html).[4] We see no reason why calculation of our measures of trade restrictiveness should not now become routine.

In section 15.1, we describe the CGE model and the various treatments of NTB's. In section 15.2, we discuss the data and various procedures for handling it prior to calculation of the TRI and MTRI. In section 15.3, we present the results of calculating the TRI and MTRI to measure trade restrictiveness in twenty-five countries relative to free trade, and the results of calculating the TRI and MTRI to analyze five cases of year-on-year changes in trade restrictiveness.

15.1 The Model

The model will be described in stages. In section 15.1.1 a general description is followed by a flowchart. Then abstract simplified equations provide a link to the general notation of the book. The detailed set of equations for the CES/CET case is provided in the appendix. Section 15.1.2 provides a formal description of the various treatments of NTBs.

15.1.1 Operationalizing the General-Equilibrium Model

The computable general-equilibrium model we design is very simple in its production structure in order to allow room for complexity in the distortion structure. Thus we have but two goods produced, while allowing for thousands of imports, both intermediate and final. The aggregation in production avoids missing and/or incompatible data across a large number of countries, while the detail of trade distortions is essential to accurate evaluation of trade policy, as we have shown in part II of this book. (Typical CGE models allow for a few dozen sectors but use trade-weighted average tariffs and tariff equivalents to summarize trade policy for each sector.)

The economy produces two final composite goods, an exportable not consumed at home and a nontraded good. The two-good specification is the minimum complexity needed to allow for a nontraded goods sector, the latter being necessary to permit policy openness to interact with "natural" openness in the application of the model across economies.

4. This effort by the World Bank reduces a very considerable information barrier prior to 2001.

Exports and nontraded goods are jointly produced with a constant elasticity of transformation (CET) production function, given the level of activity. The inputs that produce the activity include a bundle of nontraded factors of production in fixed supply, a vector of imported inputs subject to binding quota constraints, and a vector of imported inputs subject to tariffs but not subject to quotas, all related by a constant elasticity of substitution (CES) production function. The technology exhibits constant returns to scale.

As for consumption, the representative consumer's tastes are represented by a CES expenditure function. The final goods consumed are a vector of final imports subject to tariffs but not quotas, a vector of final imports subject to binding quota constraints, and the nontraded good. The Armington assumption is applied to both imports and exports. The rationale for the Armington assumption of no domestic consumption of the export good is that packaging, safety, and other requirements differentiate it from home goods, while the absence of domestic production of imports is due to other familiar dimensions of product differentiation. (The Armington structure is applied to intermediate goods that are imported and not produced at home as well.)

The flowchart in figure 15.1 emphasizes the essential structure of the model, leaving out distortions and the redistribution of revenue, and aggregating trade. The heavy outside lines represent the equilibrium conditions in nontraded goods markets and the balance-of-payments con-

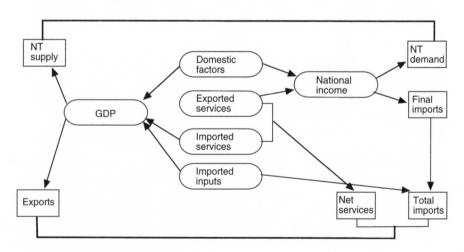

Figure 15.1
Flowchart of the simple CGE model

straint. The direction of arrows is for convenience in thinking through the logic of the model, as all cells are interdependent through dependence on the endogenous variables: real income and the relative price of the non-traded good.

Trade distortions are modeled as follows: All tariff revenue is assumed to be redistributed to the representative consumer. This includes tariff revenue collected on quota-constrained goods, where it serves to secure a portion of the quota rents. The economy is assumed to lose all quota rent other than that retained by tariffs: either to rent-seeking or to foreigners via the bargaining power they may have in narrow product lines.[5] All nontariff barriers are assumed to be quotas (or ignored as nonbinding).[6] Exports are assumed to be not subject to distortion and form a natural numéraire. Any undistorted imports also enter the composite numéraire.

The economy is assumed to be "small," facing fixed international prices. In general equilibrium the balance-of-trade constraint holds, simultaneously with market clearance for nontraded goods. The static Walrasian model is closed by imposing balance of payments with a net capital flow which is a constant share of GDP. (Trade restrictiveness index calculations are not sensitive to an alternative closure in which the net capital flow is exogenous.) The two constraints—balance of payments and nontraded goods market clearance—determine the equilibrium level of real income and the relative price of the nontraded good.

We now offer a brief formal description. We begin with the expenditure and GDP functions. Gross domestic product (GDP) is equal to the value at domestic prices of the nontraded good plus the export good (which is the numéraire) less the domestic value of imported inputs. Consumer expenditure is equal to the value of the nontraded good plus the domestic value of the final imports.

Based on the expenditure function, the distorted expenditure function is the minimum expenditure on unconstrained goods required to support a given real income u with prices for unconstrained final imports π^F, nontraded good price h, and quotas q^F. Similarly the distorted GDP function is the maximum value of GDP possible with imported input (materials) prices π^M, nontraded good price h, input quotas q^M, and shift parameters

---

5. If domestic rent-seeking exists, it uses factors in the same proportions as domestic value added.

6. This assumption is quite extreme and overstates the impact of some nontariff barriers. The alternative is to ignore the NTB as a nonbinding quota. A conservative filter (discussed in the data section below) was used to specify goods subject to NTB, which tends to understate the impact of NTBs.

γ. The distorted trade expenditure function is the difference between the distorted expenditure and GDP functions. Let the distorted consumer expenditure function be denoted $\tilde{e}(h, q^F, \pi^F, u)$, and let the distorted GDP function be denoted $\tilde{g}(h, q^M, \pi^M, \gamma)$. The CES-CET versions of these functions have closed forms, which are presented in the technical appendix to this chapter. For the CES-CET case there are natural price and quantity aggregates (the former for unconstrained and the latter for constrained goods) for final and intermediate imports based on the assumed structure.[7] The distorted functions inherit the derivative properties of the undistorted functions $e(h, p^F, \pi^F, u)$ and $g(h, p^M, \pi^M, g)$, noting that input demands are subtracted in the GDP function as opposed to final demands being added in the expenditure function. Thus $\tilde{g}_\pi$ is equal to the negative of the unconstrained input demand vector and $\tilde{g}_{q^M}$ is equal to the vector of virtual prices of quota constrained inputs.[8]

Our applications include comparisons of initial policies with free trade and comparisons of initial policies with an alternative (another year's policies) that is distorted. The discussion of chapter 8 reveals that the latter is a good deal more complex and general, reducing to the simple case when the alternative is indeed free trade. Thus we develop the complex case here, since it includes the free-trade case as a limiting case.

The model is solved for the TRI in two steps. The first step is to obtain the virtual prices $\tilde{p}$ associated with the new levels of the instruments and the old level of utility. These are found simultaneously with the nontraded good price $\tilde{h}$ associated with the new instruments and the old utility. $\tilde{h}$ is determined by the requirement that the nontraded good market clear:

$$\tilde{e}_h = \tilde{g}_h.$$

The implicit solution $\tilde{h}(q, \pi, u, \gamma)$ is substituted into $\tilde{e}_q$ and $\tilde{g}_q$ at the point $(q^{F,1}, q^{M,1}, \pi^{F,1}, \pi^{M,1}, u^0, \gamma^0)$ to evaluate the virtual prices $(\tilde{p}^F, \tilde{p}^M) = (-\tilde{e}_{q^F}, \tilde{g}_{q^M})$.

The second step is to calculate the equilibrium nontraded good price and the TRI. The new levels of the instruments (not generally at their free trade levels) imply domestic prices equal to $(\tilde{p}^F, \tilde{p}^M, \pi^{F,1}, \pi^{M,1})$. Deflating the domestic prices of tariff and tariff-equivalent ridden goods by Δ, the nontraded good market clearance equation is

7. The strong separability of the CES structure allows for closed form solutions for the price and quantity aggregates. In practice, the very large number of elements in $\tilde{p}$ need not be calculated, but only an index of them. Details of the structure are available on request.

8. The distorted trade expenditure function $\tilde{E}(q^F, \pi^F, u, \gamma)$ that subsumes the nontraded good price h is defined by $\max_h[\tilde{e}(h, q^F, \pi^F, u) - \tilde{g}(h, q^M, \pi^M, \gamma)]$.

$$e_h\left(h,\frac{\tilde{p}^F}{\Delta},\frac{\pi^{F,1}}{\Delta},u^0\right) = g_h\left(h,\frac{\tilde{p}^M}{\Delta},\frac{\pi^{M,1}}{\Delta},\gamma^0\right). \tag{1}$$

The balance of payments constraint is

$$e\left(h,\frac{\tilde{p}^F}{\Delta},\frac{\pi^{F,1}}{\Delta},u^0\right) - g\left(h,\frac{\tilde{p}^M}{\Delta},\frac{\pi^{M,1}}{\Delta},\gamma^0\right)$$

$$- \left(\frac{\pi^{F,1}}{\Delta} - \pi^{F,*}\right)\cdot e_\pi + \left(\frac{\pi^{M,1}}{\Delta} - \pi^{M,*}\right)\cdot g_\pi - t^q\cdot q^1 = b^0. \tag{2}$$

Here we use $q = (q^F, q^M)$. The quota-constrained goods are assumed to be subject to fixed tariffs at specific rate t^q, but the remaining quota rent is lost to foreigners. The system of equations (1) and (2) is solved for h and Δ simultaneously. (Note that the tariffs on quota-constrained goods are not deflated, being lump-sum, nondistortionary taxes.) The level of trade restrictiveness relative to free trade is found by setting the "new" levels of prices at their free-trade levels. The uniform-tariff-equivalent surcharge (uniform-equivalent tariff in the case of the free-trade comparison) is equal to $1/\Delta - 1$.

Calculation of the MTRI is nearly as simple. Let $p = (p^F, p^M)$ and $\pi = (\pi^F, \pi^M)$. The compensated import volume function is given by

$$M^c(h, p, \pi, u, \gamma) = \pi^{F,*}\cdot e_\pi(h, \pi^F, p^F, u) + p^{F,*}\cdot e_p$$

$$- \pi^{M,*}\cdot g_\pi(h, \pi^M, p^M, \gamma) - p^{M,*}\cdot g_\pi.$$

The constant volume constraint is expressed as

$$M^c\left(h, \frac{p^1}{\Delta^\mu}, \frac{\pi^1}{\Delta^\mu}, u, \gamma\right) = M^0 \tag{3}$$

The MTRI is calculated simultaneously with the level of utility and the nontraded goods price in the system (1) and (2), replacing the deflator Δ with Δ^μ in the first two equations.

15.1.2 Alternative Treatments of NTB-Constrained Goods

Two conceptual problems arise in practice with the evaluation of quotas. The first problem is with the meaning of the "new" trade policy in the presence of economic growth when making year-on-year comparisons. q^1 could be taken to be the actual quota in the new year. Alternatively, however, recognizing that growth will make an unchanging quota more restrictive, the new policy q^1 is defined to be the actual quota in the new year deflated by the aggregate GDP growth factor. Intuitively, for neutral growth (radial expansion of production and consumption), a quota is equi-restrictive if it grows at the growth rate. See chapter 8 for a full discussion.

The second conceptual problem with evaluation of changes in quota policy is what to do with changing levels of the rent-retaining tariff. t^q is a lump-sum (nondistortionary) instrument, so it is kept constant at the initial level for year-on-year evaluations designed to evaluate trade restrictiveness. Evaluation of the tariff equivalent of lump-sum taxes such as rent-retaining tariffs is almost trivial, and we do not consider it.

Turning to practical problems, we know that all efforts to deal with NTB's must deal with missing information on domestic prices, free-trade prices, and quota rent division between buyers and sellers. Inference of the prices in this study uses several expedients. In the evaluation of year-on-year changes, the model implies the change in domestic price (willingness to pay). Information on quota premia (which is generally missing) is not needed under the assumption that at the margin, all quota rent beyond that retained by tariffs is lost to foreigners or to rent-seeking. In contrast, in the evaluation of the hypothetical move to free trade, the missing quota premium problem means that free-trade prices (hence quantities) are unknown, so even more extreme assumptions are required. Three expedients are used in this study.

The first expedient, the *nonbinding NTB case*, assumes that rent-retaining tariffs capture all the quota rent, so the NTB is nonbinding at the margin in the initial equilibrium. Then the actual policy is fully equivalent to a tariffs only policy, and the TRI and MTRI are calculated by uniformly raising all distorted prices from the free-trade level. This means that rent-retaining tariffs are now varied in the "uniform-tariff equivalent." In other words, an implicit quota policy is combined with an efficient rent-retaining tariff policy. This is our base case.

Two other expedients are provided for sensitivity analysis. The second expedient for treating NTB-constrained goods is to assume that free trade implies a uniform 10 percent increase in NTB-constrained imports. The TRI (results for the MTRI are omitted for brevity) is calculated by (implicitly) restricting quantities so that the domestic prices of NTB-constrained goods rise uniformly, in step with the rise in tariff-ridden goods. Rent is lost save for that retained by the fixed rent-retaining tariffs. The third expedient builds on the first "as if tariffs" treatment, but with the difference that the initial rent-retaining tariffs are assumed to leave out a uniform retained rent premium worth 10 percent of the base external price. The TRI in this case also includes variation in the rent-retaining tariff so that, in effect, the policy switches from a rent-losing quota-cum-tariff policy to a full rent retention quota-cum-tariff policy. In contrast to the second expedient, there is a switch to an efficient rent-retaining tariff on formerly NTB-constrained goods. The results show that, as theory predicts, the third expedient has a larger uniform tariff equivalent, though in many instances the difference is quite small.

15.2 Data and Data Compromises

The primary data for the calculations consists of trade flows, tariffs, and nontariff barrier classifications for a detailed set of imports, consisting of about 1,200 harmonized system (HS) four-digit code categories for each of 25 countries, and for two adjacent years for the year-on-year sample. The data were assembled by the World Bank staff (mostly taken from the TRAINS data set maintained by UNCTAD). The data in the four-digit HS codes are aggregated from finer details merged from separately classified data sets for trade, tariffs, and "hard core" NTBs. These are concorded and aggregated using trade weights. (The four-digit HS codes are the finest classification for which satisfactory concordance was possible: our strategy was to preserve as much detail of distortions as feasible.) A given line of trade is deemed to be restricted by NTB's if 75 percent or more of the underlying categories are subject to NTBs. This conservative procedure eliminated a number of NTBs from further treatment. In addition to the primary data for the calculations it is necessary to enter commonly available data such as GDP, total exports, and the current account surplus, all of which are available from the *World Development Report*.

Beyond the difficulties created by missing information about NTBs, several other important limitations to the distortions information should be noted. First, the measure of the distortion wedges is subject to aggregation bias. Second, the tariff data are based on the GATT/WTO upper bound duty rates, and thus they miss the many cases where the actual rate is lower.[9] A finer classification system would permit consistent aggregation from "primitives" and might alter the ranking of countries by trade restrictiveness. Third, the analysis treats all tariffs as constant ad valorem tariffs, missing the endogeneity of the ad valorem equivalent of the many

---

9. This arises from unilateral liberalization and from regional and other trade preferences.

specific tariffs. Fourth, the analysis treats all NTBs as binding quotas, whereas in reality they are a complex set of instruments with more flexibility than a pure quota. Fifth, the analysis takes no account of the trade restrictiveness implications of domestic distortions or of export restrictions (both treated in chapter 12) due to the absence of systematic information. For these reasons if for no others, we do not claim accuracy for our measures. Our qualitative conclusions are in contrast likely to be robust to errors introduced by faulty distortion measures.

The imports data are split into final and intermediate imports on the basis of the definition of the various product lines. The split produces roughly 600 lines of each type of import.

Elasticities of substitution are assumed with little empirical foundation. In order to restrict the response of the nontraded good price in the model, the elasticity of transformation in the base case is quite high, equal to 5. Empirically, input substitution elasticities tend to be smaller than final substitution elasticities, so the base case sets them at 0.7 and 2 respectively. Sensitivity analysis shows that changes in the elasticity values do not much affect the results.

The CGE model is solved on an Excel spreadsheet, available from Anderson's Web site.[10] The data are entered into the supporting worksheets. Documentation available from the author describes the process. The model converges quickly on any modern personal computer and is usually well behaved.

For some data not used in this study, where there are very large changes in a few detailed trade distortions, the computation did not converge. Convergence failure probably indicates that the simple model is inappropriate for such large changes, and the analyst should adopt a more detailed multi-level CES specification to calculate the TRI with large asymmetric changes.

15.3   Measures of Trade Restrictiveness

In section 15.3.1, for the base case of nonbinding quotas, we first evaluate trade restrictiveness relative to free trade for twenty-five countries. Then we follow with analysis of year-on-year changes in trade policy for a five-country sample.

---

10. http://fmwww.bc.edu/EC-V/Anderson.fac.html. The accuracy of the calculations has been independently verified with GAMS calculations.

A key practical issue is the treatment of quota rents, bearing in mind that information on domestic prices (and hence on quota premia) is not available. In the base case we assume that all quotas are nonbinding at the margin. We test for sensitivity to two alternative treatments of quota rents in section 15.3.2. The alternative assumptions lead to similar qualitative results but different quantitative ones. In evaluating year-on-year changes (table 15.3) in the base case, we assume instead that binding quotas generate rents which are entirely lost to foreigners or to rent-seeking, apart from the fraction that is retained by tariffs.

In section 15.3.3 we test for sensitivity to elasticity assumptions. The results are quite insensitive to even large changes in elasticities.

15.3.1   Base Case Results

Table 15.1 presents the TRI and MTRI uniform tariffs for a cross section of twenty-five countries, along with the trade-weighted average tariff and the coefficient of variation of tariffs for reference. Table 15.2 presents the results of simple regressions and rank correlations between the columns in table 15.1. Figure 15.2 illustrates the data from table 15.1 with countries ranked by their trade-weighted average tariffs.

The first observation suggested by tables 15.1 and 15.2 and figure 15.2 is that the MTRI uniform tariff τ^μ and the trade-weighted average tariff τ^a tend to move closely together on average. (The correlation and rank correlation coefficients between the two are 0.987 and 0.972 respectively.) However, this does not mean that the two measures are interchangeable for individual countries. On the contrary, τ^a underpredicts τ^μ in all but three of the twenty-five cases. The effect is not statistically significant (as table 15.2 shows) and the underprediction is only 8.9 percent on average. However, it is important in a number of individual cases, exceeding 15 percent for Austria, Indonesia, Morocco, and the United States. This suggests that in trade negotiations, most countries would prefer to use τ^a to evaluate their own trade policies but τ^μ to evaluate their partners'. On the other hand, for India, τ^a *overpredicts* τ^μ by 7 percent. So the choice between the two measures is significant and of unpredictable sign in individual cases.

The second observation suggested by table 15.1 is that the TRI uniform tariff τ^Δ exceeds the MTRI uniform tariff by a significant margin: 48.7 percent on average. We know from chapter 5 that τ^Δ cannot be less than τ^μ (at least when both indexes are generated by the same utility-consistent model, as here). This theoretical prediction is borne out for every case in

Table 15.1
Alternative indexes of trade restrictiveness

Country and year	Trade-weighted average tariff (%)	τ^Δ: TRI uniform tariff (%)	τ^μ: MTRI uniform tariff (%)	Coefficient of variation of tariffs
Argentina 1992	14.9	19.6	15.3	0.792
Australia 1988	10.8	16.6	11.6	1.004
Austria 1988	10.6	20.0	12.4	0.928
Bolivia 1991	9.4	9.3	9.3	0.140
Brazil 1989	16.1	23.3	17.6	0.816
Canada 1990	7.0	9.5	7.9	0.732
Colombia 1991	10.0	12.4	10.9	0.523
Ecuador 1991	6.5	9.5	6.9	0.759
Finland 1988	6.0	12.6	5.9	1.355
Hungary 1991	9.1	15.3	10.3	1.001
India 1991	16.2	31.6	15.1	1.495
Indonesia 1989	12.8	30.4	16.2	1.385
Malaysia 1988	9.7	21.0	10.2	1.106
Mexico 1989	10.8	12.4	11.4	0.469
Morocco 1984	7.1	18.5	9.7	1.676
New Zealand 1988	7.9	13.6	9.1	0.985
Norway 1988	4.5	8.4	4.6	1.340
Paraguay 1990	12.5	17.8	13.2	0.795
Peru 1991	15.8	16.0	15.8	0.149
Philippines 1991	14.2	17.3	14.6	0.506
Poland 1989	8.7	14.5	9.8	1.035
Thailand 1988	32.0	44.7	34.4	0.672
Tunisia 1991	9.9	18.6	10.4	1.294
United States 1990	4.0	6.1	4.8	1.035
Venezuela 1991	12.9	21.1	14.5	0.814

Note: All three tariff indexes compare the actual tariff structure with free trade. See text for details.

the table.[11] The relationship between the two (with correlation and rank correlation coefficients of 0.886 and 0.800 respectively) is weaker than that between τ^μ and τ^a. The percentage divergence also varies considerably, ranging from over 100 percent in three cases to less than 10 percent

11. The numbers in the table are given to only three significant digits, so in one case, Bolivia, the values shown for the two indexes are equal to one another. From the raw data the percentage excess of the TRI over the MTRI for Bolivia is 0.22 percent, while the next smallest differential (Peru) is 0.88 percent.

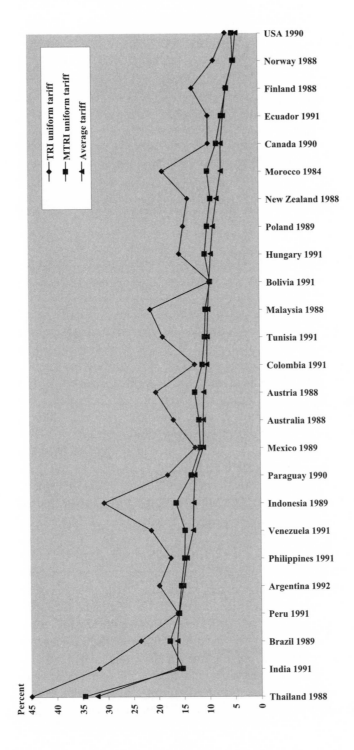

Figure 15.2
Measures of trade restrictiveness for twenty-five countries (all data from table 15.1)

Table 15.2
Regression equations based on columns in table 15.1

Regression equation	a	b	r	Rank
τ^μ on average tariff	0.4354	1.0409	0.987	0.972
	(0.4395)	(0.0353)		
τ^μ on τ^Δ	1.1993	0.6179	0.886	0.799
	(1.3096)	(0.0674)		
τ^Δ on average tariff	3.0238	1.3038	0.862	0.761
	(1.9880)	(0.1599)		
$(\tau^\Delta - \tau^\mu)/\tau^\mu$ on CV	−0.2283	0.7838	0.896	0.626
	(0.0801)	(0.0811)		

Note: a is the intercept and b the slope coefficient; standard errors are in parentheses, r is the correlation coefficient, and "rank" is the rank correlation coefficent.

for Bolivia, Mexico, and Peru. Here too the theoretical results of chapter 6 provide some insight. We see there that for small changes, τ^Δ rises by more than τ^μ if and only if the generalized coefficient of variation of tariffs rises. This suggests that the *actual* coefficient of variation of tariffs might help predict the divergence between the two indexes (since the generalized coefficient is not available in practice). The final regression in table 15.2 confirms this: the percentage excess of τ^Δ over τ^μ is positively and significantly related to the coefficient of variation of tariffs (given by the last column in table 15.1). Overall, it is clear that the uniform volume and welfare equivalents of differentiated tariff structures yield very different pictures of the relative restrictiveness of nations' trade policies.

Table 15.3 presents a small sample of year-on-year changes. We now wish to measure the *change* in the tariff structure from τ^0 to τ^1, and (as is often true) it is convenient to avoid having to estimate the level of imports in free trade. Thus we calculate the MTRI deflator μ along with comparable measures for the other indexes: the TRI deflator $\Delta = 1/(1 + \tau^\Delta)$ instead of the TRI uniform tariff, and the ratio of average tariff factors, $(1 + \tau^{a1})/(1 + \tau^{a0})$, instead of the trade-weighted average tariff. Thus a value greater than one in any of the first six numeric columns of the table indicates that according to the measure in question, trade policy became *more* restrictive between the two years indicated. Because (from the tariff-imposing country's point of view) tariffs on NTB-constrained goods serve the positive function of retaining rent rather than the negative one of restricting trade, we report average tariffs for these separately. We also distinguish between average tariffs on intermediate and final goods categories. In addition we give the (arithmetic) change in the coefficient of variation of tariffs, and three measures of NTB restrictiveness: the initial

Table 15.3
Year-on-year comparisons of the MTRI, the TRI, standard tariff measures and two measures of NTB restrictiveness

Country	MTRI	TRI	Average tariff on final goods		Average tariff on intermediate goods		CV of tariffs		Initial NTB coverage ratio		Change in NTB coverage ratio		% Change in NTBC imports	
			No NTB	NTB	No NTB	NTB	Final	Intermed.	Final	Intermed.	Final	Intermed.	Final	Intermed.
Argentina 1985–88	0.783	0.783	1.113	1.059	1.048	0.956	0.200	0.035	0.779	0.574	−0.567	−0.411	66.1	35.5
Morocco 1984–85	1.044	1.098	0.993	1.011	0.997	0.999	−0.327	−0.138	0.157	0.037	0.000	0.000	−13.8	−2.2
Morocco 1986–88	1.044	1.028	0.961	1.053	1.142	1.142	−0.086	−0.742	0.164	0.030	−0.091	−0.005	1.9	15.9
Tunisia 1987–88	0.877	0.913	0.989	0.982	1.033	0.989	0.030	−0.137	0.914	0.714	−0.320	−0.717	24.3	23.2
Tunisia 1988–89	0.903	0.862	1.045	0.991	0.981	1.039	0.039	0.006	0.851	0.649	−0.101	−0.411	21.5	13.2
Correlations with MTRI		0.955	−0.828	−0.012	0.264	0.679	−0.895	−0.687			0.897	0.789	−0.953	−0.841

Notes: MTRI and TRI are in deflator form: values greater than one indicate an increase in trade policy restrictiveness. Average tariff measures are in the form: $(1 + \tau^{a1})/(1 + \tau^{a0})$. CV: Coefficient of variation of tariffs is the arithmetic year-on-year change. NTBC: % change in volume of NTB-constrained imports. See text for further details.

level of and the (arithmetic) change in the NTB coverage ratio, and the (percentage) change in the volume of NTB-constrained imports.

In dramatic contrast to the results of table 15.1, the TRI and MTRI in table 15.3 differ considerably from the standard indexes. The large differences echo the similar results of chapter 14 for changes in quota policy. There is a good reason for the fairly high correlation among all indexes in the free-trade evaluation, on the one hand, and the very low correlation in the evaluation of annual changes, on the other hand. In the hypothetical leap to free trade, all standard indicators of trade policy move in the same direction. By contrast, in most real-world trade reforms there are conflicting tendencies that make it even more important to use a theoretically based rather than an ad hoc index number. In all cases except the disaggregated average tariffs on intermediate goods, the tariff measures and the MTRI are negatively correlated. The MTRI is more closely related to the two measures of changes in NTB's (positively to the change in the NTB coverage ratio and negatively to the proportional change in the volume of NTB-constrained imports). Many of the countries analysed had a high initial incidence of NTB's and were liberalizing NTBs in the years considered.

Comparing the changes in the MTRI and the TRI, the first columns of table 15.3 show that they always have the same sign, but no consistent ranking emerges between them. In the year-on-year changes the MTRI and TRI changes are quite highly correlated, with a correlation coefficient above 0.95. This is a surprise, since in levels they are not so closely correlated and since for changes as opposed to levels it is quite possible for mean and dispersion to move in opposite directions, amplifying differences between the two. Thus we see no reason to expect this pattern to persist with other data.

The results overall show that the TRI and MTRI are much different from standard measures in practice, enough to matter to practical policy making and to inference about the effects of trade policy. As for policy making, first, in future tariff negotiations it should be useful to come equipped with MTRI measures of proposed changes in policy, and second, the World Bank evaluation of trade liberalization for its clients under the Structural Adjustment Loan program could use the TRI. As for work by applied economists in inference, our results throw light on the appropriateness of using the trade-weighted average tariff as a measure of trade restrictiveness. Table 15.1 suggests that it may be appropriate in pure cross-sectional regressions (though not as we have seen for individual countries). However, table 15.3 suggests that in panel data studies,

Table 15.4
TRI's for alternative NTB treatments

	Nonbinding NTB (base) case	10% quantity rise, initial t^q	10% quantity rise, t^q equal to zero
India	0.760	0.860	0.964
United States	0.943	0.931	0.966

such as the estimation of cross-country growth regressions, it is likely to be a very poor proxy for the two theoretically based indexes of trade restrictiveness.

Of course, all our estimates of the TRI and the MTRI are dependent on the model used to calculate them. The next section shows that the treatment of NTBs makes a difference to results, echoing the folk wisdom of trade policy analysis that getting the distortions right matters more than many other refinements. The following section reports on sensitivity to elasticities, showing that results are not very sensitive to elasticity values. This finding is consistent with the folklore of CGE modeling. In contrast, the CGE folklore warns that specification of the model does matter.[12] We note, however, that our results are not sensitive to model closure in the sense that two treatments of capital flows (exogenous and an exogenous fraction of GDP) yield similar TRI's.

Where the magnitude of TRI and MTRI measures is important, it would be useful to have several different calculations based on differing CGE models. Despite these caveats the case seems to be made that the standard measures are likely to be very seriously misleading in practice.

15.3.2 Sensitivity, I: The TRI with Alternative Treatment of NTBs

The preceding method of dealing with NTBs is fully equivalent to evaluation with tariffs only. Two alternatives are explored in this section. The implication is, unsurprisingly, that results are sensitive to the assumptions made about NTBs. Table 15.4 presents the results of the alternatives along with the base case treatment for two sample countries.

The first alternative is to assume that all NTB-constrained categories have domestic prices inflated by a unit quota rent equal to 10 percent of the external price, in addition to the rent-retaining tariff. All quota rent

12. For an illustration that nonuniform elasticities interacting with nonuniform tariffs make a difference, see O'Rourke (1997).

(beyond that captured by the rent-retaining tariff) in the initial equilibrium is assumed to be lost to foreigners or to rent-seeking. A reversion to free trade secures a terms-of-trade improvement of 10 percent for NTB-constrained categories. The TRI for this case is calculated by assuming that a uniform tariff is levied, *including one on NTB-constrained categories*. This has the effect of potentially capturing rent that was previously lost (depending on the level of the rent-retaining tariff in the initial equilibrium). This case will subsequently be referred to as the 10 percent premium case.

The 10 percent premium case TRI measures have somewhat higher sample mean uniform tariff equivalent than those of the nonbinding NTB case (25.4 percent as compared to 18.9 percent). This indicates the initial policy is even more restrictive than in the preceding case, due to the rent loss on NTB-constrained goods. The two sets of TRIs are fairly highly correlated (a simple correlation coefficient equal to 0.88 and a rank correlation coefficient equal to 0.71). The sample mean relative error $(\tau^\Delta - \tau^a)/\tau^a$ from using the trade-weighted average tariff instead of the TRI rises from 55 to 108 percent of the average tariff. Most significant, the rank correlation of the TRI and the average tariff falls to 0.299.

The second procedure for dealing with NTBs is to assume that "free trade" causes a uniform 10 percent rise in quantities in the NTB-constrained categories. From this position the TRI finds the uniform deflator that is just as inefficient as the initial policy, where the domestic price vectors of NTB-constrained goods must be uniformly raised by implicitly tightening the quotas to do the job. Rent-retaining tariffs are maintained at the initial level in this operation, and are assumed to capture all rent (no other premium is lost). This case is presented to demonstrate the sensitivity of results to treatment of quotas rather than for any attempt at realism. The 10 percent quantity increase case has a uniform tariff equivalent which is always lower than in the nonbinding NTB case, usually quite close but sometimes substantially different. Table 15.4 shows a case in which the differences are large (India), in contrast to a case in which the differences are smaller (the United States). The table also shows the effect of different treatment of rent-retaining tariffs. A fall in rent-retaining tariffs is inefficient, other things being equal, so it matters whether the "free-trade" policy is based on zero rent retaining tariffs or on the initial rent retaining tariffs. As a further indication of the sensitivity of results to the treatment of NTBs, the uniform tariff equivalent in the 10 percent quantity increase case is uncorrelated with that in the nonbinding NTB case (a coefficient of 0.064).

A related aspect of the treatment of NTB's is to allow the share of rent retained to be an intermediate value rather than either 0 or 1. The TRI results are rather sensitive to the rent share assumption. In a typical case, that of Mexico in 1989 under the 10 percent quantity expansion assumption, a drop from complete rent loss to a 50 percent rent loss results in a more than 4 percent fall in the TRI (from 0.894 to 0.851). The initial equilibrium works out to be more distorted (liberalization results in a smaller TRI) with a rent-share assumption of 50 percent, an empirical result that can be explained theoretically by noting that the shadow price of quotas is a decreasing function of the rent-share parameter, ceteris paribus, when evaluated at the point where the rent loss is equal to 100 percent. (See chapter 7 for the formula for the shadow price of quotas in a model that encompasses the model used here.)

15.3.3 Sensitivity, II: Elasticities

Table 15.5 presents a sensitivity analysis of TRI's calculated for Mexico in 1989 with respect to variation in elasticities of substitution in intermediate and final demand for imports. The base case is in boldface. The results show that elasticity variation is not very influential. These sensitivity results are representative of the sample of countries studied.

Low sensitivity to elasticity values makes sense in terms of the theoretical structure of the TRI and MTRI. Recall from chapters 4 and 5 that the indexes can be written in the form of weighted sums of the individual tariffs, where the weights are based on marginal welfare and marginal volume responses, $\omega_i^\Delta = \pi_i^* B_i / \sum \pi_i^* B_i$ for the TRI and $\omega_i^\mu = \pi_i^* M_i / \sum \pi_i^* M$ for the MTRI. The influence of elasticities appears in both numerator and denominator of these weights and thus tends to cancel.

The limiting case where the influence of elasticity disappears entirely is found in the special case of CES preferences for final goods imports

Table 15.5
Sensitivity analysis of Mexican TRI, 1989

	Parameters	Nonbinding NTB case
Final substitution elasticity	1.05	0.8984
	2	**0.8896**
	3	0.8882
Input substitution elasticity	0.2	0.8855
	0.7	**0.8896**
	1.2	0.8918

developed at the end of chapter 6. It is shown there that the generalized mean and variance of tariffs are independent of the elasticity in the special case, while earlier in the chapter it is shown that the TRI and MTRI are functions of these variables only.

15.4 Conclusion

In this chapter we presented estimates of the TRI and MTRI for overall evaluation of trade policy systems using a simple general equilibrium model. We provided a feasible method of generating a common model across many countries given only the availability of detailed trade distortion data and a concordance with trade flows. The TRI and MTRI measures so calculated differ significantly from standard measures of trade restrictiveness, especially for year-on-year changes that typify the actual evolution of trade policy. The qualitative conclusions appear to be robust with respect to varying the expedients used to deal with the missing NTB data problem. The magnitude of the TRI and MTRI is not very sensitive to elasticity of substitution variation, but is sensitive to the assumptions used to treat NTBs.

Appendix: The CES-CET Model

This appendix lays out the mathematical formalization of the CES-CET model used to calculate the TRI. The reduced form functions we set out are able to fully exploit the special structure of the CES to avoid having to simultaneously calculate thousands of endogenous prices in quota-constrained markets. We also exploit the separability of input and output decisions and the assumption of one primary factor of production only to simplify the model. The details provided here match exactly with the computational model available on Anderson's Web site, but the simplicity of the model probably has other analytic uses.

We do not separately report on the details of the MTRI calculation because the reader should be able to use our general description to modify the details of the CGE model laid out below to calculate the MTRI.

To build intuition prior to the formalism, we provide a preliminary graphical analysis of the CES-CET model in the introduction. Then in section 15A.1 we develop the CES expenditure and distorted expenditure functions. Next we present the CES-CET cost and product functions in

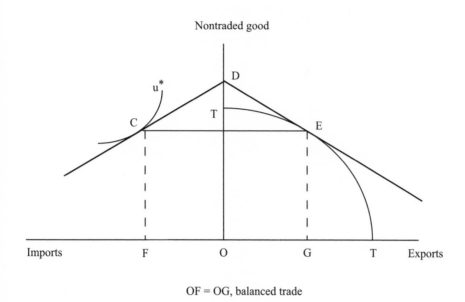

OF = OG, balanced trade

Figure 15.3
The Australian model

section 15A.2. Finally, in section 15A.3, we discuss general equilibrium in the model.

The intuition of the CES-CET model is seen in three diagrams. The first diagram (figure 15.3) shows the final output and final demand structure of the model, dubbed the Australian model for its resemblance to the Salter-Swan model. The export good is the numéraire, the external price of the final import is conventionally set equal to one, and balanced trade requires that OF, the volume of final imports (these being the only imports) equal OG, the volume of imports. The joint output of the nontraded good and of exports is selected along transformation surface TT to maximize national income at any given price of the nontraded good, represented by the inverse of the absolute value of the slope of budget line DE. With national income in terms of the nontraded good equal to OD, the representative consumer selects a utility-maximizing bundle along budget line DC, with slope equal to the inverse of the nontraded good's price.

The effect of a tariff in this model is shown in the second diagram, figure 15.4. The domestic relative price of the import is wedged above the international price, resulting in the marginal rate of substitution at C' being greater than the absolute slope of the international budget line

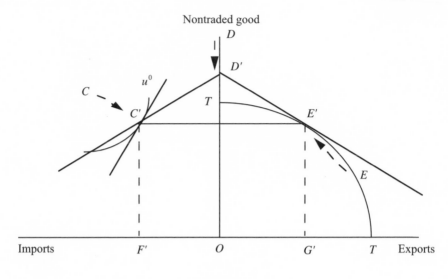

$OF' = OG'$, balanced trade

Figure 15.4
A tariff in the Australian model

$D'C'$. The international relative price, equal to the absolute slope of $D'C'$ is lower than the relative price at free trade, equal to the absolute slope of DC. This is because the price of the nontraded good is driven up as consumers are driven from tariff-ridden imports to domestic substitutes. In the analysis all tariff revenue is rebated, and trade remains balanced in both situations.

The introduction of imported inputs is heuristically shown in figure 15.5. Here the curved production function has diminishing returns to the variable imported input due to the fixed primary factor labor. With no tariff, the value of marginal product condition implies a solution at A, with domestic activity OD, implying a given distance from the origin for TT. OC is equal to gross domestic product. By convention, the price of the nontraded good is equal to one. With a tariff, the solution moves to B, with domestic activity OD', gross domestic product OC', and tariff revenue EC'. Assuming that the nontraded good price remains at one (neglecting, for simplicity, the important general-equilibrium linkage with the determination of the nontraded good price), we have the slope of the tangent at B equal to the tariff distorted input price. The elasticities of substitution in consumption, transformation, and production control the

Domestic activity

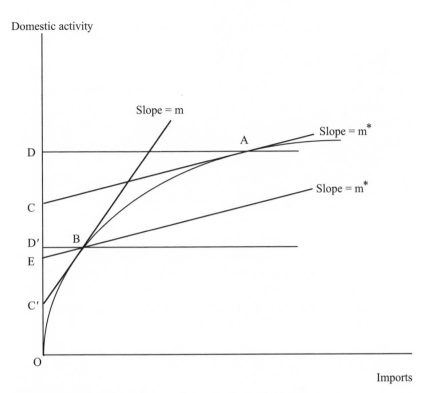

Figure 15.5
The model of imported inputs

curvature of the indifference curves, transformation functions, and production functions respectively.

15A.1 CES Expenditure and Distorted Expenditure Functions

The representative consumer is assumed to have a CES expenditure function of the form:

$$e(h, p, \pi, u) = \left(\alpha_y h^{1-\sigma^*} + \sum \beta_k p_k^{1-\sigma^*} + \sum \alpha_j \pi_j^{1-\sigma^*} \right)^{1/(1-\sigma^*)} u, \tag{4}$$

where u is the level of utility, p is the domestic price of quota-constrained goods, π is the domestic price of non–quota-constrained goods, and h is the price of the nontraded good. The superscript F (for final goods) is omitted from p and π for notational ease. The elasticity of substitution in demand is equal to the parameter σ^*, while the α's and β's are share parameters for the non–quota-constrained goods and the quota-constrained goods respectively. The true cost of living index is

$$P = \left(\alpha_y h^{1-\sigma^*} + \sum \beta_k p_k^{1-\sigma^*} + \sum \alpha_j \pi_j^{1-\sigma^*} \right)^{1/(1-\sigma^*)}. \tag{5}$$

For empirical work, the benchmark year conventionally has prices all initially equal to one, and the α's and β's are the initial expenditure share values in the data, and the initial level of expenditure is equal to u.

The distorted expenditure function is built by imposing on (4) fixed binding quotas equal to q_k for all k. (The superscript F is again omitted for notational ease.) The distorted expenditure function is defined by (Anderson and Neary 1992)

$$\tilde{e}(h, q, \pi, u) \equiv \max_p \{ e(h, p, \pi, u) - p \cdot q \}.$$

The price vector p that solves this program is a virtual price vector, and with quotas it is also a market-clearing price vector. Using Shephard's lemma, and solving the first-order (market-clearing) condition for the (virtual and market) price of each quota constrained good k, we obtain for the CES case:

$$p_k = P \left(\frac{u \beta_k}{q_k} \right)^{1/\sigma^*}, \tag{6}$$

where P is the price index defined by equation (5). Substituting (5) into (6), we have the vector of virtual prices p implicitly defined as a function of the π's and the quotas. Fortunately, an explicit solution is available. First substitute (6) into (5). Next raise both right- and left-hand sides to the power $1 - \sigma^*$. Then solve the resulting expression for $P^{1-\sigma^*}$. Finally raise both sides to the power $1/(1 - \sigma^*)$. The reduced form true cost of living index is

$$\tilde{P}(h, q, \pi, u) = \left(\frac{\alpha_y h^{1-\sigma^*} + \sum \alpha_j \pi_j^{1-\sigma^*}}{1 - u^{(1-\sigma^*)/\sigma^*} \sum \beta_k^{1/\sigma^*} q_k^{-(1-\sigma^*)/\sigma^*}} \right)^{1/(1-\sigma^*)}. \tag{7}$$

The connection of (7) to (5) is clear: if consumers face a fixed price vector for quota-constrained goods that is set at the level of the virtual price vector p defined by (6), their cost of living is the same as when constrained by quotas q.

The distorted expenditure function is obtained by substituting (6) and (7) into the definition of $\tilde{e}$:

$$\tilde{e}(h, q, \pi, u) = \tilde{P}(h, q, \pi, u)u - p \cdot q, \tag{8}$$

where $\tilde{P}$ is given by (7) and p is given by (6) using $\tilde{P}$ for P. Equation (8) factors into

$$\tilde{e}(h, q, \pi, u) = \left(\alpha_y h^{1-\sigma^*} + \sum_j \alpha_j \pi_j^{1-\sigma^*} \right)^{1/(1-\sigma^*)}$$

$$\times \left(1 - u^{(1-\sigma^*)/\sigma^*} \sum_k \beta_k^{1/\sigma^*} q_k^{-(1-\sigma^*)/\sigma^*} \right)^{-\sigma^*/(1-\sigma^*)} u. \qquad (9)$$

The constrained (by the presence of quotas) demand for unconstrained imports and for nontradables is obtained from use of Shephard's lemma:

$$\tilde{e}_{\pi_k} = \alpha_k \left(\frac{\pi_k}{\tilde{P}} \right)^{-\sigma^*} u,$$

$$\tilde{e}_h = \alpha_Y \left(\frac{h}{\tilde{P}} \right)^{-\sigma^*} u. \qquad (10)$$

The virtual price vector is obtained as

$$-\tilde{e}_k = p_k = \tilde{e} \frac{\beta_k^{1/\sigma^*} u^{(1-\sigma^*)/\sigma^*} q_k^{-1/\sigma^*}}{1 - u \sum_k \beta_k^{1/\sigma^*} q_k^{-(1-\sigma^*)/\sigma^*}}. \qquad (11)$$

15A.2   The CES-CET Cost and Product Functions

Exports and the nontraded good are jointly produced with a CES-CET technology. The level of activity of the joint process is represented by z, determined by the two outputs y, the nontraded good, and x, the export good.

Total and Variable Cost Functions

The cost of producing one unit of the activity z is equal to

$$c = \left(\sum_j \gamma_j p_j^{1-\sigma} + \sum_k \gamma_k \pi_k^{1-\sigma} + \delta_L w^{1-\sigma} \right)^{1/(1-\sigma)}, \qquad (12)$$

where p is the price vector of imported intermediate inputs subject to quota, π is the price vector of imported intermediate inputs not subject to quota and w is the price of the nontraded factor (wage rate of labor). The superscript M on p and π is omitted for notational ease. The γ's and δ_L are activity cost share parameters and σ is the elasticity of technical substitution. Total cost is equal to cz. Nontraded intermediate goods are subsumed into the production and cost structure behind (12).

The total cost function under constraint yields the variable cost function. The input quotas are denoted q_j for each good j, with the superscript M being omitted for notational ease, and the nontraded factor is in fixed supply L. Shephard's lemma and the market-clearing equations can be used to solve for the prices of the nontraded and quota-constrained inputs, just as the price of quota-constrained final goods was obtained in equation (5). Thus the input demand

$$q_j = \gamma_j \left(\frac{p_j}{c}\right)^{-\sigma} z$$

implies a value of p_j in terms of c and z:

$$p_j = c z^{1/\sigma} \gamma_j^{1/\sigma} q_j^{-1/\sigma}.$$

The resulting solution for p_j may be substituted into equation (12), and the equation solved first for $c^{1-\sigma}$ and then c (the steps are the same as those leading from equations 5 to 7) to obtain the reduced form conditional unit cost function:

$$c = C(q, \pi, L, z) = \left(\frac{\sum \gamma_k \pi_k^{1-\sigma}}{1 - z^{1/\sigma - 1}(\sum \gamma_j^{1/\sigma} q_j^{1-1/\sigma} + \delta_L^{1/\sigma} L^{1-1/\sigma})}\right)^{1/(1-\sigma)}. \quad (13)$$

Note the similarity of (13) to (7). In the reduced form cost function it is convenient to define

$$R(q, L, z) = z^{1/\sigma - 1} \left(\sum \gamma_j^{1/\sigma} q_j^{1-1/\sigma} + \delta_L^{1/\sigma} L^{1-1/\sigma}\right), \quad (14)$$

the share of total cost paid to fixed factors (the nontraded factor and the quota-constrained inputs). To see how this interpretation arises, note that Shephard's lemma implies that the share of cost paid to variable inputs is equal to $c^{\sigma-1} \sum \gamma_k \pi_k^{1-\sigma}$, where c is defined by (12). Now raise both sides of (13) to the power $1 - \sigma$, multiply both sides by $1 - R$, and divide both sides by $c^{1-\sigma}$. Then $R = 1 - c^{\sigma-1} \sum \gamma_k \pi_k^{1-\sigma}$, the right-hand side being the share of costs paid to fixed factors.

The variable cost function[13] is obtained by using (13) and (14) with (12):

$$V = cz(1 - R) = \sum_k \gamma_k \pi_k^{1-\sigma} C(\cdot)^\sigma z, \quad (15)$$

---

13. Alternatively it could be termed the distorted variable cost function to emphasize that some of the fixed inputs are fixed by policy.

where $C(\cdot)$ is given by (13). The variable cost function is more conveniently rewritten as

$$V(q, \pi, L, z) = \left(\sum \gamma_k \pi_k^{1-\sigma}\right)^{1/(1-\sigma)} (1 - R)^{-\sigma/(1-\sigma)} z, \tag{16}$$

where R is given by (14). Note the similarity of form between (16) and (9).

The properties of the variable cost function are standard. Variable input demand is

$$V_k = C_k = \gamma_k \pi_k^{-\sigma} \left(\sum_k \gamma_k \pi_k^{1-\sigma}\right)^{\sigma/(1-\sigma)} (1 - R)^{-\sigma/(1-\sigma)} z. \tag{17}$$

The marginal variable cost of competitive production is given by

$$V_z = \frac{V}{z(1 - R)} = \left(\sum_k \gamma_k \pi_k^{1-\sigma}\right)^{1/(1-\sigma)} (1 - R)^{-1/(1-\sigma)}. \tag{18}$$

Finally the virtual and market price of the constrained input is

$$-V_{q_j} = p_j = z^{1/\sigma-1} \frac{V}{1 - R} \gamma_j^{1/\sigma} q_j^{-1/\sigma}. \tag{19}$$

Equation (19) is the production analog to equation (11).

Joint Product and Gross Domestic Product Functions
For a given level of the activity z, the profit maximizing decisions of producers select nontraded output y and export output x to maximize $hy + \pi_x x$ subject to a constant elasticity of transformation production frontier $f(x, y) \geq z$. Here π_x is the export price, the numéraire. The value of total output in this setup is equal to

$$\phi(h, \pi_x)z = ((1 - \varphi)\pi_x^{1+\theta} + \varphi h^{1+\theta})^{1/(1+\theta)} z, \tag{20}$$

where θ is the constant elasticity of transformation, $\partial \log(x/y)/\partial \log(\pi_x/h)$, and φ is a share parameter. Profit maximization implies that for given z, nontraded output is equal to

$$y = \phi_h z = \varphi \left(\frac{h}{\phi}\right)^\theta z. \tag{21}$$

The aggregate rent function is the supply side analogue to the distorted expenditure function. It is a maximum value function equal to the sum of quota rents and payments to domestic fixed factors. Formally,

$$\tilde{g}(h, q^M, \pi^M, L) = \max_z \{\phi(h, 1)z - V(q^M, \pi^M, L, z)\}. \tag{22}$$

The first-order condition of (22) can be solved for a closed form solution for the activity level z:

$$z = \left(\frac{1 - (h,1)^{\sigma-1} \sum_k \gamma_k \pi_k^{1-\sigma}}{\sum \gamma_j^{1/\sigma} q_j^{-(1-\sigma)/\sigma} + \delta_L^{1/\sigma} L^{-(1-\sigma)/\sigma}} \right)^{\sigma/(1-\sigma)} = z(h, q^M, \pi^M, L). \quad (23)$$

Here ϕ is given by the right-hand side of (20). Substituting (23) into the right-hand side of (22) yields a closed form for $\tilde{g}$.

Gross domestic product is equal to the value of payments to domestic factors. This is written[14]

$$g = \tilde{g} - \tilde{g}_q \cdot q^M, \quad (24)$$

noting that $\tilde{g}_q = -V_q = p^M$ from the definition of (22) and of variable cost V. More conveniently for computations, g is equal to $-LV_L$ in using $-V_L = w$, the wage rate. The variable cost function has derivatives with respect to nontraded primary factors of the same form as (19). Thus $-LV_L$ is equal to

$$\frac{V}{1-R} (\delta_L^{1/\sigma} L^{1-1/\sigma}) z^{1/\sigma-1}. \quad (24')$$

Using (16) for V, we can rewrite the gross domestic product as

$$g(h, q^M, \pi^M, L) = \left(\sum_k \gamma_k (\pi_k^M)^{1-\sigma} \right)^{1/(1-\sigma)} (1-R)^{-1/(1-\sigma)} z^{1/\sigma} \delta_L^{1/\sigma} L^{1-1/\sigma}. \quad (24'')$$

On the right-hand side of the equation, R is understood to be replaced by its value on the right-hand side of (14) and z is understood to be replaced by its value on the right-hand side of (23).

15A.3   General Equilibrium in the CES-CET Model

General equilibrium is reached by clearance of the nontraded good market and by the balance-of-payments constraint, two equations to solve for the endogenous variables h and u. As for the nontraded goods market,

$$\varphi \left(\frac{h}{\phi} \right)^\theta z = \alpha_y \left(\frac{h}{P} \right)^{-\sigma^*} u, \quad (25)$$

---

14. It is important to note that the gross domestic product function in this setup is not an envelope function, due to the fact that the domestic value of q^M is lost. This imposes a terms-of-trade effect distortion relative to efficient production. The aggregate profit function is $\Pi(p_x, h, \pi^M, q^M, L) = \max_z \{\phi(p_x, h)z - V(\pi^M, q^M, L, z)\}$. This has the envelope property $\Pi_h = y = \phi_h z$.

where z is defined by (23) and P is defined by (7). As for the balance-of-payments constraint, we have

$$\tilde{e}(h, q^F, \pi^F, u) - \tilde{e}_q \cdot q^F - \tilde{g}(h, q^M, \pi^M, L) + \tilde{g}_q \cdot q^M$$

$$- (\pi^F - \pi^{*F})\tilde{e}_\pi - (\pi^M - \pi^{*M})\tilde{g}_\pi - t^q \cdot q = b, \qquad (26)$$

where b is a parametric trade deficit or surplus. The first line gives the difference between expenditure at domestic prices and payments to labor. The second line gives minus the sum of tariff revenue. In this setup all rent other than that retained by $t^q \cdot q$ is lost. The equation system (25) and (26) is solved for h and u.

The TRI is solved as follows: Hold u constant, deflate "new" prices of distorted goods by Δ as defined in the text equations (1) through (5), and solve (25) and (26) for h and Δ. In the text, the implicit solution for h is understood to be substituted into the various functions in (26) throughout.

16 Conclusion

Theoretically consistent aggregation of trade restrictions is important in principle, and feasible in practice. These are the large themes of this book.

We began our development of the first theme in part II by refining and extending the received theory of gradual trade reform, emphasizing dual methods to treat both tariffs and quotas in general equilibrium. On this base we constructed theoretically consistent aggregates of trade restrictions, taking as reference points two natural concerns of analysts and policy makers, welfare and market access. In part III we demonstrated the feasibility of implementing our theoretical methods with a variety of applications, all of which showed significant differences between theoretically consistent aggregation and the standard atheoretic aggregation heretofore available.

Our refinement and extension of the received theory of trade reform recast and extended the standard results to incorporate a general treatment of changes in both tariffs and quotas. We further developed new expressions for changes in welfare and trade volume in terms of generalized tariff moments, and used these tools to uncover general characterizations of the class of welfare-increasing and market-access-increasing trade reforms.

The big idea we present in the book is the development of true index numbers of trade policy. Standard atheoretic measures such as trade-weighted average tariffs fail to take account of economic behavior (especially substitution by consumers and producers in response to price changes) and lack a theoretical foundation. Hence the criticism of Afriat (1977) that they provide "answers without questions." By contrast, true index numbers start with an explicit behavioral model and provide answers to specific theoretically founded questions. In practice, this means replacing the vector of variables to be indexed with a scalar that preserves the essential link between the vector being aggregated and some other variable of concern to the analyst. In the case of trade policy aggregation, the scalar is the uniform tariff, the vector being aggregated is that of tariffs (plus tariff equivalents of quotas, and sometimes domestic policies which affect trade), and the reference variable is usually either real income or trade volume at external prices. The link between the variables being aggregated and the reference variable is provided by an economic model, with duality and the restrictions of standard general equilibrium providing the structure.

The applications of part III demonstrate the wide range of policy concerns that can be treated with our methods. The main limit to applications is the shortage and poor quality of data on trade distortions, a limitation that is shared by all applied research in trade policy. Given adequate data on distortions, our applications show that the other data and computational burdens of our methods are light.

The main theme of the applications is that our methods give substantially different measures of trade restrictiveness than the standard atheoretic indexes. The standard indexes correlate weakly with appropriate indexes when evaluating changes in trade policy, often predicting the wrong signs. For many applications it is the changes in policy that are critical, and the case is overwhelming that theoretically consistent indexes should be adopted.

The atheoretic and consistent indexes also differ significantly across countries in *levels*. Welfare equivalent uniform tariffs are guaranteed to be higher than volume equivalent uniform tariffs and are found to be higher than trade-weighted average tariffs, half again as much on average. Uniform volume equivalent and trade-weighted average tariffs are close in level, the former usually larger than the latter but not by a significant amount. Even so, the summary descriptive statistics hide individual outliers where there are significant differences between the two indexes. As a gauge of trade policy restrictiveness in the context of trade negotiations, it would presumably matter, for example, that according to our data there are three countries for which the trade-weighted average tariff underpredicts the volume equivalent by more than 15 percent while there is one case where it overpredicts by more than 7 percent. The atheoretic and consistent indexes correlate fairly well, however. So in applications where the correlation of levels alone is important, the standard indexes are useful substitutes for the consistent indexes. The high positive correlation of the two is not surprising, since in moving to free trade, all barriers fall to zero and all possible indexes of the barrier changes move in the same direction.

Future work on the lines of this book will presumably be mostly applied. It should be stressed that our indexes can be implemented using empirical frameworks other than the computable general-equilibrium methods that we develop in part III, and especially in chapter 15. For example, Kee, Nicita, and Olarreaga (2004) estimate complete systems of import demand elasticities in order to calculate the TRI. They find that because of the relatively high variances of many countries' tariff schedules, the trade-weighted average tariff typically underestimates the TRI uniform tariff by a significant margin. The effect is particularly strong in the case of the United States, where atheoretic average tariffs are about 4 percent whereas the TRI uniform tariff is approximately 15 percent. Further empirical work along these lines is very desirable to explore the robustness of the findings and to devise comparable measures of protection across time and space.

Turning to future work that goes beyond our approach, we see three lines of extensions. First, there is a great need just to document the trade restrictiveness of policy with respect to the reference points used in this book. More and better data will extend the scope of our knowledge of trade restrictiveness using the same methods. In this work it will be useful to experiment with simple alternative theoretical structures to test further the sensitivity of the results to structural assumptions.

Second, it will be very useful to apply the methods to multicountry models along the lines suggested in chapters 9 and 10. Discriminatory trade policy is becoming important and should be treated as part of this application. In doing so, it will be useful to incorporate trade costs not directly linked to trade policy. Anderson and van Wincoop (2004) show that these are considerably larger than policy costs and vary significantly across goods and bilateral trading pairs. Some trade costs reflect nontrade policies (discriminatory treatment of foreigners in property rights enforcement), while others reflect public investment decisions (transport costs) and thus have domestic policy dimensions.

Third, the methods of this book extend to domestic policy. Our methods can be used to construct index measures of the height of high-dimensional tax policy that are theoretically grounded as opposed to atheoretic measures such as the tax share of GDP. These would have advantages analogous to those that the real income-equivalent uniform tariff has over the trade-weighted average tariff, measured by tariff revenue relative to the value of imports. Our methods can also be used, mutatis mutandis, to construct index measures of high-dimensional environmental or product standard regulations that gauge the height of regulatory barriers. The methods we have used for quotas will apply, treating the regulations as quotas. As with quotas and other nontariff barriers, the practical difficulties are much greater than with taxes, but price comparisons and license prices where available can help.

In sum, we hope we have shown how the normative theory of trade and the theory of index numbers can be combined to provide guidance to all those interested in measuring the restrictiveness of international trade policy.

References

Afriat, S. N. 1977. *The Price Index*. Cambridge: Cambridge University Press.

Anderson, J. E. 1970. General equilibrium and the effective rate of protection. *American Economic Review* 78: 717–24.

Anderson, J. E. 1979. A theoretical foundation for the gravity model. *American Economic Review* 69: 106–16.

Anderson, J. E. 1985. The relative inefficiency of quotas: The cheese case. *American Economic Review* 75: 178–90.

Anderson, J. E. 1988. *The Relative Inefficiency of Quotas*. Cambridge: MIT Press.

Anderson, J. E. 1991. The coefficient of trade utilization: The cheese case. In R. E. Baldwin, ed., *Empirical Studies of Commercial Policy*. Chicago: University of Chicago Press, pp. 221–44.

Anderson, J. E. 1992. Domino dumping, I: Competitive exporters. *American Economic Review* 82: 65–83.

Anderson, J. E. 1993. Measuring trade restrictiveness in a simple CGE model; with Appendix: A manual for using the TRI spreadsheet model. Mimeo.

Anderson, J. E. 1994. The theory of protection. In D. Greenaway and L. A. Winters, eds., *Surveys in International Trade*. Oxford: Basil Blackwell, pp. 107–38.

Anderson, J. E. 1995. Tariff index theory. *Review of International Economics* 3: 156–73.

Anderson, J. E. 1998a. Effective protection redux. *Journal of International Economics* 44: 21–44.

Anderson, J. E. 1998b. Trade restrictiveness benchmarks. *Economic Journal* 108: 1111–25.

Anderson, J. E. 1999. Trade reform with a government budget constraint. In J. Piggott and A. Woodland, eds., *Trade Policy and the Pacific Rim*. London: Macmillan.

Anderson, J. E., G. Bannister, and J. P. Neary. 1995. Domestic distortions and international trade. *International Economic Review* 36: 139–57.

Anderson, J. E., and D. Marcouiller. 2002. Insecurity and trade: An empirical investigation. *Review of Economics and Statistics* 84 (2): 345–52.

Anderson, J. E., and S. Naya. 1969. Substitution and two concepts of effective rate of protection. *American Economic Review* 59: 607–12.

Anderson, J. E., and J. P. Neary. 1990. The coefficient of trade utilization: Back to the Baldwin Envelope. In R. W. Jones and A. O. Krueger, eds., *The Political Economy of International Trade: Essays in Honor of Robert E. Baldwin*. Oxford: Basil Blackwell, pp. 49–72.

Anderson, J. E., and J. P. Neary. 1992. Trade reform with quotas, partial rent retention and tariffs. *Econometrica* 60: 57–76.

Anderson, J. E., and J. P. Neary. 1994a. Measuring the restrictiveness of trade policy. *World Bank Economic Review* 8: 151–69.

Anderson, J. E., and J. P. Neary. 1994b. The trade restrictiveness of the Multi-Fibre Arrangement. *World Bank Economic Review* 8: 171–89.

Anderson, J. E., and J. P. Neary. 1996. A new approach to evaluating trade policy. *Review of Economic Studies* 63: 107–25.

Anderson, J. E., and J. P. Neary. 2003. The Mercantilist index of trade policy. *International Economic Review* 44: 627–49.

Anderson, J. E., and J. P. Neary. 2004. Welfare versus market access: The implications of tariff structure for tariff reform. NBER Working paper 10730.

Anderson, J. E., and E. van Wincoop. 2003. Gravity with gravitas: A solution to the border puzzle. *American Economic Review* 93: 170–92.

Anderson, J. E., and E. van Wincoop. 2004. Trade costs. *Journal of Economic Literature* 42: 691–751.

Armington, P. S. 1969. A theory of demand for products distinguished by place of production. *International Monetary Fund Staff Papers* 26: 159–78.

Aw, B. Y., and M. J. Roberts. 1986. Measuring quality changes in quota-constrained import markets: The case of U.S. footwear. *Journal of International Economics* 21: 45–60.

Bagwell, K., and R. Staiger. 1999. An economic theory of GATT. *American Economic Review* 89: 215–48.

Baldwin, R. E. 1984. Trade policy in developed countries. In P. B. Kenen and R. W. Jones, eds., *Handbook of International Economics*, vol. 1. Amsterdam: North-Holland, pp. 571–612.

Barro, R. J., and X. Sala-y-Martin. 1995. *Economic Growth*. New York: McGraw-Hill.

Beghin, J. C., and L. S. Karp. 1992. Piecemeal trade reform in presence of producer-specific domestic subsidies. *Economics Letters* 39: 65–71.

Bertrand, T. J., and J. Vanek. 1971. The theory of tariffs, taxes and subsidies: Some aspects of the second best. *American Economic Review* 61: 925–31.

Bhagwati, J. N. 1958. Immiserizing growth: A geometrical note. *Review of Economic Studies* 25: 201–5.

Blonigen, B. A., and S. E. Haynes. 2002. Antidumping investigations and the pass-through of antidumping duties and exchange rates. *American Economic Review* 92: 1044–61.

Boadway, R. W., and R. Harris. 1977. A characterisation of piecemeal second best policy. *Journal of Public Economics* 8: 169–80.

Bond, E. 1990. The optimal tariff structure in higher dimensions. *International Economic Review* 31: 103–16.

Boorstein, R., and R. Feenstra. 1991. Quality upgrading and its welfare cost in U.S. steel imports, 1969–74. In E. Helpman and A. Razin, eds., *International Trade and Trade Policy*. Cambridge: MIT Press, pp. 167–86.

Bordo, M. D., B. Eichengreen, and D. Irwin. 1999. Is globalization today really different than globalization a hundred years ago? In S. M. Collins and R. Z. Lawrence, eds., *Brookings Trade Forum: 1999*. Washington, DC: Brookings Institution, pp. 1–50.

Bruno, M. 1972. Market distortions and gradual reform. *Review of Economic Studies* 39: 373–83.

Cahill, C., and W. Legg. 1990. Estimation of agricultural assistance using producer and consumer subsidy equivalents: Theory and practice. *OECD Economic Studies* (Special Issue on Modelling the Effects of Agricultural Policies) 13: 13–43.

Caves, D. W., L. R. Christensen, and W. E. Diewert. 1982. Multilateral comparisons of output, input and productivity using superlative index numbers. *Economic Journal* 92: 73–86.

Chipman, J. S. 1979. The theory and application of trade utility functions. In J. S. Green and J. A. Scheinkman, eds., *General Equilibrium, Growth and Trade: Essays in Honor of Lionel McKenzie*. New York: Academic Press, pp. 277–96.

Commonwealth of Australia. 1965. *Report of the Committee of Economic Enquiry [The Vernon Committee]*. Canberra.

Corden, W. M. 1966. The effective protective rate, the uniform tariff equivalent and the average tariff. *Economic Record* 42: 200–16.

Corden, W. M. 1984. The normative theory of international trade. In R. W. Jones and P. B. Kenen, eds., *Handbook of International Economics*, vol. 1. Amsterdam: North-Holland, pp. 63–130.

Corden, W. M., and R. E. Falvey. 1985. Quotas and the second best. *Economics Letters* 18: 67–70.

Cox, D., and R. Harris. 1985. Trade liberalization and industrial organisation: Some estimates for Canada. *Journal of Political Economy* 93: 115–45.

Davis, O. A., and A. B. Whinston. 1965. Welfare economics and the theory of second best. *Review of Economic Studies* 32: 1–14.

Deaton, A. S. 1979. The distance function in consumer behaviour with applications to index numbers and optimal taxation. *Review of Economic Studies* 46: 391–405.

Deaton, A., and J. Muellbauer. 1980. *Economics and Consumer Behavior*. Cambridge: Cambridge University Press.

Debreu, G. 1951. The coefficient of resource utilization. *Econometrica* 19: 273–92.

Debreu, G., and I. N. Herstein. 1953. Nonnegative square matrices. *Econometrica* 21: 597–607.

Diewert, W. E. 1981. The economic theory of index numbers: A survey. In A. Deaton, ed., *Essays in the Theory and Measurement of Consumer Behaviour in Honour of Sir Richard Stone*. Cambridge: Cambridge University Press, pp. 163–208.

Diewert, W. E. 1983. The measurement of waste within the production sector of an open economy. *Scandinavian Journal of Economics* 85: 158–79.

Diewert, W. E. 1983. Cost–benefit analysis and project evaluation: A comparison of alternative approaches. *Journal of Public Economics* 22: 265–302.

Diewert, E. 1985. A dynamic approach to the measurement of waste in an open economy. *Journal of International Economics* 19: 213–40.

Diewert, W. E., A. H. Turunen-Red, and A. D. Woodland. 1991. Tariff reform in a small open multi-household economy with domestic distortions and nontraded goods. *International Economic Review* 32: 937–57.

Dixit, A. K. 1975. Welfare effects of tax and price changes. *Journal of Public Economics* 4: 103–23.

Dixit, A. K. 1986. Tax policy in open economies. In A. Auerbach and M. Feldstein, eds., *Handbook of Public Economics*. Amsterdam: North-Holland, pp. 313–74.

Dixit, A. K., and V. Norman. 1980. *Theory of International Trade: A Dual, General Equilibrium Approach*. Cambridge: Cambridge University Press.

Edwards, S. 1992. Trade orientation, distortions and growth in developing countries. *Journal of Development Economics* 39: 31–57.

Edwards, S. 1993. Openness, trade liberalization and growth in developing countries. *Journal of Economic Literature* 31: 1358–93.

Ethier, W. J. 1971. General equilibrium theory and the concept of effective protection. In H. Grubel and H. G. Johnson, eds., *Effective Tariff Protection*. Geneva: GATT, pp. 17–44.

Ethier, W. J. 1977. The theory of effective protection in general equilibrium: Effective rate analogues of nominal rates. *Canadian Journal of Economics* 10: 233–45.

Falvey, R. E. 1988. Tariffs, quotas and piecemeal policy reform. *Journal of International Economics* 25: 177–83.

Falvey, R. E. 1994. Revenue enhancing tariff reform. *Weltwirtschaftliches Archiv* 130: 175–90.

Feenstra, R. 1995. Estimating the effects of trade policy. In G. Grossman and K. Rogoff, eds., *Handbook of International Economics*, vol. 3. Amsterdam: North-Holland, pp. 1553–95.

Foster, E., and H. Sonnenschein. 1970. Price distortion and economic welfare. *Econometrica* 38: 281–97.

Francois, J., and W. Martin. 2003. Formula approaches to market access negotiations. *The World Economy* 26: 1–28.

Fukushima, T. 1979. Tariff structure, nontraded goods and theory of piecemeal policy recommendations. *International Economic Review* 20: 427–35.

Fukushima, T. 1981. A dynamic quantity adjustment process in a small open economy, and welfare effects of tariff changes. *Journal of International Economics* 11: 513–29.

Fukushima, T., and T. Hatta. 1989. Why not tax uniformly rather than optimally? *Economic Studies Quarterly* 40: 220–38.

Grossman, G., and E. Helpman. 1994. Protection for sale. *American Economic Review* 84: 833–50.

Hamilton, C. B. 1988. Restrictiveness and international transmission of the "new protectionism." In R. E. Baldwin, C. B. Hamilton, and A. Sapir, eds., *Issues in US-EC Trade Relations*. Chicago: University of Chicago Press.

Harrigan, J. 1993. OECD imports and trade barriers in 1983. *Journal of International Economics* 35: 91–112.

Harrigan, J. 1996. Openness to trade in manufactures in the OECD. *Journal of International Economics* 40: 23–39.

Hatta, T. 1977a. A theory of piecemeal policy recommendations. *Review of Economic Studies* 44: 1–21.

Hatta, T. 1977b. A recommendation for a better tariff structure. *Econometrica* 45: 1859–69.

Hornig, E., R. N. Boisvert, and D. Blandford. 1990a. Explaining the distribution of quota rents from U.S. cheese imports. *Australian Journal of Agricultural Economics* 34: 1–20.

Hornig, E., R. N. Boisvert, and D. Blandford. 1990b. Quota rents and subsidies: The case of U.S. cheese import quotas. *European Review of Agricultural Economics* 17: 421–34.

Jewitt, I. 1981. Preference structure and piecemeal second best policy. *Journal of Public Economics* 16: 215–31.

Jones, R. W. 1969. Tariffs and trade in general equilibrium: Comment. *American Economic Review* 59: 418–24.

Jones, R. W. 1971a. A three-factor model in theory, trade and history. In J. Bhagwati, R. W. Jones, R. Mundell, and J. Vanek, eds., *Trade, Balance of Payments and Growth: Essays in Honor of C. P. Kindleberger*. Amsterdam: North-Holland, pp. 3–21.

Jones, R. W. 1971b. Distortions in factor markets and the general equilibrium model of production. *Journal of Political Economy* 79: 437–59.

Jones, R. W. 1974. Trade with non-traded goods: The anatomy of interconnected markets. *Economica* 41: 121–38.

Jones, R. W. 1975. Income distribution and effective protection in a multicommodity trade model. *Journal of Economic Theory* 11: 1–15.

Jones, R. W., and J. P. Neary. 1991. Wage sensitivity rankings and temporal convergence. In E. Helpman and A. Razin, eds., *International Trade and Trade Policy*. Cambridge: MIT Press, pp. 270–88.

Ju, J., and K. Krishna. 2000. Welfare and market access effects of piecemeal tariff reform. *Journal of International Economics* 51: 305–16.

Kee, H. L., A. Nicita, and M. Olarreaga. 2004. Import demand elasticities and trade distortions. Mimeo. World Bank, Washington, DC.

Keen, M. 1989. Multilateral tax and tariff reform. *Economic Studies Quarterly* 40: 195–202.

Kohler, W. 1991. Income distribution and labor market effects of Austrian pre– and post–Tokyo Round tariff protection. *European Economic Review* 35: 139–54.

Krishna, K. 1991. Openness: A conceptual approach. Mimeo. Harvard University.

Krishna, K., R. Erzan, and L. H. Tan. 1994. Rent-sharing in the Multi-Fibre Arrangement: Theory and evidence from U.S. apparel imports from Hong Kong. *Review of International Economics* 2: 62–73.

Krueger, A. O. 1974. The political economy of the rent-seeking society. *American Economic Review* 64: 291–303.

Labor Statistics Bureau. 1996. *Toward a More Accurate Measure of the Cost of Living: Final Report to the Senate Finance Committee from the Advisory Commission To Study The Consumer Price Index [The Boskin Commission Report]*. Washington, DC, December 4.

Lahiri, S., and P. Raimondos. 1996. Correcting trade distortions in a small open economy. *Review of International Economics* 4: 287–99.

Lawrence, R., and P. Krugman. 1987. Imports in Japan: Closed markets or minds? *Brookings Papers on Economic Activity* 1987 (2): 517–54.

Leamer, E. E. 1974. Nominal tariff averages with estimated weights. *Southern Economic Journal* 41: 34–46.

Leamer, E. E. 1988a. Cross-section estimation of the effects of trade barriers. In R. Feenstra, ed., *Empirical Methods for International Trade*. Cambridge: MIT Press, pp. 52–82.

Leamer, E. E. 1988b. Measures of openness. In R. E. Baldwin, ed., *Trade Policy Issues and Empirical Analysis*. Chicago: University of Chicago Press, pp. 147–200.

Leamer, E. E. 1990. The structure and effects of trade barriers. In R. W. Jones and A. O. Krueger, eds., *The Political Economy of International Trade: Essays in Honor of Robert E. Baldwin*. Oxford: Basil Blackwell, pp. 224–60.

Lee, J.-W. 1993. International trade, distortions and long-run economic growth. *International Monetary Fund Staff Papers* 40: 299–328.

Lerner, A. P. 1936. The symmetry between import and export taxes. *Economica* 3: 308–13.

Little, I. M. D., and J. A. Mirrlees. 1968. *Manual of Industrial Project Analysis in Developing Countries*, vol. 2. Paris: OECD.

Lloyd, P. J. 1974. A more general theory of price distortions in open economies. *Journal of International Economics* 4: 365–86.

Lopez, R., and A. Panagariya. 1992. On the theory of piecemeal tariff reform: The case of pure imported intermediate inputs. *American Economic Review* 82: 615–25.

Loveday, A. 1931. *Britain and World Trade*. London: Longmans, Green.

Magee, S. P. 1973. Factor market distortions, production and trade: A survey. *Oxford Economic Papers* 25: 1–43.

Nathan Associates, Inc. 1990. *Comermax: A Multimarket Model of Mexico's Agriculture*. Washington, DC: Inter-American Development Bank.

Neary, J. P. 1978. Dynamic stability and the theory of factor-market distortions. *American Economic Review* 68: 671–83.

Neary, J. P. 1985. International factor mobility, minimum wage rates and factor-price equalization: A synthesis. *Quarterly Journal of Economics* 100: 551–70.

Neary, J. P. 1988. Tariffs, quotas and voluntary export restraints with and without internationally mobile capital. *Canadian Journal of Economics* 21: 714–35.

Neary, J. P. 1993. Welfare effects of tariffs and investment taxes. In W. J. Ethier, E. Help-man, and J. P. Neary, eds., *Theory, Policy and Dynamics in International Trade: Essays in Honor of Ronald W. Jones*. Cambridge: Cambridge University Press, pp. 131–56.

Neary, J. P. 1995. Trade liberalisation and shadow prices in the presence of tariffs and quotas. *International Economic Review* 36: 531–54.

Neary, J. P. 1996. Theoretical foundations of the "Geary method" for international comparisons of purchasing power and real incomes. *Economic and Social Review* 27: 161–79.

Neary, J. P. 1998. Pitfalls in the theory of international trade policy: Concertina reforms of tariffs and subsidies to high-technology industries. *Scandinavian Journal of Economics* 100: 187–206.

Neary, J. P. 2003. Simultaneous reform of tariffs and quotas. Mimeo. University College, Dublin.

Neary, J. P., and K. W. S. Roberts. 1980. The theory of household behaviour under rationing. *European Economic Review* 13: 25–42.

Neary, J. P., and A. G. Schweinberger. 1986. Factor content functions and the theory of international trade. *Review of Economic Studies* 53: 421–32.

OECD. 1991. *Producer Subsidy Equivalent and Consumer Subsidy Equivalent Tables, 1979 to 1990*. Paris: OECD.

O'Rourke, K. 1997. Measuring protection: A cautionary tale. *Journal of Development Economics* 53: 169–83.

Papageorgiou, D., M. Michaely, and A. Chokski, eds. 1991. *Liberalizing Foreign Trade*, 7 vols. Oxford: Basil Blackwell.

Pollak, R. A. 1971. The theory of the cost-of-living index. U.S. Bureau of Labor Statistics Working paper 11. Revised version in W. E. Diewert, ed. 1990. *Price Level Measurement*. Amsterdam: North-Holland, pp. 5–77.

Pritchett, L. 1996. Measuring outward orientation in developing countries: Can it be done? *Journal of Development Economics* 49: 307–35.

Robinson, S., M. Kilkenny, and K. Hanson. 1990. The USDA/ERS computable general equilibrium model of the United States. USDA/ERS Staff Report AGES 9049. Washington, DC: USDA.

Rodriguez, F., and D. Rodrik. 2001. Trade policy and economic growth: A skeptic's guide to the cross-national evidence. In B. Bernanke and K. S. Rogoff, eds., *NBER Macroeconomics Annual 2000*. Cambridge: MIT Press.

Rodrik, D. 1987. The economics of export-performance requirements. *Quarterly Journal of Economics* 102: 633–50.

Rubinstein, A. 1982. Perfect equilibrium in a bargaining model. *Econometrica* 50: 97–109.

Shephard, R. W. 1953. *Cost and Production Functions*. Princeton: Princeton University Press.

Shephard, R. W. 1970. *Theory of Cost and Production Functions*. Princeton: Princeton University Press.

Smith, A. 1982. Some simple results on the gains from trade, from growth and from public production. *Journal of International Economics* 13: 215–30.

Smith, A. 1987. Factor shadow prices in distorted open economies. In H. Kierzkowski, ed., *Protection and Competition in International Trade: Essays in Honor of W. M. Corden*. Oxford: Basil Blackwell, pp. 54–67.

Sontheimer, K. C. 1971. The existence of international trade equilibrium with trade tax-subsidy distortions. *Econometrica* 39: 1015–35.

Stern, N. H. 1990. Uniformity versus selectivity in indirect taxation. *Economics and Politics* 2: 83–108.

Tan, A. H. H. 1970. Differential tariffs, negative value added and the theory of effective protection. *American Economic Review* 60: 107–16.

Trefler, D. 1995. The case of the missing trade. *American Economic Review* 85: 1029–46.

Trela, I., and J. Whalley. 1990. Unraveling the threads of the MFA. In C. B. Hamilton, ed., *Textiles Trade and the Developing Countries: Eliminating the Multi-Fibre Arrangement in the 1990s.* Washington, DC: World Bank, pp. 11–45.

Turunen-Red, A. H., and A. D. Woodland. 1991. Strict Pareto-improving multilateral reforms of tariffs. *Econometrica* 59: 1127–52.

Turunen-Red, A. H., and A. D. Woodland. 2000. Multilateral reforms of quantity restrictions on trade. *Journal of International Economics* 52: 153–68.

UNCTAD. 1996. *A User's Manual for TRAINS (TRade Analysis and INformation System).* New York: United Nations.

Vanek, J. 1964. Unilateral trade liberalization and global world income. *Quarterly Journal of Economics* 78: 139–47.

Vousden, N. 1991. *The Economics of Trade Protection.* Cambridge: Cambridge University Press.

Woodland, A. D. 1980. Direct and indirect trade utility functions. *Review of Economic Studies* 47: 907–26.

Woodland, A. D. 1982. *International Trade and Resource Allocation.* Amsterdam: North-Holland.

Index